W9-BAZ-113

THIRD EDITION

THE HISTORY AND THEORY OF RHETORIC

An Introduction

JAMES A. HERRICK

Hope College

Boston   New York   San Francisco
Mexico City   Montreal   Toronto   London   Madrid   Munich   Paris
Hong Kong   Singapore   Tokyo   Cape Town   Sydney

For Janet

Series Editor: *Brian Wheel*
Executive Editor: *Karon Bowers*
Editorial Assistant: *Jennifer Trebby*
Marketing Manager: *Mandee Eckersley*
Editorial Production Service: *Chestnut Hill Enterprises, Inc.*
Manufacturing Buyer: *JoAnne Sweeney*
Cover Administrator: *Kristina Mose-Libon*
Electronic Composition: *Omegatype Typography, Inc.*

For related titles and support materials, visit our online catalog at www.ablongman.com.

Library of Congress Cataloging-in-Publication Data

Herrick, James A.
   The history and theory of rhetoric: an introduction / James A. Herrick.—3rd ed.
        p. cm.
   Includes bibliographical references and index.
   ISBN 0-205-41492-3
   1. Rhetoric—History.   2. Rhetoric.   I. Title.

   PN183.H47 2004
   808' .009—dc22

                                                                2004002209

Printed in the United States of America
10 9 8 7 6 5 4 3   09 08 07 06 05

CONTENTS

CHAPTER THREE

Plato versus the Sophists: Rhetoric on Trial   54

CHAPTER FOUR

Aristotle on Rhetoric   73

CHAPTER FIVE
Rhetoric at Rome   93

CHAPTER SIX

Rhetoric in Christian Europe   122

CHAPTER NINE

Contemporary Rhetoric I: Arguments, Audiences, and Advocacy   198

CHAPTER ELEVEN

Contemporary Rhetoric III: Texts, Power, and Alternatives   244

POSTMODERNISM   245

MICHEL FOUCAULT: DISCOURSE, KNOWLEDGE, AND POWER   246
Power and Discourse   247
Escape   248
Archaeology of Knowledge: In Search of the Episteme   248
Excluded Discourse   250
Power and Institutions   251
Queer Theory   252

JACQUES DERRIDA: TEXTS, MEANINGS, AND DECONSTRUCTION   253
Authors Out of Control   254
Deconstructing Texts   254

RICHARD WEAVER: RHETORIC AND THE PRESERVATION OF CULTURE   257
Critique of Modernism   257
Critique of Scientism   257
Weaver on Education   258
A True Rhetoric   258

FEMINISM AND RHETORIC: CRITIQUE AND REFORM IN RHETORIC   259
The Need for a Woman's Voice   259
Reconceptualizing Rhetoric: Voice, Gender, Invitation   261
Constructing Gender Rhetorically   261
From Conquest to Invitation   262
"Works," "Texts" and the Work of Reading   264

GEORGE KENNEDY AND COMPARATIVE RHETORIC   265
Rhetoric in Ancient China   266
"Private Speaking"   266
China Sophists and the *Intrigues of the Warring States*   267
Jian, Shui, Pien, and the Traveling Persuaders   267
Re-visioning the Greek Tradition   268

CONCLUSION   269

QUESTIONS FOR REVIEW   269

QUESTIONS FOR DISCUSSION   270

TERMS   270

Glossary   276

Bibliography   285

Index   299

PREFACE

As in the previous two editions, my goal in this edition has been to provide students with an interesting and accessible survey of the history of rhetoric, and to equip them with a conceptual framework for evaluating and practicing persuasive writing and speaking. Each chapter introduces readers to influential theories of rhetoric advanced by some of the world's greatest thinkers. Through encountering the rhetorical tradition, students are equipped to understand and participate in the symbolic practices that mark our social and private lives.

The basic structure and coverage of the third edition has been maintained from the second, though revisions have been made to all chapters. Chapter 1 still presents the defining characteristics of rhetorical discourse, as well as the social functions of the art of rhetoric. In response to recent discussions among rhetorical scholars, a section has been added on the contingent nature of the questions that rhetoric typically addresses. I have also sought, in the opening chapter, to emphasize the tension that surrounds efforts to define rhetoric, whether understood as a practice or as an art of discourse.

Chapter 2 considers the Sophists as early teachers, practitioners, and theorists of rhetoric. This edition emphasizes the major contributions these experimental rhetoricians made to our understanding of the symbolic nature of human existence. While the controversy the Sophists generated by their iconoclastic claims is discussed, their role as thinkers who achieved considerable insight into rhetoric's nature and power is emphasized. A discussion of the Sophists' social context in fifth- and fourth-century Athens is new to this edition. Moreover, new sections have been added on the centrality of oratory to public life in ancient Greece, the nature of trials in Athens, and on the Athenian approach to education. Finally, the discussion of Aspasia's contribution to the history of rhetoric has been expanded. As in the second edition, Chapter 3 considers Plato's famous criticism of the Sophistic approach to rhetoric in the dialogue *Gorgias,* as well as the philosopher's musings about a true art of rhetoric in the dialogue *Phaedrus.*

Chapter 4 explores Aristotle's highly influential theory advanced in his *Rhetoric.* The chapter discusses the details of Aristotle's affirmative answer to the question of whether rhetoric qualifies as a true art. The notions of the enthymeme, artistic proofs, and topics of argumentation are all reviewed. Chapter 5 completes the discussion of the classical period by considering Roman adaptations of Greek rhetoric to a new social situation. Key components in the rhetorical theory of Cicero, including his famous canons of rhetoric and his concern for the preparation of the orator/leader, are focal points in the chapter. The contributions of Quintilian and Longinus to rhetorical thought are also explored. New in this edition is a discussion of Roman rhetoricians' considerably greater sophistication in legal theory when compared with their Greek counterparts. Treatments of classical rhetoric in Chapters 2 through 5 have benefited from my study with the classicist David Cohen of the Department of

Rhetoric at the University of California, Berkeley, during the summer of 2003, as part of a National Endowment for the Humanities Summer Seminar.

Chapter 6 considers the theories and uses of rhetoric that characterized the era of Church dominance running from approximately the fifth through the fourteenth centuries. St. Augustine's rapprochement between the Greco-Roman rhetoric and the educational needs of the Christian church are discussed. The chapter also examines the rhetorical arts that developed in the later Middle Ages, including preaching, letter writing, and poetry. A new section on the practice of letter writing by business-women in medieval England has been incorporated into this chapter.

Renaissance rhetorical theory, particularly the contributions of the Italian Humanists, remains the focus of Chapter 7 in this new edition. The period's intense interest in classical texts and languages, and the Renaissance's fascination with rhetoric generally, are seen as forces that produced an era of extraordinary influence for rhetoric in European education, and that led to remarkable insights on the part of rhetorical theorists. New to this edition are discussions of the rhetorical contributions of both Margaret Cavendish and Madame de Scudéry, the former an English novelist and provocateur who saw rhetoric's great potential for social change, the latter a proponent of the conversational rhetoric of the French salon.

Chapter 8 is focused on eighteenth- and nineteenth-century theories of rhetoric. The chapter opens with an expanded discussion of the intriguing Italian theorist Giambattista Vico, a writer who saw rhetoric as foundational to civilization and assigned rhetoric a central role in the very evolution of human thought. Vico's determination to answer, through his rhetorical theory, the rationalist philosophy of Descartes is explored in a section new to this edition. The chapter then moves on to the writers of the Scottish Enlightenment, including Campbell, Kames, and Blair, who turned rhetoric in a more personal direction, and away from classical conceptions of oratory. A new section on the influence of the Scottish school has been added to this edition. Finally, English rhetorical theorists, including the elocutionist Thomas Sheridan and traditionalist Richard Whately, are also considered.

The dramatic renewal of interest in rhetoric during the twentieth century is taken up in three considerably amended chapters that conclude the book. Chapter 9 focuses on contemporary rhetorical theories developing around conceptions of argument and audience. Thus, Stephen Toulmin's *The Uses of Argument* and the theories of audience and argument that mark Chaim Perelman and Madame L. Olbrechts-Tyteca's *The New Rhetoric* still appear here. In addition, the chapter maintains an earlier emphasis on the rhetoric of science, but also includes a new section exploring an important criticism of this powerful movement.

Chapter 10 takes up contemporary theories that offer us rhetoric as "equipment for living" in the contemporary world of symbols. An expanded discussion of Kenneth Burke now explores his notion of identification in addition to his central theory of dramatism. Lloyd Bitzer's situational theory is also considered here. Mikhail Bakhtin's thinking about polyphony and the rhetoric of the novel receives considerably fuller treatment in this new edition. Moreover, Jurgen Habermas's theory of a rational society is now taken up in this chapter rather than in Chapter 9, and with a great deal more attention to the sources of his thought.

Chapter 11 considers the rhetorical and discourse theories influenced by Continental criticism and postmodern thought, as well as "alternative" rhetorics. A new section introduces the rise of postmodern thought in Europe, setting figures such as Lyotard and Derrida in their intellectual context. Michel Foucault's insights into the close connection between discourse and power are discussed, as is Jacques Derrida's critique of the instability of language itself. Richard Weaver's concern for rhetoric's potential to preserve cultural values over time is also explored. Two different strains of feminist thinking about rhetoric are also considered, one that develops around efforts to retrieve women's contributions to rhetoric, and another that calls for a strategy of reading the texts of the masculinist tradition that uncovers the sources of repression within it. This second school of feminist thought is explored in a section new to this third edition. The chapter closes with an expanded discussion of ancient Chinese rhetoric as representing an alternative to Western conceptions.

Each chapter includes a list of key terms, as well as questions for review and for discussion. A glossary of terms should also be useful for review of important concepts. The bibliography can be of assistance to students who wish to do additional reading on a particular topic or theorist.

This third edition incorporates insights from recent research into the history of rhetoric. A particular goal of this edition has been to represent advances in our understanding of the roles women have played in the history of rhetoric. A greater effort has also been made to accommodate critical reactions to the theorists covered. In addition, I have paid closer attention to setting the intellectual and historical contexts for each theorist and school of thought.

The centrality of symbolic activity to our social and private lives has driven the incessant human interest in symbols and their instrumental use. The written record of this interest constitutes the history of rhetoric. Our reliance on rhetorical interaction for the development and maintenance of cooperative social arrangements makes the history and theory of rhetoric a crucial study for all thinking people today. Given the pluralistic nature of contemporary society and the resulting necessity of improving our means of finding working compromises through discourse, the study of rhetoric is perhaps more relevant today than it ever has been. I hope that this new edition will convey to readers the historical centrality and continuing vitality of rhetoric as the art of the intentional and productive management of symbols.

I appreciate the insightful comments of the following reviewers: Ferald Bryan, Northern Illinois University; Kristine Hansen, Brigham Young University; Becky Michele Mulvaney, Florida Atlantic University; and John Murphy, University of Georgia. My thanks also to Mr. Hussam Kanaan for his help in preparing revisions to Chapter 11.

James A. Herrick
Hope College

■ ■ ■ ■ ■

CHAPTER ONE

AN OVERVIEW OF RHETORIC

My first problem lies of course in the very word "rhetoric."
—Wayne Booth, *The Vocation of a Teacher*

This text explores the history, theories, and practices of rhetoric. But, as literary critic Wayne Booth suggests in the quotation above, the term *rhetoric* may pose some problems at the outset because of the various meanings it has acquired in our contemporary cultural setting. For example, for some people *rhetoric* is synonymous with "empty talk," or even "deception." We may hear clichés like "That's mere rhetoric" or "That's just empty rhetoric" used as an insult when directed at someone else's comments on a subject. Meanwhile, rhetoric has become an important topic of study in recent years, and its significance to public discussion of important political, social, and even scientific issues has been widely recognized. Scholars and teachers have expressed great interest in the topic. Many colleges and universities are again offering courses in rhetoric after having banished the term from their curricula for years, and dozens of books are published every year with *rhetoric* in their titles. Clearly, *rhetoric* arouses mixed feelings—it is widely condemned and widely studied, employed as an insult and recommended to students as an important subject of study. What is going on here? Why all the confusion and ambiguity surrounding the term *rhetoric*?

The negative attitude toward rhetoric reflected in comments such as "That's empty rhetoric" is not, as we shall see, of recent origin. In fact, one of the earliest and most influential discussions of rhetoric occurs in Plato's dialogue *Gorgias,* a work written in the opening decades of the fourth century B.C. when rhetoric was popular in Athens. Plato, as his dialogue makes clear, takes a dim view of rhetoric, at least as practiced by some. The character Socrates, apparently representing Plato's own perspective, argues that the type of rhetoric being taught in Athens was simply a means by which "naturally clever" people "flatter" their unsuspecting listeners into agreeing with them and doing their bidding. Plato condemns rhetoric as "foul" and "ugly."[1] We will discuss his specific criticisms of rhetoric in Chapter 3.

Ever since Plato's *Gorgias* first appeared, rhetoric has had to struggle to redeem its tarnished public image. Rhetoric bashing continues in an almost unbroken tradition from Plato's day to the present. In 1690 another great philosopher, John Locke, advanced a view of rhetoric not unlike, and likely influenced by, Plato's. Here is Locke writing in his famous and highly influential *Essay on Human Understanding:*

> If we speak of things as they are, we must allow that all the art of rhetoric, besides order and clearness; all the artificial and figurative application of words eloquence hath invented, are for nothing else but to insinuate wrong ideas, move the passions, and thereby mislead the judgment; and so indeed are perfect cheats....[2]

We might discover many similar condemnations of rhetoric in Western literature over the past two thousand years.

But it is also true that opinion about rhetoric has always been divided. Plato's criticisms of rhetoric were themselves answers to someone else's claims about its power and usefulness, and Locke's view has often been answered as well. Recent writers have reevaluated rhetoric, and they have sometimes come to surprising conclusions. Wayne Booth is one of the twentieth-century's leading figures in literary studies. Just a few years ago Booth wrote that he believed rhetoric held "entire dominion over all verbal pursuits. Logic, dialectic, grammar, philosophy, history, poetry, *all* are rhetoric."[3] Similarly, another great literary scholar, Richard McKeon, expressed virtually the same opinion of rhetoric. For McKeon, rhetoric was best understood as "a universal and architectonic art."[4] Rhetoric is "universal," that is, present everywhere we turn. But what about *architectonic?* By this term, McKeon meant that rhetoric organizes and gives structure to the other arts and disciplines, that it is a kind of master discipline that exercises a measure of control over all other disciplines. This is because rhetoric is, among other things, the study of how we organize and employ language effectively, and thus it becomes the study of how we organize our thinking on a wide range of subjects.

In apparent agreement with Booth and McKeon, Richard Lanham of the University of California has recently called for a return to rhetorical studies as a way of preparing us to understand the impact of computers on how we read and write. Rather than developing a completely *new* theory for the computer age, Lanham argues that "we need to go back to the original Western thinking about reading and writing—the rhetorical paideia [educational program] that provided the backbone of Western education for 2,000 years."[5] For Lanham, the study that originally taught the Western world its approach to reading and writing can still teach us new things, like how to adapt to the new medium of electronic communication.

Can Booth, McKeon, and Lanham be talking about the same "rhetoric" that Plato condemned as "foul and ugly," or about those elements of eloquence that Locke referred to as "perfect cheats"? Or, are we now at a point in our cultural history, as Lanham and others have suggested, where rhetoric can reestablish itself as an important study with insights to offer about a surprisingly broad spectrum of human activities? In rhetoric do we have the disciplinary equivalent of Robert Louis Stephenson's famous and frightening two-sided character, Dr. Jekyll and Mr. Hyde, a study that dramatically and without notice changes its character from benign to malevolent? How is it that rhetoric can elicit such sharply opposed judgments about its nature or value from such eminent observers? A complete answer to this question requires some knowledge of rhetoric's long history, which is the subject of this book. But almost certainly rhetoric's mixed reviews have a lot to do with its association with persuasion, that most suspect but essential human activity. A brief digression to explore this connection between rhetoric and persuasion will be worth our while.

RHETORIC AND PERSUASION

Though I will be taking the position that there is more to rhetoric than persuasion alone, rhetoric traditionally has been closely concerned with the techniques for gaining compliance. In fact, rhetoric has at times been understood simply as the study of persuasion. This close association with persuasion has always been at the heart of the conflict over whether rhetoric is a neutral tool for bringing about agreements, or an immoral activity that ends in manipulation and deception.

Rhetoric's intimate connection with persuasion has long prompted both suspicion and interest. After all, we all are leery of persuasion. Who hasn't had a bad experience as the object of someone else's persuasive efforts? Think of the last time you knew you were being persuaded by a telephone solicitor, a religious advocate in an airport, a high-pressure salesperson, a politician, a professor, or simply a friend or family member. Something inside you may have resisted the persuasion effort, and you may even have felt some irritation. But you may also have felt you were being drawn in by the appeal, that you were, in fact, being persuaded. If the person doing the persuading had been employing the techniques of rhetoric, you would think you had some reason to distrust both rhetoric and the people who practice it. So, most of us have developed a healthy suspicion of persuasion, and perhaps a corresponding mistrust of rhetoric understood as the techniques of persuasion.

At the same time, all of us seek to persuade others on a regular basis. Many professions, in fact, require a certain understating of and capacity to persuade. Economist Deirdre McCloskey has written that "persuasion has become astonishingly important" to the economy. Based on Census Bureau data, she estimates that "more than 28 million out of 115 million people in civilian employment—one quarter of the U.S. labor force—may be heavily involved in persuasion in their economic life," a finding she regards as "startling."[6] She concludes that "economics is rediscovering the importance of words" as economists begin to understand "that persuasion is vital for the exchange of goods, services, and monies...."[7]

Outside the arena of professional endeavors, we are perpetual persuaders in our personal relationships. Who doesn't make arguments, advance opinions, and seek compliance from friends? Moreover, we typically engage in all these persuasive activities without thinking we are doing anything wrong. In fact, it is difficult *not* to persuade. We also engage in the practice on almost a daily basis in our interactions with friends, colleagues at work, or members of our family. We may attempt to influence friends or family members to adopt our political views; we will happily argue

 rhetoric everywhere

the merits of a movie we like; we *are* that salesperson, religious advocate, or politician. In fact, it is difficult to imagine a human relationship in which persuasion has no role, or a human organization that does not depend to some degree on efforts to change other people's thoughts and actions.

Consider some additional examples of how universal persuasion can be. We usually think of sports as a domain of physical competition, not of verbal battles. Yet, even sports involve disagreements about such things as the interpretation of rules, a referee's call, or which play to call. And, these disagreements often are settled by arguments and appeals of various kinds, that is, by persuasion. British writer Michael Billig notes that many of the rules governing play in a sporting event are the result of rhetorical interactions about such issues as how much violence to allow on the field of play. He writes, "the rules of rugby and soccer were formulated in order to transform informal agreements, which had permitted all manner of aggressive play, into defined codes that restricted violence." Rhetoric, especially its argumentative aspect, was crucial to the creation of these rules of play. "Above all, the rules were formulated against a background of argument."[8] Thus, even the rules by which athletes compete came into being through rhetoric.

What about a technical field, like medicine? If medicine is a science, shouldn't rhetorical practices such as argument and persuasion be nonexistent? In fact, medical decisions often are made after a convincing case for or against a particular procedure has been advanced by one doctor in a persuasive exchange with other doctors. And, the decision-making exchange often is not limited to technical issues such as the interpretation of medical data, for instance, the results of a blood test. To be sure, the arguments advanced typically will involve medical principles, but they are arguments nonetheless; they are intended to be persuasive, and they range beyond strict medical guidelines. For instance, in medical dialogue we are likely to hear ethical concerns raised, the wishes of a family considered, and even questions of cost evaluated. Moreover, the patient involved often has to be persuaded to take a particular medicine or follow a specified diet or allow doctors to perform a surgical procedure. Moreover, as physicians argue, rival medical theories may be in conflict and rival egos clash. Who should perform a needed corneal transplant on a famous politician? Shouldn't an important decision like this be resolved on the basis of medical criteria alone? Yet, even a question like this may be resolved on the basis of arguments between two well-known physicians at rival hospitals over which one of them is the best eye surgeon. Even medicine, it appears, has its rhetorical side.

Let's bring the focus down to a more personal level. Does romance involve persuasion? When I seek the attention of someone in whom I am romantically interested, I start to develop a case—though perhaps not an explicit and public one—about my own good qualities. When in the vicinity of the individual concerned, I may attempt to appear humorous, intelligent, and considerate. My words and actions take on a rhetorical quality as I build the case for my own attractiveness. I might be convincing, or may fail to convince, but in either event I have made choices about how to develop my appeal, so to speak. Once begun, romantic relationships go forward (or backward) on the basis of persuasive interactions on topics ranging from how serious the relationship should be to whether to attend a particular concert.

What about the marketplace? Business transactions, from marketing strategies to contract negotiations, frequently involve persuasive efforts. As McCloskey has pointed out, many people make their livings on the basis of their abilities as persuasive speakers. Nor is education immune from rhetorical influence. You often are aware that a professor is advocating a point of view in a lecture that ostensibly presents simple "information," or that classmates argue with one another hoping to persuade others to their point of view. As a matter of fact, you have been reading an extended persuasive case for the importance of studying rhetoric. Textbooks, it should come as little surprise, often have embedded within them a persuasive agenda. So, efforts at persuasion mark many, perhaps all, of our interpersonal activities. In fact, we even persuade *ourselves*. The internal rhetoric of "arguing with yourself" accompanies most of life's decisions, big or small.

So, though our experiences may leave us leery of persuasion, persuasion is also an important component of our occupational, social, and private lives.[9] Now, back to rhetoric. If rhetoric is in part the systematic study of persuasion, recognizing how crucial persuasion is to daily life may suggest that this controversial art deserves our attention. To recognize what we might call "the pervasiveness of persuasiveness" is not to condemn persuasion or rhetoric. Rather, it is to begin to appreciate the centrality of this activity to much of life, and to recognize that human beings are rhetorical beings. At this point it will be important to develop a more precise definition of rhetoric.

DEFINING RHETORIC

Jane Donaworth notes that "recently James Murphy suggested 'advice to others about future language use' as a good definition of rhetoric." She adds, "as the term 'rhetoric' has changed in meaning, what counts as rhetoric has also changed, from the formal public speaking of ancient Greece—political, legal, and celebratory speech making—to any spoken or written form of nonliterary discourse (and many would include a great deal of literary discourse.)"[10]

George Kennedy, a scholar writing on the history of rhetoric, has defined rhetoric even more broadly as "the energy inherent in emotion and thought, transmitted through a system of signs, including language, to others to influence their decisions or actions."[11] This also is an interesting definition, and it suggests again that rhetoric is simply part of who we are as human beings. Kennedy asserts that when we express emotions and thoughts to other people with the goal of influencing (persuading) them, we are engaged in rhetoric. And, as we have just seen, expressing ourselves in this way is a common human activity indeed. Notice that for Kennedy rhetoric involves "signs, including language." I'd like to focus attention on this important point for a moment, and suggest that rhetoric develops in the realm of symbols of one type or another. So, what are symbols?

An individual word such as *boat* is an example of a symbol, a general term referring to any mark, sign, sound, or gesture that communicates meaning based on social agreement. Individual symbols usually are part of a larger symbolic system, such as a language. Language is a familiar symbol system using written and spoken words to communicate meaning. But language is certainly not the only symbol system available for the communication of meaning. Several examples from the arts may help to establish the breadth of the human symbolic realm.

Musical notation and performance constitute a symbol system, one that employs notes, markings, sound, key, harmony, and rhythm to communicate meanings. In 1983 the musician Sting created a sinister aura in his song "Every Breath You Take" by the use of a driving bass rhythm, frequently repeated chord changes, but relatively little melodic variation. The menacing song that resulted has been called a "musical ransom note." Many of the movements in dance are symbolic because they express meaning on the basis of agreements among dancers, choreographers, and audience members. For instance, three dancers in a row performing the same robotic movement may symbolize the tedium and regimentation of modern life.

Similarly, gestures, postures, and facial expressions allow actors to communicate with audiences symbolically but without employing the symbols of spoken language. For instance, there is no actual connection between pondering a question and scratching your head, and yet a theatrical scratch of the scalp means "I don't know" or "I'm thinking about it" by a kind of unstated social agreement. In a painting, the use of form, line, color, and arrangement can be symbolic. A stark line of dark clouds may symbolize impending disaster, even though clouds do not typically accompany actual disasters. But, because storms and calamity are sometimes associated, we understand the artist's intent even when dark clouds appear in a picture in which a storm is not the likely source of danger.

The lines, shapes, and materials used in architecture often are employed symbolically to communicate meaning. The protests by veterans' groups that greeted the unveiling of the Vietnam Memorial in Washington, D.C., were responses to what some observers took to be the *meaning* of the monument, a meaning with which they did not agree.[12] For example, much of the monument is below ground, perhaps suggesting invisibility or even death. Is it significant that the monument, because it is below ground, cannot be seen from Capitol Hill? The principal material used in the monument is black granite rather than the more traditional and triumphal white marble. The memorial's polished surface is covered with the names of the 50,000 Americans who died in the war rather than with carved scenes of battle and victory. What does the Vietnam Memorial mean? One would be hard-pressed to find its meaning to be "A united America triumphs again in a foreign war."

Language is the symbol system on which most of us rely for communicating with others on a daily basis. However, arts such as music, dance, theater, painting, and architecture also provide symbolic resources for communicating. In fact, human social life depends on our ability to use various symbol systems to communicate meanings to one another. As we have seen, our social life also depends on using symbols for achieving the persuasion that brings about the cooperation, compromise, and coordination of effort inherent to forming and maintaining societies. If persuasion is central to social organization, and if the art of rhetoric takes in the study of persuasion, then our lives as members of human communities are inherently and inescapably rhetorical. It may even be the case that individual conscious thought often is rhetorical in nature. Understanding rhetoric, then, is crucial to the success and happiness of communities and of individuals.

Earlier we discussed rhetoric's connection with persuasion or influence. It is true that persuasion has long been an important goal of rhetoric, and the principal reason people have studied the art. But I would like to expand the definition of rhetoric to include other goals such as achieving clarity through the structured use of symbols, awakening our sense of beauty through the aesthetic potential in symbols, or bringing about mutual understanding through the careful management of common meanings attached to symbols. Thus, I will define the art of rhetoric as the systematic study and intentional practice of effective symbolic expression. *Effective* here will mean achieving the purposes of the symbol-user, whether that purpose is persuasion, clarity, beauty, or mutual understanding. The art of rhetoric can render symbol use more persuasive, beautiful, memorable, forceful, thoughtful, clear, and thus generally more compelling. In all of these ways, rhetoric is the art of employing symbols effectively. The systematic presentation of the art of rhetoric, descriptions of rhetoric's various functions, and explanations of how rhetoric achieves its goals are collectively known as rhetorical theory. Discourse crafted according to the principles of the art of rhetoric, that is, the product of this art, I will call rhetorical discourse or simply rhetoric. Rhetorical discourse bears certain marks of this crafting that I will discuss in the following section. I will sometimes use the term rhetor (RAY-tor) to refer to an individual engaged in creating or presenting rhetorical discourse.

As we shall see later in the text, for most of its history the art of rhetoric has focused on *persuasion* employing the symbol system of *language*. This more traditional approach to rhetoric is still important. But recently both the goals of rhetoric and the symbolic resources available to those practicing the art have expanded dramatically. Does this mean that all communication, regardless of goal or symbol system employed, is rhetoric? Some scholars make communication and rhetoric synonymous, but this seems to ignore genuine and historically important distinctions among types of communication ranging from information and reports through casual conversations to outright propaganda. I will be taking the position that rhetorical discourse is a particular type of communication possessing several identifying characteristics. What, then, are the features of rhetorical discourse that set it apart from other types of communication? The following section describes five distinguishing qualities of rhetorical discourse as we encounter it in writing, speaking, the arts, and other media of expression.

RHETORICAL DISCOURSE

This section identifies five distinguishing characteristics of rhetorical discourse, the marks the art of rhetoric leaves on messages. Rhetorical discourse characteristically is (1) planned, (2) adapted to an audience, (3) shaped by human motives, (4) responsive to a situation, (5) persuasion-seeking, and (6) concerned with contingent issues. Not all writing or speaking that might meaningfully be termed *rhetoric* clearly satisfies all of these criteria, but the criteria will serve as a starting point for identifying, understanding, and responding to rhetorical discourse. We begin by considering rhetoric's most fundamental quality.

Rhetoric Is Planned

Regardless of the goal at which it aims, rhetorical discourse involves forethought or planning. Thinking of rhetoric as planned symbol use directs our attention to the choices people make about how they will address their audiences. Issues that arise in planning a message include: Which arguments will I advance? Which evidence best supports my point? How will I order and arrange my arguments and evidence? What aesthetic resources are available to me, given my topic and audience?

The planned nature of rhetoric has long been recognized as one of its defining features. Some early rhetorical theorists developed elaborate systems to assist would-be orators in planning their speeches. The Roman writer Cicero, for instance, used the term *inventio* (invention) to describe the process of discovering the arguments and evidence for a persuasive case. He then provided specific methods for inventing arguments quickly and effectively. Cicero also discussed the effective ordering of arguments and appeals under the heading *dispositio* (arrangement), while he used the term *elocutio* to designate the process of finding the right linguistic style for one's message, whether elegant or conversational. Such concerns, already clearly defined and extensively studied in the ancient world, reflect the planned quality that characterizes rhetorical discourse. In subsequent chapters we will look more closely at a number of rhetorical systems designed to assist the planning of messages.

Rhetoric Is Adapted to an Audience

Concern for forethought or planning points up a second characteristic of rhetorical discourse. Rhetoric is planned with some audience in mind. *Audience* should not be understood strictly in the traditional sense of a large group of people seated in rows of chairs in a large hall. Some audiences are of this type, many are not. When you speak to a small group of employees at work, they are your audience, and you may adapt your discourse to them. The author of a letter to the editor of the local paper also writes with an audience in mind, though the audience is not made up of people whom the author can see or know personally in most cases. Similarly, a novelist writes with particular groups of readers in mind who constitute her audience.

Typically a rhetor must make an educated guess about the audience she is addressing. This imagined audience is the only one present when a message is actually being crafted, and it often guides the inventional process in important ways. The audience that hears, reads or otherwise encounters a message may be quite similar to the imagined audience, but even highly trained writers or speakers guess wrongly at times. Wayne Booth has spoken to hundreds of groups over his long career. He points out that even when he *thought* he knew his audience, he was sometimes mistaken:

> I always wrote with some kind of imaginary picture of listeners responding with smiles, scowls, or furrowed brows. Such prophecies often proved to be wildly awry: An imag-

ined audience of thirty teachers who would have read the materials I sent them in advance turned out, in the reality faced a week or so later, to be ten teachers, along with two hundred captive freshmen reluctantly attending as part of their "reading" assignment; the audience for a "public lecture" was discovered to contain nobody from the public, only teachers.[13]

Booth's experience is not at all unusual. Nevertheless, some effort to estimate one's audience has always been, and remains, a crucial component in the rhetorical process.

Rhetorical discourse, then, forges links between the rhetor's views and those of an audience. This means attending to an audience's values, experiences, beliefs, social status, and aspirations. Aristotle, one of the first writers to advance a complete and systematic treatment of rhetoric, emphasized a type of argument he called the enthymeme. Though scholars differ on exactly how Aristotle defined an enthymeme, most will agree that it is an argument built from values, beliefs, or knowledge held in common by a speaker and an audience.[14] In fact, Aristotle went so far as to claim that the art of rhetoric's central concern was the enthymeme. Perhaps this was because persuasion—for Aristotle, the principal goal of rhetoric—depends on commonality between a rhetor and an audience.

An example may be helpful to illustrate this point about commonality. A friend tries to persuade you that colorizing old films is wrong. He uses the following argument as part of his case:

> I think colorization violates the original filmmaker's intentions. Early directors made artistic decisions about composition, lighting, and even camera angle based on the limitations of black-and-white cinematography. Colorizing black-and-white films is no diffcrent from putting brighter clothes and a new hairstyle on the Mona Lisa because the majority of people today would find these additions more appealing.

You understand the argument as it stands, even though you may not agree with it or are not persuaded by it. But, notice, it is lacking a crucial contention that you had to supply in order to understand the argument. Your friend probably doesn't have to add this reason to his argument because you both understand that it is implied. Perhaps more to the point, you would have to *accept* this missing statement in order to be persuaded by the argument. The unstated claim in this argument is something like, "It is wrong to violate an artist's intentions by modifying a work of art to suit current tastes or desires." Your friend's hope of persuading you depended on the two of you acknowledging the principle of not violating artistic intentions. Rhetoric stresses commonality between a rhetor and an audience, something rhetorical theorist Kenneth Burke termed *identification.* Such identification is crucial to persuasion, and, thus, to cooperation, consensus, compromise, and action.

Our discussion to this point suggests that a rhetor must consider what an audience accepts as true, probable, or desirable. Rhetorical theorists Chaim Perelman and Lucy Olbrechts-Tyteca have written that in rhetoric "the important thing...is not knowing what the speaker regards as true or important, but knowing the views of those he is addressing." Changes made in a message to tailor it to a particular audience are referred to, not surprisingly, as audience adaptation. So important is this process to rhetoric that Perelman and Olbrechts-Tyteca affirm that "no orator can afford to neglect this effort of adaptation" and that rhetoric should be seen as involving "continuous adaptation of the speaker to [an] audience."[15]

No effective rhetor, then, can ignore the beliefs, values, and related concerns of her audience. But emphasizing the audience does not end with a heightened awareness of the centrality of audience adaptation to rhetoric. Perelman and Olbrechts-Tyteca argue that the audience actually "has the major role in determining the quality of argument and the behavior of orators."[16] That is to say, an ignorant or noncritical audience can be one cause of weak or unethical rhetoric, while a well-informed and critically minded audience demands that the rhetoric addressed to it be well reasoned and honestly presented.

This constant pursuit of audience approval in rhetoric has led to the longstanding criticism that rhetors decide what to say or write solely on the basis of what their audiences believe or prefer. This concern is justified in many cases. Some politicians, for instance, apparently spend more time trying to figure out what their audiences *want* them to say than speaking from their own convictions. But whether audience adaptation is done to advance a hidden and, perhaps, questionable agenda, or to promote the audience's welfare, this activity is an important defining characteristic of rhetoric.

Rhetoric Reveals Human Motives

A third quality of rhetoric is closely related to the concern for the audience. In rhetoric we find people acting symbolically in response to their motives, a general term taking in commitments, goals, desires, or purposes that lead to action. Rhetors address audiences with goals in mind, and the planning and adaptation processes that mark rhetoric are governed by the desire to achieve these goals. The motives animating rhetorical discourse include making converts to a point of view, seeking cooperation to accomplish a task, building a consensus that enables group action, finding a compromise that breaks a stalemate, forging an agreement that makes peaceful coexistence possible, wishing to be understood, or simply having the last word on a subject. Rhetors accomplish such goals by aligning their own motives with an audience's commitments. For this reason, the history of rhetoric is replete with efforts to understand human values, identify factors prompting audiences to action, and to grasp the symbolic resources for drawing people together.

Of course, human motives have a moral quality: There are good and bad motives. Imagine, for instance, a governor running for president. As you study the governor's public statements, you look for motives animating that rhetoric: Is the governor concerned to serve the public good? Does he or she hope to see justice prevail? Is fame a motive, or greed? Perhaps all of these elements enter the governor's motivation. Of course, motives may be either admitted or concealed. The same politician would likely admit to desiring the public good, but would be unlikely to admit to seeking fame, fortune, or even merely employment. Thus, you are unlikely to hear the following admission from our imaginary governor:

My principal concern in this campaign is to ensure my election to the esteemed office of president of the United States in order that I might become wealthy, powerful, and famous. If elected I promise to serve the interests of my own small group of friends, and will do my best to conceal any unscrupulous actions taken to ensure the accomplishment of my narrow, self-interested goals.

Any informed critic of rhetoric must be aware that motives may be elusive or clearly evident, hidden or openly admitted.

Rhetoric Is Responsive

Fourth, rhetorical discourse typically is a response either to a situation or to a previous rhetorical statement. By the same token, any rhetorical statement, once advanced, is automatically an invitation for other would-be rhetors to respond. Rhetoric, then, is both "situated" and "dialogic." What does it mean for rhetoric to be situated? Simply that rhetoric is crafted in response to a set of circumstances, including a particular time, location, problem, and audience. In Chapter 10 we will consider the ideas of Lloyd Bitzer, who made this factor the principal characteristic of rhetoric in a famous essay entitled, "The Rhetorical Situation."[17] For Bitzer the rhetorical situation involves an "exigence" or problem, an audience made up of individuals who can address the problem, and "constraints," which include a range of circumstantial factors including the rhetor's abilities.

The situation prompting a rhetorical response may be a political controversy concerning welfare, a religious conflict over the role of women in a denomination, a debate in medical ethics over assisted suicide, the discussions about a policy that would control visitors in university dormitories, or a theatrical performance in which a plea for racial harmony is advanced. Regardless of the topic or particular circumstances calling it forth, the rhetorical discourse advanced in any such situation is some individual's response to a particular situation. Thus, rhetoric is a matter of response-*making.*

But, rhetoric is also response-*inviting.* That is, any rhetorical expression may elicit a response from someone advocating an opposing view. Aware of this response-inviting nature of rhetoric, rhetors will imagine likely responses as they compose their rhetorical appeals. They may find themselves coaxing their mental conception of a particular audience to respond the way they think the actual audience might.

The response-*inviting* nature of rhetoric is easy to imagine when we are envisioning a setting such as a political campaign or a courtroom. In those settings one expects that a candidate's speeches will receive a response from the opposition, or that the prosecution's case will be answered by the defense. But does rhetoric also invite response in less formal settings? Think of a conversation between yourself and a friend regarding buying expensive tickets for a concert. You have given some thought to what you might say to persuade your friend to buy tickets for the concert, and you are even aware of the response your arguments will receive. Your first argument runs something like this: "Look, how often do you get to hear the Chicago Symphony live? And besides, it's only thirty bucks." You have argued from the rareness of the experience and the minimal costs involved. But your friend, ever the studied rhetor, is ready with a response: "Hey, thirty bucks is a lot of money, and I haven't paid my sister back the money she loaned me last week." Your friend has argued from the magnitude of the costs, and from the need to fulfill prior obligations. Not to be denied your goal by such an eminently answerable argument, you respond: "But your sister has plenty of money, and thirty bucks is barely enough to buy dinner out."

And so it goes, each rhetorical statement invites a response. Maybe you persuade your friend, maybe you don't. But the rhetorical interaction will likely involve the exchange of statement and response so characteristic of rhetoric. In Chapter 8 we will see that British social psychologist Michael Billig believes that the response-inviting nature of rhetoric reveals something important about how the human mind works.

Rhetoric Seeks Persuasion

As we noted earlier in this chapter, the factor most often associated with rhetorical discourse historically has been its pursuit of persuasion. Though I acknowledge that rhetoric often seeks other goals, such as aesthetic appreciation of language or clarity of expression, it is important to recognize the centrality of this particular goal throughout rhetoric's long history. Greek writers noted more than twenty-five hundred years ago that rhetorical discourse sought persuasion, and today a rhetorical theorist like Joseph Wenzel can be found stating straightforwardly that "the purpose of rhetoric is persuasion."[18] Most of the discourse referred to as rhetoric manifestly seeks to alter an audience's views in the direction of those of a speaker or writer. It may be useful, then, to examine more closely rhetoric's pursuit of persuasion.

Rhetorical discourse is usually intended to influence an audience to accept an idea, and then to act in a manner consistent with that idea. For example, an attorney argues before a jury that the accused is guilty of a crime. The attorney seeks the jurors' *acceptance of the idea* that the defendant is guilty, and in this way to bring about the *action* of finding the defendant guilty. Or, consider a more common example. I try to persuade a friend that a particular candidate should be elected mayor on the basis of the argument that the candidate has effective plans to reduce property taxes and to improve education in the city. I want my friend to *accept the idea* that this candidate is the best person for the job, and *to take the action* of voting for my candidate. Let's shift the focus to the arts. A play reveals through the symbols of the theater the vicious nature of racism. It is reasonable to conclude that the author hopes both to influence the audience's thinking about racism and to affect the audience's actions on racial matters.

How does rhetorical discourse achieve persuasion? Subsequent chapters reveal the rich variety of answers this question has received in different historical periods. Answering this intriguing question is a major goal of the discipline known as rhetorical theory. Speaking in the most general terms, we can say that rhetoric seeks persuasion by employing various resources of symbol systems such as language. Four resources of symbols have long been recognized as assisting the goal of persuasion.

For convenience I will call them: arguments, appeals, arrangement, and aesthetics. Let's look briefly at each resource.

Argument.   First, rhetoric seeks to persuade by means of argument. An argument is made when a conclusion is supported by reasons. An argument is simply reasoning made public with the goal of influencing an audience. Suppose that I wish to persuade a friend of the following claim: "The coach of the women's basketball team ought to be paid the same salary as the coach of the men's team." To support this claim, I then advance the following two reasons:

> First, the coach of the women's team is an associate professor, just as is the coach of the men's team. Second, the women's coach has the same responsibilities as the men's coach: to teach two courses each semester, and to prepare her team to play a full schedule of games.

I have now made an argument, and have sought to persuade my friend through the use of reasoning. Argument has almost always been associated with the practice of rhetoric. Chapter 5 considers the rhetorical theory of the Roman writer Cicero, who developed elaborate systems to assist students of rhetoric in discovering arguments to support their contentions.

Appeals.   Appeals are those symbolic strategies that aim either to elicit an emotion or to engage the audience's loyalties or commitments. We are all familiar with emotional appeals, such as those to pity or anger or fear. You are likely also to have encountered appeals to authority, to patriotism, or to organizational loyalty. Appeals can be difficult to distinguish from arguments at times, and the difference may be simply one of degree.

An argument is more clearly directed to reason, an appeal to something more visceral such as an emotion or a conviction. For instance, an advertisement shows a young woman standing in front of an expensive new car while cradling a baby in her arms. The caption reads: "How much is your family's safety worth?" Though we could say that an argument is implied in the picture and the caption, the advertisement seems to be structured as an appeal to one's sense of responsibility to one's family. Even if reason responded, "Yes, safety is worth a great deal, but I still can't afford that car," the advertisement's appeal could perhaps still achieve its intended effect. Chapter 4 takes up the rhetorical theory of the Greek philosopher Aristotle, who devoted a great deal of attention to the place of appeals to the emotions in rhetoric.

Arrangement.   Arrangement refers to the planned ordering of a message to achieve the greatest effect, whether of persuasion, clarity, or beauty. A speaker makes the decision to place the strongest of her three arguments against animal experimentation last in her speech on the topic. The decision is made solely on the basis of her belief that her strongest argument stands to have the greatest impact on her audience if it is the last point they hear. Clearly, speakers and writers make decisions about arrangement to achieve clarity and persuasiveness in their messages. But the designers of a public building may make similar decisions about arrangement. The Holocaust Museum in Washington, D.C., for instance, is physically arranged to make the strongest case possible against the racial hatred that resulted in the horrors of the concentration camps, and against all similar attitudes and actions. Careful planning went into decisions about which scenes visitors would encounter as they entered the museum, as they progressed through it, and as they exited. The great impact of this museum is enhanced by its careful arrangement. Like arguments and appeals, the arrangement of a message has occupied the attention of rhetorical theorists such as Cicero from very early times.

Aesthetics.   The aesthetics of rhetoric are elements adding form, beauty, and force to symbolic expression. Writers, speakers, composers, or other sources typically wish to present arguments and appeals in a manner that is attractive, memorable, or perhaps even shocking to the intended audience. Abraham Lincoln's "Second Inaugural Address" is a striking example of language's aesthetic resources employed to memorable and moving effect. Consider the use of metaphor, allusion, consonance, rhythm, and even of rhyme in the following lines:

> Fondly do we hope, fervently do we pray, that this mighty scourge of war may speedily pass away. Yet if God wills that it continue until all the wealth piled by the bondsman's two hundred and fifty years of unrequited toil shall be sunk, and until every drop of blood drawn with the lash shall be paid by another drawn with the sword, as was said three thousand years ago, so still it must be said, that the judgments of the Lord are true and righteous altogether.[19]

Lincoln engages the aesthetic resources of language in a traditional way to make his speech more beautiful and thus more moving and memorable. In some cases, however, a source may decide intentionally to offend traditional aesthetic categories to achieve persuasive effect. In the following passage, for example, Malcolm X answers some of the arguments of Rev. Martin Luther King, Jr. with provocative language that violates traditional aesthetic expectations.

> This is a real revolution. Revolution is always based on land. Revolution is never based on begging somebody for an integrated cup of coffee. Revolutions are never based on love-your-enemy and pray-for-those-who-spitefully-use-you. And revolutions are never waged singing "We Shall Overcome." Revolutions are based on bloodshed.[20]

Notice that Malcolm X, like Abraham Lincoln, employs allusion, consonance, repetition, and other aesthetic devices to enhance the impact of his discourse and to make it more vivid and memorable. Though Malcolm X employs the aesthetic resources of language, it would not be quite accurate to say that his goal has been to make his speech more beautiful or pleasant to listen to. Rather, his goal is apparently to shock his audience out of complacency, and to get them to reject one suggested course of action and to accept a different one.

The aesthetic dimension of rhetoric has always been important to the art. In the next chapter we will see that one of the early Sophists, Gorgias, believed that the sounds of words, when manipulated with skill, could captivate audiences. In the Middle Ages, the aesthetic dimension of rhetoric was central to rhetorical treatises that instructed readers in the art of poetry writing. The persuasive potential in the beauty of language is a persistent theme in rhetorical history.

Arguments, appeals, arrangement, and aesthetics each remind us that rhetoric is carefully planned discourse, adapted to a particular audience, revealing human motives, and responsive to a set of circumstances. This quality of planning is the defining characteristic of rhetoric with which we began our discussion in this section, and the one to which we now have returned. Rhetoric is intentionally fashioned discourse, and the art of rhetoric has developed around the activity of crafting discourse to achieve various effects including persuasion, clarity, and beauty of expression.

Rhetoric Addresses Contingent Issues

The ancient Greek philosopher Aristotle wrote in his work, *Rhetoric,* that "it is the duty of rhetoric to deal with such matters as we deliberate upon without arts or systems to guide us" and when "the subjects of our deliberation are such as seem to present us with alternative possibilities." He adds, "about things that could not have been, and cannot be, other than they are, nobody who takes them to be of this nature wastes his time in delineation."[21] What was this great thinker's point regarding the subject matter of the art of rhetoric? Aristotle apparently thought that rhetoric is especially important when we are faced with particular kinds of questions—practical questions about matters that confront everyone and about which there are no definite and unavoidable answers. The term rhetorical scholars use to describe such questions is *contingent,* and about contingent questions, deliberation or careful weighing of options is crucial. The art of rhetoric assists that process of weighing the options before us when issues are contingent.

To *deliberate* simply means to reason through various alternatives until we reach a decision, and Aristotle says no one does this when things cannot be "other than they are." Rhetorical theorist Thomas Farrell puts the same point this way: "it makes no sense to deliberate over things which are going to be the case anyway or things which could never be the case."[22] So, the art of rhetoric would not address a question such as whether the sun will rise tomorrow morning, nor one such as whether France should be made the fifty-first state in the American Union. The one is an inevitable fact (it is "going to be the case anyway"), the other a virtual impossibility (it "could never be the case").

Lloyd Bitzer, quoting the nineteenth-century writer Thomas DeQuincey, has this to say about contingency: "Rhetoric deals mainly with matters which lie in that vast field 'where there is no *pro* and *con,* with the chance of right and wrong, true and false, distributed in varying proportions among them.'" Bitzer adds, "rhetoric applies to contingent and probable matters which are subjects of actual or possible disagreement by serious people, and which permit alternative beliefs, values, and positions."[23] The art of rhetoric addresses contingent issues, those matters about which we must reason together because *we need to make a decision* and because *a reasoned decision is appropriate.*

Thus, we could say that the art of rhetoric has both a practical and a moral component. That is, it addresses real and unresolved issues that do not dictate to us a resolution, and it engages our decision-making capacities on matters that involve our value commitments. It is for these reasons that, according to Farrell, Aristotle treated "the very best audiences as a kind of extension of self, capable of weighing the merits of practical alternatives."[24] That is, rhetoric addresses many of the same kinds of issues that face us as individuals, practical and moral issues that demand decisions or judgments, such as, Is participating in war immoral? Of course, in a democracy similar issues face us as members of the larger public. When there are alternatives to be weighed—when matters are neither inevitable nor impossible—we are facing contingencies. And, when faced with contingencies that must be resolved, typically rhetoric comes into play.

In the following section I would like to shift the focus just a bit, and consider the social functions performed by the art of rhetoric itself. We will turn our attention away from the kind of discourse we would call rhetorical, and emphasize the art that helps to create such discourse. I will be making an argument of sorts as we proceed through these benefits, and thus will be writing rhetorically. The argument aims at this conclusion: When the art of rhetoric is taken seriously, studied carefully, and practiced well, it performs various vital social functions in the society. I will emphasize six such functions.

SOCIAL FUNCTIONS OF THE ART OF RHETORIC

We began this chapter by noting some unpleasant associations the art of rhetoric has carried with it through its history. But, though rhetoric can be used for wrong ends such as deception, it also plays many important social roles. Bear in mind that rhetoric's misuse is more likely when the art of rhetoric is available only to an elite, when it is poorly understood by audiences, or when it is unethically practiced by rhetors. What functions, then, are performed by a sound, ethically grounded practice of the art of rhetoric? The six functions I will highlight are: (1) ideas are tested, (2) advocacy is assisted, (3) power is distributed, (4) facts are discovered, (5) knowledge is shaped, and (6) communities are built. Each of the six functions introduced here will be discussed in greater detail as we consider the history of the art of rhetoric in subsequent chapters.

Rhetoric Tests Ideas (through preparation, audience & response)

One of the most important functions of rhetoric is that it allows ideas to be tested on their merits. The practice of rhetoric, both in the development and presentation of messages, provides an important and peaceful means for testing ideas publicly. In order to win acceptance for an idea in a free society, in most cases I have to advocate it. Effective advocacy, as we have already seen, means preparing and presenting arguments and appeals, considering how these will be arranged to their best effect, and asking which aesthetic resources of symbols I will employ to make my message memorable and persuasive. The process of advocacy, then, calls on our knowledge of the art of rhetoric. One of the great benefits of this process is that my ideas will be tested and refined.

In preparing my ideas for presentation, in their actual presentation to an audience, and in the responses that follow, the process of testing those ideas continues. The notion that rhetoric tests ideas brings us back to the concept of the audience. Audience is a vital element in rhetoric's capacity to test ideas. As we seek an audience's acceptance of an idea, we recognize that the audience will examine the case advanced to support that idea. Recall that Perelman and Olbrechts-Tyteca maintained that the quality of audiences determines the quality of rhetoric in a society. One way of understanding this phenomenon is to recognize that some audiences test ideas carefully, while others are careless in this responsibility. The better equipped an audience is to test the ideas a rhetor advocates, and the more care that goes into that testing, the better check we have on the quality of those ideas. Thus, *training in the art of rhetoric is just as important for audience members as it is for advocates.*

In addition to the mental testing of ideas audiences undertake, actual rhetorical responses also help ensure that ideas are tested before the public. Thus, the rhetorical response of a friendly critic, or even of an opponent, helps me strengthen my arguments and refine my ideas. These responses make my case clearer, stronger, more moving, and more persuasive. Of course, I aim to do the best job I can initially to present my ideas effectively. But whether preparing my initial message or making corrections after hearing responses to it, the process of testing and refining ideas is tied directly to understanding the art of rhetoric. Such testing answers questions such as: Is the idea being advocated clear to me or has it been intentionally obscured? Are the arguments employed clear and convincing? Is the evidence advanced recent and from reliable sources? Have emotional appeals been excessively employed to distract attention away from arguments and evidence? Are contradictions present in the case? Each of these questions finds its answer in some dimension of the art of rhetoric.

This discussion of testing ideas assumes that disagreement need not imply that one party to a dispute is completely in error. In fact, it is not unusual that both sides to a debate modify some of their views as a result of the rhetorical exchange. Rhetoric's idea-testing function means that *each* side may have to review and, perhaps, modify its arguments.[25]

Rhetoric Assists Advocacy

The art of rhetoric is the method by which we advocate ideas we believe to be important. Rhetoric gives our private ideas a public voice, thus directing attention to them. Richard Lanham actually defines rhetoric as the study of "how attention is created and allocated."[26] For this reason he also speaks of rhetoric as teaching "the economics of attention."[27]

Politics often comes to mind as an activity requiring advocacy. Clearly, political speeches and campaign ads are efforts by politicians to *advocate* their ideas. The art of rhetoric is employed in preparing such messages. The same is true when lobbyists make their case to legislators, when constituents write letters to their representatives, and when committees debate the merits of a proposal. The art of rhetoric helps judicial advocates to make their cases as well. Attorneys prepare to plead their clients' cases guided in part by their understanding of the principles that will render their advocacy clear and convincing, that is, the principles of rhetoric. Traditional courtroom pleading has involved rhetorical skill since courts resembling the ones we know first appeared. But advocates in newer legal arenas, such as environmental law, also turn to the art of rhetoric when developing their arguments.

Advocacy in less structured settings often follows the principles taught by the art of rhetoric as well. This is true whether or not advocates have had the benefit of formal education in rhetoric, though effective advocacy is perhaps more likely when actual rhetorical training has been available. When you express an artistic judgment, for example, that the films of Oliver Stone are better than those of Stephen Spielberg, you advance your reasons guided by some sense of how to present ideas effectively to an audience. In a twenty-minute video presenting interviews with AIDS patients, a student builds a case for increased funding for AIDS research. The video will be shown to funding agencies and service organizations. Editorial decisions have to be made guided by principles inherent to the art of rhetoric: Which portions of the interviews will be used in the video? Which interviews will come first, in the middle, and last? Will the interviewer be a prominent voice in the presentation, or will the people with AIDS alone speak? Such judgments are made with some sense of how an effective case is constructed in the medium of video, within a limited amount of time, and before a particular audience. Thus, whether we are considering formal contexts such as a courtroom or legislative assembly, or less structured settings such as a conversation, the art of rhetoric is important to effective advocacy.

The art of rhetoric is the study of effective advocacy. As such, it provides a voice for ideas, thus drawing attention to them and making it possible to gain adherence to them. This important function of rhetoric may easily be overlooked. But any time an idea moves from private belief to public statement, elements of the art of rhetoric are employed. For example, the women's movement made tremendous changes in the way our society understands women, their work, and their concerns. The struggle to change societal attitudes about women has been a long and difficult one, and the art of rhetoric has been a major resource for feminist advocates in their search for justice. Hundreds of feminist writers, speakers, and artists have drawn on rhetorical insights in adapting messages to particular audiences, and in rendering those messages more persuasive.[28]

In fact, among the most important resources available to individuals and groups engaged in responsible advocacy—second only to the merits of their ideas—is the art of rhetoric. But, it is important to recognize that false and destructive ideas also draw on rhetoric for achieving acceptance. Perhaps this is why the Greek philosopher Aristotle said that rhetoric's potential for advocating true ideas was one of the main reasons for studying the art. As we shall see when we overview his rhetorical theory in Chapter 4, Aristotle believed that false ideas prevail only when advocates of what is true fail to understand rhetoric.

There can be little doubt that understanding the art of rhetoric enhances one's skill in advocacy. We may at times wish that some persons or groups did *not* understand rhetoric, because we disagree with their aims or find their ideas repugnant. The solution to this problem (if it is a problem) would appear to be an improved understanding of rhetoric on our part. When we disagree with a point of view, rhetoric helps us to prepare an answer, to advance the counterargument. This brings us to the third benefit of the art of rhetoric, its capacity to distribute power.

Rhetoric Distributes Power

Our discussion of rhetoric's role in advocacy raises a closely related issue that deserves separate treatment—rhetoric's relationship to power. When we think of rhetoric and power, certain questions come to mind: Who is allowed to speak in a society, that is, whose ideas have a voice? On what topics are we permitted to speak? In which settings is speech allowed? What kind of language is it permissible to employ? Which media are available to which advocates, and why? The answers a culture provides to these questions have a lot to do with the distribution of power or influence in that culture. Issues of power and its distribution have always been central to rhetorical theory, according to James A. Berlin. "Those who construct rhetorics…are first and foremost concerned with addressing the play of power in their own day."[29] Berlin is asserting, then, that even the guidelines one sets out as normative for writing and speaking are influenced by, and maybe developed in the service of, existing power structures.

Though symbolic expression plays an enormous role in the distribution of power in a society, we sometimes minimize the power of language. For instance, when we contrast talk to action in statements like, "Let's stop talking and *do* something," we may be misleading ourselves regarding language's great power to shape our thinking and, thus, our actions. Nevertheless, people have long recognized that language and power are intimately connected. The great Chinese leader Mao Tse Dung was fond of saying, "power comes from the barrel of a gun." But power in a society is more than just sheer physical force. Because speaking and writing *are* forms of action, and because symbols shape thought and action, rhetoric as the study of how symbols are used effectively is itself a source of power.

Rhetoric is connected to power at three levels. The first I will call the personal level. Rhetoric as *personal power* provides an avenue to success and personal advancement through training the capacity to express oneself effectively. Seminars in effective speaking, writing, and even in vocabulary building suggest that the relationship between personal success and ability with language is widely acknowledged. Clear, effective, and persuasive expression is not simply a matter of demonstrating your sophistication; it is an important means of advancing toward the goals you have set for yourself.

But rhetoric is also a form of *psychological power,* that is, the power to shape the thinking of other people. Symbols and the structure of human thought are intricately connected. Thus, we may change the way people think simply by altering the symbolic framework they employ to organize their thinking. It also becomes possible to change the way people behave by the same method. Rhetoric, then, is often the means by which one person alters the psychological world of another. In fact, symbols are perhaps the only avenue into the mental world of another person.

Advertising is a ready example of rhetoric's psychological power. Through the strategic use of symbols, advertisers seek to shape our psychological frame and, thus, our behavior. The repeated symbolic association in advertising between a very thin body and personal attractiveness has led many women to become dissatisfied with their appearance. This alteration in the psychological world of the individual can have harmful consequences when it begins to affect a behavior such as eating. But other sources seek similar ends through symbols. Several years ago radio talk-show host Rush Limbaugh created controversy by introducing the term *feminazi* into English. By combining the terms *feminist* and *Nazi,* Limbaugh sought to alter his listeners' psychological frame regarding feminists and feminism. Qualities associated with the Nazis were now associated with feminists through a strategic choice of symbols. An altered way of thinking about the feminist movement and about leading feminists was sought through this new symbol, *feminazi.*

Rhetoric is also a source of *political power.* How influence gets distributed in a culture is often a matter of who gets to speak, where they are allowed to speak, and on what subjects. As we shall see in Chapter 11, French philosopher Michel Foucault has explored this intersection of rhetoric and political power in a society. He suggests that power is not a fixed, hierarchical social arrangement, but rather a fluid concept closely connected to the symbolic strategies that hold sway at any particular time.

Some rhetorical theorists point out that certain social groups have a greater opportunity to be heard in public debates than do others. This fact raises a concern for the role of *ideology* in rhetorical transactions. The "privileging" of some voices or points of view over others means that they are awarded preference or superiority in the persuasive transactions that shape public beliefs and attitudes. An ideology can be defined as a system of belief, or a framework for interpreting the world.[30] The term often carries with it the notion of concealment. That is, an unexamined ideol- ogy prevents its adherent from seeing things "as they are." The concept of ideology also reminds us to be wary of rhetoric's use to concentrate power in a few social groups.[31] When rhetoric is employed to advocate ideas, but its capacity to test ideas is subverted, the reign of unexamined ideology becomes a real possibility.

Rhetoric, ideology, and power are linked in another way as well. When one ideology dominates in a society, it can shape even our basic conceptions of rhetoric in ways that deliver power to one group. Thus, a patriarchal ideology suggests that rhetorical training and opportunities to speak be available only to men. Feminist writers have advanced a powerful analysis of this ideology's role in shaping our view of rhetoric, a topic we will return to in Chapter 11. Feminist rhetoricians have pointed out how male values, male ways of thinking, male beliefs, and male motives have dominated Western rhetoric for more than two thousand years.[32] Speeches by men often have been considered more important than speeches by women.[33] Feminist critics have demanded access by women to the rhetorical process, and have advocated that women's ways of thinking and arguing should be recognized as having value and benefit. Efforts in this direction include the publication of anthologies of speeches by women.[34]

Rhetoric Discovers Facts

A fourth important function of rhetoric is that it helps us to discover facts and truths that are crucial to decision making. Rhetoric assists this important task in at least three ways. First, in order to prepare a case, you must locate evidence to support your ideas. This investigative process is an integral part of the art of rhetoric. Though we may have strong convictions, if we are to convince an audience to agree with us, these convictions are going to have to be supported with evidence and arguments. A solid set of facts as evidence allows better decisions to be made about controversial issues.

Second, creating a message involves thinking critically about the facts available to you. This compositional process—what rhetorical theorists call "invention"—often suggests new ways of understanding facts and new relationships among facts. Third, the clash of differing argumentative cases that often accompanies rhetorical efforts brings new facts to light and refines available facts.

Audiences expect advocates to be well informed. As an advocate you are an important source of information crucial to decision making. But your audience, which may include opponents, will also be evaluating the evidence you present. Some facts may be misleading, outdated, irrelevant, or not convincing. Thus, the art of rhetoric assists not just the discovery of new facts, but determinations about which facts are actually relevant and convincing.

As we will see in Chapter 2, the insight that rhetoric assists the process of discovering facts and ideas is an ancient one. Chapter 5 considers sophisticated systems—known as *stasis* systems—that Roman orators and teachers designed to help discover the relevant facts and arguments in a criminal case.

Rhetoric Shapes Knowledge

How do communities come to agreements about what they know or value? For example, how does a particular view of justice come to prevail in one community or culture? How does a value for equality under the law become established? How do we know that equality is better than inequality? Though the answer to these questions is complex, an important connection exists between social knowledge and rhetorical practices such as speaking and writing.[35] Chapters 2 and 3 present the intense debate between the Greek Sophists and Plato over rhetoric's relationship to knowledge.

Rhetoric often plays a critical social role in making determinations about what is true, right, or probable. For this reason Robert Scott refers to rhetoric as "epistemic," that is, knowledge-building.[36] What does he mean? Through rhetorical interaction, people come to accept some ideas as true and to reject others as false. Thus, rhetoric's knowledge-building function derives from its tendency to test ideas. Once an idea has been thoroughly tested by a community or society, it becomes part of what is accepted as known by that group.

That knowledge develops rhetorically runs counter to our usual understanding of the sources of knowledge. We often think that knowledge comes through our direct experience, or through the indirect experience we call "education." In other words, knowledge is treated as an object to be discovered in the same way an astronomer discovers a new star: The star was always out there, and the astronomer just happened to see it. Some knowledge fits this objective description better than does other knowledge. A star's existence is something demonstrable, and so can be taken as known on the basis of physical evidence. Perhaps rhetoric plays a limited role in establishing this sort of knowledge. But, the star's *age* is less certain than is its existence, and may require argument among scientists to determine. Rhetoric now begins to play a role in establishing knowledge, for the scientists involved in the debate will draw on what they know of the art to persuade their peers. If the majority of scientists do reach a working agreement about the star's *known* age, members of the public might have other ideas. Knowledge about the universe's age has religious significance for many people. Do we know that the star's age should be taught in schools? Do we know that money should be invested in trying to launch a telescope to get a better look at the new star? Do we know that star has an effect on the course of our lives, as astrologers would argue? Rhetorical interactions are involved in resolving each of these questions, and the art of rhetoric becomes important to determining what finally is accepted as "knowledge." Thus, rhetoric influences every aspect of knowledge-building, from what counts as a fact through how the fact will be interpreted to how it will be employed to justify actions. We will look more closely at the issue of rhetoric in the scientific realm in Chapter 8.

Rhetoric Builds Community

What defines a community? One answer to this question is that what people value, know, or believe in common defines a community. Some observers fear that Americans may be losing their sense of constituting a community in the face of growing pressures toward fragmentation. If this is the case, and if preserving a sense of community is a goal worth striving for, what can be done about this problem of social fragmentation? Many of the processes by which we come to hold beliefs and values in common, as was suggested in the preceding section, are rhetorical in nature. Michael J. Hogan, a scholar who has studied the relationship between rhetoric and community, writes that "rhetoric shapes the character and health of communities in countless ways...." Many writers who have sought to understand the ways in which communities define themselves, and the forces that contribute either to the strength or weakness of communities, have concluded that "communities are largely defined, and rendered healthy or dysfunctional, by the language they use to characterize themselves and others."[37] If this is indeed the case, as Hogan and others have suggested, then it is important to explore the specific function played by rhetoric in building—or perhaps in destroying—communities.

I am not speaking here about communities as geographical entities bounded by certain borders or streets, or contained in particular districts of a city. Rather, I have in mind communities of people who find common cause with one another, who see the world in a similar way, who identify their concerns and aspirations with similar concerns and aspirations of other people. Thus, a church might constitute a community, a group of employees forming a union might constitute a community, and members of an ethnic group living in the same city might also be a community. Not every aspect of such communities results from the practice of rhetoric. For example, ethnicity is not a function of discourse. But developing common values, common aspirations, and common beliefs very often are a result of what is said, by whom, and with what effect.

Consider, for example, the community that developed around the civil rights advocacy of Dr. Martin Luther King, Jr. in the 1950s and 1960s. Dr. King was clearly a highly skillful and knowledgeable practitioner of the art of rhetoric. He, and others working with him, created a community of value and action. And much of their work was accomplished by means of effective rhetorical discourse. More specifically, Dr. King advocated certain values in a persuasive manner. Among the values he advocated were equality, justice, and peace. He also tested particular ideas in public settings—ideas like racism, which he rejected, and ideas like unity among races, which he embraced. He brought facts to light for his audiences, such as facts about the treatment of African American people in America. Dr. King even provided a language for talking about racial harmony in America. His notion of a "dream" of a racially unified America and of a method of "nonviolent resistance" inspired many in the civil rights movement who made his terminology part of their own vocabulary.

As Dr. King spoke and wrote, his ideas were expressed, tested, and either embraced or rejected, those who embraced his ideas became part of a larger community that King was gradually building. Through his rhetorical efforts, King built a "community of discourse" that enabled people to think and act with unity to address a wide range of serious social problems. He developed an active community around certain very powerful ideas to which he gave voice rhetorically. Rhetorical processes were central to his vital work of community-building.

It is interesting to note that often members of a particular community—examples might include feminists, Orthodox Jews, or animal rights activists—do not know all of the other members of their community personally. In fact, any particular member of a large and diffuse community might know only a very small fraction of the people who would say they belong to the group. How is a sense of community maintained when a community is geographically diffuse? Certainly the group's symbols, metaphors, and ways of reasoning function to create a common bond that promotes a strong sense of community despite physical separation. Moreover, communities are sustained over time by the rhetorical interactions of their members with one another and with members of other groups. As Hogan writes, "communities are living creatures, nurtured and nourished by rhetorical discourse."[38]

This section has discussed six functions performed by the practice of rhetoric: (1) assisting advocacy, (2) testing ideas, (3) distributing power, (4) discovering facts, (5) shaping knowledge, and (6) building community. These functions are closely related to major themes in the history of rhetoric and provide connections among subsequent chapters. The next section sets out some of these themes in greater detail.

CONCLUSION

We began this chapter by considering some common meanings of the term *rhetoric,* such as empty talk, beautiful language, or persuasion. Whereas these meanings frequently are associated with the term, *rhetoric* was defined as the study or practice of effective symbolic expression. We also noted that rhetoric refers to a *type of discourse* marked by several characteristics that include being planned, adapted to an audience, and responsive to a set of circumstances. We considered some of rhetoric's social functions such as testing ideas, assisting advocacy, and building communities.

This chapter suggests that several important issues arise when we begin to think seriously about the art of rhetoric and its various uses. We will return to these themes as we consider the ways in which the art of rhetoric has developed over the past twenty-five hundred years. The following issues will be revisited throughout this text:

1. **Rhetoric and power.** Rhetoric bears an important relationship to power in a society. The art of rhetoric itself brings a measure of power. But rhetorical practices also play an important role in distributing power. Determinations are made in any culture regarding who may speak, before which audiences, and on which topics. All of these determinations have important implications for how power is distributed. If a segment of a society lacks the knowledge of rhetoric, or is denied the ability to practice rhetoric, does this mean that their access to power is correspondingly diminished? We will examine this question at several junctures in the history of rhetoric.

2. **Rhetoric and truth.** Rhetoric discovers facts relevant to decision making. Moreover, rhetoric helps to shape what we say we know or believe. What, then, is rhetoric's relationship to truth? Does rhetoric discover truth? Or, does rhetoric simply provide one the means of communicating truth discovered by other means? Some theorists contend that rhetoric actually *creates* truth. As we explore the history of rhetoric, we will uncover various answers to these questions. The stakes could not be higher. If truth is transcendent and absolute, rhetoric's role in its discovery or creation is minimal. In fact, rhetoric might even be a threat to truth. If, on the other hand, truth is a matter of social agreements, rhetoric plays a major role in shaping our view of truth.

3. **Rhetoric and ethics.** Persuasion is a central concern in the study and practice of rhetoric. This means that rhetoric always raises moral or ethical questions. If persuasion is always wrong, then rhetoric shares this moral condemnation. If persuasion is acceptable, what are the ethical obligations of a speaker, writer, or artist with regard to an audience? What are the moral restraints within which rhetoric ought to be practiced? In a society in which various moral views are present, how do we derive a standard of ethical practice that all rhetors can accept? Clearly the question of rhetoric's relationship to ethics is an important one. Few people would want to live in a society in which rhetoric is practiced without any regard for ethical responsibility on the part of advocates.

4. **Rhetoric and the audience.** The question of the ethics of rhetoric is inseparable from the question of a rhetor's potential influence on an audience. It is because rhetoric is a form of power that ethical considerations attend rhetoric. It is because rhetorical audiences are made up of human beings that rhetoric's power poses ethical concerns in the first place. How does rhetoric achieve effects such as altering thought or prompting action? What factors in language and other symbol systems allow skilled advocates to influence their audiences? What role does the style or beauty of one's language play in affecting an audience? If audiences do have some control over the quality of rhetoric, some effort to educate audiences seems to be in everyone's best interest. Yet, as a culture we invest relatively little time and effort in such education. As we explore the history of rhetoric, the audience will often be a central concern.

5. **Rhetoric and society.** Our discussion in this chapter has also raised the larger issue of rhetoric's various roles in the development and maintenance of societies. What are rhetoric's specific functions, if any, in building and maintaining a society? Do we depend on rhetoric to forge the compromises and achieve the cooperation needed to live and work together in a democratic society? How does rhetoric shape and propagate the societal values that give us both a corporate identity and a common direction? Would it be preferable to establish a society in which rhetoric played no role at all? Issues of power and ethics will attend this critical question of rhetoric's role in society.

These themes and questions will animate our discussion of rhetoric's history. The different answers to our questions suggested by a wide range of writers, and their reasons for their answers, make the history of rhetoric a rich and intriguing source of insight into the development of human thought, relationship, and culture. In Chapter 2 we encounter most of these themes as we begin our study of rhetoric's long and rich history by looking at its controversial origins and early development in ancient Greece.

QUESTIONS FOR REVIEW

1. How are the following terms defined in the chapter?

   rhetoric
   the art of rhetoric
   rhetorical discourse
   rhetor

2. What are the marks or characteristics of rhetorical discourse discussed in this chapter?

3. Which specific resources of language are discussed under the heading, Rhetoric Is Planned?

4. What social functions of the art of rhetoric are discussed in this chapter?

5. Which three types of power are enhanced by an understanding of the art of rhetoric?

6. Given the definition and description of rhetoric advanced in this chapter, what might historian of rhetoric George Kennedy mean by saying that the yellow pages of the phone book are more rhetorical than the white pages? (*Classical Rhetoric and Its Christian and Secular Tradition,* p. 4.)

7. What is meant by the statement that rhetoric addresses contingent issues?

QUESTIONS FOR DISCUSSION

1. The following artifacts, Abraham Lincoln's "Second Inaugural Address" and Emily Dickinson's poem, "Success Is Counted Sweetest," were written at about the same time, and each is written with reference to the Civil War. The two pieces are often held to represent two different types of discourse: Lincoln's address is categorized as rhetoric, while Dickinson's work fits best into the category of poetry. Thinking back on the characteristics of rhetorical discourse discussed in this chapter, what case could be made, if any, for distinguishing Lincoln's work from Dickinson's? Do they belong in different literary categories? Refer back to the resources of language—argument, appeal, arrangement, and artistic devices—in thinking about these two pieces. Does each employ all four resources?

SECOND INAUGURAL ADDRESS

Abraham Lincoln

Fellow-countrymen: At this second appearing to take the oath of the presidential office, there is less occasion for an extended address than there was at first. Then a statement, somewhat in detail, of a course to be pursued seemed very fitting and proper. Now, at the expiration of four years, during which public declarations have been constantly called forth on every point and phase of the great contest which still absorbs the attention and engrosses the energies of the nation, little that is new could be presented.

The progress of our arms, upon which all else chiefly depends, is as well known to the public as to myself, and it is, I trust, reasonably satisfactory and encouraging to all. With high hope for the future, no prediction in regard to it is ventured.

On the occasion corresponding to this four years ago, all thoughts were anxiously directed to an impending civil war. All dreaded it, all sought to avoid it. While the inaugural address was being delivered from this place, devoted altogether to saving the Union without war, insurgent agents were in the city seeking to destroy it with war—seeking to dissolve the Union and divide the effects by negotiation. Both parties deprecated war, but one of them would make war rather than let it perish, and the war came. One-eighth of the whole population were colored slaves, not distributed generally over the Union, but localized in the Southern part of it. These slaves constituted a peculiar and powerful interest. All knew that this interest was somehow the cause of the war. To strengthen, perpetuate, and extend this interest was the object for which the insurgents would rend the Union by war, while the government claimed no right to do more than to restrict the territorial enlargement of it.

Neither party expected for the war the magnitude or the duration which it has already attained. Neither anticipated that the cause of the conflict might cease when, or even before the conflict itself should cease. Each looked for an easier triumph, and a result less fundamental and astounding. Both read the same Bible and pray to the same God, and each invokes His aid against the other. It may seem strange that any men should dare to ask a just God's assistance in wringing their bread from the sweat of other men's faces, but let us judge not that we be not judged. The prayer of both could not be answered. That of neither has been answered fully. The Almighty has His own purposes. Woe unto the world because of offenses, for it must needs be that offenses come, but woe to that man by whom the offence cometh. If we shall suppose that American slavery is one of those offenses which, in the providence of God, must needs come, but which having continued through His appointed time, He now wills to remove, and that He gives to both North and South this terrible war as the woe due to those by whom the offence came, shall we discern there any departure from those divine attributes which the believers in a living God always ascribe to Him? Fondly do we hope, fervently do we pray, that this mighty scourge of war may speedily pass away. Yet if God wills that it continue until all the wealth piled by the bondsman's two hundred and fifty years of unrequited toil shall be sunk, and until every drop of blood drawn with the lash shall be paid by another drawn with the sword, as was said three thousand years ago, so still it must be said, that the judgments of the Lord are true and righteous altogether.

   With malice toward none, with charity for all, with firmness in the right as God gives us to see the right, let us finish the work we are in, to bind up the nation's wounds, to care for him who shall have borne the battle, and for his widow and his orphans, to do all which may achieve and cherish a just and a lasting peace among ourselves and with all nations.[39]

Success Is Counted Sweetest
Emily Dickinson

Success is counted sweetest
By those who ne'er succeed.
To comprehend a nectar
Requires sorest need.

Not one of all the purple host
Who took the flag to-day
Can tell the definition,
So clear, of victory,

As he, defeated, dying,
On whose forbidden ear
The distant strains of triumph
Break, agonized and clear.[40]

2. If rhetoric accomplishes the benefits and performs the functions discussed in this chapter, it might follow that rhetorical training should be a central component in education. Has training in rhetoric or some related discipline been part of your educational experience? Should education focus more on the skills that make up the art of rhetoric?

3. Is rhetoric as pervasive in private and social life as the chapter suggests? In what realms of life, if any, does rhetoric appear to have little or no part to play? Where is its influence greatest, in your estimation?

4. Respond to the claim that rhetoric is important to the process of building community. Has it been your experience, when people come together to form a community, that ways of speaking and reasoning in common are an important part of that process?

Could a greater understanding of the art of rhetoric enhance this process of building a community?

5. Some people have criticized rhetoric for being manipulative. Do you believe that rhetoric is, by its very nature, manipulative? If not, what ethical guidelines might be important for constraining the practice of rhetoric so that it did not become a tool for manipulation?

TERMS

Aesthetics: Study of the persuasive potential in the form, beauty, or force of symbolic expression.

Appeals: Symbolic methods that aim either to elicit an emotion or to engage the audience's loyalties or commitments.

Argument: Discourse characterized by reasons advanced to support a conclusion. Reasoning made public with the goal of influencing an audience.

Arrangement: The planned ordering of a message to achieve the greatest persuasive effect.

Audience adaptation: Changes made in a message to tailor it to a particular audience.

Dispositio: Arrangement; Cicero's term for the effective ordering of arguments and appeals.

Elocutio: Style; Cicero's term to designate the concern for finding the appropriate language or style for a message.

Enthymeme: An argument built from values, beliefs, or knowledge held in common by a speaker and an audience.

Ideology: A system of belief, or a framework for interpreting the world.

Inventio **(invention):** Cicero's term describing the process of coming up with the arguments and appeals that would make up the substance of a persuasive case.

Motives: Commitments, goals, desires, or purposes when they lead to action.

Rhetor: Anyone engaged in preparing or presenting rhetorical discourse.

Rhetoric:

　Art of: The study and practice of effective symbolic expression.

　Type of discourse: Goal-oriented discourse that seeks, by means of the resources of symbols, to adapt ideas to an audience.

Rhetorical discourse: Discourse crafted according to the principles of the art of rhetoric.

Rhetorical theory: The systematic presentation of the art of rhetoric, descriptions of rhetoric's various functions, and explanations of how rhetoric achieves its goals.

Symbol: Any mark, sign, sound, or gesture that represents something based on social agreement.

ENDNOTES

1. Plato, *Gorgias,* 463; trans. W. C. Helmbold (Indianapolis, IN: Bobbs-Merrill, 1952), 23–24.
2. John Locke, *Essay on Human Understanding* (London: 1690) 3.X.34.
3. Wayne Booth, *The Vocation of a Teacher* (Chicago: University of Chicago Press, 1988), xiv–xv.
4. Richard McKeon, *Rhetoric: Essays in Invention and Discovery,* ed. Mark Backman (Woodbridge, CT: Ox Bow Press, 1987), 108.
5. Richard Lanham, *The Electronic Word: Democracy, Technology, and the Arts* (Chicago: University of Chicago Press, 1993), 51.

6. D. McCloskey, "The Neglected Economics of Talk," *Planning for Higher Education* 22 (Summer 1994): 11–16, p. 14.

7. McCloskey, 15.

8. Michael Billig, *Arguing and Thinking: A Rhetorical Approach to Social Psychology* (1989: Cambridge: Cambridge University Press, 1996), 57.

9. For a scholarly yet entertaining look at the ways we go about persuading one another in everyday life, see Robert Cialdini's insightful book, *Influence: The Psychology of Persuasion* (1984; New York: William Morrow, 1993).

10. Jane Donaworth, ed. *Rhetorical Theory by Women before 1900* (Lanham, MD: Rowman & Littlefield, 2002), xiv.

11. George Kennedy, translator's introduction to *Aristotle on Rhetoric: A Theory of Civic Discourse* (Oxford: Oxford University Press, 1991), 7.

12. Carole Blair has written an intriguing essay on the rhetoric of the Vietnam Memorial, which appears in the book, *Critical Questions* (New York: St. Martin's Press, 1994). Barry Brummett considers the rhetoric of a wide variety of cultural artifacts in *Rhetoric in Popular Culture* (New York: St. Martin's Press, 1994).

13. Booth, *Vocation of a Teacher,* xiv.

14. For a very good recent translation of Aristotle's *Rhetoric,* see the Kennedy translation cited above. For Aristotle's discussion of the *enthymeme,* see *Rhetoric,* Book I, Chapter I.

15. Chaim Perelman and Lucy Olbrechts-Tyteca, *The New Rhetoric: A Treatise on Argumentation,* trans. John Wilkinson and Purcell Weaver (Notre Dame: University of Notre Dame Press, 1969), 23–24.

16. Perelman and Olbrechts-Tyteca, *New Rhetoric,* 24.

17. Lloyd Bitzer, "The Rhetorical Situation," *Philosophy and Rhetoric* 1 (1968): 1–14.

18. Joseph Wenzel, "Three Perspectives on Argument," in *Perspectives on Argumentation: Essays in Honor of Wayne Brockriede,* ed. Robert Trapp and Janice Schuetz (Prospect Heights, IL: Waveland, 1990), 13.

19. Abraham Lincoln, "Second Inaugural Address," in *The World's Great Speeches,* ed. Lewis Copeland (New York: Dover Publications, 1958), 316–317.

20. George Breitman, ed. *Malcolm X Speaks* (New York: Grove Press, 1966), 50. Quoted in: Robert L. Scott, "Justifying Violence: The Rhetoric of Militant Black Power," in Robert L. Scott and Wayne Brockriede, *The Rhetoric of Black Power* (New York: Harper and Row, 1969), 132.

21. Aristotle, *Rhetoric,* trans. W. Rhys Roberts (New York: Modern Library, 1954), 27.

22. Thomas Farrell, *Norms of Rhetorical Culture* (New Haven: Yale University Press, 1993), 77.

23. Lloyd Bitzer, "Political Rhetoric," in *Landmark Essays on Contemporary Rhetoric,* ed. Thomas Farrell (Mahwah, NJ: Hermagoras Press), 1–22, p. 7.

24. Farrell, 79.

25. Perelman and Olbrechts-Tyteca, *New Rhetoric,* 5. See also: Chaim Perelman, *The Idea of Justice and the Problem of Argument* (New York: Random House, 1963), 140.

26. Lanham, 227.

27. Richard Lanham, "The Economics of Attention," *Michigan Quarterly Review* 36 (Spring 1997): 270.

28. See volumes in the new series from Southern Illinois University Press. *Studies in Rhetorics and Feminisms,* ed. Cheryl Glenn and Shirley Wilson Logan.

29. On the relationship of rhetoric and power, see: James A. Berlin, "Revisionary Histories of Rhetoric: Politics, Power, and Plurality," in *Writing Histories of Rhetoric,* ed. Victor Vitanza (Carbondale: Southern Illinois University Press, 1994), 112–127.

30. On ideology and rhetoric, see: Michael Billig, *Ideology and Opinion* (London: Sage, 1991).

31. Billig, *Ideology,* 5.

32. On this topic see, for example: Sally Miller Gearhart, "The Womanization of Rhetoric," *Women's Studies International Quarterly* 2 (1979): 195–201.

33. See: Karlyn K. Campbell, "Hearing Women's Voices," *Communication Education* 40 (January 1991): 33–48.

34. For example: *Women's Voices in Our Time,* eds. Victoria L. DeFrancisco and Marvin Jensen (Prospect Heights, IL: Waveland, 1994).

35. For an overview of the relationship between rhetoric and knowing, see: Richard B. Gregg, *Symbolic Inducement and Knowing: A Study in the Foundations of Rhetoric* (Columbia: University of South Carolina Press, 1984), chap. 1, "Rhetoric, Knowing, and the Symbolic."

36. One of the earliest explorations of this issue is found in: Robert L. Scott, "On Viewing Rhetoric as Epistemic," *Central States Speech Journal* 18 (February 1967): 9–16. See also: Lloyd F. Bitzer, "Rhetoric and Public Knowledge," in *Rhetoric, Philosophy, and Literature: An Exploration* (West Lafayette, IN: Purdue University Press, 1978), pp. 67–93; Walter M. Carleton, "What Is Rhetorical Knowledge?" *Quarterly Journal of Speech* 64 (October 1978): 313–328; Thomas B. Farrell, "Social Knowledge II," *Quarterly Journal of Speech* 64 (October 1978): 329–334.

37. See: *Rhetoric and Community: Studies in Unity and Fragmentation,* ed. Michael J. Hogan (Columbia: University of South Carolina Press, 1998), introduction, xv.

38. Hogan, 292.

39. Lincoln, "Second Inaugural Address," 316–317.

40. Emily Dickinson, "Success Is Counted Sweetest." Reprinted by permission of the publishers and the Trustees of Amherst College from *The Poems of Emily Dickinson,* ed. Thomas H. Johnson (Cambridge, MA: The Belknap Press of Harvard University, copyright © 1951, 1955, 1979 by the President and Fellows of Harvard College.)

CHAPTER TWO

THE ORIGINS AND EARLY HISTORY OF RHETORIC

Rhetoric did not originate at a single moment in history.
Rather, it was an evolving, developing consciousness
about the relationship between thought and expression.
—Richard Leo Enos

It is typical of histories to identify origins, and this chapter will make this history typical in that way. However, the "history" of rhetoric cannot have a beginning point any more than can the history of dance have such an unambiguous genesis. When human beings recognized in movement the capacity, not just for mobility, but also for expression, dance began. When people found in symbols the capacity, not merely for communicating meaning, but also, through some planning, for accomplishing their goals, rhetoric began. Thus, though rhetoric's precise origin as the planned use of symbols to achieve goals cannot be known, its systematic presentation within a particular cultural tradition can be located historically.

The history of rhetoric in the Western tradition begins, as do several other histories or arts or disciplines, with that ancient cluster of highly inventive societies, the Greek city–states of the eighth through the third centuries B.C. But knowing when in Greek history to date the origins of rhetoric, or of those ideas about discourse that became the Greek study of rhetoric, is difficult. Richard Leo Enos points out that theories about the power of language were already present in the writings of Homer in the ninth century B.C. In Homeric writing Enos finds three functions of language: the "heuristic, eristic, and protreptic."[1]

Briefly, the heuristic function of discourse is that of discovery, whether of facts, insights, or even of "self-awareness." The heuristic function of discourse is essential to "the inventive processes," that is the ability to discover the means of expressing our thoughts and sentiments effectively to others.[2] Second, the eristic function of discourse draws our attention to "the inherent power of the language itself."[3] Eristic expresses discourse's power to express, to captivate, to argue, even to injure. Third, the protreptic function of discourse expresses "the capacity [of words]

31

to 'turn' or direct human thought...."[4] That is, language affords human agents the possibility for persuading others to think as they think, to act as they wish them to act. It conversely affords us the ability to dissuade other people from certain thought or actions. These three functions of language—the heuristic, the eristic, and the protreptic—were recognized centuries before they became the foundation for a systematic study of rhetoric.

THE RISE OF RHETORIC IN ANCIENT GREECE

The systematic study of oratory (or rhetoric) probably originated in the city of Syracuse on the island of Sicily around 467 B.C. A tyrant named Hieron had died, and disputes arose over which families were due land that the tyrant had seized. A rhetorician named Corax offered training in judicial pleading to citizens arguing their claims in court. Corax also apparently played a role in directing Syracuse toward democratic reforms.[5] His systematic approach to teaching oratory was quickly adopted by others, and was carried to Athens and other Greek city–states by professional teachers and practitioners of rhetoric known as Sophists. Many Sophists were attracted to the flourishing city of Athens where they taught rhetoric to anyone able to pay their high fees. "In the second half of the fifth century," writes Michael Billig, "Athens offered excellent opportunities for employment to those equipped with quick wits, good speaking voices and a love of disputation." As a result, "provincials like Protagoras of Abdera, Hippias of Elis, Gorgias of Leontini and Prodicus of Iulis poured into Athens from all parts of Greece to seek their fame and fortune."[6]

But why did the Sophists find such a ready market for their rhetorical services at this particular time? Rhetoric's popularity had much to do with dramatic changes affecting several Greek city–states, particularly the major city of Athens, in the sixth and fifth centuries B.C. As historian of rhetoric John Poulakos writes, "when the Sophists appeared on the horizon of the Hellenic city–states, they found themselves in the midst of an enormous cultural change: from aristocracy to democracy." The statesman Solon (638–559 B.C.) had implemented major political reforms in Athens, and leaders such as Cleisthenes, Ephialtes, and especially Pericles (495–429 B.C.) fostered later democratic changes. Poulakos notes that these changes in the Greek political system "created the need for a new kind of education, an education consistent with the new politics of limited democracy."[7] The middle class grew in power as "family name, class origin, or property size" no longer dictated who could be involved in the courts and legislative assemblies.[8] Whereas old established families with great wealth could still afford "to buy the training necessary for leadership in the Assembly, Council and courts," the new system "guaranteed a broader distribution of power across different backgrounds, occupations, and economic statuses than ever before."[9]

As a larger number of men entered the political arena, the key factor in personal success and public influence was no longer class but skill in persuasive speaking. Democratic reforms "completed a process of democratization...allowing for, even requiring, Athenian males to develop the ability to listen, understand, and speak about deliberative and judicial affairs of the city."[10] Moreover, courts, legislative assembly, and numerous festivals and funerals that were so important to life in the Greek city–state all depended on the capacity of citizens to make speeches.

The "city" was known to the Greeks as the *polis,* the independent city–state that, more than anything else, defined what it meant to be Greek. H. D. F. Kitto writes that the Greeks had an "addiction to the independent polis—it was the polis, to the Greek mind, which marked the difference between the Greek and the barbarian: it was the polis which enabled him to live the full, intelligent and responsible life which he wished to live."[11] With democratic reforms, the political life of the *polis* came to be managed by oratory and debate. Tyrants may have ruled other nations by "torture and the lash: the Greeks took their decisions by persuading and debate."[12] Under such circumstances, the need for rhetorical training was apparent to everyone. Apparent, perhaps, but not *available* to everyone. The effect of Athenian democratic reforms on women will be considered later in this chapter.

The Sophists, then, offered Greek citizens—that is, free men—education in the arts of verbal discourse, especially training in inventing arguments and presenting them in a persuasive manner to a large audience. Newly enfranchised citizens created a market for something not previously available in Greece, education in the effective public use of reason.[13]

In most of what we think of as ancient Greece, education was divided into those studies that provided moral strength to the soul—mainly music and literature—and gymnastics that strengthened the body. Higher education in our contemporary sense, that is, advanced studies intended to sharpen the intellect, was virtually unknown. Boys began their schooling at around age seven, and typically had a music teacher, a writing and reading instructor (who also taught them numbers), and an athletic trainer. Because "the Athenian democracy functioned on the assumption that all male citizens were literate," most free males received this basic education. Education was focused on developing useful skills and cultivating traditional Greek values.[14]

For this reason Jacqueline de Romilly writes that the Sophists introduced a "great novelty" into Athenian life by offering education to any who could afford it. Formal education in Athens was rather simple, and limited in its availability to a small portion of the populace. "There was nothing that even remotely resembled what we call further education in Athens" prior to the Sophists, she writes.[15] And, success in Greece required mastery of the arts of public oratory.

Sophists "proudly advertised [their] ability to teach a young man 'the proper care of his personal affairs, so that he may best manage his own household, and also of the State's affairs, so as to become a real power in the city, both as a speaker and man of action.'"[16] Such "advertising" proved irresistible to many young Athenian men, and the Sophists grew in both wealth and influence. The new kind of education offered by the Sophists did not train one in a particular craft like masonry. Rather, rhetorical education offered its students mastery of the skills of language necessary to participating in political life and succeeding in financial ventures. The Sophists' education in rhetoric, then, opened a new doorway to success for many Greek citizens.

In Greece, rhetoric took hold as a major aspect of culture and education, a position it maintained for much of subsequent Western history.[17] The ability to speak persuasively had long been valued by the Greeks, but was viewed as a natural talent, or even as a gift from the gods. Nevertheless, training in rhetoric became the very foundation of Greek education, and eventually came to be viewed as the principal sign of an educated and influential person. "The influence of the spoken word in fifth- or fourth-century Athens was extremely strong," writes H. D. Rankin, "and can hardly be overemphasized."[18] Susan Jarratt and Rory Ong suggest that this was true in part because the Greeks assumed that "human deliberation and action are responsible for human destinies and can be shaped by thought and speech."[19] This assumption marks a profound change in thought, for it indicates that the Greek public gradually rejected the idea that human destiny was shaped by the gods, and accepted in its place a new notion: Human destiny is shaped by human rationality and persuasive speech.

The centrality of rhetoric to a democratic political system was also recognized in Greece. Richard Enos adds that "ancient Greeks considered rhetoric to be a discipline, accepted it as part of their education and, particularly in those cities that were governed by democracies, saw it as practical for the workings of their communities."[20] It was during the fourth century B.C. that the Greeks came to call the theory and practice of public oratory by the name *rhetoric* (*rhetorike*). Ironically, this art of rhetoric, so important to Greek civic life and education, was brought to Athens and other cities by foreign teachers known as Sophists. The activities, beliefs, and reputations of these intriguing rhetoricians deserve a closer look. But first, a brief description of how trials were conducted in ancient Athens will help us appreciate why personal skill in oratory was so crucial to an Athenian.

Trials in Athens

An Athenian trial consisted of two speeches—one of prosecution, the other of defense—and the jury of several hundred members did not deliberate but simply voted. Testimonial evidence had to be filed with the court preceding the trial, and was simply read aloud to the gathered citizen-jury during the trial itself. The time allowed for the all-important speeches was determined by the seriousness of the case being heard. The presiding judge's role was more that of a master of ceremonies and timekeeper than a legal expert. There were no attorneys in the modern sense of the term, nor even a highly developed legal code. A citizen had to speak for himself.

Beginning around 430 B.C. speechwriters, or *logographers* like the Sophist Antiphon, could be hired to write a courtroom speech, albeit for a hefty fee. Interpretation of what laws there were was less significant than was the individual citizen's capacity to present a persuasive speech before a large audience. Immediately following the two speeches a vote was taken and the majority prevailed. Thus, skill in speaking was paramount in Athenian courts, for the most persuasive public speaker carried the day.

THE SOPHISTS

Rhetoric as a systematic study, then, was developed by a group of orators, educators, and advocates called Sophists, a name derived from the Greek word *sophos,* meaning wise or skilled.[21] Central to their course of study was rhetoric, the art (Greek: *techne*) of *logos,* which means both "word" and "argument." The title *Sophistes* (pl. *Sophistae*) carried with it something of the modern meaning of professor—an authority, an expert, a teacher. On occasion, a Sophist might hire himself out as a professional speechwriter, or *logographos.* Others were teachers who ran schools in which public speaking was taught. A third group were professional orators who gave speeches for a fee, whether for entertainment or in a court or legislature. Of course, any particular Sophist might provide all three services—speechwriting, teaching, professional speaker. Sophists earned a reputation for "extravagant displays of language" and for astonishing audiences with their "brilliant styles...colorful appearances and flamboyant personalities."[22]

Many of the Sophists became both wealthy and famous in Greece, while at the same time they were despised by some advocates of traditional Greek social values for reasons we will consider shortly. But first we will explore how and what the Sophists taught their students. The Sophists developed a distinctive style of teaching that proved highly successful. At the same time, the Sophists were controversial from the moment they appeared in Greece. Nevertheless, recent scholarship presents the Sophists as important intellectual figures who have received a somewhat unreservedly negative press.[23] The Sophists were active in Athens and other Greek city–states from about the middle of the fifth century B.C. until the end of the fourth century. Though there never were many Sophists active at any given time, they exercised influence on the development of rhetoric and even the course of Western culture vastly out of proportion with their numbers.[24] Important Sophists include Gorgias, Protagoras, Polus, Hippias, and Theodorus.

Putting the Sophists in Context: The Flourishing of Athens

Regarding the remarkable intellectual flourishing that characterized ancient Greece and shaped subsequent European culture, Michael Gagarin writes: "the second half of the fifth century was a period of intellectual innovation throughout the Greek world, nowhere more so than in Athens. Poets, philosophers, medical writers and practitioners, religious reformers, historians, and others introduced new ways of thinking." He adds that "philosophy and oratory in particular thrived as Athens solidified its position as the intellectual and cultural capital of Greece."[25]

In fact, comparatively speaking, the study and practice of rhetoric had a greater influence on Athenian culture of the day than did now famous philosophers such as Plato. Gagarin notes that "Plato's influence on fourth-century Athenian culture was relatively slight, whereas oratory was central to the lives of most Athenian citizens, who regularly attended meetings of the courts or the Assembly in some capacity, even if they did not actively engage in legal or political affairs." The *polis* of Athens in particular "afforded more opportunities to speak in public than did other Greek cities."[26]

There has been much disagreement over the interests, character, and contributions of the Sophists. As we will see shortly, they were highly controversial even in their own day. Recent scholarship has done much to dismantle the traditional treatment of these men as merely itinerant speechwriters or rhetorically gifted con artists.

They are now often commended for their surprising insights into the power of words and the important social role of persuasion. They were also social iconoclasts who questioned assumptions at the very foundations of Greek society. "Sophists loved to experiment with arguments," writes Gagarin, "and to challenge 'traditional ways of thinking,' and the more shocking the challenge, the better."[27] Sophists employed paradoxes to shock their audiences, but also by this means to provoke debate and inquiry.[28] Though their numbers were never large, the Sophists permanently affected Greek culture.

Still, to the average Athenian some of the leading Sophists appeared to be eccentrics wrapped up in more or less irrelevant intellectual pursuits. Thus, in his famous play *Clouds* Aristophanes mocks the Sophists as preoccupied with ludicrous questions and endless debate. Interestingly, the great playwright treats Socrates himself as a Sophist, though the philosopher neither presented speeches nor taught rhetoric.

What the Sophists Taught

The Sophists were, as we have noted, teachers of the art of verbal persuasion—rhetoric.[29] However, Sophists claimed to teach more than just speech-making. Some professed to instruct their students in *arete,* a Greek term with various meanings including virtue, personal excellence, and even the ability to manage one's personal affairs in an intelligent manner so as to succeed in public life. *Arete* also suggested all of the qualities taken to be marks of "a natural leader."[30] Many Greeks doubted that the Sophists could actually teach *arete,* for virtue and personal excellence were considered gifts of birth or consequences of proper upbringing. Such qualities certainly were not to be purchased from a professional teacher, and especially not from a foreign teacher. Sophistry, then, was more than the study of persuasive speaking, as important as this was. Because the Sophists taught effective public speaking, shrewd management of one's resources, and even some aspects of leadership, it is not surprising that many young men in ancient Greece saw a sophistic education as the key to personal success.

But it was principally the study and mastery of persuasive discourse that brought the Sophists both fame and controversy. Sophists claimed that their courses of instruction would, provided enough money changed hands, teach the student to gain mastery over other people through speech. In Plato's dialogue *Gorgias,* the famous Sophist after whom the dialogue is named asserts that his art is the study of "the greatest good and the source, not only of personal freedom for individuals, but also of mastery over others in one's country." Specifically, Gorgias defines rhetoric as "the ability to persuade with words judges in the courts, senators in the Senate, assemblymen in the Assembly, and men in any other meeting which convenes for the public interest" (452). Poulakos underlines the practical nature of sophistical education by writing that it "concerned itself with rhetorical empowerment for specific, especially political and legal, purposes."[31] By what means, then, did the Sophists teach such a powerful art?

Sophists employed the method of dialectic (Greek: *dialektike*) in their teaching, or inventing arguments for and against a proposition. This approach taught students to argue either side of a case, and the Sophist Protagoras boasted he would teach his students to "make the worse case appear the better." In the dialectical method, speeches and arguments started from statements termed *endoxa,* or premises that were widely believed or taken to be highly probable. For example, an argument might develop from a premise such as, "It is better to possess much virtue than much money." One student would develop an argument or series of arguments based on this widely accepted claim. Another student would then challenge the arguments on the basis of other widely accepted notions, and by exploring the opposite points from those advanced. Thus, in dialectic, argument met counterargument in a series of exchanges that, it was believed, would yield a better view of the truth.

Because of their developed ability to argue either side of a case, the Sophists' students were powerful contestants in the popular debating contests of the day, and also were highly successful advocates in court. The dialectical method was employed in part because the Sophists accepted the notion of *dissoi logoi,* or contradictory arguments. That is, Sophists believed that strong arguments could be produced for or against any claim. We will explore this idea of *dissoi logoi* in more detail shortly when we consider the famous Sophist, Protagoras.

Closely related to the idea of *dissoi logoi* is the Greek notion of *kairos,* a term connoting various meanings such as an opportune moment or a situation. Under the doctrine of *kairos,* the truth depended on a careful consideration of all factors surrounding an event, including time, opportunity, and circumstances. Such factors often were debatable, and could be ascertained only by allowing the clash of arguments to occur. The search for truth about a crime, for example, involved considering opposite points of view. Arguments were advanced about the time or place the crime occurred and the circumstances prompting the act. Truth was discovered, or perhaps created, in the decision finally reached by a jury hearing the clash of antithetical claims and arguments.[32] Thus, the sophistic practice of rhetoric acknowledged the roles played both by *dissoi logoi* and by *kairos* in establishing the facts of a case or the truth of a claim.

The Sophists' teaching methods helped students to analyze cases, to think on their feet, to ask probing questions, to speak eloquently, and to pose counterarguments to an opponent's case. In addition to the dialectical method, Sophists also compelled their students to memorize speeches, either famous ones or model speeches composed by the teacher. Students would also compose their own speeches based on these models. This method was known as *epideixis,* a word describing a speech prepared for a formal occasion. Because of their highly trained ability to memorize speeches, Sophists sometimes performed tremendous feats of memory that left their audiences awe-struck.

In their important study, *Reclaiming Rhetorica,* Susan Jarratt and Rory Ong provide the following glimpse of a group of students learning to write speeches under the guidance of a Sophist. "Speeches were generated out of common materials arranged with some spontaneity for the occasion and purpose at hand. To prepare for performance, small seminar-type groups of students working with an accomplished rhetoician would listen to and memorize speeches composed by their teacher and would practice composing and delivering speeches among themselves." Students practiced both "the production of the whole monologues" as well as doing "closer work with topoi" or frequently used types of arguments. Finally, as already noted, Sophists involved their students in "generating arguments on contradictory propositions or *dissoi logoi.*" Thus, "rhetorical training created a critical climate within which to question, analyze, and imagine differences in group thought and action."[33]

But many Athenians doubted the high-flown claims, doubted that the Sophists really understood justice, doubted that they could teach virtue or truth. Those who were unimpressed with incredible feats of verbal and mental agility saw the Sophists as merely opportunistic charlatans ready to prey on the unsuspecting and willing to introduce into the public mind a debased understanding of truth. Plutarch wrote of the sophists as men with "political shrewdness and practical sagacity." Plato called them simply "masters of the art of making clever speeches," and Xenophon reduced them to the level of "masters of fraud." Rankin writes that the Sophists "released their pupils from the inner need to conform with the traditional rules of the city–state so that they were freer in themselves to be active in their pursuit of success without remorse or conscience."[34] This freedom to pursue one's own goals ruthlessly, unrestrained by conventional mores, while exciting to the Sophists' pupils, caused alarm among some of the more traditional members of Athenian society. As we shall see, this was only one of several reasons the Sophists provoked controversy for more than a century and a half.

Why the Sophists Were Controversial

Many traditional Greeks greeted the Sophists and their art of rhetoric with great suspicion. The Sophists' ability to persuade with clever arguments and stylistic techniques, and their willingness to teach others to do the same, led many Greeks to see the Sophists as a dangerous element in their society. Plato, who lived in Athens in the generation following the arrival of the first Sophists, encouraged such suspicion with his dialogues *Gorgias, Sophist,* and *Protagoras.*[35] Deceptive argumentation in particular was long and widely associated with the Sophists. Aristotle (384–322 B.C.), a student of Plato who was born around the time of the early Sophist Gorgias's death (d. 380 B.C.), commented on their empty arguments in *On Sophistical Refutations.* More than four centuries after Aristotle, Sophists from Greece were still plying their trade in Rome, and similar suspicions attended them.[36]

Sophists were so controversial in Athens and other city–states that their schools of rhetoric were regarded "as a public nuisance and worse."[37] A powerful debate over the Sophists and what they taught is imagined by Plato in his dialogue *Gorgias,* which still stands as a fascinating discussion of the benefits and liabilities pursuing politics and justice by means of persuasively spoken words and carefully crafted arguments. As we will see in the next chapter, Plato condemned rhetoric as "a knack of flattering with words," a criticism the art has never lived down. On the other hand, we should note that Western culture has come closer to following the argumentative model set out by Sophists like Protagoras and Gorgias in the actual conduct of its affairs than that suggested by Plato of seeking truth by means of philosophical inquiry.

What factors in their lives and teaching contributed to the popular feeling that the Sophists were "overpaid parasites"?[38] First, though it does not strike modern readers as a problem, the Sophists taught for pay. Some of the more famous Sophists, such as Hippias, Protagoras, and Gorgias, charged enormous fees for their services and became extremely wealthy. Being paid for teaching, and especially for teaching a student simply to speak persuasively, angered some Athenians. Exacting pay for instruction in something other than a trade like stonemasonry or shipbuilding was simply not done, and the practice seemed to encourage less than noble ideas about both education and work. Andrew Ford notes that the Athenian bias against teaching for pay stemmed from "an aristocratic feeling that…the professional teacher," that is, one accepting payment for teaching, "offered his services on the basis of who could pay and therefore would not base his associations on higher considerations such as character and personal loyalty."[39] In other words, aristocratic families sought to maintain exclusive access to the best education for their own children, and the Sophists threatened this system. Nevertheless, the fees charged by famous Sophists for a course in rhetoric remained out of the reach of most ordinary working Athenians.

Second, many of the Sophists were foreigners who had relocated to Athens, and some were itinerants who traveled from city to city looking for work as teachers, lawyers, entertainers, and speechwriters. People have perhaps always been suspicious of the rootless individual, the wanderer, and the foreigner. Sophistry was considered a foreign import to Athens, and all but a few of the leading Sophists were from outside of Athens. Athenians in particular were suspicious of foreigners claiming to possess knowledge or skills superior to those of the Athenians themselves.

The fact that they were from outside of the Hellenistic world and their habit of travel created a third concern about the Sophists for many Greeks. The Sophists had, as the saying goes, been around, and in their travels they noted that people believe rather different things in different places. Their cultural relativism contributed directly to another reason many in Greece were suspicious of these professional pleaders and teachers of rhetoric. The Sophists, not surprisingly, developed a view of truth as relative to places and cultures. As Susan Jarratt notes, the Sophists "were skeptical about a divine source of knowledge or value…."[40] They knew what the Athenians believed, but also what the Spartans, Corinthians, and North Africans believed. More importantly, they knew that the beliefs in different places were, in some rather important respects, different. The further one got from Athens, the more different were the customs, beliefs, and practices of a culture. In some regions of the known world, for instance, it was the custom to burn the dead, or even to eat them, whereas in other locations such acts would have been capital crimes. Marriage customs, judicial procedures, and social relationships all varied dramatically from one locale to another.

A fourth source of controversy had to do with the Sophists' view of truth. According to Sophists like Gorgias and Protagoras, truth was not to be found in transcendent sources such as the gods or a Platonic realm of universal forms. Rather, Sophists believed that truth emerged from a clash of arguments. Plato repudiated such a view of truth, arguing that it was highly dangerous. In fact, the Sophists' philosophy was even more radical than their moral relativism would suggest. John

Poulakos affirms that the Sophists believed "the world could always be recreated linguistically." That is, reality itself is a linguistic construction rather than an objective fact.[41] If truth and reality depend on who can speak the most persuasively, what becomes of justice, virtue, and social order? Truth became a completely subjective notion, with the individual capable of creating a private view of morality and even of existence. James Murphy and Richard Katula write that "knowledge was subjective and everything is precisely what the individual believes it to be." This meant that "each of us, not necessarily human beings in the collective, decides what something means to us."[42] Such a radical view of truth was a threat to conservative Athenians steeped in Homeric virtues and traditional Greek piety.

Finally, the Sophists were controversial because they built a view of justice on the notion of social agreement or *nomos.* Sophists advocated *nomos* as the source of law in opposition to other sources such as *thesmos,* or law derived from the authority of kings; *physis,* or natural law; and Platonic *logos,* a transcendent source of absolute truth.[43] The Sophists' belief in *nomos* was closely related to their rejection of transcendent truth and objective reality as discussed above. Public law and public morality are matters of social agreements and local practice, and are not derived from absolute authorities like God or a king. This view of truth, some thought, undermined the moral foundations of Greek society. For all of these reasons, then, many Athenians regarded the Sophists with considerable suspicion.

It should be noted, however, that some historians attribute the Sophists' negative image to their enemies' portrayals of them. Several ancient sources suggest that at least some of the Sophists were respectable public figures and expert politicians and diplomats. Janet Sutton has written that "Many of the ancients…paint a brilliant picture of Protagoras, Lysias, Antiphon, Gorgias, and Thrasymacus as ambassadors and statesmen, as superb stylists of poetic expression and orators of civic discourse, and as practical educators and intimates of political leaders."[44] Thus, any portrayal of the Sophists must be shaped, as they would have approved, by contradictory claims.

TWO INFLUENTIAL SOPHISTS

Regardless of the controversy raised by the Sophists in ancient Greece, the art of rhetoric caught on and was an enormous success in the Greek speaking world of the fifth and fourth centuries B.C. In fact, rhetoric came to provide the very foundation of Greek education, while the revolution in thought effected by the Sophists still influences Western ideas about education and politics. The lives of individual Sophists illuminate their thought and teaching in ways that a general survey cannot. Thus, in this section we will take a closer look at two of the most influential Sophists of ancient Greece.

Gorgias

One of the greatest early teachers and practitioners of the art of rhetoric was Gorgias of Leontini, who is reputed to have lived from 485 to 380 B.C., more than one hundred years.[45] Gorgias was originally sent to Athens as an ambassador and had a tremendously successful career as a diplomat, teacher, skeptical philosopher, and speaker. He is famous, among other things, for his three-part formulation of skeptical philosophy:

> 1. Nothing exists. 2. If anything did exist, we could not know it. 3. If we could know that something existed, we would not be able to communicate it to anyone else.

Gorgias was also known for his theory of rhetoric, which gained him both followers and critics in Athens. Richard Leo Enos calls Gorgias "one of the most innovative theorists in Greek rhetoric."[46] Gorgias was active at about the same time as the most famous of all of the early Sophists, Protagoras (485–411 B.C.). Gorgias was a teacher of rhetoric, a defender of the practice, and himself a professional persuader. He boasted of being able to persuade anyone of anything. His powers of persuasion were, indeed, legendary. For instance, he is reputed to have persuaded the Athenians to build a gold statue of him at Delphi, an honor unheard of for a foreigner, though some sources suggest that he paid for this statue. If the latter is the case, it illustrates the great wealth Gorgias accumulated as a Sophist. Gorgias was well aware of the almost magical power persuasive words can exercise over the human mind.[47] He also adhered to a philosophy of language and knowledge that suggested that the only "reality" we have access to "lies in the human psyche, and its malleability and susceptibility" to linguistic manipulation.[48]

But, what was Gorgias' opinion about the source of the power of *logos*? Bruce Gronbeck holds that for Gorgias, persuasion (*peitho*) was "an art of deception, which works through the medium of language to massage the psyche."[49] Brian Vickers writes that Gorgias' "advocacy of rhetoric was based...on its ability to make men its slaves by persuasion, not force" (*Philebus* 58 a-b). But, how was this deception or enslavement accomplished? George Kennedy suggests that Gorgias considered a rhetor to be "a *psychagogos,* like a poet, a leader of souls through a kind of incantation."[50] If this was Gorgias' view, then rhetoric worked magic on auditors, who were captured by the orator's spell-casting abilities. Jacqueline de Romilly, in her book, *Magic and Rhetoric in Ancient Greece,* confirms this view when she connects Gorgias with early practitioners of magical incantations reputed to bring healing, such as Empedocles and Pythagoras.[51] Gorgias would also have been familiar with healing practices of the day through association with his brother, who was a doctor. The "healings" that attracted Gorgias' interest included gaining control over powerful emotions. De Romilly, in fact, refers to Gorgias as "a theoretician of the magic spell of words."[52] In other words, rhetoric was for Gorgias a sort of verbal or, more to the point, poetic magic capable of exerting what one of his great critics, Plato, called an "almost supernatural" influence on audiences. And the emotions were central to controlling an audience. "The masters of rhetoric," writes de Romilly, sought "to sway the emotions of the audience." This was the magical power of rhetoric, a power like that of poetry.[53] Jane Tompkins has noted in this regard that "the equation of language with power, characteristic of Greek at least from the time of Gorgias the rhetorician, explains the enormous energies devoted to the study of rhetoric in the ancient world."[54]

Gorgias' interest in the persuasive power of language drew his attention in particular to the sounds of words. He believed that the "sounds of words, when manipulated with skill, could captivate audiences."[55] Perhaps we find here another expression of Gorgias' rejection of the view that words merely represent. If words do not represent an external reality, then their importance is as a means of shaping a verbal reality in human thought. Gorgias' experiments with sound led to his developing a florid, rhyming style that strikes modern readers as overdone. But, remember, what he is after is a magical incantation to virtually hypnotize his audience, not a tight, logical proof appealing to reason. A brief example, taken from VanHook's translation into English of part of Gorgias' famous *Encomium on Helen,* reflects something of the effect Gorgias sought to achieve with sounds:

> All poetry I ordain and proclaim to composition in meter, the listeners of which are affected by passionate trepidation and compassionate perturbation and likewise tearful lamentation.... Inspired incantations are provocative of charm and revocative of harm.[56]

This speech, a model for use in teaching argument, is also evidence of Gorgias' belief that the skilled rhetorician can prove any proposition. He argues the unlikely thesis that Helen can not be blamed for deserting Menelaus and following Paris to Troy. As George Kennedy summarizes, Gorgias enumerated four possible reasons for Helen's action: "it was the will of the gods; she was taken by force; she was seduced by words; or she was overcome by love."[57]

This hypnotic style was an adaptation of poetic devices, poetry itself being seen as a means of working magic.[58] Gorgias is best remembered in the history of rhetoric for developing stylistic devices that were later augmented and adapted by many subsequent orators and rhetorical theorists. This attention to the inherent power of words to capture and move the human spirit is at the center of Gorgias' interest in and practice of rhetoric. Jacqueline de Romilly notes that in the *Encomium on Helen,* Gorgias argues that Helen "could not have resisted the power of *logos,*" or persuasive words. Later in the speech, he emphasizes this point by calling rhetoric a type of witchcraft or magic.[59]

As poetry was considered in Greek lore to be of divine origin, the relationship between beautiful words and supernatural power was a more natural one for Gorgias than it is for modern readers.[60] Gorgias believed that words worked their magic most powerfully by arousing human emotions such as fear, pity, and longing.[61] Classical scholar G. M. A. Grube notes that Gorgias was especially fond of such rhetorical devices as "over-bold metaphors, *allegoria* or to say one thing and mean another, *hypallage* or the use of one word for another, *catachresis* or to use words by analogy, repetition of words, resumption of an argument, *parisosis* or the use of balanced clauses, *apostrophe* or addressing some person or divinity, and antithesis."[62]

Style and linguistic ornament have remained important aspects of rhetoric throughout its history. Shakespeare is probably the greatest master of the rhetorical figures in the English language. Contemporary orators such as John F. Kennedy also have revealed their knowledge of some of the ancient rhetorical figures. Kennedy, for example, employed *chiasmus* in his famous statement, "Ask not what your country can do for you, rather ask what you can do for your country." *Chi* is the Greek letter X, and *chiasmus* takes its name from the reversing of elements in adjacent clauses, forming an X in the sentence:

Ask not what your **country** can do for **you,**
rather ask what **you** can do for your **country.**

The device can be memorable and effective when well used, as Kennedy's inaugural speech proves.

Gorgias himself was perhaps most interested in the device known as *antithesis,* one that is still quite commonly used. *Antithesis* is, as the name implies, the opposing of ideas in a sentence or paragraph. Thus, a speaker might claim: "My opponent proposes a war that would bring us dishonor, while I advocate a peace that will bring us honor." Here the notions of war and peace are opposed, as are the concepts of dishonor and honor. Gorgias employed this device widely in his own speaking.

But, Gorgias' interest in antithesis extended beyond his concern for style. Like some of the other Sophists, he held that "two antithetical statements can be made on each subject," and that truth emerged from a clash of fundamentally opposed positions.[63] The idea that truth is a product of the clash of views was, as we have seen, closely related to the concept of *kairos,* the belief that truth is relative to circumstances.[64] This view also reflects the Sophists' commitment to *aporia,* the effort to place a claim in doubt. Once clouded in doubt, the orator's goal was to demonstrate that one resolution of the issue was more likely than another.

Protagoras

Whereas Gorgias was a great practitioner of rhetoric and a famous stylist, Protagoras was more important to developing the philosophy underlying rhetorical practices. He was from Abdera in the north of Greece, and probably arrived in Athens around 450 B.C., more than twenty years before Gorgias. Protagoras was active in Athens for nearly forty years, until his death or banishment around 410. Though he traveled widely, his reputation was such that "wherever he went rich and clever young men flocked to hear him."[65]

Protagoras is alleged to have been "the first person to charge for lectures," and is considered by some to be the first of the Greek Sophists.[66] His most famous maxim is that "man is the measure [*metron*] of all things; of things that are not, that they are not; of things that are, that they are."[67] But what he meant by this claim, in true sophistic fashion, has been the subject of much debate. He at least seems to have had in mind that people make determinations about what is or is not true, and that there is no ultimate or absolute appeal that can be made to finally settle such questions. Thus, the claim embodies both the concept of relative truth, and of its pursuit through *kairos.* Perhaps consistent with this relativistic view of truth, Protagoras affirmed that the existence of a god or gods was virtually unknowable given the difficulty of the subject and the shortness of human life.

In the fashion of the itinerant, Protagoras taught in Sicily, Athens, and several other Greek cities. His reputation as a scholar and teacher was widespread, and recent scholarship attributes to him a number of significant intellectual accomplishments. He is said to have made "important contributions to rhetoric, epistemology, the critical study of religion, the study of social origins, dialectic, and literary criticism."[68] But he is also thought to be the first person to systematize eristic argument, or what amounted to argumentative tricks that ignore true meaning (*dianoia*) in order to ensure rhetorical victory.

Protagoras was best known for teaching a highly practical approach to reasoning on political as well as personal questions. He advertised that he could train one, for a fee, of course, to successfully manage an estate, become a good citizen, and be prepared for political service. He apparently was convinced that contradictory arguments can always be advanced on issues of public and private significance, and that resolution of important issues depended on the clash of pro and con cases. Every logos (or argument) can be met with an antilogos or counterargument. Thus, his view of the nature of rhetorical inquiry is similar to that of Gorgias, and brings to mind the Sophists' interest in *dissoi logoi,* or contradictory claims. Protagoras is also credited with a method of questioning taken up by Socrates; presumably it was derived from his practice of generating contradictory propositions on any subject.[69]

Protagoras taught by requiring students to advance arguments for and against a variety of claims.[70] An argument could be said to have prevailed only when "it has been tested by and had withstood the attacks of the opposing side(s)." Even understanding a claim requires a consideration, not just of the claim itself, but of its opposite.[71] As John Poulakos writes, "clearly, Protagoras' notion of *dissoi logoi* provides a worldview with rhetoric at its center." Of value to the student was the fact that "this worldview demands of the human subject a multiple awareness, an awareness at once cognizant of its own position and of those positions opposing it."[72]

As we have noted, Sophists were considered less than upright citizens by many Greeks. Nevertheless, some of them had connections with very powerful people in Athens. Protagoras, for instance, was close to Pericles himself, the most powerful man in Athens. But they also had earned the disdain of a writer who was to shape conceptions of them for much of Western history—the great philosopher, Plato. The persistent bad connotations that Sophistry in particular, and rhetoric in general, has maintained in Western culture can be traced directly to Plato's famous attack on the Sophists. That famous attack, and Plato's own views of rhetoric, will be considered in Chapter 3. Despite Plato's sentiments, however, many scholars now see the Sophists as important innovators who "put the art of speaking and speech-writing on a more professional basis, equipping their pupils for success in the life of the developed *polis*."[73]

ISOCRATES: A MASTER OF RHETORIC

Another important figure often associated with rhetoric in Athens is Isocrates (436–338 B.C.), born fifty years after Gorgias and Protagoras, and fifty years before Aristotle.

He was only ten years older than Plato, and was thus a contemporary and in some respects a rival of this great philosopher. Both men studied philosophy under Socrates, and both claimed him as their model.[74] It is likely that as a young man Isocrates also studied rhetoric under Gorgias, a figure in whom Plato found little to respect.

Born into a wealthy family, Isocrates worked for a time as a *logographos* or professional speechwriter. Around 390 B.C. he founded a school in Athens, the first of the rhetorical schools, and eventually became the most respected teacher of rhetoric in the city. He also became quite wealthy. Andrew Ford writes, "For nearly half a century Isocrates was the most famous, influential, and successful teacher of politically ambitious young men in Greece. He also became one of the wealthiest teachers of his day." Ford helps us to understand just how much money Isocrates could command for his course of study. "The fee for his course was 1,000 drachmas, at a time when a day laborer was paid about 1 drachma a day."[75] If we consider what someone making minimum wage today might bring home in a day, and multiply that sum by one thousand, we get a relative idea of the cost of a course from a famous Sophist.

Whereas the great Sophists of the previous generation came from outside of Athens, Isocrates was a native Athenian. Whereas they were itinerants and cosmopolitan in their outlook, Isocrates was a devoted pan-Hellenist, that is, a Greek who believed in the unity and expansion of Greece, and in the general superiority of Greek culture to other cultures. Moreover, in some of his writings, such as the essay *Against the Sophists,* Isocrates was critical of the earlier Sophists. For these reasons, historians are reluctant to classify Isocrates as a Sophist. Still, he was a student of Gorgias, held some views in common with the early Sophists, and taught rhetoric for pay. And to the typical Athenian the term simply meant an intellectual with a special interest in words and arguments. Certainly this description applied to Isocrates.

Isocrates' approach to education was both highly practical and rigidly structured. He taught rhetoric in part by the use of model speeches that he himself composed. Many of these speeches reflect his ardent practical interest in Greek political issues. Two of the more famous are the early speech, entitled *Panegyricus* (c. 380 B.C.), and the *Plataeicus.* In the former he wrote that Athens "gave honor to skill in words, which is the desire and envy of all."[76] Some of Isocrates' speeches were circulated as written documents, and are considered perhaps the earliest polemical treatises on political topics. Among these are *Symmachicus* and *Areopagiticus.* Isocrates' tendency to write out his speeches and to circulate them in this form marks a general shift in Greek rhetoric from a predominantly spoken medium to one emphasizing written discourse.[77] It also suggests the sort of reputation Isocrates hoped to cultivate. Ford writes that "Isocrates wanted to be thought of finally not as a teacher of orators, but as the teacher of the nation, as a serious and weighty commentator on the affairs of Greece."[78]

Much of Isocrates' interest in rhetoric was a consequence of his concern for preparing Greek leaders to make wise and effective political judgments. He attracted talented students to his school, many of whom became famous and influential as statesmen and orators. His greatness as a teacher was unsurpassed, and his highly refined pedagogical approaches became models for later educators. Isocrates' teaching was not aimed at creating clever and entertaining speakers, but rather at improving the political practices of Athens. Poulakos points out that Isocrates' teaching of rhetoric "introduced two new requirements to rhetorical education—the thematic and the pragmatic." Poulakos explains that "the thematic asked that rhetoric concentrate on significant matters while the pragmatic demanded that it make a positive contribution to the life of the audience."[79]

For Isocrates, it was rhetoric—"the power to persuade each other"—that made human civilization itself possible. In his speech *Antidosis* (c. 353 B.C.) he argues that "there has been implanted in us the power to persuade each other and to make clear whatever we desire, not only have we escaped the life of wild beasts, but we have come together and founded cities and made laws and invented arts; and, generally speaking, there is no institution devised by man which the power of speech has not helped us to establish."[80] What, then, could be more significant than the study of this art?

Isocrates grounded this highly intentional, nationalistic, and morally oriented rhetorical training on three factors: natural talent, extensive practice, and education in basic principles of rhetoric. Where natural talent was lacking, there was little even a talented teacher could do to compensate for its absence. Where talent was present, Isocrates believed that it could be developed through instruction and practice. But Isocrates also insisted on high moral character in his students. This concern for *ethos,* or the speaker's character, set Isocrates apart from the Sophists whose orientation was decidedly more practical. *Ethos,* as we shall see in subsequent chapters, remained a central concern in Greek rhetorical theory.

The style of Isocrates' speeches was elegant, though some historians have accused him of being relatively unconcerned about factual accuracy. Isocrates' style influenced later orators such as Demosthenes and Cicero. Though he claimed to teach effective oratory, Isocrates did not claim to be able to teach *arete* or virtue.[81] "Let no one suppose," he wrote, "that I claim that just living can be taught; for I hold that there does not exist an art of the kind which can implant sobriety and justice in depraved natures."[82] That is, no one can be taught to be moral who does not already possess the kind of nature that desires to live a moral life. For the Sophists to claim that they could teach anyone *arete* was simply absurd. Isocrates did, however, advocate high moral standards in his students and in the citizenry generally. He upbraided the Athenians for heeding the corrupted rhetoric of politicians who promised them what they wanted, but who did not care about either the health of their souls or the city's good. Isocrates advanced the same analogy between medicine and rhetoric that Plato employs in the dialogue *Gorgias,* which we will explore in the following chapter.[83]

Isocrates taught that rhetoric should be used to advance Greek ideas and institutions, and held in disdain the shoddy rhetoric practiced in the courts and legislature. In this way he agreed with Plato. Richard Enos writes that "Isocrates was committed to the notion of a united Greece and believed that rhetoric was a tool that empowered his educational system to promote such an ideal in a number of different areas."[84] Isocrates also staunchly advocated the fair conduct of trials, including letting the accused have an equal chance to defend himself in court.[85] But his greatest cause was pan-Hellenism, which focused on urging unity among the Greek city–states (following the lead of Athens, of course) against their common foe, Persia. This goal required convincing the city–states to leave off warring with one another, a practice that drained their resources and left them vulnerable to attack by outside forces. Despite the warnings of Isocrates and others, including Demosthenes, Philip of Macedon put an end to all efforts toward pan-Hellenism by his crushing defeat of the Greek armies at Chaeronea.

Isocrates' highly developed written style and great regard for the practical uses of language have had an extraordinary influence on the course of Western education. Later rhetoricians such as Cicero considered him to be among the greatest of the Greek rhetoricians. He is also now considered the likely founder of the European humanist tradition, which we will explore in Chapter 7.

ASPASIA'S ROLE IN ATHENIAN RHETORIC

Women did not have an easy lot in ancient Athens. They were not recognized as full citizens, and were prohibited from a variety of occupations and public events. Even aristocratic women were seldom seen in public, and their "activities, movements, education, marriage, and rights as citizens and property holders were extremely circumscribed." Most women "were confined within the house at all times, except on occasions of religious festivals."[86] Because of the tremendous impact of Athens on later European culture, this practice influenced subsequent practices and attitudes in the Western world.

Making speeches was one activity from which Greek men typically barred Greek women. In the rhetorical arena, as in others, the treatment of women in ancient Greece stemmed directly from male attitudes. The Greek writer Democritus, for example, "asserts that women should not be allowed to practice argument because men detest being ruled by women. In asserting this, he describes a detestable—and not fictional—practice." Historian of rhetoric C. Jan Swearingen writes that an edict entitled "On Pleading," which dates from the sixth century A.D. "repeats the terms of Democritus' proscription: 'It is prohibited to women to plead on behalf of others. And indeed there is reason for the prohibition: lest women mix themselves up in other people's cases, going against the chastity that befits their gender.' "[87]

As democratic reforms took hold in Athens, the place of women did not improve. Because they were still denied citizenship, women "did not participate in any formal public functions."[88] In fact, the very reforms that opened the way to more Greek citizens to participate in politics seem to have worked *against* women's participation. "It remains a remarkable feature of Greek history," writes Ellen Wood, "that the position of women seems to have declined as the democracy evolved...."[89] This is likely because the larger number of men now involved in politics made it even more difficult for women to find a place in public life. Only in rural regions and in some less democratic city–states, such as Sparta, did the place of women improve slightly during the fifth and fourth centuries.

As we will note in subsequent chapters, women throughout history often have found it difficult to participate in the rhetorical life of their communities. The harshness of attitudes toward women in the ancient world makes the story of Aspasia, a female rhetorician of the sixth century B.C., particularly intriguing. As Susan Jarratt and Rory Ong write of this remarkable woman, "Aspasia left no written remains. She is known through a handful of references, the most substantial of which are several paragraphs of narratives in Plutarch's life of Pericles and an oration attributed to her in Plato's dialogue *Menexenus*." In response to the assertion by some historians that Aspasia was a legendary figure, they write, "allusions to her by four of Socrates' pupils help to confirm Plutarch's assertion that Aspasia was indeed a real person, a teacher of rhetoric who shared her knowledge and political skill with Pericles."[90]

Aspasia apparently hailed from Miletus, a Greek colony along the coast of Asia Minor. The great Greek general and orator Pericles lived with Aspasia "as a beloved and constant companion."[91] Aspasia's knowledge of politics was without equal, as was her ability as a rhetorician. She is reputed to have "taught the art of rhetoric to many, including Socrates, and may have invented the so-called Socratic method."[92] It has also been argued that Aspasia actually wrote Pericles' famous "Funeral Oration," one of the most powerful rhetorical performances of antiquity. Plato notes in his dialogue *Menexenus* that when Socrates was asked whether he could meet the challenge of giving a speech at a public funeral for men who have died in battle, "the philosopher replies, 'That I should be able to speak is no great wonder, Menexenus, considering that I have an excellent mistress in the art of rhetoric—she who has made so many good speakers, and one who was the best among all the Hellenes—Pericles, the son of Xanthippus.'"[93] Socrates himself, then, acknowledges that Aspasia was his rhetorical tutor, and that she had played the same role for the great leader Pericles. Aspasia's story underlines both the tremendous rhetorical ability of a remarkable woman, and the stringent limits placed by the ancients on women in the domain of rhetoric. As evidence of the tremendous barriers Greek women faced, Cheryl Glenn writes that "Aspasia seems to have been the only woman in classical Greece to have distinguished herself in the public domain."[94]

CONCLUSION

The number of Sophists working in Greece was never large, nor were they a major part of the scene in city–states like Athens for a long period. The greatest of the Sophists were active in Athens between about 450 and 380 B.C. Nevertheless, these provocative rhetoricians had an amazing influence over Greek life and thought. Jacqueline de Romilly is not exaggerating when she writes that "the teaching of both rhetoric and philosophy was marked forever by the ideas that the Sophists introduced and the debates that they initiated."[95] Why, we may ask, is this the case? Several reasons suggest themselves.

First, the Sophists emphasized the centrality of persuasive discourse to civilized, democratic social life. Their thinking on this matter was often insightful, and provoked discussion of rhetoric's role in democratic civic life. Second, the Sophist's appreciation for the sheer power of language also marked a theme that would continue to be important to later intellectual history in the West. Their explorations of this concept are still important to the discussion of language's centrality to thought and social life. Third, it is probably the case that the Sophist's arguments for a view of law as rooted in social conventions, and for truth as relative to places and times, influenced later philosophical and political thought. Finally, the Sophists' tendency to place rhetorical training at the center of education constituted an innovation that would continue to have influence for centuries.

There are several strikingly modern factors in the Sophists' approach to rhetoric and education, and their insights on a number of important issues in philosophy, politics, and rhetoric are only now being fully appreciated. Contemporary scholars are currently reassessing the contributions of this remarkable group of teachers, theorists, and practitioners of rhetoric. It is also important to note, however, that when studying the Sophists we are unavoidably confronted with the central ethical concern that attends rhetoric throughout its history. Rhetoric is a kind of power, and power can be used for good or for bad purposes. The Sophists were notorious in part because they disregarded conventional Greek ideas about the moral uses of language and argument. They also ignored moral conventions concerning who could or could not be educated in the powers of language. The Sophists insisted that persuasive arguments can always be made on either side of an issue, not just on the side favored by those adhering to prevailing moral assumptions. These crucial ethical questions about the power of language and who should have access to that power, once introduced by Gorgias, Protagoras, and the other Sophists, would be a permanent feature of rhetoric's history. In fact, the long debate over rhetoric, power, and ethics began in the Sophists' own day when these same questions attracted the attention of the greatest philosophical mind in Athens. His assault on the Sophists' view of rhetoric is the subject of the next chapter.

QUESTIONS FOR REVIEW

1. What beliefs, practices and personal qualities characterized the Sophists?

2. What educational revolution did the Sophists introduce into Athenian society? Why were these teachers of rhetoric controversial in Athens?

3. What was the Sophists' view of truth?

4. Why was the concept of a clash of views important to the Sophists?

5. What was *eristic* rhetoric, and why might some Athenians have been bothered by the practice?

6. Why, in your own words, was the study of rhetoric important to the citizens of ancient Athens?

7. What threat did the Sophists pose to traditional Greek society?

8. What claims did the Sophists make about their teaching?

9. What did Gorgias see as the relationship between rhetoric and magic?

10. What goal did Isocrates seek through his emphasis on pan-Hellenism?

11. Who was Aspasia?

QUESTIONS FOR DISCUSSION

1. What members of contemporary society, in your estimation, most resemble the Sophists?

2. After reading about the Sophists, do you think they deserve the bad reputation they had with many of their contemporaries?

3. In what ways, if any, does U.S. society appear to be sophistic in orientation?

4. Could the teaching and practice of rhetoric in our own society elicit the same controversy it did in ancient Greece? Why or why not?

5. Assuming that rhetoric is not a central educational concern today, where do citizens today learn to reason and to speak persuasively?

6. What, if anything, might be gained by a consistent program of rhetorical studies in schools today? Is there anything to be gained by *not* teaching people to reason and speak persuasively and effectively? Which group, if any, realizes an advantage from the absence of rhetorical training?

7. What, if anything, is the relationship between truth and argument? Persuasion and ethics?

8. The Sophists built a view of justice on conventional agreements or *nomos*. Other possible sources of law or justice included the authority of kings (*thesmos*), natural law (*physis*), and certain truth derived from philosophical argumentation (Platonic *logos*). What, in your opinion, ought to be the basis of a view of justice?

9. Do you agree with Gorgias about the great potential in language for the control of the minds of others? What, if any, are the risks associated with great eloquence? How should the public be educated so as to have a defense against the great rhetorical skill possessed by some speakers and writers?

10. What effects on the subsequent history of Western culture may have resulted from the exclusion of women from rhetorical theory and practice in ancient Greece?

TERMS

Aporia: Placing a claim in doubt by developing arguments on both sides of the issue.

Arete: Virtue; an ability to manage one's personal affairs in an intelligent manner, and to succeed in public life. Human excellence, natural leadership ability.

Chiasmus: Rhetorical device that takes its name from the reversing of elements in parallel clauses, forming an X (*chi*) in the sentence.

Dialektike: Dialectic, the method of investigating philosophical issues by the give and take of argument. A method of teaching that involved training students to argue either side of a case.

Dianoia: True meaning, as opposed to false (eristic) arguments.

Dissoi logoi: Contradictory arguments.

Endoxa: The probable premises from which dialectic began. Premises that were widely believed.

Epideixis: A speech prepared for a formal occasion.

Eristic: Discourse's power to express, to captivate, to argue, or to injure.

Heuristic: Discourse's capacity for discovery, whether of facts, insights, or even of self-awareness.

Kairos: Rhetoric's search for relative truth rather than absolute certainty; a consideration of opposite points of view, as well as attention to such factors as time and circumstances. An opportune moment or situation.

Logos: Word; argument. Also, a transcendent source of truth for Plato.

Metron: Measure; from Protagoras' "man is the measure (*metron*) of all things; of things that are not, that they are; of things that are, that they are."

Nomos: Social custom or convention; rule by agreement among the citizens.

Physis: The law or rule of nature under which the strong dominate the weak.

Protreptic: The possibility for persuading others to think as they think, to act as they wish them to act.

Psychagogos: A poet, a leader of souls through a kind of incantation.

Sophistes: (plural: *Sophistae*). An authority, an expert, a teacher. A teacher of rhetoric.

Techne: A practical art, a science, or a systematic study.

Thesmos: Law derived from the authority of kings.

ENDNOTES

1. Richard Leo Enos, *Greek Rhetoric before Aristotle* (Prospect Heights, IL: Waveland, 1993), 4.
2. Enos, 5.
3. Enos, 6.
4. Enos, 7–8.
5. Jane Sutton, "The Marginalization of Sophistical Rhetoric and the Loss of History," in *Rethinking the History of Rhetoric,* ed. Takis Poulakos (Boulder, CO: Westview, 1993), 87.
6. Michael Billig, *Arguing and Thinking* (Cambridge: Cambridge University Press, 1987), 35.
7. J. Poulakos, "Terms for Sophistical Rhetoric," in *Rethinking the History of Rhetoric: Multidisciplinary Essays on the History of Rhetoric,* ed. Takis Poulakos (Boulder, CO: Westview, 1993), 53–74, p. 56.
8. J. Poulakos, 57.
9. Susan Jarratt and Rory Ong, "Aspasia: Rhetoric, Gender, and Colonial Ideology," in *Reclaiming Rhetorica: Women in the Rhetorical Tradition,* ed. Andrea Lunsford (Pittsburgh, PA: University of Pittsburgh Press, 1995), 14.
10. Jarratt and Ong, 14.
11. H. D. F. Kitto, *The Greeks* (1951; Baltimore, MD: Penguin Books, 1968), 120.
12. Kitto, 115.
13. John Poulakos, *Sophistical Rhetoric in Classical Greece* (Columbia: University of South Carolina Press), 16–17.
14. Maurice Balme and Gilbert Lawall, *Athenaze: An Introduction to Ancient Greek* Book II (New York: Oxford University Press, 1991), 105–106.
15. Jacqueline de Romilly, *The Great Sophists in Periclean Athens,* trans. Janet Lloyd (Oxford: Clarendon Press, 1992), 30.
16. W. K. C. Guthrie, *The Sophists* (Cambridge: Cambridge University Press, 1971), 20.
17. John Poulakos, "Toward a Sophistic Definition of Rhetoric," *Philosophy and Rhetoric* 16 (1983): 35–48; Josiah Ober, *Mass and Elite in Democratic Athens: Rhetoric, Ideology, and the Power of the People* (Princeton, NJ: Princeton University Press, 1989).
18. H. D. Rankin, *Sophists, Socratics and Cynics* (London: Croom Helm, 1983), 15. Other helpful discussions of this period in Greek thought, and of the Sophists, include: Harold Barrett, *The Sophists* (Novato, CA: Chandler and Sharp, 1987); G. B. Kerferd, *The Sophistic Movement* (Cambridge University Press, 1981); J. Sallis, *Being and Logos* (Atlantic Highlands, NJ: Humanities Press, 1986).

19. Jarratt and Ong, 12.

20. Enos, ix.

21. On the meaning of *Sophist,* see: Edward Schiappa, *Protagoras and Logos* (Columbia: University of South Carolina Press, 1991), chap. 1.

22. J. Poulakos, "Terms," 58.

23. See, for example: Susan C. Jarratt, *Rereading the Sophists: Classical Rhetoric Refigured* (Carbondale, IL: Southern Illinois University Press, 1991).

24. See: Guthrie.

25. Michael Gagarin, *Antiphon and the Athenians: Oratory, Law and Justice in the Age of the Sophists* (Austin, TX: University of Texas Press, 2002), 1.

26. Gagarin, 5, 6.

27. Gagarin, 16–17.

28. Gagarin, 18.

29. See: Mario Untersteiner, *The Sophists* (Oxford: Oxford University Press, 1954).

30. Guthrie, 25. Rankin writes that *arete* "combines the factors both of high moral virtue and worldly success" (13).

31. J. Poulakos, "Terms," 57.

32. Dale Sullivan, "*Kairos* and the Rhetoric of Belief," *Quarterly Journal of Speech* 78: August 1992, 320.

33. Jarratt and Ong, 16.

34. Rankin, 14.

35. See: Schiappa, chapter 1.

36. See: G. W. Bowersock, *Greek Sophists in the Roman Empire* (Oxford: Clarendon Press, 1969).

37. Andrew Ford, "The Price of Art in Isocrates: Formalism and the Escape from Politics," in *Rethinking the History of Rhetoric,* ed. Takis Poulakos (Boulder, CO: Westview, 1992), 37.

38. Ford, 37.

39. Ford, 37.

40. Jarratt, xx.

41. J. Poulakos, *Sophistical Rhetoric,* 25.

42. *A Synoptic History of Classical Rhetoric,* eds. Richard Katula and James J. Murphy (Davis, CA: Hermagoras Press, 1995), 28.

43. Jarratt, 42.

44. Sutton, 87.

45. On Gorgias' philosophy of *logos,* see: Charles P. Segal, "Gorgias and the Psychology of the *Logos*," *Harvard Studies in Classical Philology* 66 (1962): 99–155.

46. Enos, 72.

47. See: John O. Ward, "Magic and Rhetoric from Antiquity to the Renaissance: Some Ruminations," *Rhetorica* VI (Winter 1988): 57–118, especially p. 58.

48. Segal, 110. Quoted in Bruce E. Gronbeck, "Gorgias on Rhetoric and Poetic: A Rehabilitation," *Southern Speech Communication Journal* 38 (Fall 1972): 27–38.

49. Gronbeck, 33.

50. George Kennedy, *Classical Rhetoric and Its Christian and Secular Tradition,* 2d ed. (Chapel Hill: University of North Carolina Press, 1999), 35.

51. Jacqueline de Romilly, *Magic and Rhetoric in Ancient Greece* (Cambridge, MA: Harvard University Press, 1975).

52. de Romilly, 16.

53. de Romilly, 6.

54. Jane P. Tompkins, "The Reader in History: The Changing Shape of Literary Response," in *Reader Response Criticism,* ed. Jane P. Tompkins (Baltimore, MD: Johns Hopkins University Press, 1980), 203–204.

55. G. M. A. Grube, *The Greek and Roman Critics* (Toronto: University of Toronto Press, 1965), 16.

56. Gorgias, *Encomium on Helen* 9 and 10, trans. LaRue VanHook, *Classical Weekly* 6 (1913): 122–123. Quoted in Gronbeck, 34.

57. Kennedy, 35.

58. Kennedy, 64.

59. de Romilly, *Magic,* 3.

60. de Romilly, *Magic,* 4.

61. de Romilly, *Magic,* 5.

62. Grube, 16.

63. Kennedy, 66.

64. On Gorgias' philosophy of language and knowledge, see: Gronbeck.

65. Balme and Lawall, 106.

66. Billig, 40. Billig cites Philostratus, *Lives of the Sophists,* trans. W. C. Wright (London: Loeb Classical Library, 1965); Rankin, 30, ff.

67. Plato, *Theaetetus,* 151e–152a.

68. Rankin, 32.

69. Jarratt and Ong in *Reclaiming Rhetorica,* 15.

70. Billig, 41.

71. J. Poulakos, "Terms," 58–59.

72. J. Poulakos, "Terms," 60.

73. Robin Sowerby, *The Greeks: An Introduction to Their Culture* (London: Routledge, 1995), 107.

74. de Romilly, *Great Sophists,* viii.

75. Andrew Ford, "The Price of Art in Isocrates: Formalism and the Escape from Politics," in *Rethinking the History of Rhetoric,* ed. Takis Poulakos (Boulder, CO: Westview, 1992), 37.

76. Quoted in Sowerby, 108.

77. On the importance of writing as an intellectual activity at this time, see: Kathleen E. Welch, *The Contemporary Reception of Classical Rhetoric: Appropriations of Ancient Discourse* (Hillsdale, NJ: Lawrence Erlbaum, 1990), 16–17.

78. Ford, 38.

79. J. Poulakos, *Sophistical Rhetoric,* 134.

80. *Antidosis, 254.* Quoted in Brian Vickers, *In Defense of Rhetoric* (Oxford: Clarendon Press, 1988), 156.

81. Vickers, 150.

82. The quote is from *Against the Sophists.* Quoted in Vickers, 150.

83. Vickers, 154,

84. Enos, 114.

85. Vickers, 155.

86. Jarratt and Ong, 13.

87. C. Jan Swearingen, "A Lover's Discourse: Diotima, Logos, and Desire," in *Reclaiming Rhetorica: Women in the Rhetorical Tradition,* ed. Andrea Lunsford (Pittsburgh, PA: University of Pittsburgh Press, 1995), 25–26.

88. Jarratt and Ong, 14.

89. Ellen Meiksins Wood, *Peasant–Citizen and Slave: The Foundations of Athenian Democracy* (London: Verso, 1988), 115. Quoted in Jarratt and Ong, 13.

90. Susan Jarratt and Rory Ong, 10.

91. Jarratt and Ong, 12.

92. Jarratt and Ong, 13.

93. Jarratt and Ong, 15. *Menexenus,* par. 235.

94. Cheryl Glenn, "Locating Aspasia on the Rhetorical Map," in *Listening to Their Voices: The Rhetorical Activities of Historical Women,* ed. Molly Meijer Wertheimer (Columbia: University of South Carolina Press, 1997), 19–41, p. 21.

95. de Romilly, *Great Sophists,* 4.

CHAPTER THREE

PLATO VERSUS THE SOPHISTS
RHETORIC ON TRIAL

Your way, Callicles, has no value whatever.
—Socrates in Plato's *Gorgias* (527e)

As noted in Chapter 2, the Sophists were highly controversial in Greece for over a century. One of their chief critics was the great philosopher Plato (427–347 B.C.), who attacked the sophistic practice of rhetoric in his dialogue entitled *Gorgias,* and suggested the possibility of a "true rhetoric" in another dialogue called *Phaedrus.*[1] Sophists and their philosophy are also mentioned in Plato's dialogues *Sophist* and *Protagoras,* as well as other places in his dialogues.[2] Whereas Plato's thirty-year-long attack on rhetoric has been called "idiosyncratic and extreme" by historian of rhetoric Brian Vickers, Plato's views do point up the long rivalry between rhetoric and philosophy.[3] It is not exaggerating to say that rhetoric and philosophy have been at odds at various crucial points throughout Western history.[4]

Because Plato so successfully anticipates the major issues that attend rhetoric throughout its long history—issues like power, the potential for manipulation, and rhetoric's relationship to truth—*Gorgias* has long been viewed as a valuable treatment of the Sophists in particular and rhetoric in general. But, it should also be borne in mind that because Plato is arguing against the Sophists in *Gorgias,* his own ability as a rhetorician is itself on display. In fact, historian of rhetoric George Kennedy calls Plato "a consummate rhetorician," adding "no dialogue of Plato is untouched by rhetoric."[5] Plato himself suggests a good use for rhetoric in his dialogue *Phaedrus,* a point that often has attracted the attention of rhetorical theorists. A towering philosophical genius, Plato's thoughts on the potential for good and for harm in rhetoric continue to prompt thought and debate. His withering criticism of the Sophists in *Gorgias* undoubtedly has shaped attitudes toward them and toward rhetoric ever since. But, as will be shown, it may be the case that even *Gorgias* points the way to the "right" uses of rhetoric. We will take a close look at his treatment of sophistry in *Gorgias* first, and then turn to Plato's thoughts about the potentially good uses of rhetoric in *Phaedrus.*[6]

PLATO'S *GORGIAS:* RHETORIC ON TRIAL

In Plato's intriguing dialogue, *Gorgias,* the protagonist Socrates, a character modeled on Plato's great teacher but apparently representing Plato's own views, takes on three Sophists in a debate over rhetoric's effects on politics and justice.[7] The debate that transpires in *Gorgias,* one of Plato's early dialogues, written around 387 B.C., mixes elements drawn from actual debates with imagined dialogue representing the views of Socrates, Plato, and the famous Sophist Gorgias. Though Plato aims his arguments at Sophists in particular, he builds a case against anyone depending on rhetoric for a living, especially politicians. Such wielders of persuasive words Plato refers to collectively as *rhetores* (rhetors or politicians), and it is clear that he has little respect for them. As Vickers points out, "Plato crudely lumped all politicians and rhetors together as flatterers and corrupters of the people."[8] The Sophists were the most prominent and controversial of the rhetoricians in Athens, and thus were a convenient target for Plato's attack. But Plato held no great regard for Athenian politicians, the same people who had put his teacher Socrates to death, and many of his arguments in *Gorgias* are directed against them as well. Thus, Kennedy calls the *Gorgias* "a criticism of all rhetoric and all rhetoricians."[9]

In *Gorgias,* Plato addresses major questions attending rhetoric throughout its history, many of which are as important to contemporary society as they were to the ancient Greeks. What is the nature of rhetoric? Does rhetoric by its very nature tend to mislead? What happens to a society when persuasion forms the basis of law and justice? The dialogue transpires before a small audience of Sophists and other guests gathered in a home for a dinner party. The drama of *Gorgias* develops around Socrates' dialogues first with Gorgias himself, then with a young Sophist named Polus, and finally with the villainous Callicles, a more mature Sophist in whose home the play is set.

Plato was critical of the Sophists on a number of grounds, including their "taking money," "making exaggerated pedagogical claims," and "boastfulness."[10] But his general contention in *Gorgias* is that rhetoric as practiced by the Sophists, or at least by some of the more notorious Sophists, does not embody an adequate conception of justice, and is thus a dangerously deceptive activity for both the individual and the state.[11] The Sophists' rhetoric, according to Plato, aimed only at *persuasion* about justice through the manipulation of public opinion (*doxa*), whereas an adequate view of justice must be grounded in true knowledge (*episteme*), and aim at the well-being of the individual and of the city–state (*polis*).[12]

The Debate with Gorgias: Rhetoric's Nature and Uses

As *Gorgias* opens, Socrates states that he wants to ask the famous Sophist after whom the dialogue is named, and who was still living when the dialogue was published, about "the power of his art, and what it is he professes to teach" (447).[13] More to the point, Socrates wants to know, "With what class of objects is rhetoric concerned?" This question reflects Plato's conviction that any *true art or discipline,* the translation of the Greek term, *techne,* involves knowledge of some class of objects, just as medicine involves knowledge of the human body. The practitioner of any *techne* must be able to give an account (*logos,* here meaning rational explanation) of the art, that is, explain in clear and logical terms how it achieves its ends.

This opening question about rhetoric's subject matter should be a simple one for a great master of rhetoric like Gorgias to answer. If weaving is concerned with fabrics, and music with composing songs, with what is rhetoric concerned? Gorgias responds initially, and perhaps glibly, that he instructs in rhetoric (Greek: *rhetorike*), an art concerned "with words." This is the earliest recorded use of the Greek term *rhetorike,* which has led some scholars to conclude that Plato coined the term.[14] Socrates is not satisfied with this answer, suggesting that rhetoric would take in many other arts such as arithmetic, which also achieve their ends using words and other symbols. Socrates takes a slightly different tack in response to Gorgias' answer, and asks what good result rhetoric produces (451). True arts, according to Plato, have some good result that they both aim at and regularly achieve. Piloting a boat, for example, has the good result that the pilot can, with regularity, get his passengers and cargo to the correct destination.

Again, Gorgias' answer is more eloquent than substantive. Rhetoric, he asserts, produces "the greatest good and [is] the source, not only of personal freedom for individuals, but also of mastery over others in one's own country" (452). Clarifying his point, Gorgias affirms that rhetoric offers one "the ability to persuade with words judges in the law courts, senators in the interest" (452). That is, the great Sophist Gorgias teaches the use of *persuasive* words that grant one personal power. The power of rhetoric is simply this, to persuade with words.

Gorgias, then, narrows the scope of rhetoric to persuasive words from his first answer that it deals with *all* words. But, is this a sufficient definition of the domain of the art of rhetoric? Socrates thinks not. Doesn't all teaching, regardless of subject matter, involve persuasion about the subject under study? Do not all teachers seek to gain our adherence to their teachings? Do not all of the arts, in the final analysis, involve persuasion? Gorgias agrees they do, and that the field of rhetoric has not yet been defined. Throughout the opening passages of the dialogue, Gorgias is surprisingly willing to "go along with" Socrates as he scrutinizes the subject of rhetoric with a series of probing questions.

Pressed on the point of rhetoric's proper subject matter, Gorgias affirms, perhaps with some frustration, that "the sort of persuasion I mean, Socrates, is the kind used in the law courts and other public gatherings, as I said, just a moment ago, and it deals with justice and injustice" (454). Socrates is willing to grant Gorgias that he may now be in the realm of an identifiable art which he calls Justice. But Socrates is unrelenting, for there is an important distinction to be made between "true knowledge" (*episteme*) about justice on the one hand, and "mere belief" (*pistis*) or "mere opinion" (*doxa*) about it on the other. Socrates contends that Gorgias deals only in beliefs and opinions about justice, and not in true knowledge.

According to Plato, justice, like any *techne,* takes a long time to understand, and such an understanding comes only through careful study. Clearly, Socrates argues, a Sophist could not instruct a jury about a subject as difficult as justice in the short time allotted to a trial. The Sophist must, therefore, deal only with popular beliefs and opinions about justice. Gorgias agrees that what rhetoricians do in the law courts is to produce beliefs about justice, and not real knowledge. Socrates counters with this important summary statement on rhetoric as practiced by the Sophists: "So rhetoric, it seems, effects a persuasion which can produce belief about justice and injustice, but cannot give instruction about them." Gorgias answers, perhaps surprisingly, "Yes" (455). Socrates then advances one of his condemnations of Sophistic rhetoric: "The rhetorician, then, is not a teacher of law courts and other public gatherings as to what is right or wrong, but merely a creator of beliefs; for evidently he could never instruct so large a gathering in so short a time" (455).

To teach about justice, one must really understand the subject, have true knowledge about it, and take considerable pains to communicate that knowledge to one's students. This is a far cry from creating "mere belief" about justice in a jury in a speech of an hour or two. That rhetoric produces persuasion, no one can doubt. That it makes people *think* they grasp the concept of justice is also perhaps beyond question. That it *teaches* justice is highly unlikely. The danger in all this, Plato is arguing, is that the public is left thinking they have learned about justice when they have not. Moreover, this is a dangerous situation, for a person in such a state of mind is likely to commit injustices, and a society so deceived about justice might do the same. Later Socrates adds that this dependence on mere belief rather than on true knowledge is why rhetoric works best before a large audience, that is, "among the ignorant" (459). Before a knowledgeable audience the rhetorician will not be able to persuade by merely creating beliefs.

Here we encounter Plato's greatest concern about the Sophists: that they profess to teach about justice without any real understanding of justice itself. This is truly a dangerous undertaking because of the Sophists' power to mislead their students and their audiences on the most important issue. Interestingly, Gorgias agrees with Socrates that one must understand justice before one can teach others about it. In the course of his conversation with Gorgias, Socrates has made the surprising assertion that one who truly understands justice could never choose to do injustice. This is because to understand justice is to love it, and at the same time to recognize just how repulsive injustice is.

Socrates versus Polus: Rhetoric as Power

Gorgias knows enough about Socrates' skill in debate to let him make his point, and does not risk further embarrassment at the hands of the old barefoot stonemason. But Gorgias' young student Polus, whose name means "colt," is not so wise. This character is apparently based on an actual Sophist who had written a treatise in which he claimed that rhetoric was a true art, or *techne*.[15] He comes carelessly and perhaps bravely to his master's defense. Polus angrily denounces Socrates' implication that Gorgias does not understand justice, claiming that the philosopher has shown himself "downright rude." How could Socrates be so arrogant as to suggest such a thing about the greatest advocate and teacher in Athens? Socrates tells Polus to calm down, and make his own argument, though not long speeches, in defense of rhetoric.

Polus claims unabashedly that rhetoric is "the noblest of the arts" (448 c). He may represent the many young Athenians infatuated with the Sophists' teaching, the generation of young men who viewed rhetoric as a path to fame and wealth as was noted in Chapter 2. This social phenomenon was of great concern to Plato, himself a member of the aristocracy of Athens. Nobility, status, and power attracted Polus to rhetoric, much as a life of prestige and influence in law, finance, the military, or politics might attract a young person today.

Polus takes pride in the power of rhetoricians such as Gorgias. Orators exercise "the greatest power in the country," but Polus defines power as the ability to "act like tyrants and put to death any one they please and confiscate property and banish any one they've a mind to" (466b–c). Here we encounter another of Plato's concerns about rhetoric: It attracts practitioners by its power to manipulate and coerce. Adele Spitzer has noted that "Polus is concerned to conquer...[and] power must be unbridled force if Polus is its example."[16]

Rhetoric as Knack.   In the interaction between Socrates and Polus, Plato develops a famous set of comparisons among true and false arts. When Polus asks what kind of thing Socrates thinks rhetoric is, the philosopher responds that he finds it to be a "foul" and an "ugly" one. He compares rhetoric to the "knack" (Greek: *tribe*) some people have of cooking pleasing foods or, perhaps, of concocting folk remedies that make one feel better. This pursuit involves no real knowledge of medicine or of restoring health to the body. This and similar activities are not true arts, but rather examples of "flattery" (Greek: *kolakeia*) because they "aim at pleasure without consideration of what is best" (465). Socrates proceeds to develop a series of analogies to show what he thinks rhetoric is really like. As these comparisons afford considerable insight into Plato's condemnation of rhetoric, and into his thoughts about the possibility of a "true rhetoric," we will take some time to examine them.

Plato presents us with a view of the arts that bring health to both the body and the soul, and of their imitations or counterfeits. The true arts govern the health of each, and each of these true arts has a counterfeit that only flatters people into thinking they have achieved health. Real health, for Plato, is a state of well-being in which one is in full possession of mental and physical powers, and is directing these powers toward good ends such as justice. Health also involves self-control and peace of mind. Physical and mental health is an ideal state pursued through various arts that demand effort, discipline, and even pain. However, the result is worth the effort.

Now, returning to Plato's analogies, some true arts are concerned with maintaining health, while others restore health when it is lost or threatened. Thus, there are four true arts of health, two for the body and two for the soul, an art of maintenance and an art of restoration for each. The art that governs the maintenance of physical health is gymnastics (we might substitute the term physical education). The practitioner of this art is the trainer or the coach. The art that restores lost physical health is medicine, and its practitioner is the physician.

The art that assists us in maintaining the health of our souls is called "legislation" by Socrates. What did Plato mean by this? He apparently viewed the job of a legislator as laying down laws that would help people act properly, and not go wrong morally. Thus, a legislator must have true knowledge of human virtue and vice, and how to ensure that virtue would be pursued and vice avoided. This was a vocation of the highest importance. When the individual *did* do wrong, there was an art to assist the restoration of the soul's lost health. That art is called *justice,* and its practitioner is the judge who metes out penalties to help bring the soul warped through crime or immorality back into line. It is of utmost importance, then, that a judge understand the true nature of justice.

We have now overviewed the four true arts of health in the body and soul. The boxed diagram helps us to apprehend this first set of health-related arts.

THE ARTS OF HEALTH

	Body	Soul
	coach	
Maintain	Gymnastic	Legislation – *legislator*
Restore	Medicine	Justice – *judge*
	physician	

Plato was not only concerned with these true arts, however. He was also keenly interested in what he took to be counterfeits or "shams" of each art that only created the impression of well-being without delivering the real product. These imitation arts flatter people into thinking they are healthy when they are not. The imitation of gymnastic Plato called the knack of makeup, which involved the use of colorings, beautiful clothing, and other artificial aids to help a middle-aged man look younger and healthier than he actually was. Notice that only the appearance of health is achieved by the sham art of makeup, and that no real knowledge of health is required of the cosmetologist.

The imitation of the art of medicine has been translated "cookery," and refers to preparing pleasing foods that make one feel satisfied, or perhaps concocting home remedies for various kinds of ailments. In short, Plato has in mind the chicken soup approach to medicine. The point seems to be that some people possess a knack for preparing foods that make one feel temporarily satisfied or even healthier, but which achieve their effect with no knowledge of the body, its ailments, or true medicines. Again, the knowledge of illnesses and their cures is not required of the cook or of the folk healer, only a knack for making a suitable dish, soup, drink, or narcotic that creates the impression that health has been restored.

The imitation of legislation Plato calls *sophistic,* or the making of long speeches in the legislature to influence legislation to benefit oneself or one's constituents. When a Sophist uses rhetoric to affect the form of laws, he is not concerned to discover what is likely to ensure the moral goodness of the people, but rather to pass laws that will protect his own interests or those of his employers. Such laws benefit no one. From the individual's point of view, these laws do not assist living a just life. Rather, they deceive one into thinking that he or she is living justly, when the opposite may be the case.

Finally, the counterfeit of the art of justice is rhetoric itself. True justice, recall, is aimed at restoring health to a soul that has been made sick through illegal, unjust, or immoral activity. Rhetoric as practiced by the Sophists in court is not concerned to restore the health of a sick soul, but rather to pervert the judgments of judges and juries. Because they are not knowledgeable about justice, but only skilled in creating beliefs about justice, Sophists may mislead their audiences into committing injustice. And doing injustice, living an unjust life, is for Plato the worst evil. Thus, to be the victim of injustice is *not* the worst condition in which you might find yourself. Committing injustice is worse even than suffering it.

The four "sham arts" or knacks, then, are diagrammed in the box.

THE SHAM ARTS OF HEALTH

	Body	*Soul*
Maintain	makeup	sophistic
Restore	cookery	rhetoric

Here, then, is Plato's assessment of rhetoric as practiced by the Sophists. It is a sham art that imitates the true art, or *techne,* of justice. As such, rhetoric has no power to bring about the well-being of the individuals who practice it or who are influenced by it. Rather, it creates a false impression about justice in individual minds, and thus eventually in an entire society. Moreover, young people are attracted to rhetoric because it promises, not truth and justice, but power and wealth. For all of these reasons, Socrates asserts that rhetoric is a dangerous and "ugly" undertaking.

Polus sought the power rhetoric provided, power even to control the lives of other people. Accordingly, he had argued that to suffer wrong was worse than to do wrong. Socrates attempts to show Polus that power and honor belong, not to the life of tyrannical caprice, but rather to the life of wisdom and justice. He brings Polus to accept a conclusion that seems absurd to the young man, and that represents an important paradox at the center of *Gorgias:* "That to do wrong and not to be brought to justice is the first and greatest of all evils." Perhaps even more remarkably, Socrates argues that rhetoric ought to be employed to bring oneself and one's friends to justice. But, as we have seen, this is consistent with Plato's view of justice as an art that restores health to sick souls. Rhetoric must thus be used to reveal one's crimes, and to seek the appropriate cures. "Crime must not be concealed, but be brought to light so that the criminal may pay the penalty and grow well again. A man must force himself and his friends to grit the teeth without flinching and ignore the pain" (480c–d). Rhetoric, the art Polus loved because it brought honor and power, ought to be valued for its power to bring justice, the true source of honor.

Socrates versus Callicles: The Strong Survive

We turn now to Socrates' dialogue with Callicles, the last interaction in *Gorgias.* Callicles is presented as a hardened and cynical defender of a rhetoric of ruthless power, and as an advocate of the principle that the strong should dominate the weak. Such "natural justice" should be the rule in human society just as it is in nature. Callicles asserts, "This I conceive to be justice according to nature: he who is better and more intelligent should rule and have the advantage over baser men" (490). He despises law based on convention (*nomos*), that is, all laws and rules rooted in social agreements. "The manufacturers of laws and conventions are the weak, the majority, in fact" (483). Weak people, according to Callicles, have to find some way to control strong people like himself, and the way they do this is by binding the strong with laws.

In addition to dominating the weak, the strong person should, according to Callicles, pursue desire without any reservation. This is the "beautiful and just" life:

> What is beautiful and just by nature I shall now explain to you without reserve. A man who is going to live a full life must allow his desires to become as mighty as may be and never repress them. When his passions have come to full maturity, he must be able to serve them through his courage and intelligence and gratify every fleeting desire as it comes into his heart (492–493).

Callicles, then, redefines morality as following pleasure or desire (Greek: *hedone*) rather than excellence or virtue (*arete*). In the process, he turns traditional Athenian morality upside-down.

Socrates answers this revolutionary argument by affirming that Callicles is *not* free, but is a slave to both his own desires and those of his audience, *the people* (*demos*). This fact is evident any time Callicles steps before the people's assembly to make a speech. "If you are making a speech in the Assembly," Socrates remarks, "and the Athenian Demos disagrees, you change and say what it desires" (481d–e). Socrates says Callicles is actually a slave to his desires and to his audiences. Despite his "cleverness" or rhetorical skill, he cannot resist the pull of these forces.

Callicles is not his own master, but rather is driven by his lusts for power and for pleasure. Socrates tempts his opponent with a true love—philosophy—in contrast to Callicles' fickle love represented by the people. Thus, we could say that Socrates' has adapted his own rhetoric to the audience he is addressing, that is, to Callicles. Having identified Callicles as someone who wants power and pleasure, Socrates constructs arguments that suggest that those things will come to Callicles if only he will lead a life devoted to justice.

But Callicles is not convinced. He argues that strong people like himself are sometimes successfully "charmed" and "enslaved" by the weak whom they threaten. He will have nothing to do with Socrates' view of life as the pursuit of true justice, which Callicles sees as simply the product of convention (*nomos*):

> [W]e mold the nature of the best and strongest among us, raising them from infancy by the incantations of a charmed voice, as men do lion cubs; we enslave them by repeating again and again that equality is morality and only this is beautiful and just. Yet I fancy that if a man appears of capacity sufficient to shake off and break through and escape from all these conventions, he will trample under foot our ordinances and charms and spells, all this mass of unnatural legislation; our slave will stand forth revealed as our master and the light of natural justice will shine forth! (483d–484a)

But Socrates is not shaken by this rejection of his arguments. He continues to argue for a just life guided by philosophy—the love of wisdom—and leading to true happiness. Notice how rhetoric is employed to persuade others to live justly as well: "[T]his is the best way to spend one's days: to live and die in the pursuit of justice and the other virtues. Let us follow it, then, and urge others to do the same and to abandon the way in which you put your confidence and your exhortations; for your way, Callicles, has no value whatever" (527e).

Callicles proves impossible to persuade because he has practiced an unjust rhetoric for so long that he is convinced of its truth. He mocks philosophy as an occupation for weak men content to spend their time with a few "lisping boys." His only interest is raw power, the kind of power rhetoric brings him. Thus, Callicles has become a victim of the very phenomenon that Socrates warned Polus and Gorgias against, leading an unjust life and hating wisdom, while all the time thinking oneself to be living justly. This is, according to Plato, the worst possible existence.

The Outcome of the *Gorgias*

In the dialogue *Gorgias,* then, Plato presents his criticism of sophistic rhetoric. In sum, the Sophists' rhetoric is simply a knack for creating persuasive speeches lacking any foundation in justice. Practicing debased rhetoric is dangerous as it leads to an unjust society. Educating young people to practice such rhetoric is also reprehensible because it perpetuates injustice.

Does Socrates "win" this debate? None of the major contestants—Gorgias, Polus, Callicles—is clearly convinced by Socrates' arguments. The outcome of the dialogue with Callicles is particularly uncertain, and this conclusion may suggest that Plato held serious reservations about reversing the direction of an unjust life. Notice that Socrates himself acts as a rhetorician in this dialogue, and that even his great skill in argument is not enough to change Callicles' mind. Nevertheless, Plato's *Gorgias* hints that there exists a true art of rhetoric with justice as its goal.

Is Plato Fair to Rhetoric and the Sophists?

Has Plato been fair to rhetoric and the Sophists in *Gorgias*? Some historians of rhetoric, like Brian Vickers, think not.[17] Vickers notes, for instance, that though Socrates says he rejects the rhetorical way of arguing based on probabilities, witnesses, beliefs, and even ridicule, he engages in these tactics when they serve his ends. Similarly, Richard Leo Enos writes that Plato's case in *Gorgias* should be viewed as "rhetorical argument of the kind associated with sophistic rhetoric."[18]

Plato might also be unfairly representing the Sophists, portraying them as worse offenders against justice than they actually were. Callicles, for instance, may be an extreme example rather than a typical Sophist. Then again, Plato likely had a hidden agenda in the dialogue, as the real-life Callicles apparently encouraged the trial leading to the death of Socrates, Plato's beloved teacher. But Enos finds the portrayal of Gorgias himself so exaggerated as to be unrecognizable. "The biased characterization of Gorgias of Leontini in Plato's famous dialogue," writes Enos, "was a gross misrepresentation...."[19]

Plato's criticism of rhetoric is that it brings about "a condition which seems to be good, but really isn't." Specifically, sophistic rhetoric deceives audiences into thinking they are dealing with truth when they are dabbling in opinions, that they are rendering justice when they are committing injustice, and that they are completely healthy when they are desperately sick. Moreover, rhetoric dupes even its practitioners into thinking they wield real power when they are, in fact, slaves to public opinion. But, if this is the point he wishes to prove, why has Plato endangered his opposition by engaging in sophistic rhetoric to refute both the Sophists and rhetoric? The great Roman orator, Cicero, wrote after reading *Gorgias* during a visit to Athens more than two centuries after it was written, "What most surprised me about Plato in that work was that it seemed to me that as he was in the process of ridiculing rhetors he himself appeared to be the foremost rhetor."[20] Other observers of the rhetorical scene throughout history have been equally surprised, and the puzzle resulting from the tension between Plato's goal and his methods in *Gorgias* remains unsolved.

Nevertheless, the condemnation of rhetoric as trafficking in opinions about justice has dogged the art ever since Plato wrote *Gorgias*. Here we encounter one of the themes mentioned in Chapter 1—rhetoric's relationship to truth. The Sophists in *Gorgias* hold that rhetoric creates truth that is useful for the moment out of *doxa,* or the opinions of the people, through the process of argument and counterargument. Socrates will have no part of this sort of "truth" which, nevertheless, is essential to a democracy. Truth to the philosopher is transcendent and absolute, and thus is not to be had by persuading an uninformed audience that they understand a complicated idea like justice in a short time and with little effort. In some respects, then, Plato's argument against rhetoric extends to any aspect of democracy (rule by the *demos*) that seeks truth by weighing arguments for and against an idea.

This observation brings us back to one of Plato's central concerns in *Gorgias:* the rhetor's relationship to an audience. The Sophists, according to Plato, are willing to tell their audiences whatever they wish to hear in order to persuade them. Thus, the character Socrates asserts that the audience ends up in virtual control of the rhetor. The Sophists seek to manipulate their audiences, but often the equation is reversed. No one benefits under these circumstances because the truth is ignored while the audience is flattered. Truth, for Plato, exists independently of audiences. To make truth a matter of audience agreement is dangerous, for audiences are easily deceived by a clever speaker promising them what they want.

Of course, rhetoric's relationship to power is a concern in the dialogue as well. The power of rhetoric (the methods of persuasion) is pitted against the power of philosophy (the earnest search for truth). The Sophists want the power that persuasion brings them. But power for them is control over an audience gained by flattery and deceit, with injustice as its outcome. For Socrates, power is self-control grounded in true knowledge, and its goal is justice. Is this latter version of power something sophistic rhetoric can deliver? Plato's answer is an emphatic "No." In the next section we will consider Plato's other great statement on rhetoric, the *Phaedrus,* in which rhetoric takes on a different quality, and may even achieve the status of a *techne,* or genuine and useful art.[21]

RHETORIC IN PLATO'S *PHAEDRUS:* A TRUE ART?

Scholars have often noted that in *Phaedrus* Plato hints at a true art of rhetoric. Clearly, this would not be the same art as that practiced by the Sophists and criticized in *Gorgias*. In fact, this Platonic art of rhetoric may not have been practiced by anyone in Athens, except Plato himself! Jacqueline de Romilly writes, "in the *Phaedrus,* Plato was to recognize another kind of rhetoric," which she terms "a science of dialectics." She adds, "the contrast [to *Gorgias*] constituted by [*Phaedrus*] emphasizes the inadequacies of the rhetoric of the Sophists; but it certainly does nothing to diminish the force of Plato's first reaction as expressed in the *Gorgias,* where, in the name of morality, he wanted to reject rhetoric utterly."[22] Thus, in *Phaedrus* Plato suggests a rhetoric used for the good of the individual and of the society, but he does not retract his criticism of sophistic rhetoric. The true rhetorician, it turns out, must be a philosopher like Plato.

Some introduction to this great dialogue will be helpful to understanding its presentation of rhetoric. *Phaedrus* is not devoted strictly to discussing rhetoric, but summarizes Plato's views on several issues including love, immortality, the soul, and poetry. However, rhetoric is given a prominent place in the dialogue. Plato argues that a true art of persuasive speech would aim to bring order to society through a thorough study of the human soul, the different types of people, and the power of words. Of particular significance to Plato's thinking about rhetoric, and coming as a surprise to many first-time readers of *Phaedrus,* is the interaction of the themes of love and rhetoric in this dialogue.

The *Phaedrus* presents a conversation between Socrates and a young man named Phaedrus, a student of the Sophist, Lysias. Phaedrus is "an immature youth intoxicated with rhetoric."[23] He loves speeches, and is taken with the beauty of words at the command of great orators. It is also clear from the opening pages of the dialogue that Socrates finds this young man attractive, physically as well as intellectually. Thus, the themes of erotic love and of rhetoric arise as natural consequences of the interests of both parties. But Plato also sees them as intimately linked.

The early portion of the dialogue develops around three speeches. Phaedrus reads the first of these speeches to Socrates, asserting that Lysias wrote it himself (231–234). The theme of this speech is love, and Phaedrus considers it a brilliant piece of work, "marvelously eloquent, especially in its use of language."[24] But it proves a rambling and sophomoric affair of no merit whatever. The speech argues that it is better to be a "nonlover" than a true lover. That is, to care nothing for a lover is better than actually to care for him.

Socrates listens to the speech, is unimpressed, and offers to deliver a better speech on the same topic. Though defending the same thesis, Socrates' speech is better organized and argued than is the speech of Lysias. Socrates feigns embarrassment at delivering a speech on such an impious theme, but he wishes to demonstrate the ineptitude of the earlier speech by contrast to a better one. Later, Socrates makes yet another speech that contains many of the dialogue's important themes. Love is described as a "divine madness" like the trance a poet enters. Socrates also discusses the human soul, its immortality, and its various types. In this second and longer speech, Socrates also introduces the famous myth of the charioteer to illustrate the relationships among the three parts of the human soul. Before exploring this important myth and its relationship to rhetoric, it will be helpful to overview Plato's understanding of human psychology.

The Complexity of the Soul. Plato believed the human mind or soul (Greek: *psyche*) was complex, consisting of three parts. Moreover, each of these three parts pursues its own interests and is engaged in a more or less constant struggle with the other two parts for control of the individual's thoughts and actions.[25] Plato distinguished the soul's three parts by their characteristic loves. One part, he argued, loves wisdom. The true philosopher's soul is governed by this part. A second part loves nobility and honor, and people of a military cast of mind are controlled by this part of the soul. Last, and least in Plato's opinion, are the lovers of appetites or lusts. The people controlled by this part of their souls spend their lives pursuing pleasure, and never know either peace of mind or self-control; they are spiritually unhealthy people who are headed toward ruin. Plato coupled this view of the soul with a view of justice as a transcendent and absolute concept that our individual conceptions of justice should imitate, and to which our lives should conform. It is only when we understand the nature of true justice that we can begin to think and act justly.

The Myth of the Charioteer. Plato's view of the soul helps us to understand the myth of the charioteer. In his second speech, Socrates states that the soul "is like the composite union of powers in a team of winged horses and their charioteer" (246a). In the myth, he had "divided every soul into three parts, two of which had the form of horses, the third that of a charioteer" (253). The "wisdom-loving" part of the human soul is portrayed as the charioteer trying to control two very different kinds of horses. "One of them is noble and handsome and of good breeding," says Socrates, "while the other is the very opposite, so that our charioteer necessarily has a difficult and troublesome task." The driver's task is, in fact, to control these two powerful horses.

The first horse, the "noble and handsome" one, is easily controlled. The charioteer speaks and it responds readily to his "word of command alone." Socrates calls this horse a "lover of honor." This horse is a picture of the nobility-loving part of the soul, but it also must be under the charioteer's control, that is, under the control of the lover of wisdom. The other horse is wild, strong, ugly, and unwilling to respond to the driver's commands. In fact, this horse will "hardly heed whip or spur." This horse represents the "appetite-loving" part of the soul. If the charioteer does not control this part it will take control of the chariot and its driver.

The charioteer must know the different kinds of horses under his command, and control each accordingly. When the charioteer masters these horses, order is achieved in the soul, and happiness is the result. Socrates argues: "If, then, the better part of the intelligence wins the victory and guides them to an orderly and philosophic way of life, their life on earth will be happy and harmonious since they have attained discipline and self-control: They have subdued the source of evil in the soul and set free the source of goodness" (256).

The story of the charioteer is told principally to illustrate Socrates' understanding of erotic love rather than his view of rhetoric. The discussion between Phaedrus and Socrates that follows the telling of the myth, however, is all about speech writing, speech making, and a true art of rhetoric. There is, then, some connection between love and rhetoric in *Phaedrus* that makes the myth of the charioteer relevant to each concern. What is that connection?

Components of a *Techne* of Rhetoric

As we have already noted, in the *Phaedrus* a *techne* of rhetoric is suggested, an art useful for bringing about justice and harmony. Of what specific studies would such an art consist? Certainly it must be founded on a true knowledge of justice and the other virtues. Repeating a theme from *Gorgias,* Socrates notes that "when an orator who knows nothing about good or evil undertakes to persuade a city in the same state of ignorance," the results are disastrous. The first thing a lover of wisdom who wishes to use rhetoric well must learn, then, is "the truth." "I bring no compulsion to learn the art of speech on anyone who is ignorant of the truth," says Socrates. And truth comes via the arduous study of philosophy.

Socrates proceeds to define rhetoric as "an art of influencing the soul [*techne psychagogia*] through words [*logoi*]" (261). Notice that Plato chooses the same word, *psychagogia,* that the Sophist Gorgias often used to describe his version of rhetoric. The term *psychagogia* means something closer to "leading the soul" than "influencing the soul." Because Plato uses one of the Sophists' own terms to define rhetoric, we have some evidence that he is attempting in *Phaedrus* to do what the Sophists in *Gorgias* could not do, give a full, rational account of the art of rhetoric.

Rhetoric is the art of leading the human soul toward truth through *logoi,* a Greek term that means both words and arguments. Thus, foundational to a true art of rhetoric is knowledge of truth, but also knowledge of the human soul. Plato confirms this point in writing that anyone "who addresses words to another in a scientific manner" must be equipped to "accurately describe the nature of the object" to which the speech is addressed. "And this," adds Socrates, "I suppose, will be the soul" (270). So, a rhetor must know souls. Socrates now set about to sketch the outline of this knowledge of the soul. "Since it is in fact the function of speech to influence souls," he writes, "a man who is going to be a speaker must know how many types of souls there are. Let us, then, state that they are of this or that number and of this or that sort, so that individuals also will be of this or that type" (271).

Guided by this deep understanding of different psychological types, a practitioner of the *techne* or science of soul management "must discover the kind of speech that matches each type of nature" (277b). Rhetoricians must be skilled psychologists or soul-knowers. If, moreover, this *techne* relies on a knowledge of *logoi* (words and arguments), then he or she must also study arguments. Specifically, the rhetor studies arguments persuasive to each type of soul. Thus, Jacqueline de Romilly writes that Plato's *techne* of rhetoric is built on "a thorough classification of the different kind of *logoi* and of the different kinds of souls."[26] Similarly, G. M. A. Grube notes that "the speaker must learn the parts of the soul, their number and the nature of each. He must then classify the different kinds of argument, when each is appropriate and why, thus relating his technique to his psychology."[27]

Thus, in the *Phaedrus* Plato suggests that the ability to adapt arguments to various types of people is central to a true art or *techne* of rhetoric.[28] The speaker "must discover the kind of speech that matches each type of nature."

How, then, does one compose a speech? Socrates describes a knowledge-based process by which a rhetor would "arrange and adorn each speech in such a way as to present complicated and unstable souls with complex speeches, speeches exactly attuned to every changing mood of the complicated soul—while the simple soul must be presented with simple speech" (277). Only when one has gained a thorough knowledge of souls and of *logoi* "will it be possible to produce speech in a scientific way, in so far as its nature permits such treatment, either for purposes of instruction or of persuasion" (277b).

Rhetoric, Harmony, and Justice. The goal of rhetoric for Plato is to establish order in the individual and in the city–state. This occurs when the wisdom-loving part of the soul persuades the other two parts to submit to its control. Similarly, wisdom-loving people in the city–state would also be engaged in the activity of persuading others to submit to their control. The goal of the *techne* of rhetoric, then, is voluntary submission of the lower parts to the wisdom-lover, a submission producing harmony and justice in the soul as well as the state.[29] Any true *techne* has a goal or product, and the product of true rhetoric is order in the soul and a corresponding order in the state.

Where does love enter the rhetorical picture? The wisdom-lover's art of rhetoric is guided by a thorough understanding of the *loves* of the other two parts. Thus, to be a true rhetorician, according to Jon Moline, "the wisdom-loving part…must learn what each part loves and must construct discourses which are effective owing to their promising each part what it loves."[30] Moline adds that "the business of the wisdom-loving part is to guide the other parts by persuasion, to transplant into alien parts its own opinions." This is why the wisdom-lover must know souls, for "it is not likely to succeed in doing this unless it recognizes the number and nature of those alien parts."[31] Once the wisdom-lover has this knowledge, it can design arguments to bring these "alien parts" under its control.

To be more precise, the wisdom-lover's rhetoric is guided by a thorough understanding of the *loves* of the other two parts. Thus, to be a true rhetorician, "the wisdom-loving part, like the wisdom-loving person ruled by this very part, must learn what each part loves and must construct discourses which are effective owing to their promising each part what it loves."[32] Grube holds that part of the "method a rhetorician must learn" is to discern "the different kinds of love existing."[33] The goal of true rhetoric, then, is the voluntary submission of the lower parts to the wisdom-lover. Of course, this implies that the wisdom-lover knows what is best for the other two parts of the soul.

In sum, a true or just rhetoric employs persuasion toward "the good ordering of our lives which is called virtue," and this "depends on the right ordering of the two lower parts so that they obey reason, in the same way as good government depends on the lower orders obeying the wise rulers."[34] Plato's *techne,* or "true art" of rhetoric, then, involves two related studies: (1) a psychological study of the human soul, focused on its three different types or parts and the loves of each, and (2) a logical study of arguments (*logoi*) directed to each type of soul. The goal of this true art is harmony, virtue, health, or, to use a favorite term of Plato's, *justice*. Again, this goal is realized only when the soul's lower parts submit to the lover of wisdom.

Rhetoric's Relationship to Truth.   Among the persistent questions that attend Plato's discussion of rhetoric is whether rhetoric discovers truth or simply propagates it in the soul and the state. Opinion is divided on this question. Susan Jarratt suggests that Plato's rhetoric does not discover truth; this is the role of philosophy employing dialectic.[35] Thus, rhetoric has only an advocacy role, while the more philosophically rigorous art of dialectic reveals the truth.

Patricia Bizzell and Bruce Herzberg take a different view. They argue that rhetoric is a means of "attaining truth" in *Phaedrus,* and in two different ways. First, rhetoric attains truth in its capacity to "convey" that truth to others, a process we have examined. But, of course, this is not actually a matter of discovery but of propagation. Second, rhetoric attains truth in its ability to sharpen understanding through conversation. Bizzell and Herzberg see Socrates in *Phaedrus* actually "working out the truth in his own mind by talking to Phaedrus about it and correcting the less experienced thinker's misconceptions."[36] If this is a discovery function for rhetoric, it is limited to attainment through refinement; rhetoric does not discover truth *per se,* but corrects and refines truth already discovered by some other means.

It seems, then, that Plato intends a true rhetoric to be one of the tools employed by the philosopher to help bring about justice. It does this by assisting the recognition of higher truths. Truth certainly is not discovered through political speech making, a sophistic idea that Plato utterly repudiates. He may not intend that truth is attained through any function of rhetoric, for that matter, unless we make dialectic—rigorous, critical questioning—a part of rhetoric. There is some justification for doing this, if Plato's conversations in both *Gorgias* and in *Phaedrus* are examples of the true art of rhetoric in action, as I take them to be.

As a final consideration, Plato's treatment of rhetoric in *Phaedrus* may be an answer to Isocrates' tendency to make rhetoric and philosophy tools in the service of politics. This is not a high enough view of truth for Plato, nor even of a true art of persuading the soul.[37] Even though he holds out to us the possibility of a true art of rhetoric in *Phaedrus,* Plato does not provide the details of the art in this dialogue. We do not have from Plato, then, what we could properly call *techne* of rhetoric, a scientific treatment of the practice. In the next chapter we will see his most famous student, Aristotle, attempt to provide us with the details of just such a science of rhetoric.

CONCLUSION

Plato recognized the great power of persuasive language, particularly when employed by a trained practitioner of rhetoric. But he also saw a great danger in this power. The Sophists represented for him that danger manifested in Athenian society.

The power of rhetoric in the service of personal motives, and appealing to an ignorant public, would lead a society to ruin. In *Gorgias* he attempts to reveal the problems inherent in the practice of rhetoric when it is not joined to a love of wisdom and a true knowledge of justice. Plato is also asking his readers, however, to consider what constitutes "the good life." Is it personal power in the service of pleasure and mastery over other people, or is it perhaps the practice of virtue and the pursuit of wisdom? Rhetoric can serve either goal, and it is up to the individual practitioner to decide on the proper uses of the art.

But, can there actually be a true art of rhetoric, one founded on a love of wisdom and a knowledge of justice? Perhaps, as Plato suggests in *Phaedrus,* there can be such an art. It would consist of a thorough knowledge of the different types of human souls, as well as a thorough knowledge of how to make arguments that would appeal to each type of soul. Moreover, the true rhetorician would have to understand truth and justice. The goal of this art would be to order society properly so that a healthy nation would result.

In *Gorgias* Plato presents us with two pictures of rhetoric—one evil and one virtuous. His view of the evil uses of rhetoric may be exaggerated, his view of a good rhetoric utopian. Nevertheless, Plato anticipated many of the important themes that have colored the history of rhetoric, including its connection to power, its relationship to conceptions of truth, and its potential for shaping a society. The ethical questions raised by the rhetor's relationship to his or her audience are also considered in these dialogues, as is the question of the proper content of rhetoric as a discipline. Thus, Plato's *Gorgias* and *Phaedrus* still reward the study of anyone interested in better understanding the art of rhetoric and its many implications for free societies.

QUESTIONS FOR REVIEW

1. What were Plato's main objections in *Gorgias* to rhetoric as practiced by the Sophists?

2. Why is Plato concerned about the difference between mere belief and true knowledge, particularly concerning the issues of justice?

3. What criteria must a pursuit satisfy in order to be considered a *techne* by Plato?

4. Plato argues in *Gorgias* that rhetoric is a sham art. He also discusses a number of true arts. What is the true art to which rhetoric corresponds? What does Plato apparently mean by this comparison?

5. What are the various types of souls Plato discusses in *Phaedrus*?

6. What is the specific role assigned to a true art of rhetoric by Plato in *Phaedrus*?

QUESTIONS FOR DISCUSSION

1. Do you agree with Socrates that rhetoric works best "among the ignorant"? Can rhetoric still be employed when an audience becomes better informed? Does the quality of an audience govern the quality of the rhetoric it is likely to hear?

2. Based on your reading of this chapter and Chapter 2, has Plato been fair to the Sophists? Does he have a good argument against them?

3. Does Plato make a convincing case in *Phaedrus* that there may be a true and just art of rhetoric? When he calls it an art, or *techne,* of "leading the soul" (*psychagogeo*) through words, is he suggesting a role for rhetoric that cannot be defended as ethical? That is, is his rhetoric any different from that of the Sophists?

4. Plato suggests in *Gorgias* that certain arts, such as justice and medicine, are essential to society. Others, such as the Sophist's brand of rhetoric, are imitations of these essential arts. If you had the opportunity to set up a society's system of government, what role, if any, would the study of rhetoric play in it? Would you place any restrictions on the practice of this art?

5. Do you think that Plato has a point when he suggests in *Phaedrus* that there are different types of human souls dominated by the different things they love? Is his brand of psychology too simple, or does he perhaps have an insight?

TERMS

Demos: The people.
Dialectic: Rigorous, critical questioning.
Doxa: A belief or opinion. Also, "mere opinion."
Episteme: True knowledge.
Kolakeia: Flattery. Promising people what they want without regard for what is best for them.
Logos (**pl.** *logoi*):   An account. A clear and logical explanation of a true art or *techne.* Word. Argument.
Pistis: Mere belief.
Polis: The city–state, particularly the people making up the state.
Psyche: Mind or soul.
Rhetores: Rhetors or orators. Those making their living and wielding power by means of persuasive words.
Techne: A true art or discipline. A scientific or systematic pursuit capable of a full account and arriving regularly at a good product or outcome.

ENDNOTES

1. To view the complete text of any of Plato's dialogues, visit www.persues.tufts.edu. For a discussion of Plato's *Phaedrus* as rhetoric, see: Jane V. Curran, "The Rhetorical Technique of Plato's *Phaedrus,*" *Philosophy and Rhetoric* 19 (1986), 66–72. There are many excellent sources on Plato, his philosophy, and his thought on specific topics. Such works that take up issues discussed in this chapter include: I. M. Crombie, *An Examination of Plato's Doctrines,* v. I (London: Routledge and Kegan Paul, 1961); Michael Despland, *The Education of Desire: Plato and the Philosophy of Religion* (Toronto: University of Toronto Press, 1985); R. M. Hare, *Plato* (Oxford: Oxford University Press, 1982).

2. On these dialogues, see, for example: Plato's *Sophist,* trans. William S. Cobb (Savage, MD: Rowman and Littlefield, 1990); Plato, *Protagoras,* trans. C. C. W. Taylor (Oxford: Clarendon Press, 1991); B. A. F. Hubbard and E. S. Karnofsky, *Plato's Protagoras: A Socratic Commentary* (Chicago: University of Chicago Press, 1982).

3. Brian Vickers, *In Defense of Rhetoric* (Oxford: Oxford University Press, 1988), 148.

4. For a detailed discussion of this question, see Vickers, Chapter 3, "Territorial Disputes: Philosophy versus Rhetoric," 148–213.

5. George Kennedy, *Classical Rhetoric and Its Secular and Christian Tradition,* 2d ed. (Chapel Hill: University of North Carolina Press, 1999), 54.

6. A good introduction to these dialogues and their relationship to one another is Seth Benardete's *The Rhetoric of Morality and Philosophy: Plato's Gorgias and Phaedrus* (Chicago: University of Chicago Press, 1991). Also helpful: Adele Spitzer, "The Self-Reference of the *Gorgias,*" *Philosophy and Rhetoric* 8 (1975): 1–22.

7. All passages are from *Gorgias,* trans. W. C. Helmbold (Indianapolis, IN: Bobbs-Merrill, 1952). Other translations include: Plato, *Gorgias,* trans. T. Irwin (Oxford: Clarendon Press, 1979). For a detailed introduction to and commentary on *Gorgias,* see: George Kimball Plochmann and Franklin E. Robinson, *A Friendly Companion to Plato's Gorgias* (Carbondale, IL: Southern Illinois University Press, 1988).

8. Vickers, 153.

9. George Kennedy, *The Art of Persuasion in Greece* (Princeton, NJ: Princeton University Press, 1963), 185.

10. Bruce Gronbeck, "Gorgias on Rhetoric and Poetic: A Rehabilitation," *Southern Speech Communication Journal* 38 (Fall 1972), 35.

11. For discussions of Plato's theory of art as it relates to rhetoric, see: Hans-George Gadamer, *The Idea of the Good in Platonic-Aristotelian Philosophy* (New Haven, CT: Yale University Press, 1986), 46–49, 78–80; and Rupert C. Lodge, *Plato's Theory of Art* (1953; New York: Russell and Russell, 1975), chaps. III and IV.

12. Crombie suggests that rhetoric's product would be "spiritual order," evidenced in "justice and self-restraint," and that these are "the qualities that the scientific orator would aim to produce in his hearers" (197).

13. On the themes treated in Gorgias, see: Edwin Black, "Plato's View of Rhetoric" *Quarterly Journal of Speech* 44 (December 1958): 361–374.

14. Kennedy, 59; Edward Schiappa, "Did Plato Coin *Rhetorike?*" *American Journal of Philology* 111 (1990), 457–470.

15. Vickers, 97.

16. Spitzer, 10.

17. Vickers, 113–120.

18. Richard Leo Enos, *Greek Rhetoric before Aristotle* (Prospect Heights, IL: Waveland, 1993), 92.

19. Enos, 72.

20. Cicero, *De Oratore,* 1. 11. 47. Quoted in Enos, 91.

21. Some scholars have argued that as Plato criticizes rhetoric in *Gorgias,* he also employs the art. See, for example: Jan Swearingen, *Rhetoric and Irony* (Oxford: Oxford University Press, 1991).

22. Jacqueline de Romilly, *The Great Sophists in Periclean Athens,* trans. Janet Lloyd (Oxford: Clarendon Press, 1992), 71.

23. John Poulakos, *Sophistical Rhetoric in Classical Greece* (Columbia: University of South Carolina Press, 1995), 79.

24. Plato, *Phaedrus,* trans. W. C. Helmbold and W. G. Rabinowitz (Indianapolis, IN: Liberal Arts Press, 1956), 12. All passages from *Phaedrus* are taken from this edition unless otherwise indicated.

25. This view may remind you of Freud's id, ego, and superego, and, while there are some similarities in the two theories, the analogy is not exact.

26. Jacqueline de Romilly, *Magic and Rhetoric in Ancient Greece* (Cambridge, MA: Harvard University Press, 1975), 51.

27. G. M. A. Grube, *Plato's Thought* (1935; rpt. Boston: Beacon Press, 1958), 214–215.

28. T. Benson and M. Prosser, *Readings in Classical Rhetoric* (Boston: Allyn and Bacon, 1969), 22.

29. Regarding the relationship between the harmony of the individual and the harmony of the state, Moline explains that on Plato's view: "[T]he individual is wise in the same way, and in the same part of himself, as the city.... And the part which makes the individual brave is the same as that which makes the city brave, and in the same manner, and everything which makes for virtue is the same in

both.... The city was just because each of the three classes in it was fulfilling its own task." Jon Moline, *Plato's Theory of Understanding* (Madison: University of Wisconsin Press, 1981), 55.

30. Moline, 65.

31. Moline, 65.

32. Moline, 65.

33. Grube, 212.

34. Hare, 54.

35. Susan Jarratt, *Rereading the Sophists: Classical Rhetoric Refigured* (Carbondale, IL: Southern Illinois University Press, 1991), xvi.

36. Patricia Bizzell and Bruce Herzberg, *The Rhetorical Tradition: Readings from Classical Times to the Present* (Boston: St. Martin's Press, 1990), 28.

37. de Romilly, *Magic,* 58.

CHAPTER FOUR

ARISTOTLE ON RHETORIC

Rhetoric is the faculty (dunamis) *of observing in any given case the available means of persuasion.*
—Aristotle, *Rhetoric*

Michael Billig writes of rhetoric's place in Western educational tradition that "from the time of the ancient Greeks almost without exception until the last century every well-educated person in the Western world was expected to have a grounding in rhetoric, or the art of speaking well." Moreover, "rhetoric was not a specialist study, confined to the ambitious few who hoped to make a career from public speaking. On the contrary, it was an established intellectual tradition, which offered practical skills of articulate expression and theoretical insights into the nature of communication."[1]

One major contributor to the development of Western thinking about rhetoric is the great Greek philosopher, Aristotle (384–322 B.C.). A native of the city of Stagira in northern Greece, Aristotle came to Athens in 367 B.C. as a young man, just thirty years before Athens' defeat by Philip of Macedon. Tradition marks the origins of rhetoric around the year 467 B.C., exactly one century before Aristotle arrived in the great city–state, and forty years before Gorgias made his own emigration to Athens in 427 B.C.

Aristotle's early education "probably included the usual study of language, poetry, music, and geometry, as well as athletic training in the gymnasium." George Kennedy notes that Aristotle also "learned something about medicine from his father," who was court physician to King Amyntas of Macedon.[2] Entering Plato's Academy on his arrival in Athens at about the age of 17, he thus joined an intellectual circle that "included some of the most eminent philosophers and scientists of the age."[3] The chief rival to Plato's school in Athens was that established by Isocrates, whose ideas about rhetoric we encountered in Chapter 2.[4] Forbes Hill notes that "Aristotle began his career as an orthodox Platonist who carried forward a running battle with the Sophists."[5] That battle would certainly have included issues regarding rhetoric. Rhetoric, both as a subject of study and as a topic of controversy, was an important part of the intellectual scene in Athens at this time.

As a student and later a teacher in Athens, Aristotle took an interest in the art of rhetoric. Early in his career, and under the influence of Plato, Aristotle was critical of rhetoric. Later, however, he turned his attention to a more careful study of the art. Aristotle's disposition and upbringing inclined him toward science. He was a prolific writer and a universal genius possessing limitless curiosity and intellectual energy. It is estimated that he wrote as many as 550 books and a total of more than 6,000 pages in modern print.[6] Only a fraction—perhaps one third—of his works survive. One of those works is his highly influential *Rhetoric*.[7]

Aristotle's teaching of rhetoric probably began around 350 B.C., "while still a member of [Plato's] Academy." Kennedy writes that Aristotle's course in rhetoric "seems to have been open to the general public—offered in the afternoon as a kind of extension division of the Academy and accompanied by practical exercises in speaking."[8] In his work *Rhetoric,* Aristotle set out a systematic course in rhetoric for the benefit of his more advanced students and in an effort to legitimate the study of rhetoric in his school, the Lyceum. Avoiding the moralizing tone of his beloved teacher of twenty years, Plato, Aristotle's approach to rhetoric was both pragmatic and scientific.

Much of Aristotle's theory of rhetoric is a response to Plato's criticisms, and to sophistic treatises on rhetoric that Aristotle found inadequate. Previous works on rhetoric by Sophists "deal mainly with non-essentials" and focus on courtroom speaking. Aristotle, then, agrees with Plato that the sophistic tradition of rhetoric is unsophisticated (1354a). The art deserves better. Aristotle thus sought to improve on the shallow rhetorical treatises circulating in Athens. But at the same time he wanted to answer Plato's charges that rhetoric was not a *techne,* or true art. Though he is responding both to the Sophists and to Plato, Aristotle likely borrowed some of his ideas about rhetoric from both sources. The system of rhetoric he introduced still offers valuable insights into various aspects of public and private discourse. Hill notes that many claims in Aristotle's *Rhetoric* stand "in direct contradiction to some part of the *Gorgias.*"[9] One of those claims opens the *Rhetoric.*[10]

ARISTOTLE'S DEFINITIONS OF RHETORIC

Before examining Aristotle's *Rhetoric,* it should be noted that the book confronts scholars with several perplexing questions.[11] Thus, the conclusions of recent scholarship on the *Rhetoric* are not univocal on topics we will be considering. Some of this difficulty of interpretation stems from the fact that the early manuscripts of the *Rhetoric* derive from student notes rather than from Aristotle's own complete presentation of his theory. In addition, some scholars believe that portions of the *Rhetoric,* perhaps even an entire additional book (on humor?), have been lost. With these cautions in mind, we will overview some of Aristotle's major themes as they emerge from the pages of the *Rhetoric.*

Aristotle's *Rhetoric* as we have it is divided into three books. Book I defines and establishes the domain of rhetoric, and describes the three types of oratory. Book II discusses rhetorical proofs derived from character and emotion, while Book III deals with matters of style and arrangement.

Rhetoric and Dialectic

The opening words of the *Rhetoric* assert that "rhetoric is the counterpart of dialectic" (1354), the latter art being discussed in another of Aristotle's books, the *Topics*. The term *counterpart* is a translation of the Greek word *antistrophos,* and it is the same term used in Plato's *Gorgias* when Socrates asserts that rhetoric is the "counterpart of cookery" (465). Thus, by asserting that rhetoric is the counterpart to the *techne* of dialectic, Aristotle answers his teacher's claim that rhetoric is a mere analogy to the knack of cooking. Aristotle understood dialectic as a logical method of debating issues of general interest, starting from widely accepted propositions. Aristotle writes in the *Topics* that "the purpose of this treatise is to find a method from which we shall be able to syllogise about every proposed problem on the basis of generally accepted opinions [*endoxa*] and while upholding an argument ourselves say nothing self-contradictory."[12] Dialectic resolved foundational questions in philosophy. However, the dialectical method had a more general use as well, and could be employed to reason through any number of practical issues.[13] Dialectic allowed one to critically examine both sides of a question, thus testing old ideas and discovering new ones.[14]

Rhetoric and dialectic both start with commonly held opinions, and address a wide range of questions. However, rhetoric employs proofs dialectic avoids—proofs from character and emotion. Moreover, rhetoric is a public art for resolving practical issues in the political and judicial arenas.[15] Thus, the typical form of rhetoric is the public speech, while dialectic was a more private activity involving briefly stated questions and similarly brief answers. Rhetoric addressed a large audience that lacked special logical training, while dialectic addressed the skillful interlocutor or small group of trained advocates. Finally, rhetoric usually resolved specific issues such as, "Is Cleanthes guilty of robbing Chaerophon?" Dialectic, on the other hand, addressed general questions such as one debated in *Gorgias:* "Is it better to suffer injustice, or to commit injustice?"

Thus, rhetoric and dialectic, discussed in the *Rhetoric* and the *Topics* respectively, represent two complementary arts of reasoning to probable conclusions on a wide range of topics. By calling rhetoric the "counterpart of dialectic," Aristotle hoped to distinguish rhetoric from sophistry or groundless persuasion. He discussed sophistical fallacies and how to guard against them in his work, *Sophistici Elenchi,* or *On Sophistical Refutations.* He also hoped, however, to distinguish rhetoric from the strict logic of formal philosophical inquiry discussed in *Analytics.* And, though rhetoric is concerned with matters of style, it is not itself the study of beautiful and moving language, a topic Aristotle addresses in his *Poetics.* Rhetoric is something other than sophistry, logic, or poetry. What, then, distinguishes this art from other uses of language?

Near the beginning of his *Rhetoric,* Aristotle advances the most famous definition of rhetoric ever formulated, and the most influential. "Rhetoric," he writes, "is the faculty (*dunamis:* also capacity, power) of observing in any given case the available means of persuasion" (1355b). In making this claim, Aristotle aligns rhetoric with inventional (creative) rather than practical (oratorical) considerations. In other words, Aristotle presents rhetoric principally as a study of finding persuasive arguments and appeals, and not as a technique for making persuasive and impressive speeches. The Sophists taught their students to memorize great speeches and to debate in order to learn persuasion by imitation and practice. Aristotle taught his students the investigative, rational ability to discover what is persuasive in any setting.

DIALECTIC AND RHETORIC: SIMILARITIES AND DIFFERENCES

Similarities

Each deals with questions that concern everyone.
Each deals with questions that do not belong
  to a specific science or art.
Each can reason on either side of a case.
Each starts with *endoxa* or common opinions.

Differences

	Dialectic	Rhetoric
Purpose:	Testing an argument	Defending an idea or self
Practitioner:	Experts in reasoning	Ordinary citizens
Method:	Question and answer	Speech
Issue:	General question	Specific questions
Audience:	Small audience	Large audience
Argument:	Syllogism	Enthymeme
Proofs:	Arguments	Argument, character, and emotion

Rhetoric as *Techne*

In apparent response to Plato's criticism of the practice, Aristotle sets out to define the territory of rhetoric as a practical and systematic art, or *techne*. A *techne* must first have as its domain concerns not addressed by other arts. Aristotle's affirms that rhetoric's domain—discovering the "available means of persuasion"—is not "a function of any other art." In other words, rhetoric has purposes and goals not accomplished by any other art, including dialectic, logic, or poetry. "Every other art," he explains, "can instruct or persuade about its own particular subject matter; for instance, medicine about what is healthy and unhealthy, geometry about properties of magnitudes, arithmetic about numbers, and the same is true of the other arts and sciences" (1355b). Each *techne*, then, has its own set of concerns not addressed by other arts.

Like these other arts, rhetoric has its own subject matter: the means of persuasion. Aristotle's concern with the proper domain of rhetoric is so similar to that expressed in the opening pages of *Gorgias,* where Socrates asks Gorgias about rhetoric's object of study, that it is hard not to conclude that he is answering Plato's charge that rhetoric has no identifiable study of its own.

Aristotle also points out that no art achieves its goals in every case. Medicine proves this point: It only helps us to get as healthy as we can be under the circumstances, but it by no means guarantees health in every instance. Similarly, rhetoric's "function is not simply to succeed in persuading but rather to discover the means of coming as near such success as the circumstances of each particular case allow" (1355b). Thus, it is Aristotle's opinion that rhetoric is an art, and that it can thus be studied systematically. In what, then, does the systematic study of this art consist?

Why Rhetoric Is Useful.   Aristotle begins his treatment of rhetoric, in Book I, Chapter 1 of *Rhetoric,* by suggesting four reasons why the art is useful. First, rhetoric is useful because "things that are true and things that are just have a natural tendency to prevail over their opposites, so that if the decisions of judges [audience members] are not what they ought to be, the defeat must be due to the speakers themselves, and they must be blamed accordingly" (1355a). That is, if all other things were equal, then true and just ideas would usually prevail on their own. But, clearly, all other things are not equal, and we cannot depend on true and just notions prevailing in the give-and-take of public debate. Ideas need the advocacy of rhetorically capable speakers and writers. Recall that Chapter 1 of this text discussed the advocacy of ideas as one of the important benefits of rhetoric. Similarly, Aristotle argues that knowing rhetoric is useful in order to ensure that just and true ideas prevail over unjust and false ones.

His second reason for the utility of rhetoric derives from the nature of some audiences, again recalling a point made in Chapter 1 regarding rhetoric's constant concern with audiences. "Before some audiences," Aristotle writes, "not even the possession of the exactest knowledge will make it easy for what we say to produce conviction." Why is this? Aristotle's answer is that "there are people whom one cannot instruct" (1355a). Is this a harsh condemnation of the general public, or is it simply an observation about the nature of some members of some audiences? For most of us, experience would confirm that it is very hard to inform and persuade certain individuals with a simple presentation of "the facts." "Here, then," writes Aristotle, "we must use, as our modes of persuasion and argument, notions possessed by everybody...when dealing with the way to handle a popular audience." Aristotle is not, then, advocating verbal trickery or specious arguments, nor is he urging us to water down the content of our messages. He is suggesting, however, that it is important to make connections between the point we are arguing and beliefs already held by our listeners. This is perhaps the most important dimension of audience adaptation—connecting our case to others' experiences, values, and beliefs. Rhetoric offers instruction in this skill, according to Aristotle.

Aristotle's third reason for rhetoric's usefulness is reminiscent of an aspect of the Sophists' approach to rhetoric: "We must be able to employ persuasion," writes Aristotle, "on opposite sides of a question...in order that we may see clearly what the facts are, and that if another [advocate] argues unfairly we on our part may be able to confute him" (1355a). As was noted in Chapter 2, the Sophists' instruction in rhetoric involved practice in arguing opposite sides of an issue. This was thought valuable training for the two reasons Aristotle mentions: It helped one to see all of the facts in the case or to discover all of the "available means of persuasion," and it taught one to answer any argument with a well-framed counterargument. Aristotle is certainly not suggesting that we are obliged to actually *present* both sides of a case to our audience. Rather, he is stating a practical fact: Rhetoric teaches one to think out the pros and cons of any issue, and this is a very useful skill. This skill both provides arguments for a case and helps us in refuting the opposition's case. Thus, this skill in argument advances the three benefits inherent to the practice of rhetoric as discussed in Chapter 1: testing ideas, advocating points of view, and discovering relevant facts and truths.

The fourth and last reason Aristotle presents for the usefulness of rhetoric involves an interesting analogy to self-defense. It's absurd, he contends, that people should be taught to defend themselves with their hands and feet, and yet be unable to "defend [themselves] with speech and reason." Aristotle argues that "the use of rational speech is more distinctive of a human being than the use of his limbs." To those who object that people who know rhetoric can "do great harm," Aristotle responds with some indignation that "*that* is a charge which may be made in common against all things except virtue, and above all against the things that are most useful, as strength, health, generalship." The most useful things are also sometimes the most dangerous, and rhetoric is very useful.

It is important to notice that Aristotle sees rhetoric as a practical art, one he can recommend to his readers and his students as beneficial. As we have seen, Plato did not view the art in this way in *Gorgias,* though he suggests there might be a useful rhetoric in *Phaedrus.* But beyond its being personally useful to one skilled in its practice, rhetoric is also beneficial for the citizenry of a democracy to understand and practice. It allows for the advocacy of true and just ideas, and the refutation of weak arguments. Rhetorical knowledge encourages critical examination of a wide range of political issues on which judgments must be rendered. And, rhetoric assists one to communicate clearly and persuasively to the large, public audiences that make important decisions in a democracy.

The Enthymeme.   At one point early in the *Rhetoric,* Aristotle calls the *enthymema,* or enthymeme, "a sort of syllogism," that is, *a rhetorical syllogism* (1354). A syllogism is *a deductive argument moving from a general premise, through a particular application of that premise, to a specific and necessary conclusion.* Aristotle's own famous example is often still used to illustrate syllogistic reasoning: All men are mortal, and Socrates is a man, so Socrates is mortal. This is a syllogism, but what makes a syllogism an enthymeme, that is, a *rhetorical* syllogism? We will return to this question shortly. Aristotle contrasts this sort of rhetorical syllogism with a rhetorical induction, which he terms the *paradeigma,* or *example, an argument from a particular instance or small number of instances to a probable generalization.*[16] He summarizes by writing that "the *paradeigma* [example] is an induction, the *enthymema* a syllogism," or deduction (1356).

But this initial definition of the enthymeme is too narrow to represent the complete concept as Aristotle develops it throughout the *Rhetoric.* He suggests at some points in his treatise that the substance of *all* rhetoric was the enthymeme. Because of these varied and apparently inconsistent references, there has been some debate about what Aristotle actually meant by his term, enthymeme.

It does seem clear that Aristotle held rhetoric to be constructed of arguments and appeals involving premises shared by the speaker and audience.[17] The Greek term *enthymema* literally means "held in the mind," and enthymemes always have at least one reason or claim that both the speaker and members of the audience believe or hold in common. In fact, so clear was the agreement on the shared claim that it might not even be stated in the speech itself. Such an unstated reason is, literally, "held in the mind" of the audience and the rhetor. Thus, the argument itself was being constructed or completed by rhetor and audience at the same time. Lloyd Bitzer has written that the enthymeme's "successful construction is accomplished through the joint efforts of speaker and audience, and this is its essential character."[18] For example, suppose I were to argue: "Our football team must be good, for even our rivals praise us." Notice that it was not necessary for me to state the obvious missing premise: "One does not praise a rival team unless it is exceptionally good." Or, again, if I argue in a judicial setting, "Watson and Jones should receive the same sentence, for their crimes were the same," it is clearly understood and likely accepted by the audience that my unstated claim is that "similar crimes should receive similar sentences." Aristotle believed that all rhetoric was characterized by such enthymemes, or arguments marked by premises that are unstated because they are accepted mutually by the speaker and the audience.

There is another aspect to the enthymeme that we can use to conclude our general discussion of Aristotle's rhetoric. First, however, let's recall that rhetoric is useful when arguing about contingent matters, issues about which decisions must be based on probabilities, because absolute certainty is not possible. Recall also that rhetoric was used to argue before an audience of the general public, and not a group of highly trained experts. Finally, rhetoric was the type of discourse most important to a democratic society in which issues are resolved by a free exchange of views among the general public. The idea of enthymeme, then, becomes crucial. An enthymeme depends on a previous agreement about a belief, a value, or preference. Thus, to argue rhetorically is to argue with a keen awareness of the values of the public before which you are arguing. Rhetoric must connect with what that audience believes. By its very nature, then, rhetoric is a communal and democratic approach to resolving issues. Aristotle recognized this fact, and for that reason placed the enthymeme at the very center of his art of public discourse. Enthymemes are arguments that obligate the rhetor to consider the beliefs, values, and experiences of the audience. The people themselves cannot be ignored in the practice of rhetoric, and the enthymeme stands as an emblem of this fact.

THREE RHETORICAL SETTINGS

Speeches and arguments are of different types and presented in varied settings. Any complete study of oratory, thus, must take into account the various kinds of speeches, their settings, and the types of issues each deals with. Aristotle invented what has become a famous division of speeches into three categories reflecting both the different settings in which speeches occur and the three corresponding rhetorical purposes for which they are made. He discusses these three categories in Book I of the *Rhetoric,* Chapters 4–15.

First, Aristotle discusses deliberative oratory, speeches presented in the legislature as laws were being debated, that concerned the use of resources and the solution to problems facing the city–state. He called this first type of rhetoric by the name *symbouleutikon*. Second, ceremonial speeches of the type given at funerals or following a great victory Aristotle called by the name *epideiktikon,* from which the term epideictic oratory is derived. Ceremonial speeches praised citizens for some great accomplishment, publicly condemned someone for a vicious action, or eulogized people at their funerals. Third, courtroom pleading (Greek: *dikanikon*) Aristotle called forensic oratory.[19] Courtroom speeches usually involved accusation and defense of an individual accused of a crime.

In order to understand Aristotle's systematic approach in the *Rhetoric,* it will be important to consider each type of oratory in more detail. Jane Sutton has argued that Aristotle's preference for the first of these three types of speeches—deliberative or legislative—is itself something of a rhetorical statement by Aristotle against the Sophists and their preference for the third type—judicial.[20] Clearly, Aristotle spends the most time discussing deliberative oratory and seems relatively less concerned with judicial pleading.

Deliberative Oratory

As discussed in Chapters 2 and 3, the Sophists were known principally for their courtroom pleading, a kind of rhetoric that depended largely on one's ability to sway a jury and to win a favorable judgment in a short time. Judicial rhetoric often emphasized emotional appeals and appeals to personal character. Indeed, these appeals could at times become rather ridiculous displays. Aristotle apparently thought that deliberative oratory taking place in legislative assemblies was both more substantial and, because it affected the whole *polis,* of benefit to a larger number of people. He thus may have found it a better model for all rhetoric than was judicial speaking.[21] Aristotle writes that "in political oratory there is less inducement to talk about nonessentials. Political oratory is less given to unscrupulous practices than forensic, because it treats wider issues" (1354b).[22]

Each of the three types of oratory deals with a different kind of question that might arise in any number of public and private contexts. Deliberative oratory, discussed in Chapters 4 through 8 of Book I of the *Rhetoric,* focused on questions of the best or most advantageous (*sympheron*) course of action to be taken by the state. Thus, deliberative rhetoric involved weighing evidence for and against a policy or course of action. It was also typically oriented toward the future; that is, it influenced judgments about what *should* be done. The guiding principle of deliberative speaking was a concept known as *eudaimonia,* which meant human well-being, happiness, or fulfillment.[23] That is, the most general goal of deliberative speaking was to establish policies and pursue actions that would contribute to the well-being of the citizens of Athens. Thus, a well-trained deliberative speaker must understand not only matters of law, politics, economics, trade, and warfare, but such a speaker must also have a grasp of the factors in civic life that contribute to the general good of the citizenry.

We should note that the kind of reasoning common to deliberative oratory occurs in many kinds of decision making. Deliberative reasoning addresses questions of the expedient use of time, money, and other resources. Thus, if you are trying to decide what type of car to buy, or whether to even buy a car, you are engaged in what Aristotle would call deliberative reasoning. By the same token, if a school board is trying to decide whether to go to a year-round format rather than the traditional "summer off" format, the board is engaging in deliberative reasoning and will be hearing deliberative oratory. In sum, deliberative oratory is concerned with actions, is future oriented, and deals with questions of the best uses of resources. Deliberative orators would need, then, to know what the audience envisions as a good future, what they consider to be in their best interests, and what they consider to be wasteful. The deliberative orator also needs a good grasp of such issues as the available resources, how much time is needed for a particular course of action to be completed, and what obstacles stand in the way of pursuing a given plan.

Epideictic Oratory

The second type of speaking Aristotle identifies in Chapter 9 of Book I of the *Rhetoric* is ceremonial or epideictic oratory. Epideictic oratory (*epideictikon*) was characteristic of public ceremonies such as funerals or events commemorating war heroes. It dealt with issues of praise (*epainos*) and blame (*psogos*). We have already noted in Chapter 2 the Sophists' use of *epideixis,* or speeches of display in which they both practiced and demonstrated their rhetorical skills. Aristotle also noted the importance of such ceremonial speaking, but he was more interested in the speaking that occurred on public occasions than with flashy performances designed to entertain audiences.

In epideictic oratory the rhetor's task often was to praise a person being honored. On other occasions a citizen might be publicly blamed for some notorious action. If deliberative oratory dealt with questions of expedience, and forensic oratory with justice, ceremonial or epideictic oratory, then, dealt with virtue and vice. This kind of speaking played a more important role in Athens than might be immediately apparent, for it provided opportunities to reinforce important values having to do with right behavior, or to uphold virtues such as courage, honor, or honesty.

As with deliberative oratory, epideictic has a broader scope than it might seem. Any time that we offer reasons why someone has done a good, honorable or courageous thing, we are reasoning epideicticly. We uphold a virtue, and we show how some individual has exhibited it. For example, if an athlete showed good sportsmanship under great pressure, and if a sports writer wrote an editorial praising that sportsmanship, we would be reading epideictic discourse. At the same time, if a political columnist wrote a piece condemning a politician for corruption, the journalist's writing would be epideictic. Martin Luther King's famous "I Have a Dream" speech can be seen as an example of epideictic oratory in which King upholds the values of justice, harmony, and peace. Epideictic oratory elevates virtuous people for emulation, and emphasizes certain values that are deemed important to the well-being of the citizenry.

Forensic Oratory /judicial

Forensic or judicial speaking, discussed in Chapters 10 through 15 of Book I of the *Rhetoric,* differs in several respects from deliberative. In judicial speaking the main concern is deciding questions of justice rather than questions of policy. "In the law courts," writes Aristotle, "there is either accusation (*kategoria*) or defense (*apologia*)" rather than argumentation about the expedient uses of resources.[24] Moreover, when a lawyer makes a case in court, the focus is not on the future, but rather on questions of past fact such as "What was done?" and "Who did it?" Other judicial questions included the seriousness of the offense and appropriate punishment.

Forensic oratory reconstructs the past, rather than arguing about the future good of the city–state. Thus, forensic speakers must be skilled in convincing a jury that the available evidence supports a particular hypothesis. The judicial advocate must also be a careful observer of human character so as to be able to argue effectively that a defendant either was or was not capable of committing the crime in question. This pleader should, in addition, have a very good grasp of what the citizens think is just, and so must be familiar with public values about justice.

Of course, questions of justice are argued outside of court as well. Any time we seek to determine what occurred, and whether it was right or wrong, we are reasoning along forensic lines. In such instances we infer from evidence to a plausible hypothesis, and we call on our beliefs about justice. Thus, if I argue that a new banking law was passed because of pressure brought to bear on legislators by lobbyists, and that the law is unfair to the poor, I am reasoning forensically. I might support my claims with evidence about the amount of money the banking industry spent on lobbying efforts, and additional evidence that shows that the new law makes it more difficult for poor people to borrow money for business or housing purposes. In the process of making my argument, I also try to forge connections with widely held values about equality of opportunity. Thus, questions of what is right or just come up frequently outside of the formal courtroom setting, but much of the reasoning employed to argue these questions is of the same type: Evidence is sifted to support a particular hypothesis about a past action, a standard of justice is applied, and the action is judged to be either just or unjust.

THE ARTISTIC PROOFS

If rhetoric is an art, as Aristotle has argued, then what is it the study of? That is, what does the art of rhetoric teach, and what does a student of rhetoric study?[25] This would likely have been Plato's question to Aristotle, as it was Socrates' question to Gorgias. In Book I, Chapter 2 of the *Rhetoric,* Aristotle gives his initial answer to that question, identifying three technical or artistic proofs (*entechnoi pisteis*) that make up the *techne,* or art of rhetoric. He also identifies several inartistic proofs (*atechnoi pisteis*), things such as documents or "testimony obtained under torture." Such things may be useful in arguing, but are not part of the proper study of rhetoric.

The three artistic proofs, or proofs taught specifically by the art of rhetoric, are (1) logical reasoning (*logos*), (2) the names and causes of various human emotions (*pathos*), and (3) human character and goodness (*ethos*). We can take a closer look at each of these proofs characteristic of rhetoric as Aristotle conceived the art.

Logos: The Logic of Sound Arguments

The first of these artistic proofs, *logos,* Aristotle begins to discuss in Book I, Chapter 2. *Logos* is a Greek term with many nuances of meaning. It can mean simply a word, or it can refer in a plural sense to the words of a document or speech. It also carries the sense of a thought expressed in words, a discourse, an argument, or a case. *Logos* could also suggest intellect or rationality generally, and the possession of *logos* was the distinctly human characteristic that separated us from other animals. Thus, John Randall writes that to act in accordance with *logos* was "to act intelligently."[26]

Greeks of the fourth century B.C. did not make a sharp distinction between thinking and speaking; one activity was intimately associated with the other.[27] Words implied oral expression, a fact that was revealed in various aspects of their lives. Silent reading, for example, was unknown to the Greeks or to the later Romans; all reading was done aloud. Written words, then, were always also spoken words. *Logos,* even in written form, suggested spoken words.[28]

In the *Rhetoric* Aristotle uses *logos* to refer to proofs available in the words, arguments, or logic of a speech. *Logos* was the study of inference making or reasoning, a study closely related to logic. However, he was more concerned with the ways people commonly reason as decisions are made about important public issues than he was about the formal logic of the logician or dialectician. *Logos* was the study of the arguments typical of the reasoning employed in practical decision making, and in particular of the enthymeme.

Pathos: The Psychology of Emotion

Though he was critical of speakers who manipulated the emotions of their audiences, Aristotle nevertheless thought a study of human emotion, or *pathos,* to be essential to a systematic treatment of rhetoric. He defines *pathos* as "putting the audience in the right frame of mind" (1358a). He discusses this type of proof in detail in Book II, Chapters 1 through 11 of the *Rhetoric.* The term *pathos* is often used to refer to the affective or emotional appeals that give persuasive messages their power to move an audience to action, but Aristotle's interest in emotion has to do specifically with emotion's ability to affect the *judgment* of audiences. Jonathan Barnes writes that "the orator wants to persuade, or in other words to affect judgment—and stimulation of the emotions is therefore relevant to him only insofar as the emotions do affect judgment."[29] Having "suggest[ed] a connection between emotion and judgment," writes Larry Arnhart, this connection "becomes the underlying theme of [Aristotle's] subsequent discussion of the passions," that is, of emotions.[30] A knowledgeable speaker can engage those strong beliefs and feelings that both affect the judgment of audience members and move them to action. However, Aristotle's concern that the audience be placed "in the *right* frame of mind" suggests that the orator has a moral concern for *correct* judgment, not simply a pragmatic or sophistic concern for winning a debate. The study of *pathos,* then, is the study of the psychology of emotion, governed by a moral concern for discovering and acting on the truth.

In his discussion of *pathos,* Aristotle examines the emotions we all experience, such as anger, fear, shame, and pity. In his typically systematic way, he defines the different emotions and their opposites. Thus, for example, indignation is said to be nearly the opposite of pity. Aristotle discusses the reasons we experience each emotion, and his treatment of the various emotions is often extensive and detailed. For instance, at the opening of Book II, he defines anger as "an impulse, accompanied by pain, to a conspicuous revenge for a conspicuous slight directed without justification towards what concerns oneself or towards what concern's one's friends" (1378a). He then proceeds to note that "there are three different kinds of slighting—contempt, spite, and insolence." Each of these three causes of feeling slighted is then discussed. Thus, this treatment of *pathos* is not simply a "how to" of arousing different emotions. It is, rather, a detailed psychology of emotion intended to help the student *understand* human emotional response toward the goal of adjusting an audience's emotional state to fit the nature and seriousness of the particular issue being argued.

"Fear," writes Aristotle, "may be defined as a pain or disturbance due to a mental picture of some destructive or painful evil in the future" (1382). Fear appeals, he notes, often derive from three fears common to most of us. First, there is the fear of death or physical harm, either to ourselves or loved ones. Second, we fear loss, either of health, wealth, or security, as in the loss of occupation. Third, we know the fear of deprivation of rights or freedoms. Pity appeals usually involve suggesting or stating that someone or something helpless is being harmed, and these appeals are intensified if the harm is being done carelessly or intentionally by another. Thus children and defenseless animals are often the sources of pity appeals.

Emotions, as Aristotle views them, are not irrational impediments to decision making. Rather, they are rational responses to certain kinds of circumstances and arguments. W. W. Fortenbaugh writes that "Aristotle's analysis of emotion made clear the relationship of emotion to reasoned argument."[31] Fortenbaugh argues that Aristotle "showed that emotional response is intelligent behavior open to reasoned persuasion."[32] Thus, emotional appeals need not be irrational and irrelevant elements of persuasive discourse, but can become part of a carefully reasoned case. Aristotle's view differs from, and may be a response to, that of "rhetoricians like Thrasymachus and Gorgias [who] spoke of emotional appeals as charms and enchantments."[33] He adds that "it was Aristotle's contribution to offer a very different view of emotion, so that emotional appeal would no longer be viewed as an extra-rational enchantment."[34]

Ethos: The Sociology of Good Character

Aristotle discusses *ethos* in Book II, Chapters 12 through 17, where he acknowledges the persuasive potential of the speaker's character or personal credibility. This proof should develop from what the speaker says in the course of a speech, and not be imported on the basis of prior reputation with the audience (1356). Aristotle breaks down character into its three constituent parts. In order to establish *ethos,* the speaker must "exhibit *phronesis* (intelligence, good sense), *arete* (virtue), and *eunoia* (good-will)."[35] As with *pathos,* Aristotle seeks to rehabilitate the study of character, or *ethos,* from what he took to be the abuses of earlier rhetors and teachers of rhetoric. He may have particularly in view the courtroom pleaders, descendents of the Sophists, whose exaggerated use of both *pathos* and *ethos* had given rhetoric a bad name.

A trained rhetor must also understand what the community believes makes a person believable. If Aristotle's study of *pathos* is a psychology of emotion, then his treatment of *ethos* amounts to a sociology of character. It is not simply a how-to guide to establishing one's credibility with an audience, but rather it is a careful study of what Athenians consider to be the qualities of a trustworthy individual. Aristotle discusses the character traits typical of young, middle-aged, and elderly people (1388–1390). He also examines the character qualities associated with wealth, power, and "good birth" (1390–1391). Aristotle apparently held that of the three artistic proofs—*logos, pathos,* and *ethos*—this last one, *ethos,* was potentially the most persuasive. When people are convinced that a speaker is knowledgeable, trustworthy, and has their best interests at heart, they will be very likely to accept as true what that speaker has to say.

Aristotle, then, saw the art of rhetoric as combining a logical study (*logos*), a psychological study (*pathos*), and a sociological study (*ethos*). *Logos, pathos,* and *ethos* provide the rhetor with sources of proof, that is, of persuasive possibilities. A skilled rhetor has "the faculty of discovering" such proofs or "means of persuasion." Moreover, this faculty is adaptable to "any given situation." Once these proofs have been discovered, they can be employed in a carefully achieved persuasive balance.

THE TOPOI, OR LINES OF ARGUMENT

Each of the artistic proofs—*logos, pathos,* and *ethos*—might be employed in any of the three rhetorical settings described by Aristotle, the deliberative, the epideictic, and the forensic. But it is also true that certain kinds of proof seemed to be used more often in one setting than in the others. At this point it is important to introduce the Greek term *topos,* which is often translated "topic" (pl. *topoi*).[36] *Topos,* which literally means "place," came eventually to mean location for an argument, and then a line of argument or type of argument that could be used in making a case.

Special Topics

Focusing his attention on the arguments employed in the three oratorical settings— deliberative, epideictic, and forensic—Aristotle wrote about what he called the *eidei topoi,* or special lines of argument, also called special topics. These were lines of argument and specific claims that were especially important to one type of rhetorical setting or question. For instance, Aristotle spends a good deal of time in Book I, Chapters 4 through 8, discussing the specific arguments and information that a deliberative orator must command in order to argue effectively in the legislature. Such an orator must understand "finances, war and peace, national defense, imports and exports, and the framing of laws" (1359b).[37] Aristotle examines the constituents of human happiness, and of what people consider to be the good life. All such knowledge is especially useful to the deliberative orator. Thus, any argument or bit of information that could prove something to be useful or useless, expedient or inexpedient, wise or foolish was an argument of special use to the deliberative orator.

The epideictic orator's special topics had to do with understanding human virtue and vice, and with being able to prove someone to be praiseworthy or blameworthy. Thus, arguments and information that assisted an orator in demonstrating that someone possessed a virtue, or, conversely, that they were vicious, might be among the special arguments of the epideictic orator. Similarly, the judicial orator must understand such things as the causes of wrongdoing, the nature of human desire that drives people to do wrong, and the types of human character that lead one to commit crimes. And the deliberative orator needed a thorough grasp of arguments regarding what was best for the citizen and the polis.

Common Topics

Arguments and strategies useful in any of the three rhetorical settings Aristotle called *koinoi topoi,* or universal lines of argument, also sometimes referred to as common topics. In Book II, Chapter 23, Aristotle listed twenty-eight of these common topics in the *Rhetoric.* This list includes a wide range of arguments and strategies that might be employed in all sorts of debate and speaking contexts. A consideration of opposites appears in this brief catalogue. Thus, someone argues that, because peace has brought economic woes, so war is needed to bring prosperity. Or, one might reason from correlative ideas, so that if someone *gave* you a gift, you must have *received* a gift.

Among the twenty-eight lines are such strategies as turning the tables, or using the same charge against your opponent that he has used against you. Also included are linguistic devices like working with a crucial word in order to derive the desired conclusion. For example, a pleader might reason: "You have said that you benefited from the action of which you accuse my client. If you *benefited* from his action, it must have been a *beneficial* action, and beneficial actions cannot be prosecuted."

The common topics also include lines of argument such as reasoning from general to particular, or by division of possibilities. For instance, division arguments proceed like this: "There are only three causes of such a disaster, A, B, and C. A and B are not even suspected in this case, so the cause must have been C." The twenty-eight *koinoi topoi* are not an exhaustive but rather a suggestive list of the kinds of arguments that might be used in any of the three rhetorical settings. The combination of the special and universal lines of argument constituted much of what went into the study of *logos.*

There has been considerable discussion of what Aristotle intended his topics, both universal and special, to do. It is typically assumed that they were to be guides to inventing or discovering arguments.[38] Other understandings of the topics are also worth consideration, however. William Grimaldi, for example, has argued that the topics may also have been intended by Aristotle as suggesting a method, not just of producing arguments, but of thinking productively about a range of problems that face individuals and societies.[39] Thomas Conley has suggested, however, that the topics were means of "justifying" claims already arrived at.[40] Yet a third scholar, Donovan Ochs, has argued that the topics of Aristotle are not intended as a system of inventing arguments at all, but rather should be understood as the primary elements of enthymemes.[41]

Some Common Fallacies

In addition to understanding good arguments, a rhetor must be aware of the various forms of fallacious reasoning. Toward the end of Book II, Aristotle catalogued nine types of enthymemes that seem serious or reasonable, but are not. These are, to his thinking, fallacies. Aristotle discusses such tactics as wordplay, the fallacy of reasoning from part to whole, and even the use of indignant language such as, "Why, it's just plain rude to make such claims!"

Aristotle also notes that an opponent might make what appears to be a sound argument by reasoning from a single atypical instance to a generalization. Thus, I might argue that, because Carl Sagan was a highly paid academic, therefore academics are well paid. He also notes causal fallacies such as the *post hoc* fallacy. This fallacy suggests that because one event followed another, the former caused the latter. Thus, someone might reason: "The recession hit hardest after the victory in the Gulf, so military victories cause economic troubles." One can also reason deceptively by omitting relevant facts. Thus, one might argue that, because the teacher scolded the children in her class, she is an angry person who should not be allowed to teach children. What is omitted is that the children were misbehaving and would not be quiet.

ARISTOTLE ON STYLE

Book III of Aristotle's *Rhetoric* discusses the issues of the delivery, style, and arrangement of speeches. Aristotle says that he considers the matter of delivery to be "unworthy" of systematic discussion, but, because it is part of rhetoric, it must be discussed. He admits that delivery can be important to how an audience receives a speech, for "the way in which a thing is said does affect its intelligibility" (1404a). Nevertheless, really effective delivery is hard to teach because "dramatic ability is a natural gift." If interested, one can seek out a teacher of diction to help with delivery.

The style of a speech, its linguistic manner, should be appropriate to the occasion. Above all, a speaker must be clear. "Clearness is secured," writes Aristotle, "by using words (nouns and verbs alike) that are current and ordinary" (1404b). Thus, a speaker must have a good ear for everyday spoken language. The effective orator should not use so many artistic devices in speaking that the speech takes on an artificial feeling, for "naturalness is persuasive." It is difficult to escape the conclusion that Aristotle's advice on style is in many ways a reaction against the highly stylized speaking of the Sophists.

Aristotle advises his readers on the use of metaphors, writing that "metaphor…gives style clearness, charm, and distinction as nothing else can." A good metaphorical comparison "must be fitting, which means that they must fairly correspond to the thing signified.…" The "inappropriateness" of a bad metaphor "will be conspicuous" because the "want of harmony between two things is empha-sized by their being placed side by side." Thus, great care must be devoted to the construction of apt comparisons. Aristotle offers his readers practical advice on con-structing striking metaphors. For instance, if you wish to compliment an action or person, "you must take your metaphor from something better in the same line; if to disparage, from something worse" (1405a). Thus, if I wished to elevate or compli-ment a homeless person's request for money in a prose piece, I might compare it to an act of prayer. If I wished to disparage the act, I might compare it to theft.

Though he offers such advice on composing metaphors, real skill with this de-vice, according to Aristotle, "is not a thing [that] can be taught by one man to an-other" (1405a). He goes on to discuss a wide range of stylistic devices such as simile, rhythm, and antithesis. Those of his students who wish to study the qualities that bring beauty to language in greater detail, Aristotle refers to his book, *Poetics*.

As was discussed in Chapter 2, some of the Sophists, most notably Gorgias, maintained a strong interest in the stylistic or aesthetic aspects of rhetoric. But, as was also noted, Gorgias seems to have been interested in linguistic beauty only for its ability to captivate an audience. Aristotle's inclusion of stylistic considerations such as metaphor in a systematic and comprehensive art of rhetoric, as we shall see in subsequent chapters, will remain a persistent theme in the history of rhetoric. In fact, in the works of some of the rhetorical theorists whom we will be considering, aesthetic matters such as the style of one's writing or speaking will take precedence over issues like argument and arrangement.

CONCLUSION

Aristotle set out to present a systematic treatment of the art of rhetoric, and, by most accounts, he succeeded. His treatment of rhetoric remains one of the most complete and insightful ever penned. Still, some historians have noted that Aristotle's rhetori-cal theory has been of greater interest to historians of the subject than to practicing orators in his own and subsequent centuries. Rhetoric was, for Aristotle, "the faculty of discovering the available means of persuasion in any setting." Like the art of dia-lectic, it was not limited to one class of subjects, and reasoned to probable conclu-sions. Like the art of poetry, it was concerned for the beauty of language. But rhetoric was unique in its capacity to adapt messages to large audiences made up of people who lacked special training in dialectic. Moreover, rhetoric was unique in its application to questions of public significance that engaged the community's most important values, such as those regarding happiness, virtue, and justice.

As we have seen, Aristotle held that, in order to be a successful rhetorician, one certainly needed to understand arguments. But it was also necessary to have a thorough understanding of human emotion, and of the constituents of good character. The rhetorician must also understand a range of substantive issues associated with the particular kind of oratory being practiced. And, it helped if an orator had some natural dramatic ability, and a very good grasp of the aesthetic dimension of language. Thus, to be a truly accomplished speaker was a very demanding occupation indeed.

The major themes of Greek rhetoric continued to play an important role in the thinking of rhetorical theorists for several centuries. In fact, it is no exaggeration to say that Greek rhetorical theory still provides the foundation for much instruction in both speaking and written composition. In the next chapter we will see how the tradition of Greek rhetoric was translated into the cultural context of another great civilization, that of the Roman republic.

QUESTIONS FOR REVIEW

1. How is Aristotle's view of rhetoric different from Plato's?

2. Aristotle called rhetoric the counterpart (*antistrophos*) of dialectic. In what ways are the two arts similar, and how are they different?

3. What does Aristotle mean by "artistic proofs" (*entechnoi pisteis*)?

4. What are the three types of artistic proofs Aristotle identifies, and with what is each concerned?

5. What is an enthymeme?

QUESTIONS FOR DISCUSSION

1. Describe the courses someone might take in a modern university in order to learn the components of the art of rhetoric as Aristotle describes that art in the *Rhetoric*.

2. Many Greeks of Aristotle's day believed that good character was a more reliable form of proof than was physical evidence. The reasoning behind this preference, apparently, was that it is much easier to fake physical evidence than it is good character. What do you think of this view of the relative reliability of physical evidence, which Aristotle treats as an inartistic proof about which he has little to say, and good character, which he makes perhaps the most important and persuasive of the three artistic proofs?

3. What is your response to Aristotle's argument that studying rhetoric is useful for (a) defending the truth, (b) adapting complicated ideas to a large and untrained audience, (c) thinking through both sides of a case, and (d) self-defense? Are these still good reasons for studying the subject, or have things changed too much since Aristotle's day for these reasons still to hold? Is there any use of rhetoric that should be added to Aristotle's list?

TERMS

Apologia: Defense; one type of pleading common to forensic oratory, the other being accusation.

Arete: Virtue; a component of *ethos.*

Artistic proofs: *(Entechnoi pisteis)* Proofs taught specifically by the art of rhetoric—*logos, pathos,* and *ethos.*

Common Topics: *(koinoi topoi)* Arguments and strategies useful in any rhetorical setting.

Contingent matters: Matters where decisions must be based on probabilities, because absolute certainty is not possible.

Deliberative oratory: *(symbouleutikon)* Speaking in legislative assemblies.

Dialectic: A method of reasoning from common opinions, directed by established principles of reasoning to probable conclusions. A logical method of debating issues of general interest, starting from widely accepted propositions.

Dikanikon: Courtroom or forensic oratory.

Dunamis: Faculty, power, ability, or capacity.

Eidei topoi: The special topics of Aristotle, appropriate to special rhetorical settings such as the courtroom.

Enthymeme: *(enthymema)* A rhetorical syllogism or a rhetorical argument based on a premise shared by speaker and audience.

Epainos: Praise; one of two functions of epideictic oratory, the other being blame.

Epideictic oratory (*epideixis*): Speaking characteristic of public ceremonies.

Ethos: The study of human character; one of the three artistic proofs; The persuasive potential of the speaker's character and personal credibility.

Eudaimonia: Human well-being or happiness; goal of deliberative oratory.

Eunoia: Goodwill; a component of *ethos.*

Forensic oratory: *(dikanikon)* Courtroom speaking.

Inartistic proofs: *(Atechnoi pisteis)* Proofs not belonging to the art of rhetoric.

Kategoria: Accusation; one of the two functions of forensic oratory, the other being defense.

Logos: The study of arguments; one of the three artistic proofs.

Paradeigma: Argument from an example or examples to a probable generalization; the inductive argument that complements the deductive enthymeme.

Pathos: The study of the psychology of emotion; one of the three artistic proofs.

Phronesis: Intelligence, good sense; a component of *ethos.*

Psogos: Blame; one of two functions of epideictic oratory, the other being praise.

Syllogism: A deductive argument moving from a general premise, through a specific application of that premise, to a specific and necessary conclusion.

Sympheron: Advantageous course of action and actions.

Topos: Line of argument.

ENDNOTES

1. Michael Billig, *Arguing and Thinking* (Cambridge: Cambridge University Press, 1989), 31.

2. George Kennedy, trans. *Aristotle on Rhetoric: A Theory of Civic Discourse* (New York: Oxford University Press, 1991), introduction, 3. To view the complete text of Aristotle's *Rhetoric* visit www.perseus.tufts.edu.

3. *The Cambridge Companion to Aristotle,* ed. Jonathan Barnes (Cambridge: Cambridge University Press, 1995), 4. On Aristotle's life, and his relationship to Plato, see: G. E. R. Lloyd, *Aristotle: The Growth and Structure of His Thought* (Cambridge: Cambridge University Press, 1968), chaps. 1–3.

4. *Cambridge Companion,* 4.

5. Forbes I. Hill, "The Rhetoric of Aristotle," in *A Synoptic History of Classical Rhetoric* (Davis, CA: Hermagoras Press, 1983), 19.

6. *Cambridge Companion,* 8.

7. Kennedy's recent translation, cited above, is very helpful. Other widely used translations of the *Rhetoric* include those by Lane Cooper (New York: Appleton-Century-Crofts, 1932) and W. Rhys Roberts (New York: Modern Library, 1954). Larry Arnhart's overview of the *Rhetoric* in *Aristotle on Political Reasoning* (DeKalb: Northern Illinois University Press, 1981) is very accessible and helpful. See also: Aristotle: *The Classical Heritage of Rhetoric,* a collection of essays edited by Keith V. Erickson (Metuchen, NJ: Scarecrow Press, 1974).

8. Kennedy, 5.

9. Hill, 24.

10. Unless otherwise indicated, all quotations from *Rhetoric* are from: Aristotle, *Rhetoric,* trans. W. Rhys Roberts (New York: Modern Library, 1954).

11. Kathleen Welch quotes Ellen Quandahl to the effect that "the *Rhetoric* is difficult to read, full of discrepancies, gaps, repetitions," in *The Contemporary Reception of Classical Rhetoric: Appropriations of Ancient Discourse* (Hillsdale, NJ: Lawrence Erlbaum, 1990), 22; Quandahl, "Aristotle's *Rhetoric.* Reinterpreting Invention," *Rhetoric Review* 4 (January 1986): 128.

12. Kennedy, appendix I, 289–290.

13. See: Larry Arnhart, *Aristotle on Political Reasoning* (DeKalb: Northern Illinois University Press, 1981), 18–19.

14. Arnhart, 19.

15. Arnhart, 39.

16. See: Gerard A. Hauser, "The Example in Aristotle's *Rhetoric:* Bifurcation or Contradiction?" *Philosophy and Rhetoric* 1 (1968): 78–90.

17. On Aristotle's theory of the enthymeme, see: Lloyd Bitzer, "Aristotle's Enthymeme Revisited," *Quarterly Journal of Speech* 45 (1959): 399–408.

18. Bitzer, 408.

19. The Kennedy translation of Aristotle's *Rhetoric* has been very helpful in preparing this section.

20. Jane Sutton, "The Marginalization of Sophistical Rhetoric and the Loss of History," in *Rethinking the History of Rhetoric,* ed. Takis Poulakos (Boulder, CO: Westview 1993), 75–90.

21. Sutton, 84.

22. Quoted in Sutton, 84.

23. On Aristotle's thinking about happiness, see: Anthony Kenny, *Aristotle on the Perfect Life* (Oxford: Clarendon Press, 1992).

24. Kennedy trans., Bk. 1, Ch. 3, sect. 3 (Emphasis added).

25. For a detailed answer to the question of rhetoric's subject matter, see Fr. Michael Grimaldi's, "The Role of the *PISTEIS* in Aristotle's Methodology," appendix to *Aristotle, Rhetoric I: A Commentary* (New York: Fordham University Press, 1980), 349–356.

26. John H. Randall, Jr., *Aristotle* (New York: Columbia University Press, 1960), 253.

27. On the difference between ancient and modern understandings of the relationship of thought and expression, see: Welch, 15 ff.

28. See, for example: G. M. A. Grube, translator's introduction to Longinus, *On the Sublime* (Indianapolis, IN: Library of Liberal Arts, 1957), x.

29. *Cambridge Companion,* 267.

30. Arnhart, 37. See also: David Charles, *Aristotle's Philosophy of Action* (Ithaca, NY: Cornell University Press, 1984), 176–188.

31. W. W. Fortenbaugh, *Aristotle on Emotion* (New York: Barnes and Noble, 1975), 17.

32. Fortenbaugh, 17.

33. Fortenbaugh, 17.

34. Fortenbaugh, 18.

35. James M. May, *Trials of Character: The Eloquence of Ciceronian Ethos* (Chapel Hill: University of North Carolina Press, 1988), 2.

36. On *topoi* and Roman *loci,* see: Michael Leff, "The Topics of Argumentative Invention in Latin Rhetorical Theory from Cicero to Boethius," *Rhetorica* 1 (Spring 1983): 23–44.

37. Kennedy translation.

38. See, for instance, Leff.

39. On this view, see: Fr. William M. A. Grimaldi, "The Aristotelian Topics," *Traditio* 14 (1958): 1–16.

40. Thomas M. Conley, "'Logical Hylomorphism' and Aristotle's *Koinoi Topoi,*" *Central States Speech Journal* 29 (Summer 1978): 92–97.

41. Donovan J. Ochs, "Aristotle's Concept of Formal Topics," *Speech Monographs* 36 (1969): 419–425.

■ ■ ■ ■ ■

CHAPTER FIVE

RHETORIC AT ROME

*In Lucian's day the open sesame to a professional career was public
speaking; once [one] had the rhetorician's arsenal at [one's] command
the way was open to riches and reputation.*[1]

—Lionel Casson

*By developing his powers of oratory, as if these were the wings which
would carry him to the heights of public life, he clearly showed that he
had no intention of remaining inactive.*

—Plutarch on Gaius Gracchus

"Rhetoric," writes Manfred Fuhrmann, "like all subjects of instruction in the ancient
world, was created by the Greeks; the Romans dutifully adopted both its forms and
its subject-matter, which had acquired their ultimate outlines in the Hellenistic period."[2] Greek-based rhetorical studies resided at the center of a liberal education in
Rome for several reasons. First, rhetoric was a means of achieving personal success
in politics. Second, rhetoric provided a method for conducting political debates.
Third, the study of rhetoric developed the verbal skills that signaled refinement, wisdom, and accomplishment. In other words, in order to play a significant role in
Roman society, it was virtually a requirement that one be skilled in rhetoric. Thus,
rhetorical education was vitally important to the Romans.

Rhetoricians such as Cicero (106–43 B.C.), the greatest orator and rhetorical
theorist of Rome; and Quintilian (A.D. 35–100), Rome's most famous and successful
teacher of rhetoric, wrote extensive treatises on and developed methods of teaching
rhetoric. These writers were so successful in this regard that their methods of teaching rhetoric were employed in Europe right up until the time of the American Revolution. Never in human history has a subject and an approach to teaching that subject
achieved such dominance in education as did rhetoric and the Roman methods of
teaching that art. This chapter explores the aspects of Roman society that made rhetoric so important, the Roman practice of rhetoric, and Roman approaches to teaching rhetoric. Considerable time will be devoted to examining the rhetorical thought
of the most influential Roman orator and rhetorical theorist, Cicero.

ROMAN SOCIETY AND THE PLACE OF RHETORIC

When we speak of Rome or the Roman world, we are really talking about a society that existed in various political forms over a very long period of time, at least the seven hundred years from approximately 300 B.C. to about A.D. 400. During this time much of the Mediterranean world was dominated by one culture with its capital at the city of Rome in Italy. We must also talk about Rome under two quite different systems of government: one a limited democracy called the Roman Republic and the other a monarchy, or tyranny, called the Roman Empire.

Rhetoric and Political Power

At the time of its founding as a sovereign political entity, Rome was a republic governed by elected executives, a senate, and popular assemblies. This is not to suggest, however, that Rome was a popular democracy in the modern Western sense. In order to vote or wield power, one had to own land or be a member of some important group such as the military or a powerful family. The most important governing body in the Republic was the Senate, which had power over both domestic and foreign policy.

The Senate was made up of men who were supposed to possess political wisdom, and the Latin word *senatus* literally means "council of elders." The Senate had about three hundred members, and they held their positions for life, as long as they met certain financial qualifications. Most of these men had held other political offices either in Rome or in one of its colonies.

Roman thinking about political power, as reflected in the rule of a Senate of elders, was bound up with assumptions about human character. "Character was an extraordinarily important element in the social and political milieu of Republican Rome," writes James May, "and exerted a considerable amount of influence on native Roman oratory." May explains that "the Romans believed that character remains essentially constant" throughout an individual's life. Moreover, it "demands or determines" a person's actions.[3] As a result, demonstrating one's good character through one's rhetoric—what Aristotle referred to as *ethos*—was vital to being a successful orator.

Rome was a patriarchy, and power in the Roman Republic usually belonged to men fortunate enough to belong to a *gens* or clan, a group of influential families. These family groups were so powerful that it was difficult for a person from the outside to achieve political prominence. This is not to say that it was impossible, for Cicero, one of the most important politicians in Rome, was not from a politically influential family. He was considered a "new man" in Roman politics, a political outsider with sufficient intellect and rhetorical talent to become influential without family connections.

The Roman Republic operated on the basis of a very complex system of checks and balances among representative assemblies of common people, assemblies of ruling elites, and powerful individuals. In this complex system, it was possible for one group, or even an individual, virtually to stop the progress of government by objecting to a policy. Persuasive speaking in the Senate and other bodies was crucial to forging the agreements and alliances essential to Roman government and expansion during this period. "The practice of oratory," writes Harold Gotoff, was "the stock in trade of the professional politician" during the period of the Roman Republic. Thus, proficiency in speaking was vital to political success. A senator like Cicero "put his competence and authority on the line every time he performed" by making a speech.[4] Rhetoric reigned in the Senate, but also in the courtroom and in the public forum, where all manner of important issues were discussed. "The orator could not afford to pander in facts or trifle in words; he had to be a man of true wisdom and eloquence. For on his speech hung the fate of an accused, the reputation of an opponent, indeed the tenor of a society, the strength of its resolve, the focus of its worship, the direction of its future."[5]

Through military might and participative government, the Romans were able to consolidate their rule of the Italian peninsula, and, by about 200 B.C., to extend their influence to other areas of the Mediterranean world. Through a long series of wars occurring between about 240 and 140 B.C., Roman armies conquered much of what was then the known world. Rhetoric and the cooperative policymaking it allowed was as important as military might to the success of the Republic.

But success did not come without crises. By 130 B.C. Rome was a rich and powerful empire, but one made up of many competing forces. Tensions between the landed rich and working poor became acute, and the government grew more and more to depend on a powerful army to maintain control of an increasingly unhappy populace. As the Senate became more ruthless in wielding power, certain generals decided to take control of the situation in Rome themselves. This development, which began around 100 B.C., led eventually to the creation of the Roman Empire, with Rome transformed into a virtual monarchy. Combining their forces, the two powerful generals, Pompey and Crassus, took total control of Rome in 70 B.C. Under the rule of the Consuls, the Senate continued to function as a policymaking body. It was during this period that the most important Roman orator, Cicero, was prominent in the Senate. Rhetorical prowess was still a crucial element in achieving and holding power, as well as in the conduct of government in Rome.[6] No one better illustrates this fact than does Cicero, whose views on rhetoric we will consider.[7]

Rhetoric and Roman Education

To be formally educated in the Roman Republic was to be immersed in Greek language and culture. Rhetoric occupied the very center of such instruction. Classicist G. M. A. Grube puts the point even more strongly when he writes that rhetoric "remained, through Greco-Roman times, the essential content of higher education."[8] Calvin Troup expresses a similar judgment in writing that "rhetoric was *the* system of education in the Roman Empire."[9] The rhetorically centered educational system of Rome differed from modern educational approaches in important ways. As our own educational methods depend heavily on written texts, it would be easy to assume that ancient Greek or Roman education was transmitted in a similar fashion. But such was not the case. Education, like other aspects of earlier social life, developed principally in the medium of oral expression. This meant that the spoken word was crucial to education just as it was to politics. For this reason, eloquence, or facility with the spoken word, was a key to influence and success. Another consequence of the primarily oral culture of the ancient Mediterranean world is that training the memory was considered much more important than it is in a culture based on written texts. Where written texts are relatively rare, memory becomes essential to expression, to influence, and to education.

For students in the Roman Republic, instruction in all subjects was conducted in the Greek language, and instruction in rhetoric followed Greek rhetorical theories. Roman treatises on rhetoric were based on earlier Greek *technai,* or textbooks. Roman rhetorical education emphasized both practical rhetorical skill and ingenuity in debate. The education of a male Roman youth from a privileged family involved "a number of years of instruction in rhetoric."[10] Moreover, this education "proceeded according to a strictly methodical system."[11] Declamatory exercises, memorizing and delivering great speeches from the past, and debates were stressed. Education in rhetoric was provided "not only by rhetoricians, but also by philosophers."[12] Roman rhetorical training also emphasized style and diction, making the aesthetics of language central to effective speech. Grube notes that the Roman writer Longinus, whom we will consider later in the chapter, emphasized "sound and rhythm" in his treatise on rhetoric, that is, "the music of language."[13]

THE RHETORICAL THEORY OF CICERO

Marcus Tullius Cicero was born on the third of January, 106 B.C., and died in December of 43 B.C. That we can be so precise about his birth and death is emblematic of the fact that more is known about Cicero than about any other figure in Roman history. Christian Habicht writes that "no one else in antiquity is as well known as Marcus Tullius Cicero, with Julius Caesar and the emperor Julian far behind."[14] Cicero took great pains to ensure that this would be the case. He was the greatest speaker and one of the most prolific writers of his day, an unparalleled master of argument with an astonishing understanding of his Roman audiences.[15]

One scholar has written that Cicero "embodied an age in which to be educated meant to command the skills of eloquence."[16] A studied and virtuoso performer in the public oratorical arena, brilliant eloquence was the hallmark of Cicero's career. Gotoff writes: "Every rhetorical stance, every anecdote, every argument, every inflection of a speech, and the manner in which each of these is presented, is calculated to control and direct the attitude of a defined audience in a particular situation."[17] Fifty-eight of his one hundred and six major public addresses survive. Moreover, copies exist of more than 800 letters by Cicero to others, and of 100 letters of others to him. Also surviving are at least six books on rhetoric, and parts of seven on philosophy. Throughout his long political career he demonstrated "an unfailing willingness to talk about himself, both publicly and in confidential letters."[18]

De Inventione

As we have already noted, the Romans adhered closely to Greek methods of rhetorical education, a fact reflected in such well-known Roman treatises as Cicero's *De Inven-*

tione and the anonymous *Rhetorica ad Herennium.*[19] Both works were written at about the same time, around 85 B.C. The former was Cicero's youthful effort to adapt Greek rhetorical theory to Roman purposes, and the latter has been called "our first complete Hellenistic rhetoric," that is, an essentially Greek rhetorical treatise written for Romans by a Roman.[20] These treatises emphasize judicial argument, thus expressing a preference for the sophistic tradition over the legislatively focused Aristotelian tradition. Both *De Inventione* and *Rhetorica ad Herennium* were enormously popular in the Roman world. Brian Vickers writes that they were "the two most popular rhetoric-books of antiquity, and perhaps the two most disseminated books of any kind."[21]

De Inventione (87 B.C.), Cicero's first book on rhetoric, was written when he was about nineteen. A collection of notes and musings on the art of oratory, *De Inventione* provides a glimpse of how rhetoric was taught to young men like Cicero in the late Roman Republic.[22] It is not, however, a mature work on the nature or practice of rhetoric. One modern scholar has called it "severely technical," and Cicero himself later called *De Inventione* "inchoate and rough."[23] This work seems to draw on Greek Stoic approaches to logic and discourse. Cicero's efforts in bringing Greek philosophy and rhetorical theory to a Roman audience were both unique and significant. He was skilled at "creating the Latin terms capable of expressing the meaning of the Greek ones."[24]

In *De Inventione,* Cicero sounds one of the major themes that characterized his rhetorical career—the union of wisdom and eloquence. He writes: "I have been led by reason itself to hold this opinion first and foremost, that wisdom without eloquence does too little for the good of states, but that eloquence without wisdom is generally highly disadvantageous and is never helpful.[25] Wisdom was the virtue Romans admired perhaps above all others. But the Roman conception of wisdom differed somewhat from the Platonic notion of the philosopher as a contemplative "lover of wisdom." Wisdom to a Roman was "gained through practical experience, expert knowledge, and a sense of responsibility in both private and public life."[26]

On Cicero's model, then, the rhetorician studied philosophy, ethics, and other disciplines important to careful thinking and good government. There is always a practical bent to Cicero's interest in rhetoric and in wisdom. He argues that rhetoric is *the* civilizing force that makes human social life possible. By skill in rhetoric we overcome our human tendency toward violence and the rule of the strong over the weak, a theme reminiscent of Plato's debate with Callicles in *Gorgias.* But rhetoric's great power is useful only when tempered by great wisdom. "For from eloquence," he writes, "the state receives many benefits, provided only it is accompanied by wisdom, the guide of all human affairs."[27] Cicero addressed the problems arising when persuasion is cut free from truth, making advocacy untruthful and providing truth inadequate advocacy.

The Canons of Rhetoric

In *De Inventione,* Cicero advances what is probably his best remembered contribution to the history of rhetoric, his five canons of oratory. He admits, however, that these divisions are not new with him: "The parts of [rhetoric], as most authorities have stated, are Invention, Arrangement, Expression, Memory, and Delivery."[28]

Cicero's canons provide a useful means of dividing the work of the orator into units, each of which suggests a course of study.

The first of the canons is invention (*inventio*), which Cicero described as "the discovery of valid or seemingly valid arguments." In the following sections we will examine methods that were employed for teaching the skill of developing appropriate and effective arguments. Much of Roman rhetorical training was focused on the canon of invention, and most of *De Inventione* is devoted to this one concern.

The second canon is arrangement (*dispositio*) or "the distribution of arguments thus discovered in the proper order." In addition to discovering materials for a speech, the orator composes or orders those materials intelligibly and effectively. The third canon, expression (*elocutio*), focused the would-be orator's attention on "the fitting of the proper language to the invented material." Rhetors needed a command of language sufficient to allow them to convey their arguments in striking and persuasive phrases.

The fourth canon of rhetoric in Cicero's scheme is less likely to fit with modern conceptions of rhetoric than are the first three. "Memory [*memoria*] is the firm mental grasp of matter and words" of a speech. We have already noted the centrality of memory to an oral culture. Because orators delivered long and complex arguments from memory, a trained memory was essential. Students were required to memorize long speeches to develop skills of memory.

Finally, "delivery [*pronuntiatio*] is the control of voice and body in a manner suitable to the dignity of the subject matter and the style."[29] A speech in a Roman courtroom or in the Senate was a performance, and the skilled orator needed the presence, poise, power, and grace of an actor. Orators studied movement, gesture, posture, facial expression, and vocal tone and volume. Accounts of Roman orators slapping their thighs, stamping their feet, and even ripping open their togas to reveal war wounds suggests that delivery in Rome was quite a different matter from the stolid "talking-head" approach to speaking characteristic of contemporary politicians.

Stasis and Topical Systems

As the following sections will suggest, the Romans had an extraordinary interest in judicial argument. This was a consequence of their equally intense interest in law itself. The Roman legal code (and commentary on it) was vastly more complex than that used by the Athenians. In fact, the Romans invented the concept of jurisprudence—the science or philosophy of law. Mastering the Roman legal code as well as the art of Rhetoric involved many years of rigorous study.

Invention—the discovery of arguments—received much attention in training judicial orators. Roman educators employed two closely related methods of teaching invention. These two approaches to finding persuasive arguments are the *stasis* and the *topical* systems.

In Book I of *De Inventione,* Cicero discusses a system for thinking through a judicial case, called the stasis (struggle or stopping point) system.[30] An aspiring rhetorician could learn the skill of analyzing a case by dividing the debate into the likely issues of conflict, or stopping points. For example, in legal disputes there are issues of fact or conjectural issues that involve questions such as, *"What occurred?"* and *"When did it occur?"* The issue of fact would become a point of potential clash between two sides arguing the case, a point at which agreements would "stop," and arguments on both sides would be advanced.

Other stopping points in argumentation were also likely, and arguments would be expected at each. For instance, once issues of fact have been argued, issues of definition are often engaged. Cicero writes, "the controversy about a definition arises when there is agreement as to the fact and the question is by what word that which has been done is to be called."[31] Questions arise such as: "How shall we classify this act?" "Was this a case of murder?" The issue of definition may be followed by arguments occurring at another point of stopping or clash. For example, if it is determined that a murder has occurred—a definitional concern—an issue of quality may arise which, again, becomes a point where arguments must be advanced. Issues of quality address the severity of an act, and its appropriate categorization: "Was the killing committed in a moment of great passion?" "Was it carefully planned ahead of time for personal gain?"

Fourth, issues of procedure or translative issues could provide points of *stasis* as well, if either party wished to raise an objection to how the case was being pursued by the other side. Cicero writes that questions will arise "as to who ought to bring the action or against whom, or in what manner or before what court or under what law or at what time, and in general where there is some argument about changing or invalidating the form of procedure."[32] Cicero further subdivides each of these four points of *stasis* into additional questions or issues that might arise in pleading a case.

Students studying a *stasis* system learned to think through cases by following the points at which disagreements were likely to arise. These points of *stasis*, or struggle, as shown above, divided a complex case into its component parts or questions. Arguments relevant to questions of fact, definition, and quality were rehearsed and thus integrated into the student's pattern of thinking. As we shall see, the *stasis* system closely resembles another teaching method common to Roman rhetorical training, the topical system.

In addition to systems for thinking through the parts of a case, Cicero also wrote about systems for discovering and organizing arguments. The Latin name for these arguments was *loci communes,* which translates as commonplaces. The systems themselves were called topical systems (*topica*) from the Greek term *topos* or "place" (pl. *topoi*). We encountered the concept of *topoi* in our discussion of Aristotle's universal and special lines of argument in Chapter 4. Topical systems probably began as memory devices and later evolved into methods for discovering arguments. These systems were brought to a high level of development by Romans, who saw in them great practical utility as aids to analyzing a case and developing one's arguments. Cicero's own topical systems were highly influential in Roman and in later European rhetorical theory and practice.

Because orators spoke from memory, often for a very long time, training the memory was crucial to rhetorical education. The *loci* or "places" systems for developing memory were particularly effective in this regard. These mnemonic (memory) systems involved envisioning physical settings or locations. A rhetor would associate arguments in a long oration with places in, for instance, a familiar public building, putting each argument, literally, in its place. Recalling the arguments, then, might involve a mental walk through the building. By such means, orators in Greece and Rome were able to accomplish amazing feats of memory, reciting speeches of two or three hours in length.

Loci systems eventually developed into methods for helping a rhetor both think through a case and discover appropriate arguments. From places in which to store an argument for later recall, the *loci* became categories for organizing persuasive arguments by general types. As such, *loci* became part of rhetorical education in *invention* rather than in *memory*. Learning these rudimentary and prescriptive categories of argument types trained the prospective orator to work routinely through various established lines of argument in developing a case.

More sophisticated topical schemes suggested possibilities for thinking through a complex rhetorical problem, rather than prescribing a particular argument suited for a given situation. Thus, Donovan Ochs writes that the system presented in Cicero's later work, *Topica,* "is considerably less mechanical than that offered in *De Inventione.*"[33] Topical systems probably were intended to organize and discipline natural thought processes. Thus, Edward P. J. Corbett writes that topical systems "represent the natural way in which the human mind reasons or thinks," rather than being simply an "artificial gimmick" for coming up quickly with arguments.[34]

Attributes of Person and Act.   Most Roman topical systems were oriented to courtroom pleading. Judicial arguments were often arranged under two headings discussed in Cicero's *De Inventione.* The first of these is called "attributes of the person," while the second is termed "attributes of the act."[35] That is to say, when one went into court to prosecute or to defend an accused person, two types of questions often came up, and these broad categories suggested lines of argument regarding each type.

First, in a culture in which personal character was elevated, questions surrounding the accused person's reputation had to be addressed. Such questions, for the Roman courtroom pleader, included "such straightforward matters as the person's name, nature, manner of life, and the like." Cicero writes, "we hold the following to be the attributes of the person: name, nature, manner of life, fortune, habit, feeling, interests, purposes, achievements, accidents, speeches made."[36] Under these divisions a judicial pleader might consider some issues that modern readers would likely find irrelevant to courtroom pleading. For example, the accused's place of birth and nationality (nature), or even the manner in which he or she was reared (manner of life) might be developed into an argument for accusation or defense. Michael Leff notes that Cicero's list of eleven attributes of the person "is not exhaustive (later authorities list more than twenty divisions), nor is there any apparent attempt to rationalize the items in this inventory into a coherent structure."[37] Thus, these *loci* are apparently intended to suggest arguments about the likelihood that the accused could have or would have committed the crime in question.

Second, questions surrounding the alleged act had to be argued. These issues are still vital to judicial pleading. Cicero's list of attributes of the act in *De Inventione* is longer and more detailed than is that concerning the person.[38] Divisions include:

1. Topics coherent with the act itself, which would include issues such as motive and summary statements representing the nature of the act;
2. Topics involved in the performance of the act, which would focus attention on considerations of time, place, and occasion;
3. Adjuncts of the act or topics of relation in which the act in question is compared to, contrasted with, or somehow brought into relation with another act;
4. Consequence, which were topics based on things that follow from the performance of the act, which meant principally public reactions to the act.[39]

Such *topoi* were a common feature of Roman rhetorical treatises, and remained important to rhetorical education for centuries.

Hermagoras and the Development of Topoi

As was true of many aspects of Roman rhetoric, the Greeks were the source of the original topical systems. Hermagoras of Temnos, a Greek rhetorician of the second century B.C., was particularly important in this regard.[40] Though his own works no longer exist, his rhetorical theories are known through Roman writers who followed his model. He classified judicial arguments according to what he called "issues." His three types, recorded in the later Roman rhetorical treatise, the *Rhetorica ad Herennium* are: (1) conjectural, (2) legal, and (3) juridical issues.

A conjectural issue concerns a matter of fact. For example: "Did Person A steal money from Person B?" A legal issue revolved around the interpretation of an important text or document. For example: "Does the contract between A and B mean that A is required to pay B rent for land on the first of each month?" Finally, a juridical issue considered the rightness or wrongness of a particular act. "If A did steal from B, was it wrong if the purpose was to feed her family?"

Hermagoras also developed a famous method for analyzing arguments. He divided arguments into a "thesis" and a "hypothesis." The thesis was a general premise useful in various arguments, the equivalent of the first claim or "major premise" of a syllogism. For example, a thesis regarding plausible human motives might be: "A man may kill even his friend if he sees him as a rival for the object of his love." The hypothesis would be a conclusion drawn by applying the thesis to a specific case. Thus, for this thesis, the attending hypothesis might be: "Mr. Y did kill his friend, Mr. Z." The move from thesis (general or major premise) to hypothesis (specific conclusion) requires the mediation of a minor or specific premise. In this case, the minor premise would be: "Mr. Y viewed Mr. Z as a rival for the object of his love." Hermagoras' approach to classifying and analyzing arguments was highly influential in Roman rhetorical treatises.[41]

De Oratore

After a long and distinguished political career, Cicero was banished in 58 B.C. by Clodius for alleged illegalities in his fight with Catiline. A year later, Pompey allowed Cicero back to Rome, but he was not important to the political scene there. He was, however, very popular with the citizenry.[42] In 55 B.C. Cicero retired to his country estate to write. One of the works from this period of leisure, *De Oratore,* was probably published that same year. This mature work on rhetoric was "written in response to Plato's *Gorgias,*" and in particular to what Cicero held was Plato's separation of eloquence from clarity of thought.[43]

De Oratore, which Cicero said he had written "in Aristotelian fashion," is composed in the form of a dialogue, but it is not like the dialogues of Plato.[44] Here the participants—Crassus, Antonius, Rufus, Cotta—interact to contribute insights into the topic of rhetoric. There is no effort to refute or discredit one another, as is typical of Platonic dialogues. Observations on the topic at hand provide insights as the conversation unfolds.

Union of Wisdom and Eloquence.   As already noted, one of Cicero's persistent themes, and the one for which he is best known, is that eloquence and wisdom must be united in the true orator. "I hold that eloquence is dependent upon the trained skill of highly educated men."[45] Like other Roman writers on rhetoric, Cicero sought to prepare the diligent student of rhetoric to take the role of the perfect or complete orator. This finished or complete orator (perfectus orator) would be a leader manifesting the values of the state, "a public servant whose ability with words is informed by a command of the entire cycle of learning."[46] Cicero invested his vision of the complete orator with the highest dignity and the greatest erudition. He writes: "In the orator we must demand the subtlety of a logician, the thoughts of the philosopher, a diction almost poetic, a lawyer's memory, a tragedian's voice, and the bearing of the most consummate actor." Not often does such a person emerge from human society. "No rarer thing than a finished orator," Cicero concludes, "can be found among the sons of men."[47]

Because this concern for education as preparation for eloquent moral leadership has been largely lost in the educational theory of our own day, it may take some effort to recognize the importance of the issue to Romans like Cicero. Oratory was absolutely essential to Roman government and life, so knowing how to prepare an individual to be a morally responsible rhetor was a pressing educational concern. Cicero viewed the eloquence of the wise as civilization's foundation: "In every free nation, and most of all in communities which have attained the enjoyment of peace and tranquility, this one art has always flourished above the rest and ever reigned supreme."[48]

Implied in his emphasis on wisdom is Cicero's concern for personal character. An individual's moral character does not emerge from the words of a speech, as Aristotle suggested in making *ethos* a technical proof in rhetoric. This earlier Greek view suggested that moral character could be studied and used persuasively by the orator. Rather, in keeping with Roman thinking on the subject, character was a natural trait of an individual that gradually revealed itself through the course of a life. James May writes, "The Roman view is succinctly...expressed by Cicero in *De Oratore:* 'Feelings are won over by a man's dignity (*dignitas*), achievements (*res gestae*), and reputation (*existimatio*).' Aristotle's conception of personal character portrayed through the medium of a speech was, for the Roman orator, neither acceptable nor adequate."[49]

In *De Oratore,* Cicero blames Plato for separating wisdom and eloquence in the philosopher's famous attack on the Sophists in *Gorgias.* "Socrates," writes Cicero, "separated the science of wise thinking from that of eloquent speaking." Moreover, "this is the source from which has sprung the undoubtedly absurd and unprofitable and reprehensible severance between the tongue and the brain, leading us to have one set of professors to teach us to think and another to teach us to speak."[50] Cicero sought to reunite "the tongue and the brain," and in the process to produce great speakers who also were great thinkers.

The Audience's Centrality.   The audience, like the complete orator, is always a central concern in Cicero's rhetorical theory. Though himself a person of great learning, intellect, and power, Cicero recognized that rhetoric required the orator to look always to the audience of ordinary citizens. The rhetor could not stand aloof from the concerns of the populace, and was in this way different from the practitioners of other arts. "Whereas in all other arts that is most excellent which is farthest removed from the understanding and mental capacity of the untrained, in oratory the very cardinal sin is to depart from the language of everyday life, and the usage approved by the sense of the community [*sensus communis*]."[51] This is an important observation, for it reveals political and judicial rhetoric's constant dependence on and adaptation to the public's language and values. Rhetoric's arguments, ornaments, and appeals must all be accessible and acceptable to the ordinary audience member. Plato, recall, criticized rhetoric's pandering to "ignorant" audiences. Cicero, however, viewed the audience's centrality as a fact to be faced in rhetorical practice rather than as a fatal flaw in rhetoric's nature.

The Orator's Qualities.   What are the qualities, then, of the orator? Cicero devoted much thought to this question. The rhetor must be, above all, a broadly educated person. "To begin with, a knowledge of very many matters must be grasped, without which oratory is but a ridiculous swirl of verbiage."[52] The orator must understand law, politics, domestic and foreign economics, military affairs, and international issues such as trade. But the accomplished orator should also appreciate poetry and the other arts. Knowing philosophy is essential. Moreover, the orator must strive for "a distinctive style" in both language and delivery, arranging and presenting words and arguments to the most forceful effect.

Like Aristotle, Cicero argues that the orator must understand the emotions fully. "All the *mental emotions* [*animorum motus*], with which nature has endowed the human race, are to be intimately understood, because it is in calming or kindling the feelings of the audience that the full power and science of oratory are to be brought into play (emphasis added)."[53] Thus, Cicero makes *pathos* central to powerful and systematic rhetoric. In Book II of *De Oratore* he discusses emotions at length, and explains how orators arouse powerful feelings in their audiences.[54] Not only must a good orator *arouse* appropriate emotions in an audience, but simultaneously *experience* those same emotions as well. In a famous passage, Cicero writes that "it is impossible for the listener to feel indignation, hatred or ill-will, to be terrified of anything, or reduced to tears of compassion, unless all those emotions which the advocate would inspire in the arbitrator, are visibly stamped or rather branded on the advocate himself."[55] In other works such as *Brutus* and *Orator,* Cicero assigns three functions to oratory: to teach (*docere*), to delight (*delectare*), and to persuade (*movere*). Persuasion is principally concerned with moving the audience's emotions, the crucial function to which he devotes great attention in Book II of *De Oratore.*

What other knowledge and skill must the effective orator possess? "Humor, flashes of wit," "culture," as well as "charm and urbanity" are all important. The orator must also be well versed in history, and have the stage presence and vocal control of an outstanding actor. Is there anything the orator *doesn't* need to know? Apparently not, Cicero maintaining that real orators are hard to find because very few people can master the knowledge of so many arts. "Indeed, in my opinion, no man can be an orator complete in all points of merit, who has not attained a knowledge of all important subjects and arts."[56] But the orator's calling is such a high one, and his role so important to the society, that any amount of study is warranted to attain this office. The health and welfare of the entire nation depend on orators. "The wise control of the complete orator [*perfecus orator*] is that which chiefly upholds not only his own dignity, but the safety of countless individuals and of the entire state."[57] Perhaps it is a measure of his modesty that Cicero considered himself the leading orator in Rome.

Cicero on Humor in Rhetoric.   Many topics related to oratory are discussed in *De Oratore,* too many to cover adequately in this chapter. However, Cicero's discussion of humor can stand as an example of his thorough and insightful discussion of rhetorical concerns. In fact, one of the many important Ciceronian contributions to the history of rhetoric is his elaborate theory of humor's role in oratory.

The basic problem of humor in rhetoric is stated in two observations. First, there is "great and frequent utility" in humor. However, second, it is an "absolute impossibility" to learn wit by studying it.[58] Facing such a dilemma, the best that can be done in a rhetorical treatise is to present a few guidelines for humor's use in rhetoric. First and foremost, it is vital to maintain dignity in the use of humor, which means respecting the audience's sensibilities. "Regard ought to be paid to personages, topics and occasions, so that the jest should not detract from dignity."[59]

This cardinal rule—respect for one's audience—must be followed if humor's advantages are to be realized. And, clearly, humor affords the orator several distinct and desirable advantages in oratory and debate. It "wins goodwill for its author," and audiences admire someone who is quick witted enough to "repel or deliver an attack." Humor also reveals the rhetor to be a person of "finish, accomplishment and taste." But, "best of all [humor] relieves dullness" in a speech. In spite of these advantages, there are definite "limits within which things laughable are to be handled by the orator," an issue that requires "most careful consideration." Some things one simply ought not to make fun of, including "outstanding wickedness, such as involves crime, [and] outstanding wretchedness," that is, misery or real human suffering. "The public would have the villainous hurt by a weapon rather more formidable than ridicule; while they dislike mockery of the wretched." In all circumstances the rhetor "must be especially tender of popular esteem" so as not to "inconsiderately speak ill of the well-beloved." Respect for one's audience is, again, "the restraint that, above all else, must be practiced in jesting."[60] Cicero adds that the orator must not "let his jesting become buffoonery or mere mimicking," for an orator who employs humor runs the risk of looking foolish if the joking becomes excessive or indecorous.

Cicero classified two types of wit (*facetiae*) in rhetoric, "one employed upon facts, the other upon words." Of the type that deals with facts, he writes that there are, again, two types. First is the amusing presentation of a narrative or anecdote, and second, the mimicking of something or someone well known.[61] The wit of words, on the other hand, "is awakened by something pointed in a phrase or reflection." Thus, the rhetor must not unwittingly (so to speak) make himself or herself look foolish while trying to be funny. It is interesting to note that Cicero considers puns and related wordplay as legitimate sources of rhetorical wit. "Regard then to occasions, control and restraint of our actual raillery, and economy in bon-mots, will distinguish an orator from a buffoon," he cautions.[62] Admitting that perhaps the most difficult aspect of humor in rhetoric is knowing when to use it, Cicero writes, "would that we had some theory of the use of these qualities!"

Cicero notes repeatedly in *De Oratore* that "there is no source of laughing-matters [*ioci: jokes*] from which austere and serious thoughts are not also to be derived."[63] Thus, orators must ensure that they have a good sense of what is worthy of humor, and of what their audiences consider as appropriate matter for humor. Nothing is more disastrous for a rhetor than to make light of a topic the audience considers a serious matter. "All is not witty that is laughable." The buffoon or clown [*sannio*] is laughable in a low manner, and this is not humor "in the sense that I would have an orator humorous."[64]

Cicero warns that mimicry of the mannerisms of other persons (*imitatio*) should be avoided by the rhetor, or used sparingly or with care; the risks of looking foolish are just too great. Grimacing is also beneath the dignity of a true orator, as is obscenity.[65] Certain types of humor, however, reveal sophistication, but are not likely to get a laugh. For example, equivocation (*ambigua*), can be a sign of scholarship, but does not raise big laughs. Thus "the notorious Titius, who was devoted to ball-play and also under suspicion of mutilating the holy statues by night: when his associates missed him, as he had not come to the Playing Fields, Vespa Terentius apologized for his absence on the plea, 'He has broken an arm.'"[66] Get it? Broken an *arm*.

Successful word play of this kind can garner the approval of an audience, "for the power to divert the force of a word into a sense quite different from that in which other folk understand it, seems to indicate a man of talent," but it just isn't very funny. Thus, "the jest arouses wonder rather than laughter, except when it also falls within some other category of the laughable."[67] Particularly effective humor of this type occurs, however, when "a word is snatched from an antagonist used to hurl a shaft at the assailant himself, as was done by Catulus against Philipus." Philipus, during a particularly heated debate, demanded of Catulus (whose name means "young dog"), "What are you barking at?" To which Catulus replied coldly, "I see a thief." Philipus really set himself up for that one.

Laughs can also be raised by skillfully juxtaposing words that are similar in spelling, or using a portion of a well-known verse at just the right place in a speech, or an old expression where its meaning is taken in an unexpected way. Taking a term literally when it is meant figuratively, or figuratively when meant literally, are also possibilities for humor based on words.[68] In the former category Cicero includes the humorous response of Lucius Nascia when asked by Cato the censor, "On your conscience, are you satisfied that you are a married man?" "Married for certain," returned Nascia, "but verily not to my entire satisfaction!"[69]

Sources of humor "dependent upon facts" are "more numerous, and provoke heartier laughter" than those based on words.[70] Narrative or storytelling, a really difficult subject, must "present to the mind's eye, such things as bear the semblance of truth." Caricature of well-known individuals is also amusing, though comparisons between people and things they resemble may be a little unseemly at times. Caesar, the speaker at this point in the Cicero's dialogue, relates his own quip to Titus Pinarius, "who kept twisting his chin when he was speaking, that the time for his observations, if he wished to say anything, would come when he had finished cracking his nut."[71]

For the accomplished orator, humor demonstrates mental agility while at the same attracting and holding audience interest. However, Cicero cautions the would-be wit at every turn, for humor also runs the dual risk of offending the audience and making the orator look foolish. Cicero's treatment of humor remains one of the most complete and insightful in the history of rhetoric.

The End of Cicero's Life

Cicero's life ended abruptly as the result of his enmity with Julius Caesar. Tensions developed between the ruling Consuls, often generals of the army, and powerful members of the Senate such as Cicero. With the rise of the general Julius Caesar, Rome was near a civil war in which several powerful Senators were set against Caesar. In 49 B.C., Caesar returned from Gaul and invaded his own country, seizing ultimate control of the entire Roman Empire and taking the title "Perpetual Dictator." After Caesar's murder in 44 B.C., Cicero was ordered killed by the powerful general Mark Antony. Cicero's head and hands were cut off and hung in the forum over the podium, a grim reminder to any other potential opponents of how eloquence employed against the emperor would be dealt with. Other emperors followed, and for four centuries Rome was ruled by a series of dictators of widely varying levels of skill, humaneness, and sanity.

With the possible exception of Aristotle, Cicero's influence on subsequent rhetorical thought and practice was unparalleled. As we shall see in the next chapter, he is the source of virtually all of the rhetorical theory of the Middle Ages. For Cicero, the truly skilled orator had a very high calling—to provide moral as well as political leadership to the state, and to serve as a conduit of a society's values. Thus, rhetoric was for him a kind of power, and a power that went beyond Aristotle's *dunamis* (faculty, power) of discovering available means of persuasion. Certainly Cicero was interested in persuasion, and even in the power of rhetoric to "move the minds and bend the wills of hearers."[72] But he was also convinced of the potential for one person, equipped with sufficient natural ability and willing to expend enough effort, to shape the character and course of a society through the power of speech.

Quintilian

Just as Isocrates was the most famous and successful teacher of rhetoric in ancient Athens, the Roman whose method of rhetorical education achieved the highest degree of sophistication was Marcus Fabius Quintilianus (c. A.D. 35–100). So renowned was Quintilian for his contributions to education of Roman youth that the Roman poet Martial wrote of him:

> Quintilian, premier guide of wayward youth,
> Quintilian, glory of the Roman toga![73]

Like Isocrates, Quintilian had many students who went on to great achievements, and who spread his fame and advocated his ideas on education. Among his more famous students were the historian, Tacitus, and the statesman, Pliny the Younger.

Quintilian was born in the Roman province of Spain, and studied rhetoric in Rome. He became famous first as a judicial advocate, and later as a teacher of rhetoric.[74] His massive work, *Institutes of Oratory,* is a "cradle to grave" guide to achieving excellence as a public speaker.[75] Such training begins virtually at birth, and Quintilian warns parents of children destined to be great orators that even their nurses should speak proper Latin. He urges them to "be particular concerning your child's earliest training." The child's "nurses must be of good character and speak correctly." Nor are the parents themselves off the hook. Quintilian writes that "both parents should be as highly educated as possible, mothers included." Even the child's friends "ought to be carefully chosen."[76] Clearly, a great deal is at stake in developing a great orator.

Rhetoric and the Good Citizen

Quintilian is perhaps best known in the history of rhetoric for defining rhetoric as the art of the good citizen speaking well. This formulation clearly implies a moral function for rhetoric. The rhetoric of deception or of "mere persuasion" was of no interest to Quintilian. Rather, he cast the orator in the role of a good citizen intent on employing rhetorical powers for the benefit of the society. For Quintilian, then, the true orator must be a culturally conservative Roman citizen and an honorable person, one who adds to such virtues certain natural gifts that have been honed through practice and careful instruction.

A vicious individual cannot counterfeit morally good eloquence through rhetorical training. But the study of rhetoric may develop and enhance the moral character already evident in a good person. The preface to his *Institutes of Oratory* states, "My aim, then, is the education of the perfect orator. The first essential for such a one is that he should be a good man, and consequently we demand of him not merely the possession of exceptional gifts of speech, but of all the excellences of character as well."[77] Prentice Meador writes that "it is this sensitivity to the orator's need for moral rectitude that distinguishes Quintilian's contribution to classical rhetoric."[78]

Quintilian brings us back to one of the central ethical concerns always attending rhetoric: Can the power of rhetoric be limited to only morally good individuals?

By restricting access to rhetorical training to the select few who possessed particular traits of character and a particular moral perspective (and, we might add, certain political views), Quintilian answered this question affirmatively. But this act of educational rationing on Quintilian's part does not, of course, resolve the issue. Other teachers in first-century Rome, as was the case in Athens five centuries earlier, when the Sophists were flourishing, took fewer pains to ensure that rhetoric did not fall into the wrong hands.

Educating the Citizen–Orator

Studying rhetoric under Quintilian meant a great deal of hard work for the handpicked student. But, then, one was fortunate to be studying under the great master, and such a privilege was worth a little effort. "Eloquent speeches," he wrote, "are not the result of momentary inspirations, but the products of research, analysis, practice, and application."[79] Quintilian's system of rhetorical education under which students learned to make such "eloquent speeches" was worked out in great detail. The *Institutes of Oratory* reveal the strong influence of Cicero's rhetorical theory as presented in *De Oratore,* and also incorporate elements from Greek rhetoricians like Hermagoras.

Indefinite and Definite Questions. Rhetoric, for Quintilian, addressed two kinds of questions, which he termed "indefinite" and "definite." Indefinite questions are discussed without specific reference to persons, time, place, or other particular limitation. Hermagoras and other Greek writers had referred to this kind of general question as a *thesis.* Examples would include theological questions such as, "Is the universe governed by providence?" and more mundane issues such as, "Should one enter politics?"

Definite questions include issues concerning specific individuals, facts, places, and times. Thus, the question, "Should Cato marry?" and "Is Crassus guilty of theft?" were definite questions. Aristotle had limited rhetoric to this second type of question, assigning indefinite questions to dialectic. Quintilian broadened the scope of rhetoric by finding it appropriate to the resolution of both factual (definite) and speculative (indefinite) issues.

Bases. Quintilian also discussed the bases, or the specific issues addressed in resolving a judicial case. If your case were limited to a single line of argument, this would be its basis. However, typically cases were built on several bases or issues. The bases are closely related to points of *stasis* in a debate. Quintilian found three bases in forensic cases, which he termed existence, definition, and quality. Existence was a question of what had occurred, a question, that is, of fact. "Did Crassus take money from the council treasury?" is a question of the existence of the event in question. Definition involves arguments concerned to categorize the event. "Was this a theft, or an effort to protect the money from actual thieves?" "Was the money taken as a loan that would be repaid?" Finally, quality concerned the severity of the act once it had been defined. Supposing that Crassus' act was found to be a theft; a question would still remain regarding the severity of the theft. "Did Crassus steal money in order to feed his family?" "Was he, perhaps, well off and stealing only out of greed?" The answers to such questions resolved the basis of quality.

Proof. Quintilian found proof to derive from four sources. First, there are the things that we perceive by our senses that are admissible as evidence. Thus, eyewitness testimony is a strong form of evidence. Aristotle had classified such evidence as inartistic proof, or proof not taught by the art of rhetoric. Second, I might advance as proof things about which there is general agreement, similar to the Greek concept of *endoxa.* Thus, a proof might be derived from the observation that people will perform desperate acts when they are in desperate circumstances. Third, proof can be drawn from the laws and common agreements. This is similar to Hermagoras' concept of a legal issue. Thus, a proof might be based on a statute or a contract. Finally, what both parties to a dispute have admitted may be a source of proof. If both parties admit that Crassus took the money he is accused of taking, this can be entered as a kind of proof.

Loci. In his *Institutes of Oratory,* Quintilian also advances a topical system much like Cicero's. But, rather than seeing the *topica* primarily as devices for discovering arguments, Quintilian was interested in exploiting their potential as means of teaching argumentation. His *loci* were not to be memorized for quick recall when needed, but rather they were to be practiced in order to develop particular habits of thought that would serve the student well when the need arose.

As Michael Leff points out, Quintilian found that the "authentic function" of topical systems was to "help promote the argumentative skills of the student, to foster the development of natural talents and to sharpen insight into cases that arise in the public arena."[80] The goal of training in types of arguments, or *loci,* was to create intellectual habits that would assist the would-be orator in any setting where quick argumentative thinking was imperative. This facility required "constant practice" with arguments, so that

> just as the hands of the musician, even though his eyes be turned elsewhere produce bass, treble, and intermediate notes by force of habit, so the thought of [an] orator should suffer no delay owing to the variety and number of possible arguments, but that the latter should present themselves uncalled, and just as letters and syllables require no thought on the part of a writer, so arguments should spontaneously follow the thought of the orator.[81]

Topical systems following those of Cicero and Quintilian continued to appear between A.D. 200 and 500, remaining a key feature of rhetorical training. Variations on a central theme were endless. In one popular system, *loci* of the act were arranged according to spatial and temporal considerations such as what preceded the act (*ante rem*), what occurred in the act itself (*in re*), what circumstances surrounded the act (*circa rem*), and what events followed the act (*post rem*).

The Parts of a Judicial Speech. Quintilian taught his students to think of judicial speeches—the type with which he was most concerned—as divided into five parts, an approach common to other Roman rhetorics such as Cicero's *De Inventione* and the anonymous *Rhetorica ad Herennium.* The first part, the *exordium,* was an introduction designed to dispose the audience to listen to the speech. The second part, the *narratio,* was a statement of the facts essential to understanding the case, and intended to reveal the essential nature of the subject about which they were to render a decision.

The third part of the judicial speech was the proof or *confirmatio,* which was a section designed to offer evidences in support of claims advanced during the narratio. Fourth came the *confutatio,* or the refutation, in which counterarguments were answered. Finally the *peroratio* or conclusion was presented, a section in which the orator demonstrated again the full strength of the case presented.[82]

Quintilian's highly refined and technical approach to teaching rhetoric proved remarkably successful. His students went on to become some of the most influential and famous citizens of Rome, and they frequently credited Quintilian's rigorous education in rhetoric with their success.

TEACHING ARGUMENT AT ROME

CICERO'S FIVE CANONS OF ORATORY

1. Invention
2. Arrangement
3. Expression
4. Memory
5. Delivery

THE STASIS SYSTEM: CICERO, *DE INVENTIONE*

1. Issues of Fact
2. Issues of Definition
3. Issues of Quality
4. Issues of Procedure

HERMAGORAS'S ISSUES, SOURCE OF CICERO'S CATEGORIES

1. Conjectural issues
2. Legal issues
3. Juridical issues

THE TOPICAL SYSTEMS, CICERO, AND OTHERS

1. Attributes of the person:
   name, nature, manner of life, fortune, habit, feelings, interests, purposes, achievements, accidents, speeches made
2. Attributes of the act:
   Topics coherent with the act
   Topics involved in the performance of the act
   Adjuncts of the act
   Consequences of the act

QUESTIONS OF QUINTILIAN

1. Definite questions
2. Indefinite questions

BASES OF QUINTILIAN

1. Existence (like fact or conjecture)
2. Definition (like juridical or definition)
3. Quality

SOURCES OF PROOF OR QUINTILIAN

1. From senses
2. From common belief
3. From laws, contracts, and agreements
4. From admission

LOCI OF THE ACT

1. Ante rem
2. In re
3. Circa rem
4. Poste rem

LONGINUS: ON THE SUBLIME

On the Sublime is a famous Roman rhetorical treatise that emphasizes the principles of good writing.[83] Many scholars have seen this work as an early application of rhetorical theory to literary criticism, that is, to the discussion of how great writing is achieved, and how it in turn achieves its ends. Brian Vickers, for example, calls *On the Sublime* "the outstanding union of rhetoric and literary criticism."[84] Grube refers to this work as "certainly the most delightful of all the critical works of classical antiquity."[85]

The Emotive Power of Language

The author of *On the Sublime* is particularly concerned with the emotive power of language. Its authorship is uncertain though it has traditionally been attributed to Longinus (c. A.D. 213–273), and I will, mainly for convenience and because his name is still conventionally attached it, treat him as the actual author of this important work. Estimates about the date of authorship of *On the Sublime* range from the first to the third centuries A.D. Though the details of authorship and dating are uncertain, the author's insights into the means by which the principles of rhetoric can guide effective expression are seldom doubted.

Language, Style, and Power. If Aristotle and Hermagoras' interest in argument was perpetuated in Rome by Cicero and Quintilian, then Gorgias' interest in the sheer power of language and the effects of rhetorical style was advanced in Rome by Longinus. Jane Tompkins writes that "for Longinus, language is a form of power and the purpose of studying texts from the past is to acquire the skills that enable one to wield that power."[86] Longinus' theory of language's potency is organized around a concept he terms "the sublime" or perhaps "sublimity," a measure of the impact that literature combining emotion combined with great ideas has on readers. Tompkins emphasizes that "Longinus' notion of the sublime is equivalent to a conception of poetry as pure power."[87]

Five Sources of Great Writing. Longinus advises his readers that there are "five sources most productive of great writing [Greek: *hypsos,* also translated "the sublime"]. All five," he adds, "presuppose the power of expression without which there is no good writing at all."[88] Though Longinus mentions writing as his concern, the connection in the ancient world between writing and speaking was more intimate than it is for us. Even written discourse was typically read aloud; silent reading was almost unknown to the Romans.

So, what are the five sources of great writing? The "first and most important," Longinus writes, "is vigor of mental conception," while the "second is strong and inspired emotion." But having great and passionate ideas to inform your writing is not something anyone can teach you. Longinus comments, "both of these are for the most part innate dispositions." Nevertheless, Longinus spends a long time—six chapters—discussing the qualities of mind that distinguish a great writer. Literary genius of the type exhibited by Sappho, Demosthenes, or Plato is more interesting to Longinus than is technical perfection.

The other qualities of great writing "are benefited also by artistic training." And they are "the adequate fashioning of figures (both of speech and of thought), nobility of diction which in turn includes the choice of words and the use of figurative and artistic language; lastly, and including all the others, dignified and distinguished word-arrangement."[89] The rhetorical art, then, can assist you to become a great writer by teaching you the various devices that enhance expression, the ability to choose words appropriate to your ideas, and the most effective arrangement of those words, that is, composition.

The Use of Examples. Longinus advances numerous examples of these principles from the writers of his own day, as well as from earlier Roman and Greek authors. One of his favorite examples is Sappho, a Greek author of, among other things, erotic love poetry. "Sappho, for example, selects on each occasion the emotions which accompany the frenzy of love," writes Longinus. "How does she excel? In her skillful choice of the most important and intense details and in relating them to one another." Longinus then provides his readers with one of Sappho's most famous poems, which illustrates these principles:

> *Peer of gods he seemeth to me, the blissful*
> *Man who sits and gazes at thee before him,*
> *Close beside thee sits, and in silence hears thee*
> *Silvery speaking,*
>
> *Laughing Love's low laughter. Oh this, this only*
> *Stirs the troubled heart in my breast to tremble,*
> *For should I but see thee a little moment,*
> *Straight is my voice hushed;*

Yea, my tongue is broken, and through and through me
'Neath the flesh, impalpable fire runs tingling;
Nothing see mine eyes, and a noise of roaring
Waves in my ears sounds;

Sweat runs down in rivers, a tremor seizes
All my limbs and paler than grass in autumn,
Caught by pains of menacing death, I falter,
Lost in the love trance.[90]

Figures of Speech.   Longinus also advances a great deal of advice about the use of figures of speech or rhetorical devices to enhance writing and speaking. For instance, he writes that "the best use of a figure is when the very fact that it is a figure goes unnoticed."[91] Rhetorical figures can be powerful enhancements to writing and speaking, but the author or orator must be subtle in their use for audiences are a little suspicious of them:

> The cunning use of figures arouses a peculiar suspicion in the hearer's mind, a feeling of being deliberately trapped and misled. This occurs when addressing a single judge with power of decision, and especially a dictator, a king, or an eminent leader. He is easily angered by the thought that he is being outwitted like a silly child by the expert's use of pretty figures; he sees in the fallacious reasoning a personal insult; sometimes he may altogether give way to savage exasperation, but even if he controls his anger he remains impervious to persuasion.[92]

Longinus spends considerable time discussing rhetorical figures. Regarding the device known as *asyndeton*—leaving out connectives such as *and* in a descriptive list—Longinus writes, "the words burst forth without connective, pour out, as it were, and the speaker himself cannot keep up with them. 'Shield on shield,' says Xenophon, 'they were pushing, fighting, killing, dying.'"[93] But Longinus' principal concern in his discussion of rhetorical figures, perhaps his central concern in *On the Sublime,* is the power of words to evoke powerful emotions in an audience. As Brian Vickers writes, "what sets him apart is his recognition of the functional relationship between figures and feeling: 'they all make style more emotional and excited,' and emotion (*pathos*) is 'an essential part of sublimity.'"[94]

Longinus is careful to add that the emotional impact of writing is always to be governed by a refined concern for decorum, that is, for what is dignified or proper and in keeping with the subject at hand. The true rhetorician should never stoop to simply tricking an audience into reacting emotionally, such debased tactics being a mark of a Sophist. The content of literature or speech should warrant the emotional response aroused by skillfully employed rhetorical figures.

On the Sublime, then, advances the rhetorical tradition of exploring the sheer emotional power of words, a tradition that extends back to Gorgias. At the same time Longinus introduces a concern for the relationship between subject matter and emotional content in writing and speaking, hardly a central concern to Gorgias, who believed that he was creating reality linguistically in his speeches. *On the Sublime* also marks a shift in emphasis from the primarily spoken rhetoric of Cicero to a new interest in the rhetoric of the written word. This emphasis on writing continues to play an important role in the history of rhetoric right up to the present day. Finally, Longinus may be viewed as the inventor of literary criticism, the careful analysis of texts and how they achieve their effects on an audience. In this role, Longinus stands as the greatest figure in the Greek and Roman rhetorical tradition.

RHETORIC IN THE LATER ROMAN EMPIRE

Not surprisingly, as the power of the emperors increased over against that of the Senate, the importance of rhetoric as a means of shaping policy declined. However, rhetorical training remained a means preparing people to serve as administrators in the vast Roman Empire.

The Second Sophistic

The Second Sophistic refers to the period from about A.D. 50 to 100 during which some of the oratorical elements associated with original Greek Sophists were reintroduced in parts of the Roman Empire. G. M. A. Grube writes that the Second Sophistic "can best be described as the triumph of display oratory, mainly in the Greek part of the empire, especially in the province of Asia."[95] The Second Sophistic followed times of great crisis for the Greek sections of the Empire. In the preceding centuries, Greece had experienced "the wars of Alexander's successors, the Roman wars of conquest, the exactions of Roman proconsuls under the late Republic, and the Roman civil wars."[96] Following this period of war, the cities of the Eastern Empire began to flourish again. In cities such as Smyrna, Ephesus, and Antioch orators could make a living by entertaining large crowds with speeches that emphasized style over content.

These new Sophists "made speeches of display at games and international festivals," sometimes amazing the crowds with their feats of memory and dramatic delivery. At this time, "any Sophist of repute could be sure of a good audience and a good fee in almost any city of Asia."[97] Dio Cocceianus (A.D. 40–120), also known as Chrysostomos or "golden tongued," was among the popular orators of this period. He was a wandering Stoic philosopher who spoke on a variety of apolitical topics such as the merits of sculpture and poetry, how to prepare to be a public speaker, and Greek tragedy. Another prominent orator of the Second Sophistic was Aelius Aristides (b. A.D. 117). He also specialized in topics that avoided political controversy, including a famous series of speeches on medicine. He was reputed to have been helped to health by the god Asclepius who, he claimed, spoke to him through dreams. Aelius also made speeches defending rhetoric against the attacks of Plato.[98]

As the examples of Chrysostomos and Aelius suggest, in spite of the renewed interest in rhetorical practice, the Second Sophistic represents a serious demotion of rhetoric from its former prominence as a means of shaping public policy and influencing judicial decisions. Rhetoric, in effect, had to be restrained because of the nature of empirial government. "It became a capital crime to insult the Emperor." Even the simple act of defacing a coin "could be construed as an offense punishable by death" because the coin bore the Emperor's image. "Roman orators were therefore effectively denied the safe exercise of the first major type of speaking, the deliberative or political speech."[99]

But this is not to say that the Second Sophistic represents rhetoric employed solely as a form of entertainment. It is possible to identify substantial roles performed by the rhetoricians of this period. First, these Greek orators working in a Roman world sought to preserve Greek culture. Historian of rhetoric George Kennedy writes that these later Sophists "differ from the older Greek Sophists in that they were cultural conservatives, intent on preserving the heritage of Hellenism in language, literature, rhetoric and religion."[100]

Thomas Conley suggests a second important role for rhetoricians during the Second Sophistic. As was true of those who preceeded them, the rhetoricians of this period were educators. Conley notes that chairs of rhetoric were established and funded at Roman universities in cities such as Antioch, Gaza, Alexandria, Athens, and Constantinople.[101] In fact, as in Athens, rhetorical training remained the principal vehicle for an ambitious young person to enter political life, albeit as a provincial administrator or perhaps as a lawyer. No longer did citizen–orators wield significant power in the Assembly.

Rhetoric's reduction in the late Roman Empire to a method of training administrators and a form of entertainment point up an important connection between rhetoric and democracy. When democracy flourishes, so does rhetoric and its study. When democracy declines, rhetoric also declines as its role as the method of free public discourse is diminished.

Though rhetoric's significance as the art of public discourse dwindled in empirial Rome, the art of rhetoric as it evolved in Rome outlived the civilization that produced it. Ironically, an essentially Roman rhetoric was reborn in a culture that shared relatively little with either the Roman Republic or the Roman Empire. This curious and important phenomenon in the history of rhetoric will be explored in the next chapter.

CONCLUSION

Rhetoric in the Roman world provided a center for a rigorous education that prepared citizens for personal success and advancement, for participation in civic life, and for public service. Rhetoric's connection with power, both personal and political, then, is clearly evident in the Roman tradition. Rhetorical training was a key to influence and personal advancement. Under the guidance of Longinus and other early literary critics, rhetoric came to be viewed as the means of achieving distinction and grace in writing.

Though the Romans learned rhetoric from the Greeks, they lent the art their own particular emphases. Roman theorists such as Cicero and Quintilian developed the *loci* of judicial pleading, for example, to a very high level of sophistication. But writers such as Longinus also employed the insights of Greek rhetoric to transform the Latin language, considered rough and vulgar by the Greeks, into one of great beauty, power, and subtlety of expression.

The audience was a key component in the rhetoric of Rome. In Cicero, as in other great Roman rhetoricians, a concern for the audience's tastes, sensibilities, and values is consistently evident. In addition, whether in Cicero's desire to unite wisdom and eloquence or Quintilian's definition of rhetoric as the good citizen skilled in speaking, an ethical dimension attends Roman thinking about rhetoric.

Rhetoric, the ability to speak and write clearly and persuasively, was for the Romans the most practical and potent of linguistic abilities. In the best of Roman rhetorical theory, this ability carried with it a moral responsibility to serve the people of Rome well.

QUESTIONS FOR REVIEW

1. What are Cicero's five canons of rhetoric?

2. Into what two general categories did Cicero divide his *loci* of judicial pleading?

3. Who was Hermagoras of Temnos, and why was he significant to Roman rhetoric?

4. According to Cicero, of what must speakers be wary when using humor?

5. Cicero held that eloquence had been separated from some other crucial factor in Roman rhetoric. What is that other factor, and why was he concerned to bring these two qualities together?

6. What were the five parts of a speech that Quintilian taught to his students?

7. What did Quintilian mean by suggesting that an orator must be a good person?

8. What were the qualities and skills that Longinus suggested helped an author to achieve the quality of sublimity?

9. What factors characterized the Second Sophistic?

QUESTIONS FOR DISCUSSION

1. For Cicero, the complete orator represented Roman civic values. Is such a conception of a single public figure—whether speaker or writer—possible today? Which persons in our society might take on such a role? Who comes closest? Why?

2. Is skill in argumentation still important to courtroom pleading today, or have procedural matters taken over the practice of law in courts? Is argumentation widely taught in our schools? If not, is it assumed that skill in this art is either natural, learned through studying other subjects, or just not important?

3. Longinus found in rhetoric an avenue to beautiful and expressive writing. Can studying examples of great writing, particularly the rhetorical figures employed by great writers, help you to improve your writing? Is great writing still valued, or has visual expression overshadowed writing in contemporary society?

4. If rhetorical practices and democratic forms of government tend to flourish together, how would you characterize the present state of rhetoric and democracy in U.S. culture? Are both flourishing? Are both in decline?

TERMS

Ambigua: The kind of equivocation involved in making puns.
Animorum motus: The emotions.
Ante rem: Events *preceding the act* in one *loci* system.
Arrangement: [*dispositio*] The distribution of arguments in the proper order; the second of Cicero's five canons of rhetoric.
Bases: In Quintilian's system, the specific issues that would have to be addressed in resolving a case.
Circa rem: Circumstances *surrounding the act* in one *loci* system.
Confirmatio: A section of a judicial speech offering evidences in support of claims advanced during the statement of the facts, or *narratio.*
Confutatio: In a judicial speech, the refutation or section in which counterarguments are answered.
Conjectural issues: In Cicero's stasis system, questions of fact, such as "What occurred?" and "When did it occur?"
Definite questions: Issues concerning specific individuals, facts, places, and times.
Definition: In Quintilian's system, a concern for categorizing an event.
Delectare: To delight; one of Cicero's three functions or goals of rhetoric.
Delivery: [*pronuntiatio*] The control of voice and body in a manner suitable to the dignity of the subject matter and the style; the fifth of Cicero's five canons of rhetoric.
Docere: To teach; one of Cicero's three functions or goals of rhetoric.
Existence: A question of what had occurred, a question of fact.
Exordium: An introduction designed to dispose the audience to listen to the speech.
Expression: [*elocutio*] Fitting proper language to arguments; the third of Cicero's five canons of rhetoric.
Facetiae: Wit or humor.
Gens: A clan, a group of influential families in Rome.
Hypothesis: In Hermagoras' system, a conclusion drawn from a thesis or general premise combined with a particular premise that applies the thesis to a given case.
Hypsos: Sublimity or great writing, the theme of Longinus' *On the Sublime.*
Imitatio: Imitation or mimicry.
Indefinite questions: In Quintilian's system of rhetoric, questions discussed without specific reference to persons, time, place or other particular limitation.
Invention: [*inventio*] The discovery of arguments; the first of Cicero's five canons of rhetoric.
In re: What occurred in the act itself, a locus of argument in one *loci* system.
Ioci: Jokes; discussed in Cicero's theory of humor in *De Oratore.*
Issues: Hermagoras of Temnos' *topoi,* which included three classifications of judicial arguments. The three types include:

1. Conjectural issues, or a concern for matters of fact.
2. Legal issues, or a concern for the interpretation of a text or document.
3. Juridical issues, or a concern for the rightness or wrongness of an act.

Issues of definition: Questions regarding by what name an act should be called.

Issues of fact: Questions concerning such questions as "What occurred?" and "When did it occur?"

Issues of quality: Questions concerning the severity of an act.

Loci communes: Commonplaces; types of arguments.

Memory: [*Memoria*] The firm mental grasp of matter and words; the fourth of Cicero's five canons of rhetoric.

Movere: To persuade or move an audience's emotions; one of Cicero's three functions or goals of rhetoric.

Narratio: In a judicial speech, a statement of essential facts.

Perfectus orator: Complete orator, a leader who embodied and articulated the society's values.

Peroratio: The conclusion or final section of a judicial speech in which the orator reiterated the full strength of a case.

Post rem: The events *following an act* in one *loci* system.

Pronuntiatio: The control of voice and body in a manner suitable to the dignity of the subject matter and the style.

Quality: In Quintilian's system of bases, a concern for the severity of the act, once defined or categorized.

Sannio: Clown or buffoon, a classification the orator must avoid in using humor.

Senatus: Senate; Roman governing body. Literally, a council of elders.

Stasis **system:**   Method for discovering arguments by identifying points where clash or disagreement was likely to occur in a case or debate.

Thesis: [pl. theses] A general premise in an argument under Hermagoras' system.

Topical systems: [*topica*] Systems for discovering arguments.

Translative issue: Issues of procedure; objections regarding how a case was being pursued.

ENDNOTES

1. Lionel Casson, *Selected Satires of Lucian* (New York: Norton, 1968), xiii.

2. Manfred Fuhrmann, *Cicero and the Roman Republic,* trans. W. E. Yuill (Oxford: Blackwell, 1992), 18.

3. James M. May, *Trials of Character: The Eloquence of Ciceronian Ethos* (Chapel Hill: University of North Carolina Press, 1988), 6.

4. Harold C. Gotoff, *Cicero's Caesarian Speeches: A Stylistic Commentary* (Chapel Hill: University of North Carolina Press, 1993), x.

5. Michael Mooney, *Renaissance Thought and Its Sources* (NY: Columbia University Press, 1979), 36.

6. Graham Anderson, *Sage, Saint, and Sophist: Holy Men and Their Associates in the Early Roman Empire* (London: Routledge, 1994).

7. See: Ann Vasaly, *Representations: Images of the World in Ciceronian Oratory* (Berkeley: University of California Press, 1993).

8. G. M. A. Grube, translator's introduction to Longinus, *On the Sublime* (Indianapolis, IN: Library of Liberal Arts, 1957), ix.

9. Calvin Troup, *Temporality, Eternity, and Wisdom: The Rhetoric of Augustine's Confessions* (Columbia: University of South Carolina Press, 1999), 13.

10. Fuhrmann, 19.

11. Fuhrmann, 19.

12. Fuhrmann, 19.

13. Longinus, *On The Sublime,* trans. G. M. A. Grube (Indianapolis, IN: Library of Liberal Arts, 1957), x.

14. Christian Habicht, *Cicero the Politician* (Baltimore, MD: Johns Hopkins University Press, 1990), 1.

15. See: Christopher P. Craig, *Form as Argument in Cicero's Speeches: A Study of Dilemma,* American Classical Studies, #31 (Atlanta, GA: Scholars Press, 1993).

16. Mooney, 8.

17. Gotoff, xii.

18. Habicht, 2. Habicht provides a brief and readable account of Cicero's political career. For a more detailed account of Cicero's life, see: D. R. Shackleton-Bailey, *Cicero* (New York: Charles Scribner's Sons, 1971).

19. On the *Rhetorica ad Herennium,* see: James J. Murphy, "The Age of Codification: Hermagoras and the Pseudo-Ciceronian *Rhetorica ad Herennium,*" in *A Synoptic History of Classical Rhetoric,* eds. Richard Katula & James J. Murphy (Davis, CA: Hermagoras Press, 1983), 77–89. For a detailed discussion of *De Inventione* (and Cicero's other works on rhetoric), see: Donovan J. Ochs, "Cicero's Rhetorical Theory," in *A Synoptic History of Classical Rhetoric,* 90–150.

20. Craig, 14.

21. Brian Vickers, *In Defense of Rhetoric* (Oxford: Oxford University Press, 1988), 28.

22. Cicero, *De Inventione,* trans. H. M. Hubbell (Cambridge, MA: Loeb Classical Library, 1976).

23. M. L. Clark, *Rhetoric at Rome* (New York: Barnes & Noble, 1953), 53.

24. Habicht, 2.

25. *De Inventione,* I. 1.

26. May, 6.

27. *De Inventione,* I. iv. 5.

28. *De Inventione,* I. vi. 9.

29. *De Inventione,* I. vii. 9 (emphasis added).

30. *De Inventione,* I. 11–19.

31. *De Inventione,* I. viii. 11.

32. *De Inventione,* I. viii. 16.

33. Donovan J. Ochs, "Cicero's *Topica:* A Process View of Invention," in *Explorations in Rhetoric: Essays in Honor of Douglas Ehninger,* ed. Ray E. McKerrow (Glenview, IL: Scott, Foresman, 1982), 117. Quoted in Kathleen E. Welch, *The Contemporary Reception of Classical Rhetoric: Appropriations of Ancient Discourse* (Hillsdale, NJ: Lawrence Erlbaum, 1990), 60.

34. Edward P. J. Corbett, "The *Topoi* Revisited," in *Rhetoric and Praxis: The Contribution of Classical Rhetoric to Practical Reasoning,* ed. Jean Deitz Moss (Washington, DC: Catholic University of America Press, 1986), 47. Quoted in Welch, 60–61.

35. Cicero discusses these *loci* in *De Inventione,* Book I. xxiv–xxviii. See also: Michael Leff, "The Topics of Argumentative Invention in Latin Rhetorical Theory from Cicero to Boethius," *Rhetorica* 1 (Spring 1983): 23–44.

36. ___, *De Inventione,* I. xxiv. 34.

37. Leff, 27.

38. *De Inventione,* I. xxvi–xxviii.

39. Leff, 28.

40. On Hermagoras' work and influence, see: Murphy, "Age of Codification."

41. See: Vickers, 26–27.

42. Cicero, *De Oratore,* trans. E. W. Sutton, H. Rackham (Cambridge, MA: Harvard University Press, 1976), ix ff.

43. Michael Mooney, *Vico in the Tradition of Rhetoric* (Princeton, NJ: Princeton University Press, 1985), 8.

44. On the Aristotelian influences in *De Oratore,* see: May, 3ff.

45. *De Oratore,* I. ii. 5.

46. Mooney, 8–9.

47. *De Oratore,* I. xxviii. 128.Quoted in Mooney, 36.
48. *De Oratore,* I. vii. 30.
49. May, 9.
50. *De Oratore,* III. xvi. 60–61.
51. *De Oratore,* I. iii. 12.
52. *De Oratore,* I. v. 17.
53. *De Oratore,* I. v. 18 (emphasis added).
54. *De Oratore,* II. xliv. 187 ff.
55. *De Oratore,* II. xliv. 188.
56. *De Oratore,* I. v. 20.
57. *De Oratore,* I. viii. 34.
58. *De Oratore,* II. lvi. 228.
59. *De Oratore,* I. vi. 229.
60. *De Oratore,* II. lviii–lix. 338–9.
61. *De Oratore,* lx.
62. *De Oratore,* II. lx. 247.
63. *De Oratore,* II. lxi. 250.
64. *De Oratore,* II. lxi. 251.
65. *De Oratore,* II. lxi. 252.
66. *De Oratore,* II. lxi. 253.
67. *De Oratore,* II. lxi. 254.
68. *De Oratore,* II. lxiv. 258–259.
69. *De Oratore,* II. lxiv. 260.
70. *De Oratore,* II. lxvi. 264.
71. *De Oratore,* II. lxvi. 266.
72. R. G. M. Nisbet, "The Speeches," in *Cicero,* ed. T. A. Dorey (New York: Basic Books, 1965), 56.
73. Quoted in Prentice A. Meador, Jr., "Quintilian and the *Institutio Oratoria,*" in *A Synoptic History of Classical Rhetoric,* 151–176.
74. On Quintilian's teaching, see: James J. Murphy, "Roman Writing Instruction as Described by Quintilian," in *A Short History of Writing Instruction,* ed. James J. Murphy (Davis, CA: Hermagoras Press, 1990), 19–76.
75. Quintilian, *Institutio Oratoria,* 4 vol., trans. H. E. Butler, (Cambridge, MA: Harvard University Press, 1959–1963), Loeb Classical Library. See also: Quintilian *On the Early Education of the Citizen Orator,* ed. James J. Murphy, trans. John S. Watson (Indianapolis, IN: Library of Liberal Arts, 1965).
76. Quintilian, *Institutes of Oratory,* I. 1.
77. Quoted in Meador, 155.
78. Meador, 157.
79. Quintilian, *Institutes,* II. 11.
80. Leff, 33.
81. Quintilian, *Institutes,* V. 10.125. Quoted in Leff, 34.
82. For a more detailed discussion of ancient systems for dividing speeches, see: Vickers, 67–72.
83. Longinus, *On the Sublime,* trans., G. M. A. Grube (Indianapolis, IN: Library of Liberal Arts, 1957). All passages from *On the Sublime* are from this translation.
84. Vickers, 307.
85. Grube, x–xi.
86. Jane Tompkins, "The Reader in History: The Changing Shape of Literary Response," in *Reader Response Criticism,* ed. Jane P. Tompkins (Baltimore, MD: Johns Hopkins University Press, 1980), 203.
87. Tompkins, 203.
88. Longinus, 10.
89. Longinus, 10.
90. Longinus, 17.Translation of the love ode of Sappho by J. A. Symonds (1883).
91. Longinus, 29.

92. Longinus, 29.
93. Longinus, 31.
94. Vickers, 310. Longinus quote from *On the Sublime,* 29. 2.
95. Grube, 325.
96. Grube, 325.
97. Grube, 325, 326.
98. Grube, 328.
99. Katula and Murphy, 206.
100. George Kennedy, *A Comparative Rhetoric* (New York: Oxford University Press, 1998), 211.
101. Thomas M. Conley, *Rhetoric in the European Tradition* (New York: Longman), 60.

■ ■ ■ ■ ■

CHAPTER SIX

RHETORIC IN
CHRISTIAN EUROPE

Since preaching and teaching are necessary for the
Church of God, that science which presents the form of preaching
artistically is equally necessary, or even more so.
—Robert of Basevorn

Emperor Constantine legalized Christianity for Romans in A.D. 313, suggesting that Christianity had gained a considerable foothold in the late Roman Empire. When Rome fell in the fifth century A.D., its successor, European Christendom, was already present in embryonic form within its boundaries. With the barbarian conquest of the Empire, rhetoric initially suffered a significant decline, as did many other disciplines. The tribes of northern and western Europe did not maintain Roman and Greek traditions, and often hastened the passing of classical learning by acts such as destroying libraries.

This is not to say, however, that the classical tradition in rhetoric disappeared entirely. As George Kennedy writes, "classical rhetoric did not die. A few private teachers of grammar and rhetoric could probably be found at most times in cities of Italy and Gaul."[1] As the cities of Italy started to reestablish a recognizable civic life, rhetoric again became an important study. As it had been in the past, rhetoric was central to both legislative and judicial functions in cities such as Venice and Bologna. The art also ascended to a position of great importance in a new theater of power—the Church.

RHETORIC, TENSION, AND FRAGMENTATION

By far the most important cultural phenomenon in the West in the period following the fall of the Roman Empire was the rise of Christianity, and its eventual domination of Europe. The Church came to control virtually every aspect of public and even of private life. This meant that the legislative assemblies and courts of law that had characterized Greek and Roman culture, and that had much to do with the development of the classical rhetorical tradition, were largely absent from the medieval European scene. Nevertheless, true to its nature as a public and practical art, rhetoric was adapted to the needs of Christian European society between the fifth and fifteenth centuries. But, medieval Europe's adaptation of Greek and, especially, Roman rhetoric was, as we shall see, a somewhat constricted and fragmented appropriation of the rich classical tradition.

As suggested, medieval Europeans were more familiar with Roman than with Greek rhetoric, and their familiarity extended to only a small portion of Roman theory at that. Much of Greek rhetoric was simply unknown in the Middle Ages. Aristotle's *Rhetoric,* for instance, "was not known to the Latin West before Hermannus Alemannus translated it into Latin (from Arabic) in 1256 and William of Moerbeke again translated it (from Greek) in about 1270."[2] Because of barbarian conquests in what had been the Roman Empire, ensuing social fragmentation, and the destruction of ancient libraries such as the famous one in Alexandria, many other texts of classical antiquity were not widely available in medieval Europe, and many were permanently lost. Quintilian's *Institutio Oratio,* the Roman master's massive multivolume treatment of rhetoric, survived only in incomplete sets of often mutilated copies.

Still, there were exceptions to the rule of lost and damaged classical works on rhetoric in the Middle Ages. Two of these exceptions proved particularly important. Cicero's early work on rhetoric, *De Inventione,* along with the anonymous *Rhetorica ad Herennium,* were widely known and provided a foundation for the vast majority of medieval rhetorical treatises and practices.[3] Commentaries on *De Inventione* by medieval scholars such as Victorinus influenced how Cicero was interpreted and taught.[4] Kathleen Welch writes that "it is interesting to note that *On Invention* was the only text of Cicero available to most of the medieval period and therefore was frequently cited during this period." Thus, two works—*De Inventione* and *Rhetorica ad Herennium*— were "the major works of Latin antiquity for the Middle Ages."[5] The content of these rhetorical treatises often was preserved and communicated in commentaries, works by later writers intended to explain the rhetorical systems being presented. Some of these commentaries date from as early as the fourth century A.D.

Some educated people in the Middle Ages viewed much of the classical tradition with suspicion, and this for the same reasons that Augustine found it difficult to reconcile his interest in rhetoric with his work as a Christian minister. The Greek and Roman classics were, after all, the products of people who were not Christians. Rhetoric in particular was viewed with suspicion. A "strong hostility...marked the attitudes of Christian scholars toward an art which they viewed as reminiscent of all the immorality of pagan Rome."[6] For this reason—and because of the limited availability of many classical sources—a small number of antiseptically technical Roman works formed the basis of much of the medieval rhetorical curriculum. Cicero's works, and a few other sources, may have benefited from Augustine's endorsement of them in *De Doctrina.*[7] Because of the Church's suspicion of pagan antiquity, medieval scholars often lifted components from classical works on rhetoric and shaped them to serve the purposes of a Christian culture. For this reason some historians of rhetoric view the medieval period as one during which classical rhetoric was dismantled or fragmented.[8]

During the Middle Ages rhetoric increasingly was identified with written style and used to assist the oral exposition of biblical texts. Rhetoric's traditional role of assisting the development of persuasive cases through the discovery and arrangement of arguments was gradually lost to view. Dialectic and logic took over these crucial inventional functions. In order to trace the dramatic changes in both rhetoric's scope and social functions in medieval Europe, it will be helpful to consider the place it occupied in the educational curriculum.

RHETORIC AND THE MEDIEVAL CURRICULUM

As educational practices developed over the long course of the Middle Ages, an intellectual movement known as Scholasticism became dominant in parts of Europe. Scholasticism was a closed and authoritarian approach to education centered on disputation over a fixed body of premises derived largely from the teachings of Aristotle. Scholasticism developed around the medieval tendency to treat ancient sources—both the Bible and certain texts of classical antiquity—as authoritative. So strong was this tendency that individual sentences from a respected source, even when taken out of context, could be employed to secure a point in debate. These isolated statements from ancient sources were called *sententiae.* Some authors collected large numbers of *sententiae* into anthologies for educational and disuputational purposes. Disputes centered on debatable points suggested by one or more sententiae, these debatable notions being called *quaestiones.* Education by debating general topics drawn from authoritative statements reveals one way in which rhetorical and dialectical practices made their way into the Middle Ages.

The scholastic method did afford certain advantages for students trained under it. As Charles G. Nauert writes, "its great virtue was that it probed each issue in an orderly and rational way, collecting the various possible opinions and making a determination of what seemed to be the correct opinion."[9] Unfortunately for students trained by the use of *sententiae,* however, the actual meaning of a statement in its original context often was lost by the practice of separating sentences from the texts in which they originally appeared. The classical authors tended to disappear in this process, leaving a fragment of a thought to represent a whole book, theory, or body of work. As Nauert notes, Scholasticism "simplified and distorted the opinions of authorities by reducing each author's opinion to a single statement, totally divorced from its original context."[10]

Despite such limiting textual practices, Marjory Curry Woods has argued that rhetoric as a component in the medieval curriculum exhibited remarkable consistency over a long period. "For example," she writes, "the techniques of teaching grammar and rhetoric that John of Salisbury, writing in about 1150, describes in his eulogy of his master, Bernard of Chartres, were used consistently throughout the thirteenth, fourteenth, and fifteenth centuries." Some rhetorical texts formed the basis of educational approaches for virtually the entire medieval period. In fact, rhetoric's duration in this regard is astonishing. Woods writes, "the books that formed the basis of rhetorical education in composition at the beginning of the Middle Ages continued to be taught more than a thousand years later."[11] Such remarkable continuity points up both the significance of rhetorical training to medieval education and the heavy cultural reliance on portions of the classical tradition of rhetoric. It will be worth our while to take a closer look at some specific rhetorical components of the medieval curriculum, and the scholars who advocated rhetoric's study.

RHETORIC IN THE EARLY MIDDLE AGES: AUGUSTINE, CAPELLA, AND BOETHIUS

Ciceronian rhetoric in the Middle Ages shaped education, civic administration, private life, and Church practice in a variety of ways. We will begin our study of this phenomenon with the writer who initially translated classical rhetoric into the language of the Church, Augustine of Hippo, otherwise known as St. Augustine. We will then consider another early medieval writer, Martianus Capella, who authored perhaps the most successful textbook on rhetoric ever. This section concludes with a discussion of the philosopher Boethius, who revived Cicero's topical system in his effort to import classical rhetoric into a new domain—Christian Europe.

ST. AUGUSTINE

In the period between A.D. 450 and 1000, rhetoric became important to the functioning of the Church. For guidance in their teaching, debates with opponents, and evangelism, Church leaders looked to the rhetorical tradition. Cicero occupied the center of that tradition as it was known to them. His influence on medieval thought was great in other related academic areas as well. For example, Christian Habicht writes that Cicero "made Greek philosophy accessible" to scholars in the Middle Ages.[12] Cicero's comprehensive influence is evident from the very beginning of the period, as is apparent when we consider early medieval rhetorical theory. But, as we shall see, even where Cicero's influence is great, originality is still possible.

St. Augustine of Hippo (A.D. 353–430) was the greatest of the Early Church Fathers, a group of theologians writing between about A.D. 180 and 450 who did much to shape Christian theology. Augustine was born in northern Africa, then part of the waning Roman Empire. His mother, Monica, was a devout Christian, though his father did not embrace the faith. Augustine was sent to the great Roman port of Carthage to study rhetoric as a teenager, but fell victim to the temptations of the city. He fathered a child by his mistress before he was eighteen.

For nearly ten years, until the age of twenty-eight, Augustine followed a secret religious sect known as the Manichaeans. He also became a professor of rhetoric in the imperial city of Milan, a faculty position he later referred to as "a chair of lies."[13] The rhetoric Augustine taught was based on works by Cicero that he had studied in the famous school of rhetoric at Carthage. Augustine's understanding of rhetoric and its place in society was also heavily influenced by the practices of the Second Sophistic, a late Roman development discussed in Chapter 5. Calvin Troup has written of this rhetorical movement, "the Second Sophistic rewarded delivery, style and ornamentation with little or no attention to substance" and that this approach to rhetoric "dominated the fourth-century Roman schools...." Troup affirms that for Augustine "rhetoric and the Second Sophistic were synonymous."[14]

While teaching this brand of Sophistic rhetoric in Milan between the years A.D. 384–386, Augustine became acquainted with the Christian leader, Ambrose. Through a series of sermons and discussions, Ambrose contributed to Augustine's decision to convert to Christianity. Ambrose baptized Augustine in 387.[15] Augustine was ordained a priest in 391 and was later elevated to the office of Bishop of Hippo, after Carthage, the largest port city in Roman North Africa. Over the three decades that he served as bishop, Augustine spent much of his time writing against various heretical groups such as the Donatists and the Pelagians. In 397 he published *Confessions,* one of the most famous works of Western literature. The *Confessions* describes his early life and his conversion to Christianity. The book also contains a scathing attack on the type of rhetoric Augustine had at one time taught. Between 413 and 426, he wrote and published his great *City of God,* which views the Church as a new order replacing the old Roman Empire. The end of Augustine's life marks the end of the Roman Empire in the West, for the Vandals under Genseric laid siege to Hippo in 430, and Augustine died three months into the siege.

Augustine's Rhetorical Theory

Augustine's early education had been conducted on a classical Roman model, which meant that the core of his curriculum was rhetoric. The young Augustine excelled at rhetoric and saw it as a path to wealth and fame. Rhetoric would allow him to "succeed in this world and excel in those arts of speech which would serve to bring honor among men and to gain deceitful riches."[16] He went on to teach the subject at universities in Italy and in other parts of the Mediterranean world. Thus, during this period of his life, Augustine lived, believed, and taught much like a Sophist of the fifth century B.C. in Athens. Moreover, when he attacks rhetoric, as he does at points in his *Confessions,* it is a sophistical model of rhetoric he has in mind. "Augustine never abandons rhetoric qua rhetoric in practice," writes Troup, "but rejects only the abuses of the Second Sophistic."[17] As we shall see, Augustine thought much in the rhetorical tradition was useful in the Christian church and in Christian society generally.

Following his conversion to Christianity—which he at one point said was a conversion *from* rhetoric—Augustine wrestled with the potential uses of Roman rhetoric in the Christian Church.[18] Like Plato in *Phaedrus,* Augustine sought a true art of rhetoric that could be used in the service of transcendent truth, in his case, the truth of the Christian scriptures. Thus, the ancient theme of rhetoric's relationship to truth becomes a central issue in rhetorical theory at the opening of the Middle Ages. Augustine believed that there are two tasks for the Christian teacher: to discover and then to teach the contents of scripture.[19] His voluminous apologetic writings suggest

Augustine identified a third task—to defend scriptural truth when it was attacked. Rhetoric, in spite of its pagan origins and frequent misuse, could assist the Christian teacher in fulfilling each of these obligations. But the classical theory of rhetoric had to be adapted to a new Christian understanding of truth.

The Preacher's Dilemma: Expressing the Inexpressible.   God was the source of truth in the Christian system, and this central fact posed a serious problem for the Christian rhetorician. Language, the medium of rhetoric, is a finite system of symbols, while God is infinite and thus cannot adequately be described by means of finite signs. However, Augustine was convinced that God commands that the preacher *must* speak of Him. Thus, Augustine faced a dilemma: A rhetoric of God is both impossible and essential. He sought to adapt the resources of the classical rhetoric he had once taught in Italian schools to the Christian purpose of creating a rhetoric capable of expressing truth about God.

The rhetorical theory Augustine developed in response to his dilemma is at several points Platonic. Augustine held that in order to contemplate God, the mind should be cleansed. Part of this process of preparing the mind for divine thoughts is rhetorical: The preacher corrects through good preaching the errors that have corrupted the mind. This is reminiscent of Plato's conception of "true rhetoric" as a kind of medicine for sick souls that works by refuting error. But rhetoric also guides the preacher in preparing truthful messages for maintaining the health of souls now put into a receptive attitude. Augustine's Christian rhetoric, then, assisted the work of the preacher by curing the ailments of the human soul through the refutation of error, and by making possible the soul's health through communicating divine truth. Augustine's rhetoric, again, strikes one as Platonic in its orientation toward both correcting error and teaching truth.

Rhetoric assists the preacher to discover divine truth in the scriptures, and to teach this truth to the congregation. But rhetoric is also an aid to the clear, forceful, and stylistically appealing presentation of one's message. Augustine also endorses the Ciceronian ends of rhetoric, to teach, to delight, and to move, though he gives each goal a Christian significance. The preacher must know his subject matter in order to *teach* it well. He must also know how to reach his congregation's emotions (to *delight*), and to persuade them to Christian living (to *move*).

The Teacher's Dilemma: Roman Rhetoric in Christian Schools?   We have considered the dilemma Augustine faced as a preacher, that is, finding in finite rhetoric a means of communicating truth about an infinite God. But Augustine faced a second dilemma as a Christian educator. He found this art of rhetoric both indispensable to his educational work as a priest and later a Bishop, and yet he held that the received tradition of rhetoric was inconsistent in many respects with Christian principles. It was, after all, an art developed by pagans such as Cicero. It was also an art aimed at a suspicious goal, persuasion, sometimes by verbal trickery.

Thus, rhetoric posed Augustine a second dilemma: It was useful, even vital to confuting the heretics and teaching his own congregation, but it was also a suspect and potentially dangerous art. Augustine resolved his dilemma by reasoning that rhetoric should not be at the disposal only of the unbelieving. Moreover, the Bible itself was a model of eloquence for the Christian.[20] He treats these problems in his most important work on rhetoric, *De Doctrina Christiana.*

De Doctrina Christiana

Augustine's major work on rhetoric is his guide to preaching, entitled *De Doctrina Christiana (On Christian Doctrine)*, a work with strong connections to Cicero's *De Oratore* and *Orator.* W. R. Johnson has referred to the book as "not merely the most influential but perhaps the most precious book in the tradition of humanistic rhetoric."[21] James J. Murphy calls *De Doctrina,* "one of the most significant works of the early middle ages."[22] Murphy's assessment is based on Augustine's ability to treat the dilemma facing Christian writers at the beginning of the Christian era in Europe, namely, what to do with a rich classical tradition rooted in pagan culture and belief. Murphy explains Augustine's solution to the dilemma as follows:

> The *De Doctrina* begins by pointing out that the means of finding material for understanding Scripture (the *modus inveniendi*) is different from the means of expressing the ideas found (the *modus proferendi*). Augustine urged the Church to study the human arts of discourse—in particular, rhetoric—either through formal schooling or through study of great models.[23]

Thus, Augustine urged the Church to use what was useful in the classical rhetorical treatises. But, he was concerned that education not be given over to learning the systems so characteristic of Roman rhetoric. Rather, education in Augustine's view should be centered not on learning "rhetorical ornament and structures," but on what John O. Ward has called "the inculcation of appropriate thought and content."[24]

Augustine's commitment to education is everywhere evident in his treatments of rhetoric. Johnson finds the purpose of *De Doctrina* to have been largely educational. Christians needed training in reading the Bible, and even in defending it, if the Christian gospel was to be preserved and propagated. "The *De Doctrina* was written for clergy and highly educated members of the laity," writes Johnson, "to help them in their efforts to read the Bible and to give them advice about how to go about sharing what they had learned with fellow Christians who were less educated than themselves."[25]

In resolving his ambivalent feelings about rhetoric—arising from its pagan origins and its Christian usefulness—Augustine posed his readers this question: "For since by means of the art of rhetoric both truth and falsehood are urged, who would dare to say that truth should stand in the person of its defenders unarmed against lying?"[26] The strongly implied answer to this question is, of course, an endorsement of the Christian study of classical rhetoric. The reasoning behind the answer runs like this: The happiness of all people can be achieved if all can be brought to understand and accept the truth of the gospel. And the truth of the gospel can be more effectively advanced and defended if Christians, and particularly Christian ministers, understand the principles of rhetoric.[27]

Augustine on Signs

[handwritten: semiotics – study of signs / signifier + signified]

In *De Doctrina* Augustine sets out a sophisticated theory of the relationship between words or "signs," and the things they represent. In Book II Augustine divides the world into two broad categories: things, and signs pointing to things. Words are one set of signs, but Augustine also held that the world itself could be understood as a system of signs pointing people to God. Human beings themselves, in fact, are a kind of symbol in that they are created in the image of God. The whole world of physical things, then, is to be used to return us to God, not to be enjoyed for its own sake.

This distinction between the sign and the thing signified helps the Christian preacher discern two different kinds of meanings in objects encountered in scripture. For example, a rock or a tree in a biblical story are physical objects, signified by the words *rock* and *tree*. However, the rock or the tree may also themselves be signs with their own spiritual meaning. The rock may refer to Christ, as St. Paul suggested that a rock in one Mosaic story did. The tree may represent everlasting life.

Augustine's Contribution to Rhetoric

As preacher and polemicist, Augustine showed himself a master of rhetorical practice. In his books on Christian teaching and preaching, he writes as a studied theorist of the art as well. Though Augustine professed great mistrust of rhetoric and found the art at points inconsistent with Christian principles, he also made a concerted effort to bring Roman rhetoric into the service of the Christian gospel. Augustine is in these ways perhaps reminiscent of that other great critic of rhetoric who yet showed his vast understanding of the art and practical mastery of it—Plato. We might also speculate that the critic of rhetoric is always bound to employ the art even to frame a criticism of it.

Augustine's ambivalence about rhetoric was productive, for he successfully negotiated the tension between the emerging Christian consensus in the West, and its pagan Greek and Roman literary heritage reflected in the rhetorical tradition. Augustine taught the Church how to employ pagan writers without paganizing Christianity. He thus provided a model to many later teachers and preachers.

Rhetoric provided a valuable means of discovering, presenting, and defending the truth of scripture.[28] The rules of rhetoric—the topics and figures—are not as important for Augustine as are good models of eloquence, especially when joined with a thorough knowledge of scripture. Here we have Augustine's version of the Ciceronian ideal of the union of wisdom and eloquence. However, in Augustine wisdom is not worldly but heavenly, not political but divine. Specifically, wisdom consists in knowing the contents and sense of scripture. Augustine thus takes what is of use in the theory and practice of classical rhetoric, especially some principles of Cicero, and appropriates this knowledge for the proclamation and defense of the Christian gospel.

MARTIANUS CAPELLA

Martianus Capella was one of the rhetoricians responsible for creating the impression among people living in the fifth and sixth centuries A.D. that the rhetorical tradition was incompatible with Christianity. A lawyer with a strong interest in mysticism and little regard for Christianity, Capella lived in the North African city of Carthage around the same time that Augustine was presiding over his parish not far away. Carthage at this time was home to "the best school of rhetoric in all of Roman North Africa."[29]

Capella is best known for a single work, broken into several books, that presented in prose and poetry the seven liberal arts. It is difficult to overestimate the influence of his work, *The Marriage of Philology and Mercury* (A.D. 429), which included his *Book of Rhetoric.* One scholar has called *The Marriage of Philology and Mercury* "the most successful textbook ever written," and it certainly was one of the most widely used books in medieval schools.[30] In his strange, massive, and thoroughly pagan book, Capella imagines a wedding in which the god Mercury gives his bride a gift of the seven liberal arts constituting the core of the medieval curriculum. These seven are grammar, dialectic, rhetoric, geometry, arithmetic, astronomy, and harmonics.[31] The liberal arts were divided between the four major or advanced studies of arithmetic, geometry, astronomy, and harmonics called the *quadrivium* (four roads); and the three fundamental studies of grammar, rhetoric, and logic, called the *trivium* (three roads). Cappella represents rhetoric as a heavily armed woman, a tradition that continued throughout the Middle Ages.

Grammar, rhetoric, and logic, then, were important foundational studies for anyone preparing for public service or for service in the Church. Grammar involved the study of significant literary sources such as Homer, as well as the studies of composition, style in writing, and proper syntax. Composition and literary criticism might be the closest parallels in the modern curriculum. Logic presented the rules governing deduction. But it was rhetoric that dominated the curriculum in schools at the time that Capella wrote, and the study of rhetoric was largely Ciceronian in conception. Rhetoric was divided according to Cicero's canons from *De Inventione:* invention, arrangement, style, memory, and delivery. Capella's summary of Cicero in his *Book of Rhetoric* influenced other important rhetorical scholars. For instance, Isidore of Seville's (A.D. 560–636) *Etymologiae* presented the rhetorical tradition following the accounts of Quintilian and Cicero found in Capella.

BOETHIUS

Anicius Manlius Severinus Boethius (A.D. 475–524) was a late Roman statesman and philosopher, who, around A.D. 500, became an important figure in the court of the Gothic king, Theodoric, who was at that time ruling Italy from Rome. He is most famous for writing *The Consolation of Philosophy,* a work he penned while in prison for daring to challenge Theodoric's oppressive tendencies. Boethius also translated many works of Aristotle from Greek to Latin, and he may have been the last of the great Roman philosophers to understand Greek. Just as he served as a bridge be-

tween Greek and late Roman culture, he was also a transitional figure in the movement from Roman to Christian culture in Europe. He is said to have begun "an
eclecticism that finds a place for all of the great authors of antiquity, from Plato and
Aristotle down to Cicero."[32] Boethius was executed on Theodoric's orders in 524.

Boethius was interested in a wide range of subjects, including mathematics,
philosophy, dialectic, and rhetoric. He advanced a modified Roman topical system in
his work, *De Differentiis Topicis.*[33] One medieval scholar has noted that Boethius'
book was "the only text which seems to have enjoyed a currency approaching, but
not equaling, the *ad Herennium* and *De Inventione*" in schools of the Middle Ages.[34]
Boethius' work on rhetoric is, not surprisingly, heavily influenced by Cicero's *De Inventione* and *Topica* where Cicero appears to be "a teacher of rules and precepts"
rather than the reflective master of the art we find in the later *De Oratore.*[35] Thus,
Boethius' work itself is sometimes criticized as excessively prescriptive, system-
bound, and impractical. In Boethius, rhetoric looks something like the technical
study known in classical times as dialectic. Nevertheless, as we have noted, *De Dif-
feretiis Topicis* remained one of the most popular medieval rhetoric manuals. The dry
and systematic treatment rhetoric receives at Boethius' hands may reflect the oppressive circumstances under which the book was written. Rhetoric's role under any tyrannical or authoritarian government is always severely circumscribed and limited,
rendering rhetoric either the technical study of argument, the formal rules of official
communication, or perhaps a form of entertainment. With these concerns in mind,
Boethius' highly influential book does merit a closer look.

Differentiis Topicis

In *Differentiis Topicis* (c. A.D. 520), Boethius discussed what he termed topical maxims, which were rational principles or major premises in arguments. One was the
maxim of material cause, which is the premise: "Where the material needed to produce an object is absent, the object also is absent." Thus, in an argument from the
maxim of material cause, the advocate might reason:

> Our enemies do not have a source of iron.
> Where the material needed to produce an object is absent, the object also is absent.
> Thus, our enemies cannot be in possession of iron weapons.

Boethius grouped these maxims according to what he called *differentia,* or
general categories of argument. For example, all of the maxims regarding *cause*
were grouped together to facilitate memory and use. This category included both
maxims having to do with the causes of objects, as illustrated in the example, and
maxims about what will cause a person to commit a particular crime. For instance:
When a man feels threatened, he may strike another man. Boethius' topical system
reveals the influence of both Aristotle and Cicero.[36]

Boethius' topics are the concluding chapter in the Greek and Roman tradition
of topical inventional systems. The Middle Ages witnessed a decline in the kind of
courtroom pleading that originally gave rise to the great classical interest in topical
invention. Thus, as Michael Leff points out, "Boethius' efforts center much more on

the construction of a theoretically coherent art of rhetorical topics than on the application of topics to public argument."[37] Boethius' systematic presentation of a classical rhetoric influenced later rhetorical theory in Europe, particularly in the schools of Paris in the thirteenth century.[38]

THREE RHETORICAL ARTS IN THE TWELFTH AND THIRTEENTH CENTURIES

Between 1100 to 1300, the high-water mark for medieval European rhetoric, the art came to be codified in manuals on preaching, letter writing, and poetry.[39] Each art had particular uses in a complex societal setting, each reflected its classical heritage in a different way, and each appealed to a different medieval audience. John O. Ward writes regarding the adaptability of rhetoric and the practical orientation of medieval theorists, teachers, and practitioners: "[as] each generation of medieval students of rhetoric succeeded another, our sources pinpoint ways in which contemporaries kept their teaching and study of the classical rhetorical corpus close to the needs of their day."[40] It is interesting to note, however, that the medieval rhetorical writers produced little or no original theory of speech-making outside of church settings. As James J. Murphy has written, "the middle ages did not produce any major original works on secular speaking" because "the political climate which had encouraged such writing in ancient Greece and Rome simply did not exist in medieval Europe."[41] We will look first at the rhetorical art that most nearly approximates the traditional conception of rhetoric as oratory, and then at the adaptation of rhetoric to instruction in writing.

THE ART OF PREACHING

Rhetoric was appropriated to the needs of a vast Church hierarchy that developed its own peculiar forms of government, discourse, education, and art. The art most easily associated with the purposes of the church was preaching (*ars praedicandi*). From the late eleventh century through the fifteenth, preaching was an important and popular art in Europe. Orders of preachers, such as the Dominicans and Franciscans, emerged in the Church.[42] Numerous preaching manuals were authored during the Christian Middle Ages, particularly during the thirteenth century.[43]

Themes, Sermons, and Moral Persuasion

Typical of the preaching manuals of the late Middle Ages is Robert of Basevorn's *Forma Praedicandi* (*The Form of Preaching*).[44] The preaching instruction one received from such manuals emphasized expanding on the meanings of *brief biblical texts,* or themes, toward the goal of improving the moral conduct and religious understanding of one's audience, presumed to be Christians. It was recognized that many members of the preacher's audience would be illiterate and generally unfamiliar with the contents of scripture. Thus, thematic preaching, as it is called, emphasized the selection of appropriate and accessible texts, as well as careful audience adaptation.[45] James J. Murphy, a leading expert on medieval rhetoric, suggests that treatments of thematic preaching began making appearances in European university centers such as Paris around A.D. 1230. As an approach to preaching, it became, he writes, "extremely popular" and "extremely influential."[46]

In his treatise, *The Form of Preaching,* Robert complains that most preaching is done with no understanding of the structure of a sermon. Such knowledge is, however, essential to the Church. "Since preaching and teaching are necessary for the Church of God," he writes, "that science which presents the form of preaching artistically is equally necessary, or even more so."[47] Thus, just as Aristotle set about to provide his listeners with an art, or *techne,* of rhetoric, so Robert intends to provide his readers with an art of preaching.

"Preaching," he writes, "is the persuasion of many, within a moderate length of time, to meritorious conduct."[48] Preaching was not, then, conceived of principally as theological investigation. It was, rather, moral persuasion. And, like Cicero, Robert holds out that a preacher must be a knowledgeable person, one who unites wisdom and eloquence. A preacher must have "competent knowledge." This implied that the adequately prepared preacher must at least "have explicit knowledge of the Articles of Faith, the Ten Commandments, and the distinction between sin and nonsin."[49]

In his search for methods of preaching, Robert turns to Christ himself. "It is not easy to understand all the methods which Christ used in preaching. He, as I believe, included all praiseworthy methods in His own, as the fount and origin of good." The list of preaching methods is interesting, including promises, threats, examples, and reason.[50] The question of audience enters into the selection of method. For example, "good and agreeable" audiences are drawn to "sweet and beautiful promises," such as the promise of heaven. "Stubborn" listeners require the use of threats, such as the threat of divine judgment. Examples are stories or parables, which Robert notes that Christ used extensively. The Apostle Paul is said to have used "reason with great success."[51]

Robert turns to a discussion of the method of preaching by developing themes. Interestingly, themes ought to "contain not more than three statements or convertible to three." He is insistent on this point, devoting an entire chapter, Chapter XIX, to the discussion of divisibility by three. "No matter how many statements there may be, as long as I can divide them into three, I have a sufficient proposition."[52] This notion that sermons ought to be divisible into three sections persists in preaching to this day.

Good themes ought also to "immediately excite the audience to devotion, no matter what idiom is used." Thus, the audience is made central to developing a sermon just as in antiquity it had been central to structuring cases in court and in the legislature. The classical idea of rhetoric as persuasive audience-adapted discourse was maintained in the art of preaching, though concern for the audience and persuasion are considerably less evident in the other two major rhetorical arts of the Middle Ages. For Robert, the audience influences decisions regarding composition and style of the sermon. He advocates brevity of expression to keep the audience's attention and stylistic devices that make the sermon easier to listen to.

Robert, in fact, devotes a lengthy section to "Winning-over the Audience," in which he makes practical suggestions such as "to place at the beginning something subtle and interesting, [such] as some authentic marvel which can be fittingly drawn in for the purpose of the theme." If this doesn't work to get the attention of the audience, the preacher can always "frighten them by some terrifying tale or example."[53] Such adaptive decisions assisted the preacher's goals of illuminating the passage under consideration, enlightening the audience's understanding, and moving them to more virtuous actions.

Ornaments

Robert devotes much of the rest of his work to discussing what he terms the "ornaments" for introducing and developing the theme of a sermon. For instance, a theme, a verse such as "the righteous shall be delivered out of distress," can be introduced by ornaments such as "examples." "Examples" include analogies such as comparing Christ to a doctor, and people to the doctor's patients. Just as the doctor seeks to heal the patients, so Christ seeks to heal us of our spiritual maladies.[54] Themes can be developed by a variety of ornaments such as division of the text into its component parts, declaration or presentation of the parts to the audience, proof of parts or a kind of defining and explanation, and amplification or discussion of the spiritual implications of each part. The next chapter discusses the important role ornaments played in subsequent centuries.

THE ART OF LETTER WRITING

Because of the hierarchical nature of ecclesiastical Europe, correspondence among various Church and government officials came to be highly formalized. Letters became increasingly important to civic, commercial, and clerical life during the Middle Ages. "Official letters," write Bizzell and Herzberg, "were often the only record of laws or commercial transactions and hence had legal standing."[55] For these reasons, letter writing or *dictamen* became a highly developed rhetorical art of composing official letters and other documents, the *ars dictaminis* (*dictare:* to dictate). Teachers and practitioners of dictamen were referred to as *dictatores,* a term that also carried a somewhat more general reference for any person skilled in rhetoric.

Italian rhetoricians developed letter writing to a high art in the eleventh through the thirteenth centuries. Murphy notes that "a Benedictine monk, Alberic, is generally credited with the first systematic application of Ciceronian rhetoric to the matter of letter writing, which he wrote at the monastery of Monte Casino in central Italy in the year 1087."[56] Thousands of such treatises on *dictamen* would follow in the next two centuries. The central focus of letter writing treatises became recording and transmitting legal documents within the rigidly structured medieval society. Nicholas Mann writes that "the study of what in classical times had been the art of public speaking had by the twelfth century become the *ars dictaminis,* the art of letter writing; those who practiced it, the *dictatores,* applied their knowledge to the needs of their patrons and the legal profession."[57] In the development of the *ars dictaminis,* rhetoric again demonstrated its adaptability and utility, now being shaped into a method for communicating legal agreements, commercial contracts, and personal requests by letter. However, as it developed into a technical method for composing letters, this rhetorical art gradually lost a vital connection to its classical sources and thus to the broader rhetorical tradition of Greece and Rome.

The rise of letter writing reveals European culture "shifting toward the primacy of the written text" over against the orally presented speech.[58] The change from oral to written rhetoric takes place in part because, as Renato Barilli points out, "in the late Middle Ages…civic life offers little opportunity for public debate."[59] This significant cultural shift toward the written text intensified with the advent of Gutenberg's printing press in the middle of the fifteenth century. Rhetoric, as the study of effective expression, also turned toward written expression, a change evident as well in the rise of poetry writing to be discussed in the next section. We also see during this period that rhetoric's center begins to shift from matters of argument to matters of arrangement and style. This trend is encouraged by the entry into Europe of Aristotle's works on logic in the thirteenth century, which sparked tremendous interest in oral dialectical disputation. But argumentation was treated as a concern of logic rather than rhetoric, and rhetoricians often were left to codify components of written style.

The Italian city of Bologna became the center for the study of letter writing, and many treatises on the art were published there. Charles Faulhaber writes that Bolognese letter-writing manuals reached their highest point of development under "three masters, Boncompagno of Signa (c. 1165–c. 1235), Bene of Florence (fl. 1220), and most especially Guido Faba (c. 1190–c. 1243), whose *Summa Dictaminis* was published around 1228."[60] Faba wrote eight major books, "all of them dealing with *dictamen*," a fact that indicates the importance accorded to the art.[61] For writers like Faba, for many years a professor of *dictamen* in Bologna, the art of letter writing "was an eminently *practical* discipline."[62] Thus, according to Faulhaber, "his major theoretical work, *Summa Dictaminis*, is organized not as a complete treatise on dictaminal theory…but rather as a practical handbook with a limited number of short and succinct precepts."[63]

Many letter writing manuals conveyed what amounted to various form letters to be employed as persons of different social ranks communicated with one another on a variety of clerical, legal, personal, and business matters. As the structure of such letters will reveal, their purpose was usually to make a request.

The Parts of a Letter

According to the treatises on letter writing, a letter should be divided into five parts. George Kennedy explains that the "standard five-part epistolary structure" is reminiscent of typical Roman divisions of a speech: "The *salutatio,* or greeting; the *captatio benevoluntatiae,* or exordium, which secured the goodwill of the recipient; the *narratio* [the body of the letter setting out the details of the problem to be addressed]; the *petitio,* or specific request, demand, or announcement; and a relatively simple *conclusio*."[64] Of these parts, the *salutatio* received a disproportionate amount of attention, probably because establishing the correct relationship between yourself and the person to whom you were writing was crucial to gaining a hearing for your request. However, as the *salutatio* did not deal with matters of substance but of formality, rhetoric was in this way removed from addressing important matters of public concern.

Typical of the letter writing manuals is that by an anonymous Bolognese author, entitled, *The Principles of Letter-Writing*. This author writes that a letter's salutation is "an expression of greeting conveying a friendly sentiment not inconsistent with the social rank of the persons involved."[65] Whereas this may be obvious, how to write a proper salutation apparently is not. Titles such as deacon or bishop or clerk should always be employed. The respective ranks of the writer and the recipient must also be considered, as well as the subject of the letter. The author includes the following as a model of a salutation from the pope:

> Bishop Innocentius, servant of the servants of God (*servus servorum dei*) in his beloved son Christ, to N—, august emperor of the Romans, sends greetings and papal blessings.[66]

Other formal salutations included those of "prelates to their subordinates," "of close friends and associates," and "of subjects to their secular Lords."[67] Close friends, for instance, might open letters according to the formula, "To N—, the closest of friends," or "the most beloved of comrades," or "the dearest of favorites," or

> Guido, already bound by a sincere bond of affection, N—, follower of the profession of logician, wishes to be bound further to him by a mutual chain of affection and to be disturbed by no hostility, wishes him to live forever and to abound in all good things, to live always honorably and never to cease in his affection, to possess always wisely a happy life, and to hold always more firmly to the rightful ways.[68]

Such an elaborate greeting certainly makes "Dear Guido" sound a little hollow.

The possible salutations are numerous, and the relationships covered are intriguingly various. For example, the author includes these salutations from a "delinquent son" to his parents:

> "To Peter and Mary his parents, N—, once their son but now deprived of filial affection," "once dear to them but now without cause become worthless, does whatever he can though he seems to be able to do nothing."[69]

Again, though a florid and formal salutation may establish your relationship to the person receiving your letter, such writing certainly does not bring one into the realm of important civic concerns.

The anonymous writer of our treatise also considers other parts of a letter in detail. Securing goodwill—the role of the *captatio benevoluntatiae*—for example, can be achieved in a variety of ways. "Goodwill will be secured by the person sending the letter if he mentions humbly something about his achievements or his duties or his motives."[70] Other details of letter writing are also considered, such as how to shorten an overlong letter.

So elaborate and extensive were the treatments of topics such as composing a salutation that Brian Vickers writes that the letter-writing manuals contained "the most elaborate development of techniques for the manipulation of words in human history."[71] He notes by way of example that "of Guido Faba's eight books, four are simply collections of hundreds of *exordia*," or methods of securing a reader's goodwill. Such extraordinarily elaborate treatments were intended to cover every possible purpose and "every possible combination of rank between sender and receiver, in a highly structured society."[72]

Interest in letter writing was extensive during the later Middle Ages, particularly, as already noted, in Italy. Lawyers, secretaries, and notaries all had to understand the intricacies of the formal letter and the official document. The number of published *dictamen* treatises is quite remarkable. Paul Kristeller writes that "the body of literature that belongs to *dictamen* and its related enterprises is very large indeed, and exceeds by far in bulk anything comparable that has been preserved from classical antiquity, and anything else remotely rhetorical, such as the rhetorical commentaries on Cicero, produced in the Middle Ages."[73]

The *ars dictaminis* teaches us several things about rhetoric and its role in medieval society. First, rhetoric provided a framework for pursuing the complex social relationships that characterized a hierarchically organized world. Rhetoric facilitated social interaction. Second, rhetoric brought a measure of grace and decorum to the harsh and difficult lives of people living in Europe at this time. Third, rhetoric allowed a link to classical antiquity for the descendants of barbarian Europe. Important in this regard was the capacity of rhetoric to communicate something of the educational theory and philosophy of the classical past. Finally, the *ars dictaminis* placed rhetoric at the center of civic life. As Faulhaber writes, letter writing "formed an indispensable step in the training of all those who made their living running the administrative machinery of church and state." This also meant that "practitioners of *dictamen* were much in demand, and their positions were lucrative."[74]

Women and Letter Writing

In an intriguing essay on women and the letter-writing tradition in England, Malcolm Richardson explores the ways in which a rhetorical form can actually impose gender-related restrictions on an author. With a special interest in women responsible for small family businesses, Richardson notes that "the rhetoric of medieval business writers was, at the base, the same as that used by all other writers of nonliterary prose: the *dictamen,* or that part of medieval rhetoric that governed letterwriting." And, he notes that dictamen, or the rhetorical form of letter writing, "was universally accepted for public and private correspondence."[75]

Richardson writes that the "daily lives" of even relatively prosperous people of the Middle Ages "plainly had more to do with buying and selling and dealing with lawyers than with tournaments and troubadors." And, because women often had responsibility for managing a family's business affairs, they were necessarily involved in practicing the art of letter writing.[76] But, Richardson also notes that, due to a variety of factors peculiar to the age, the style of males and females does not vary in any noticeable way. "The great unasked question in this essay so far must be this: 'Does the writing of medieval women in commerce differ from that of men'? On the limited basis of this study, the answer, it should be clear by now, is 'no.' If a sizable number of these letters by both sexes were mixed together and the writers' identities concealed, it would be difficult to detect and difference."[77]

Why is this? The first part of Richardson's answer has to do with how letters were written. Very often a literate secretary wrote what an employer dictated, but adapted the dictation to the accepted form of a letter as described in the many manuals on the subject. And, "the letters were almost always physically written by male secretaries or professional scribes." Richardson comments, "while the inability to write was not a sign of poor education or low social status in the Middle Ages, there is little question that we would have a different view of the medieval world had more women's thoughts been written down by women."[78]

The second reason for the absence of any stylistic variation between letters by women and those by men has to do with the rather rigid form imposed by the letter-writing tradition itself. "The notarial form of the dictamen cast its hand over everything," writes Richardson. Authority for a letter was borrowed from the form it assumed, not the author's skill as a writer nor even the merits of her case. "A letter that did not at least make gestures toward following the dictamenal formulas had no authority. It would have violated the medieval sense of rhetorical decorum and, however serious its purpose, risked being taken lightly, as would a modern attorney appearing in court without a tie." Thus, a woman's voice, of necessity, became a man's voice in the letter. "[W]hen women began using correspondence to do business, they (and their secretaries) had no real option but to adopt the patriarchal voice. There was, after all, no feminine dictamen."[79] Because this form carried with it a "universal, authoritative voice," one notably masculine voice become "a constant in commercial rhetoric."[80]

Thus, in a rather subtle fashion we see again that control of rhetorical theory leads to control of rhetorical practice. And, as women seldom wrote theory prior to the twentieth century, their rhetorical practice in earlier ages often conformed to male-inspired models. But, there may be a hidden benefit in this imposition of one universal rhetorical voice across medieval culture. Richardson adds, "to end on a fairly positive note, however, we can with justice claim that the chief virtue for women of following the standard commercial rhetoric was (and is) that it rendered them rhetorically equal to men."[81]

THE ART OF POETRY

In the twelfth century, interest in written style dominated. This interest evolved into new and highly prescriptive approaches to the writing of poetry, or the art of poetry (*ars poetriae*). Treatises on poetry writing included Matthew of Vendome's *Ars Versificatoria* (1175), Geoffrey of Vinsauf's *Poetria Nova* (1213), and Gervais of Melkley's *Ars Poetica* (early thirteenth century). These books exhibit close attention to the aesthetic potential of the rhetorical devices that had long been discussed in rhetorical treatises.

Recall that Aristotle, for example, discusses metaphor and other stylistic devices in Book III of his *Rhetoric*. However, the treatment of style in the medieval poetry manuals has often been described as disappointing, and one scholar finds the manuals themselves "superficial" and "lacking a deeper logic."[82] Brian Vickers explains that such flaws in the poetry manuals result from the fact that they were "essentially exercise-books for schoolboys learning to write Latin verse."[83] The central concern of the art of poetry in the Middle Ages appears to have been to arrange words in such a way as to achieve a pleasing effect. Unlike letter-writing manuals, relatively few poetry manuals were written. We will consider the most famous one of these, that by Geoffrey of Vinsauf.

Geoffrey of Vinsauf

Geoffrey of Vinsauf's *Poetria Nova* (*New Poetry*) was the most widely circulated of the medieval poetry manuals, and more than 200 manuscripts of it still exist.[84] Written around 1210, it was "extremely influential on Latin verse writing of the thirteenth century [and] it continued to exercise authority, especially in France and England, until as late as the fifteenth century."[85] Geoffrey apparently intended his *new* approach to poetry to replace "the 'Old Poetics' of Horace," a famous and widely studied Roman poet of the first century B.C.

Geoffrey of Vinsauf's *Poetria Nova* has as "its central concerns," according to James Murphy, "the style and structure considered proper to poetic narrative."[86] Geoffrey emphasizes the need for a plan in writing poetry, in much the way that Robert of Basevorn emphasized the need for a form to guide preaching. In a famous opening passage, Geoffrey writes:

> If a man has a house to build, his hand does not rush, hasty, into the very doing: the work is first measured out with his heart's inward plumb line, and the inner man marks out a series of steps beforehand, according to a definite plan; his heart's hand shapes the whole before his body's hand does so, and his building is a plan before it is an actuality.[87]

Geoffrey's building metaphor is intended to point up the need for a mental plan before one sets about to write a poem. Poetry is personified as a woman who comes to dress thoughts in beautiful words:

> When a plan has sorted out the subject in the secret places of your mind, then let Poetry come to clothe your material with words. Inasmuch as she comes to serve, however, let her prepare herself to be apt for the service of her mistress; let her be on her guard, lest either a head of tousled hair, or a body clothed with rags, or any minor details be displeasing.[88]

Despite this apparent concern for a plan that guides writing, scholars have found little real attention to teaching composition in the poetry manuals. Most of the advice offered a student focuses on minor details such as choosing the right beginning for a sentence or developing a fitting rhetorical figure to make a passage more pleasing.

Geoffrey provided his readers advice on various means of creating vivid metaphors. While metaphors and their development may be familiar to modern readers, other components of Geoffrey's instruction in poetry writing are less so. For example, one section of *Poetria Nova* is devoted to the discussion of the method of *conversio* (conversion), which Ernest Gallo defines as "a systematic method of varying a given sentence so that one may choose its most pleasing form." Gallo explains that conversion required a student to "take an important noun in a sentence and vary its cases," that is, its grammatical role in a sentence. Thus, "if the basic sentence is *Splendour illuminates his features,*" where *splendour* is the subject of the sentence, one possible change is *"His face dazzles with the light of splendour,"* where *splendour* is used in the genitive or possessive case. A second possible conversion is *"His face is wed to splendour,"* where "splendour" is now in the dative case as an indirect object.[89] The utility of such an approach as a teaching device is evident, but its value as a guide to creating great poetry is questionable.

The discussion of conversion brings us back to the fact that the medieval treatises on poetry often were rigid and rule-bound in their discussion of the ornaments and other devices. One can imagine that writing poetry according to "minute captious rules" might render the final product rather stiff and uninspiring. In fact, this was the case, with some poetry of the thirteenth through the fifteenth centuries taking on a "paint by numbers" quality, while some of Geoffrey's advice seems intended to help students learn to create a long poem out of relatively little material.

To grant them their due, some teachers of poetry stressed imitation of great Latin masters, particularly Ovid. Woods notes that

> medieval student compositions that have come down to us illustrate how students reworked material from the literary texts that they read. Most of those that have survived are based on the works of Ovid, especially the *Metamorphoses,* whose interwoven narratives provided medieval teachers with perfect topics for short composition assignments.[90]

More advanced students could move beyond rehearsing various rhetorical devices in their own writing, and begin "to analyse the larger structure of works."[91] Thus, some medieval poetry instruction provided students with a rigorous introduction to both the rudiments of writing and methods of critical analysis. As a method for teaching writing, Woods concludes that "the medieval approach is pedagogically sound."[92] Perhaps, but, as Brian Vickers concludes, "whatever Dante, or Chaucer, or the *Gawain* poet knew about form, they did not learn from the arts of poetry."[93]

Ernest Gallo argues that writing style, however, may not always have been the poet's central concern. Using Virgil's *Aeneid* as their prime example, some medieval poetry instructors pointed out that Virgil crafted his great poem, not as an aesthetic experience, but rather as an argument in support of the heroism of its main character, Aeneas. The very fact that the poem opens with an act of heroism that actually occurs chronologically in the middle of the story makes Virgil's method similar to that of a great orator who might place the strongest argument first. Virgil is viewed as "a master rhetorician" who "manipulated the facts of the case so as to amplify the good qualities of Aeneas and to diminish the impact of certain facts that seem to detract from the hero's glory. The poet's aim is that of the orator: Each is arguing a case."[94]

Geoffrey of Vinsauf develops such rhetorical sense in aspiring poets reading his manual. If you wish to teach a lesson through a poem, "let the sentiment you begin with not sink to any particular statement, but rather raise its head to a general pronouncement."[95] That is, begin the poem with a proverb or some similar device that makes a general point. Gallo comments that "the poet can control our response to his material by starting in a way that will lead us to see the subject matter in just the way that he wants us to see it." This suggests that the poet is principally a rhetorician, adapting materials to an audience to achieve the greatest possible persuasive, even argumentative, effect. "In short, poetry is essentially rhetorical; the poet is arguing for a certain point of view."[96] If Gallo's interpretation of Geoffrey is correct, then perhaps the criticism of Vickers and others is blunted just a bit. Poetry manuals may not always have been intended principally to teach style following Ovid, which they admittedly did not always do well. Perhaps their goal on occasion was to teach the effective selection and arrangement of the materials in an argumentative case, following Virgil.

Marie de France

There are a few examples extant of the work of women poets in the twelfth and thirteenth centuries. Marie de France, for instance, wrote widely read poetry between the years 1160 and 1215. That she saw a connection between poetry and eloquence is clear from her verse:

> *Whoever has received knowledge*
> *and eloquence in speech from God,*
> *Should not be silent or conceal it*
> *but demonstrate it willingly.*[97]

According to Joan M. Ferrante, Marie de France's three known works are the *Lais,* the *Fables,* and *St. Patrick's Purgatory.*[98] So popular were her poems in the late Middle Ages that they were "translated or adapted in many languages," including "Old Norse, Middle English, Middle High German, Italian and Latin."[99]

CONCLUSION

During the Middle Ages, the thousand years between about A.D. 400 and 1400, the rhetoric of Cicero's *De Inventione* and a few other classical sources was adapted to a variety of educational and social ends. St. Augustine stands as a vital link between the period of Greco-Roman classical antiquity and Christian European hegemony. A trained rhetorician himself, Augustine both employed rhetoric to defend Christianity, and argued for Christian education in the art of rhetoric in order that Christian truths might have effective advocates. Boethius represents a somewhat different effort to import the insights of classical rhetoric into a new social setting through his development of a topical system.

The three medieval rhetorical arts identified by James J. Murphy—preaching, letter writing, and poetry writing—adapted Greco-Roman rhetoric to the social needs of later Christian Europe. The need for maintaining records and for preserving social hierarchies gave rise to the art of letter writing. The need to teach Christian principles to a largely illiterate and almost entirely Christian public called for a rhetoric of preaching. A rising interest in the aesthetic potential of written language contributed to the adaptation of rhetorical insights from antiquity to the writing of poetry.

Scholars have only recently begun to understand the specific ways in which the uses of classical rhetoric in medieval Europe represent, not just imitation of ancient systems, but practical application of an available ancient set of theories and practices to pressing cultural exigencies. However, a classical rhetoric developed to address the practical needs of the Athenian democracy or Roman republic did not always fit well with "medieval Christian learning," which was largely "elitist and hierarchical." As John O. Ward points out, medieval rhetoric "could not, therefore, adopt the principal tenets of an art that assumed a more popular focus of learning and was initially designed for theatres other than the schoolroom."[100]

But other realities of medieval life must be accounted for in understanding the medieval tendency to find a source of inspiration in Greek and Roman rhetoric. Perhaps the most significant of these factors is, according to Ward, the individual "confronted with situations that required persuasion at a nontechnical level." Whether that persuasion was pursued from a pulpit or in the office of an Italian civic official, the insights of classical rhetoricians remained critical to its success.[101]

QUESTIONS FOR REVIEW

1. Which classical rhetorician had the greatest influence on the shape of rhetorical theory and practice in the Middle Ages?

2. Why are the Middle Ages considered a period of fragmentation in rhetorical theory?

3. What for St. Augustine were the two functions of rhetoric within the Church?

4. What dilemmas faced Augustine of Hippo regarding rhetoric? What was Augustine's response to these dilemmas?

5. How can Boethius be seen as perpetuating the classical tradition of writers like Cicero?

6. What were the three rhetorical arts that characterized the middle and later portions of the Middle Ages?

7. What was the goal of preaching as a rhetorical art in the Middle Ages?

8. What social functions did the art of letter writing serve in the medieval period?

9. What particular aspect of rhetoric is stressed in the art of poetry?

QUESTIONS FOR DISCUSSION

1. How does Augustine's approach to rhetoric resemble Plato's? In what ways is Augustine's relationship to sophistic rhetoric similar to Plato's?

2. In what ways was classical rhetoric used to maintain the hierarchical structure of medieval Europe? From your study of classical and medieval rhetoric, does it seem to you that rhetorical theory is often used to maintain existing social orders?

3. Excluding preaching itself, which rhetorical practices of our own time seek goals similar to those of medieval preaching?

4. Do we pay less attention to social hierarchy than the Europeans of the later Middle Ages? If so, what has changed in Western society? If not, how do we acknowledge and maintain these hierarchies?

TERMS

Captatio benevoluntatiae: Section of letter securing the goodwill of the recipient.

Conclusio: The conclusion of a letter.

Conversio: A teaching method in which the structure of a sentence was varied so as to discover its most pleasing form.

Dictaminis (Ars):   The rhetorical art of letter writing; the craft of composing official letters, contracts, and other documents.

Dictatores: Teachers and practitioners of dictamen or letter writing; also any persons skilled in rhetoric.

Differentia: Topics of Boethius divided according to major premises.

Exordia: In letter writing, methods of securing goodwill.

Modus inveniendi: In Augustine, the means of understanding scripture.

Modus proferendi: The means of expressing the ideas found in scripture.

Narratio: Body of the letter setting out the background of the problem to be addressed.

Petitio: Specific request, demand, or announcement in a letter.

Poetriae (Ars):   The art of poetry; one of three medieval rhetorical arts. Highly prescriptive approaches to writing poetry.

Praedicandi (Ars):   The art of preaching; one of three medieval rhetorical arts.

Quadrivium: The four major studies in medieval schools, consisting of arithmetic, geometry, music, and astronomy.

Quaestiones: Debatable points suggested by sententiae, or passages from ancient authorities.

Salutatio: The greeting in a letter.

Scholasticism: A closed and authoritarian approach to education centered on a disputation over a fixed body of premises derived largely from Aristotle.

Sententiae: Isolated statements from ancient sources.

Theme: In medieval preaching theory, a biblical text that provided the basis for developing a sermon, toward the goal of improving the moral conduct and religious understanding of the audience.

Topical maxims: In Boethius, rational principles or major premises in arguments.

Trivium: The three minor studies of grammar, rhetoric, and logic in medieval schools.

ENDNOTES

1. George A. Kennedy, *Classical Rhetoric and Its Christian and Secular Tradition from Ancient to Modern Times* (Chapel Hill: University of North Carolina Press, 1980), 174.

2. Karin Margareta Fredborg, "Twelfth-Century Ciceronian Rhetoric: Its Doctrinal Development and Influences," in *Rhetoric Revalued,* ed. Brian Vickers (Binghamton, NY: Center for Medieval and Early Renaissance Studies, 1982), 88.

3. Roger P. Parr writes that "Geoffrey's [of Vinsauf] primary source, particularly for the devices of style, was *Rhetorica ad Herennium.*" Translator's introduction to Geoffrey of Vinsauf's *Documentum do Modo et Arte Dictandi et Versificandi* (Milwaukee, WI: Marquette University Press, 1968), 2.

4. Fredborg, 88.

5. John O. Ward, "From Antiquity to the Renaissance: Glosses and Commentaries on Cicero's *Rhetorica,*" in James J. Murphy, ed. *Medieval Eloquence: Studies in the Theory and Practice of Medieval Rhetoric* (Berkeley: University of California Press, 1978), 54, n 74. Quoted in Vickers, 216.

6. *Readings in Medieval Rhetoric,* ed. J. Miller, M. Prosser, and T. Benson (Bloomington: Indiana University Press, 1974), xiii.

7. *Readings in Medieval Rhetoric,* xiii.

8. See, for example, Vickers, Chapter 4: Medieval Fragmentation, 214–253.

9. Charles G. Nauert, Jr., *Humanism and the Culture of Renaissance Europe* (Cambridge: Cambridge University Press, 1995), 18.

10. Nauert, 18.

11. Marjory Curry Woods, "The Teaching of Writing in Medieval Europe," in *A Short History of Writing Instruction* (Davis, CA: Hermagoras Press, 1990), 80–81.

12. Christian Habicht, *Cicero the Politician* (Baltimore, MD: Johns Hopkins University Press, 1990), 2.

13. Quoted in Calvin Troup, *Temporality, Eternity, and Wisdom: The Rhetoric of Augustine's Confessions* (Columbia: University of South Carolina Press, 1999), 1. Augustine, *Confessions,* 9.2.4.

14. Troup, 4.

15. Kennedy, 149 ff.

16. *Confessions* 1.9.14. Quoted in Troup, 11.

17. Troup, 27.

18. James J. Murphy, "Saint Augustine and the Debate about a Christian Rhetoric," *Quarterly Journal of Speech* 46 (1960): 400–410.

19. Augustine, *On Christian Doctrine,* trans. D. W. Robertson (Indianapolis, IN: Library of Liberal Arts), 7.

20. Renato Barilli, *Rhetoric,* trans. Giuliana Menozzi (Minneapolis: University of Minnesota Press, 1989), 42.

21. W. R. Johnson, "Isocrates Flowering: The Rhetoric of Augustine," *Rhetoric and Philosophy* 9 1976: 220.

22. *Three Medieval Rhetorical Arts,* ed. James J. Murphy (Berkeley: University of California Press, 1971), xiii.

23. Murphy, *Arts,* xiii (Emphasis added).

24. John O. Ward, "From Antiquity to the Renaissance: Glosses and Commentaries on Cicero's *Rhetorica,*" in *Medieval Eloquence,* ed. James J. Murphy (Berkeley: University of California Press, 1978), 27.

25. Johnson, 220.

26. Augustine, *Christian Doctrine,* 118.

27. Johnson, 221.

28. Augustine, *Christian Doctrine,* 118.

29. Troup, 13.

30. Percival Cole, *Later Roman Education in Ausonius, Capella, and the Theodosian Code* (New York: Columbia University Press, 1909), 16. Quoted in *Readings in Medieval Rhetoric,* 1.

31. On Capella, see: Kennedy, 175–177.

32. Barilli, 42.

33. Boethius, *De Topicis Differentiis,* trans. Eleanor Stump (Ithaca, NY: Cornell Press, 1978). See also: Michael Leff, "The Logician's Rhetoric: Boethius' *De Differentiis Topicis,* Book IV," in *Medieval Eloquence: Studies in the Theory and Practice of Medieval Rhetoric,* ed. James J. Murphy (Berkeley: University of California Press, 1978), 3–24.

34. Ward, 55.

35. Barilli, 43.

36. See: Michael Leff, "The Topics of Argumentative Invention in Latin Rhetorical Theory from Cicero to Boethius," *Rhetorica* 1 (Spring 1983): 23–44.

37. Leff, "Topics," 41.

38. Kennedy, 179.

39. In this section I am following Murphy's analysis of later medieval rhetoric as manifested prin cipally in three arts.

40. Ward, 44.

41. James J. Murphy, *Three Medieval Rhetorical Arts* (Berkeley: University of California Press, 1971) xxiii. Quoted in Vickers, 225.

42. Kennedy, 190.

43. Margaret Jennings, C. S. J., "The *Ars compendi sermones* of Ranulph Higden," in *Medieval Eloquence,* 113.

44. Murphy, *Arts,* 109–216.

45. Murphy, *Arts,* 112.

46. Murphy, *Arts,* 112–113.

47. Murphy, *Arts,* 114.

48. Murphy, *Arts,* 120.

49. Murphy, *Arts,* 124.

50. Murphy, *Arts,* 128.

51. Murphy, *Arts,* 129.

52. Murphy, *Arts,* 138.

53. Murphy, *Arts,* 146.

54. Murphy, *Arts,* 156.

55. *The Rhetorical Tradition,* eds. Patricia Bizzell and Bruce Herzberg (Boston: St. Martin's Press, 1990), 377.

56. Murphy, *Arts,* 3.

57. Nicholas Mann, "The Origins of Humanism," in *The Cambridge Companion to Renaissance Humanism,* ed. Jill Kraye (Cambridge: Cambridge University Press, 1996), 5.

58. Barilli, 49.

59. Barilli, 49.

60. Charles B. Faulhaber, "The *Summa Dictaminis* of Guido Faba," in Murphy, *Medieval Eloquence,* 85.

61. Faulhaber, 87.

62. Faulhaber, 86.

63. Faulhaber, 86.

64. Kennedy, 186 (Emphasis added). See also, Murphy, *Arts,* 7.

65. Murphy, *Arts,* 8. This translation of *The Principles of Letter-Writing* is by Professor Murphy.

66. Murphy, *Arts,* 11.

67. Murphy, *Arts,* 13–14.

68. Murphy, *Arts,* 13.

69. Murphy, *Arts,* 15.

70. Murphy, *Arts,* 17.

71. Vickers, 235.

72. Vickers, 235–236.

73. Paul Kristeller, "Philosophy and Rhetoric from Antiquity to the Renaissance," part 5 in *Renaissance Thought and Its Sources,* ed. Michael Mooney (New York: Columbia University Press, 1979), 241. Quoted in James J. Murphy and Martin Camargo, "The Middle Ages," chap. 2 in *The Present*

State of Scholarship in Historical and Contemporary Rhetoric, ed. Winifred Bryan Horner (Columbia: University of Missouri Press, 1990), 59.

74. Faulhaber, 108.

75. Malcolm Richardson, "Women, Commerce, and Rhetoric in Medieval England," in *Listening to Their Voices: The Rhetorical Activities of Historical Women,* ed. Molly Meijer Wertheimer (Columbia: University of South Carolina Press, 1997), 133–149, p. 136.

76. Richardson, 140.

77. Richardson, 145.

78. Richardson, 146.

79. Richardson, 147.

80. Richardson, 146.

81. Richardson, 147.

82. Edmond Faral, *Les Artes Poétique du XIIe et XIIIe Siècle* (1924, rpt. Paris, 1971), xv. Quoted in Vickers, 239.

83. Vickers, 239.

84. Ernest Gallo, "The *Poetria Nova* of Geoffrey of Vinsauf," in *Medieval Eloquence,* 68.

85. Murphy, *Arts,* 29.

86. Murphy, *Arts,* 30. Vinsauf's *The New Poetics* in Murphy's collection is translated by Jane Baltzell Kopp.

87. Murphy, *Arts,* 34.

88. Murphy, *Arts,* 35.

89. Gallo, 71.

90. Woods, 84.

91. Woods, 86.

92. Woods, 87.

93. Vickers, 242.

94. Gallo, 76.

95. *Poetria Nova,* lines 126–131. Quoted in Gallo, 77.

96. Gallo, 77.

97. From: Joan M. Ferrante, "The French Courtly Poet, Marie de France," in *Medieval Women Writers,* ed. Katharina M. Wilson (Athens: University of Georgia Press, 1984), 65.

98. Ferrante, 64.

99. Ferrante, 64.

100. Ward, 64.

101. Ward, 64.

CHAPTER SEVEN

RHETORIC IN THE RENAISSANCE

There is nothing more pleasing to God who governs the
world than men united by social bonds....
—Petrarch

This chapter considers some major trends in rhetoric during the European Renaissance. From the fourteenth through the seventeenth centuries, enormous intellectual and social changes took place in Europe. Assumptions and institutions that had held sway for centuries were radically challenged, including the Christian worldview and the Catholic Church. Gutenburg developed the printing press in the early 1450s, thus making possible the wide dissemination of printed material in Europe. Exploration revealed a larger world than Europeans had assumed existed, as evidenced in Columbus's famous voyage of 1492. Europe was split by wars, as well as by the Protestant Reformation, which takes the year 1517 as its traditional starting date.

During this period of social upheaval, the classical rhetorical tradition attained a place of prominence in European education and social life. In fact, as we shall see, rhetoric flourished in the Renaissance as a method of instruction in writing and persuasion, an avenue to personal refinement, a means of managing the intricacies of civic and commercial interests, and a critical tool for studying a variety of literary texts both ancient and contemporary.

This chapter considers some important trends in the study of rhetoric between 1350 and 1600. We will focus attention first on the important role rhetoric played in Renaissance education, and on the activities of women rhetoricians in this period. We will then turn our attention to a fascinating group of writers, known collectively as the Italian Humanists, who made rhetorical studies the foundation for a new understanding of the origins and flourishing of civilization. The Italian Humanist school found in rhetoric a means of both self-improvement and social development. The last sections of this chapter consider influential European writers who criticized rhetoric toward the middle of the sixteenth century and how it flourished in England during the same period.

FEATURES OF RENAISSANCE RHETORIC

While rhetoric was a prominent element in the education and culture of Greece, Rome, and Christian Europe, perhaps rhetoric's greatest influence over a civilization was achieved in Europe during the period known as the Renaissance. Historian of rhetoric Brian Vickers has written that "during the European Renaissance—a period which, for convenience, I take as stretching from 1400 to 1700—rhetoric attained its greatest preeminence, both in terms of range of influence and in value."[1]

Classical and Medieval Sources

Jerrold Seigel traces Renaissance interest in rhetoric, particularly as manifested in the Humanist tradition, directly back to a "medieval intellectual movement" that had two prominent features: "[I]t was a species of professional rhetoric, and it was primarily an Italian phenomenon."[2] Thus, though Renaissance treatments of rhetoric certainly vary from those we explored in Chapter 6, there is evidence of a continuous strand of rhetorical tradition running from the Middle Ages to the Renaissance. And, as Seigel points out, that medieval strand originates in Italy with a professional class of rhetoricians practicing primarily the *ars dictaminis,* or the art of letter writing and drafting legal and commercial documents.

But Renaissance interest in rhetoric, despite its connection to medieval letter writing, was classical in conception and grounded in a renewed appreciation for the place of speech in human experience. The Dutch Humanist Erasmus (1466–1536) wrote that "I have learned from Galen that what differentiates man from the animals, or brutes [*alogi*]…is not reason, but speech."[3] This fundamental interest in speech, and particularly in public oratory, led to serious study of classical rhetoric and to speculation about the role of persuasive speech in shaping civilization.

The study of Greek and Roman writers dominated the intellectual culture of Northern Italy and other centers of humanist research. Paul Oskar Kristeller writes that as Europe moved from the rhetoric of the Middle Ages to that of the Renaissance, the principal change had to do with the rediscovery of a wide range of classical sources. "It was the novel contribution of the humanists," he writes, "to add the firm belief that in order to write and to speak well it was necessary to study and to imitate the ancients."[4] Many Renaissance rhetoricians looked back past the medieval tradition to Athens and especially Rome in the hopes of rediscovering the entire classical rhetorical tradition. Such "classicism" was, as we shall see, consistent with the general tenor of Renaissance humanism.

Renaissance rhetoricians such as George of Trebizond (1395–1472) sought to reunify the various genres and methods of rhetoric, which he took to have been dismantled during the Middle Ages, into a synthetic and systematic whole.[5] A Greek scholar of note, Trebizond worked to retrieve the rhetorical theory of Greek writers such as Hermogenes. Trebizond was a tireless translator of Greek manuscripts into Latin, an effort that made a much wider range of Greek thought available to Humanist scholars, many of whom were unfamiliar with Greek. His most important work was the *Five Books of Rhetoric* (1434), which brought together both Greek and Latin rhetorical theories. It has been called "the first new full-scale rhetoric of the Renaissance," and stands as a prime example of the work of Renaissance Humanists to reclaim the entire classical rhetorical tradition of antiquity.[6] Trebizond admired the ancient Greek Sophists such as Gorgias, and disparaged Plato's attack on them in the dialogue *Gorgias.*

Assisting the rapidly advancing interest in the classical period was the discovery of a large number of ancient Greek and Latin texts in the Renaissance. Though a Ciceronian influence is evident in medieval rhetoric, as we saw in Chapter 6, that influence was limited to a narrow range of concepts derived from a small number of Cicero's works, especially *De Inventione.* In the Renaissance, however, serious study of a large number of classical sources, Latin and Greek, was closely tied to the theory and practice of rhetoric. James Murphy points out, for instance, that "by the year 1500, only four decades after the advent of printing, the entire Ciceronian corpus was already available in print all over Europe."[7] In addition, one hundred editions of Quintilian's *Institutes of Oratory* had been printed in Europe by the middle of the sixteenth century.[8]

Many other classical sources were also becoming more widely available, and translation of ancient sources into contemporary European languages was taking place. Plato as well as Aristotle enjoyed wide popularity among Renaissance scholars, and a vibrant Platonism (or Neoplatonism) developed in sixteenth century Italy.[9] Still, in spite of the many newly discovered works, the *Rhetorica ad Herennium* remained a great favorite of Renaissance rhetoricians even after its Ciceronian authorship was disproved in the late fifteenth century. In the following sections we will consider some of the ways in which rhetoric wielded its influence during this period of social and intellectual upheaval.

Rhetoric and Renaissance Education

Rhetoric's influence was felt perhaps most strongly in the arena of education during the Renaissance. Vickers writes that "the quantity of rhetoric texts known to have been published" during the period "is immense." Astonishingly, more than 2,500 *different* books on rhetoric appeared in Europe between the late fourteenth and early eighteenth centuries. If each of these books had enjoyed even ordinary usage in schools of the time, it would mean that "several million Europeans had a working knowledge of rhetoric" during this period, an amazing figure that would include persons from many professional groups, and women as well as men.[10] A single rhetoric book, Erasmus of Rotterdam's *On an Abundant Style,* "went through 150 editions in the sixteenth century," a remarkable record in any century.[11] Renaissance scholar Don Abbott, noting the extensive reach of rhetoric in Renaissance Europe, calls it "*the* Renaissance subject." He adds, "Rhetoric dominated the thoughts of Renaissance intellectuals and the curriculum of Renaissance schools to a degree that is extraordinary."[12]

Rhetorical Ornaments.   Rhetoric enjoyed tremendous prestige as a discipline, and entire academic curricula were structured around it. Extraordinary efforts were made to systematize rhetorical knowledge for educational purposes. Vickers notes that in the *Thesaurus Rhetoricae* of 1559, Giovani Baptista Bernardi defined over 5,000 rhetorical terms![13] Students were drilled repeatedly in rhetorical figures, and were expected to memorize large numbers of them. But Thomas O. Sloane has pointed out that emphasis on classical rhetorical education in two-sided argument also characterized Renaissance writers such as Valla and Erasmus.[14] For younger students in the Renaissance schools "letter-writing manuals, handbooks of tropes and figures, and dictionaries of proverbs" were used for rhetorical training. While "learning the figures of speech and their names may have encouraged students to overuse them," writes historian Peter Mack, "it may also have made students more sensitive to the manner of their use." Similarly,

> reading the examples of 200 ways of saying 'your letter pleased me greatly' from Erasmus' *De copia* may well have encouraged a tendency towards dense and repetitive writing. But it may also have helped students understand that in using any given expression they were choosing among alternatives, since there were 199 other inflections that could be given to the same material. It must also have encouraged students to rewrite their sentences and paragraphs, and shown them how rewriting could bring out different aims and emphases.[15]

Thus, this rigorous and repetitive rhetorical training had practical benefits to students who must themselves have questioned its utility at times. Erasmus also offered students more than two hundred ways to say in Latin, "I shall remember you as long as I live."[16] *De Copia* or *On an Abundant Style* was well named.

Richard Lanham provides a fascinating account of the human attraction to rhetorical ornaments such as metaphor that was so pronounced in the Renaissance—the brain's own need for economy. Following the famous biologist, Edward O. Wilson, Lanham writes that "rhetorical figures" may represent "a basic evolutionary strategy for our species." Lanham quotes Wilson to the effect that "the brain depends upon elegance to compensate for its own small size and short lifetime." Over the course of human development, Wilson speculates that the brain "was forced to rely on tricks to enlarge memory and speed computation." These tricks included developing a facility with "analogy and metaphor" that allowed for a "sweeping together of chaotic sensory experience into workable categories labeled by words and stacked into categories for quick recovery." Lanham concludes that "such a raison d'être" for rhetorical figures of speech would mean that they were "a kind of data compression, an immensely rapid substitute for iterative searching." That is, rhetorical figures saved us time in recalling information, and valuable space in the human cerebral cortex.[17]

The Universal Man.   Skill in rhetoric, then, became the hallmark of the educated person in the Renaissance, much as it had been in Cicero's Rome. As Donald R. Kelley writes, "in many ways indeed the master of rhetoric fulfilled the idea of the *uomo universale* [the universal man] in moral and political as well as in literary and philosophical terms. The Orator, in other words, was the very prototype and paradigm of the

Renaissance man."[18] As this statement implies, wisdom was joined to eloquence in the thought of many Renaissance rhetoricians. Bringing wisdom to eloquence implied study of topics such as law, theology, and even medicine. But no discipline's intersection with rhetoric was more difficult to navigate than that of philosophy, a theme we will return to repeatedly in this chapter.

The effort to join wisdom to eloquence raised the question of rhetoric's relationship to several other disciplines, particularly philosophy. Though it may be hard for modern readers to understand, the debate over this issue was intense and often personal. In the late fifteenth century, for instance, the Humanist Ermolao Barbaro sent a letter to Pico della Mirandola in which he condemned philosophers as "dull, rude, uncultured barbarians."[19] Several prominent Renaissance scholars, as we shall see, insisted that the study of philosophy be subordinate to the study of rhetoric. The issue revolved around the distinction rhetoricians made between *res,* or the substance or matter of one's arguments, and *verba,* or the words in which that matter was advanced. To possess the *res* of the philosophers without possessing the *verba* that came by way of rhetoric rendered philosophy a tedious and almost meaningless study, at least according to the rhetoricians.[20]

Renaissance education's preoccupation with rhetoric was also encouraged by a rising European interest in classical languages, particularly Greek. Accordingly, interest in classical authors such as Aristotle and Cicero, as we have already noted, also rose dramatically in this period. Classicism actually became popular, a development assisted in the sixteenth century by the appearance of rhetorical treatises in vernacular languages, particularly English. At this point, education in rhetoric became a possibility for anyone who could read, and not just for scholars. Classical treatments of rhetoric eventually provided the basis not just for rhetorical studies, but even for personal conduct.

LORENZO VALLA: RETRIEVING
THE RHETORICAL TRADITION

We will be exploring the intellectual movement known as Italian Humanism momentarily. Renaissance interest in rhetoric, as we shall see, is virtually inseparable from the Humanist movement in Europe. At this point it will be helpful to introduce a Humanist writer who was particularly significant to establishing rhetoric as central to education in the Renaissance period. Lorenzo, or Laurentius, Valla (1407–1457) has been called "not only the most wide-ranging, but also perhaps the most influential of all humanist scholars."[21] His works, *Dialectical Disputations* (1435) and *Elegancies of the Latin Language* (1444)—the latter work referred to as "the Bible of the later humanists"—attacked scholasticism and "suggested a new approach to human understanding based on rhetoric."[22]

Valla's works had enormous influence on educational practices in their day and throughout the Renaissance. Peter Mack writes that Valla's *Elegancies,* in which he sought "to restore the rich distinctions of classical Latin was much read and greatly valued in the late fifteenth and sixteenth centuries."²³ Valla sought to broaden the conception of proper Latin beyond the model established by Cicero, and was a great advocate of Quintilian's writings. The point of much of Valla's work is that rhetoric, not the dialectic and philosophy of the universities, is the proper basis for education. Rhetoric was more comprehensive than dialectic, and more informative than philosophy.

The spread of Humanist ideas in Renaissance Europe, and with them interest in rhetoric, was greatly aided by educational institutions in Italy, France, England, and other sites in Europe. Historian Peter Burke writes that "the contribution of the schools to the spread of the concepts, methods, and values of Italian humanists was obviously crucial."²⁴ And no one's ideas were more important to Humanist education in such schools than those of Lorenzo Valla.

Born in Rome, Valla studied classical literature and philosophy in Naples and Milan. He is credited with translating a number of Greek classical texts into Latin, and with developing New Testament studies by comparing the Greek and Latin versions of the Bible. Jerrold Seigel finds Valla to have "built, through his enthusiasm for linguistic study, the foundations of philology and historical criticism."²⁵ And, in the estimation of Donald R. Kelley, "the great 'triumvirate' of sixteenth-century learning— Erasmus, Bude, and Vives—were all Valla's disciples in one way or another."²⁶

Valla's vast study of ancient sources was guided by his intense interest in rhetoric, which he usually referred to as oratory or eloquence, and to his Christian piety. Valla himself wrote to Pope Eugene IV that the goals of his life were "to please God and help men through the study of oratory."²⁷ Valla argued in his *De Voluptate* that Christian culture was superior to that of earlier pagan Greece.²⁸ Thus, Humanism in the Renaissance did not imply rejection of Christian principles, though for Valla it *did* mean the rejection of the monastic idea of contemplative piety.²⁹ His religion was active and public.

Valla was a vigorous advocate of oratory, the public practice of the rhetorician's art. In Valla's view, oratory was the master of philosophy. "Philosophy is like a soldier or a tribune under the command of oratory," he writes.³⁰ Moreover, Seigel points out that in Valla's view "orators treated questions of ethics 'much more clearly, weightily, magnificently' than did 'the obscure, squalid, and anemic philosophers.'"³¹ Philosophers dealt only with academic questions, which they debated endlessly within the confines of their universities. Orators employing rhetoric, on the other hand, were active in civic life working for the good of the society. A consequence of the subordination of philosophy to rhetoric was that Valla also came to subordinate the ethical disputations of philosophers to the moral sense of ordinary people. Moral truth, for Valla, was to be found in "the standards of common sense," and rhetoric had a role in shaping and perpetuating the moral precepts of common sense.³²

Thus, rhetoric's relationship to truth was explored in the Renaissance as it had been by rhetoricians since the time of the Sophists. Though not all rhetoricians agreed with Valla that ethical standards could be derived strictly from community standards apart from philosophy, many did elevate and venerate the active life of involvement in the affairs of the city. Rhetoric had a practical role to play in guiding ethical deliberations in the noisy deliberations of day-to-day life in a busy community.

WOMEN AND RENAISSANCE RHETORIC

Women were more likely to have access to education during the Renaissance than at earlier periods in Western history, and one of the subjects they would have studied was rhetoric. However, women's access to education, and especially the social mobility such education afforded women, should not be overstated.

Katharina Wilson, perhaps the leading authority on women writers of the Renaissance, notes that access to education for Renaissance women came to them principally through the privilege of birth into a high social rank. "Women of the 'middling rank' or of the lower estate, on the other hand, lacked such opportunities, and neither group was free to pursue unidirectionally learning and scholarship."[33] Nor did education provide women the same sort of opportunity to rise above their social station, as it often did for men of the period. "Very little, if any, opportunity existed in the power structure of Renaissance courts, principalities, universities, or professional organizations for the woman scholar to rise above her born position through education and intellectual accomplishments," writes Wilson.[34] Some women who had the opportunity to study rhetoric, however, became ardent advocates for women's education.[35]

Among the women who wrote in favor of women's education during the period are Louise Labe, Laura Cereta, and Madeleine des Roches (1520–1587) and her daughter Catherine (1542–1587).[36] In 1487, a woman named Cassandra Fedele "addressed the students and faculty of the University of Padua on the value of humanistic learning."[37] Another woman, Laura Cereta, was the "author of a spirited letter to an imaginary male opponent in defense of liberal education for women."[38] Some male writers of the period, such as Giovanni Boccaccio and Juan Luis Vives, also advocated education for women.

Joanna Vaz

Though there was considerable opposition to women actually speaking in public during the Renaissance, some women gained reputations for their public oratory. Joanna Vaz, for instance, enters the recorded history of the Renaissance based on her reputation for eloquence. Unfortunately, our knowledge of figures such as Vaz is limited at the present time, but a number of scholars are at work retrieving the historical record of female rhetoricians in the Renaissance period. We do know that Vaz could read and write Greek, Latin, and Hebrew, and that she was appointed a tutor to the daughter of the King and Queen of Portugal. She was apparently an eloquent speaker, but no known written record of her speeches survives.[39] Another woman of the seventeenth century renowned for her eloquence was Publia Hortencia de Castro. She is reputed to have argued with theologians of her day, and to have been invited to speak before King Philip of Spain.[40]

Christine de Pisan

In the early fifteenth century a woman of great rhetorical power appeared on the European scene.[41] Christine de Pisan (1364–c.1430) was the daughter of Thomas de

Pisan, a professor of astrology and Councilor in the Republic of Venice. She became "Europe's first professional woman writer."[42] Christine's life was unusual for a woman of her day. She lived for a time in the court of King Charles V of France, a situation that allowed her access to libraries as well as association with learned people. She was largely self-educated, and spent a great deal of her time reading and writing. Jenny Redfern, a scholar who has studied the life of Christine de Pisan, writes, "her self-education…included history, science, and poetry from Greek and Roman authors as well as from contemporaries such as Dante and Boccaccio."[43] Christine would, then, have been exposed to classical rhetorical theories in her vast reading. She also studied languages, becoming familiar with French, Italian, and probably Latin as well.

Christine was one of the rare female writers of this period who attracted a wide audience, and she used her prominence to correct the prevailing view of women. As Jenny Redfern writes, Christine urged women "to discover meaning and achieve worthy acts in their lives." Redfern adds, "her objective was to counteract the slander of the female sex so prominent in texts of the time."[44] In particular, Christine identified the power of language as a key to women's advancement. "Her most important lesson," writes Redfern, "is that women's success depends on their ability to manage and mediate by speaking and writing effectively," skills still closely connected to success.[45]

Christine modeled what she advocated, using the power of language as a studied rhetorician over a long career. As Redfern notes, Christine was a prolific writer of poetry and prose, with "forty-one known pieces written over a career of at least thirty years" from 1399 to 1429.[46] One of the factors contributing to the popularity of her work was that she wrote in the vernacular language of French rather than in academic Latin.[47] As Latin was the domain of men, Christine's authorial decision made it possible for any literate woman to become part of her audience.

Perhaps Christine de Pisan's most popular work was *The Treasure of the City of Ladies,* which originally appeared in 1401 with the title, *Book of the City of Ladies.* This work was extraordinarily popular, went through eighteen manuscript editions, and eventually was translated into French, Dutch, and Portuguese. The book includes an "outspoken defense of women," which was "an anomaly in her time."[48] Christine sought in her books to answer the harsh criticism of women expressed in popular books such as Jean de Meun's *Romance of the Rose,* which portrayed women as immoral and incapable of genuine accomplishments. What Redfern calls "woman-hating stories" were popular in the late Middle Ages.[49] Christine sought to defend women against the many false charges leveled against them in these stories. Her other works include *The Changes of Fortune* (1400–1403) and *Vision of Christine* (1405).

Margaret Cavendish

One of the most intriguing and provocative rhetoricians of the late Renaissance was Margaret Cavendish, Duchess of Newcastle. Born in 1623, the eighth child of Sir Thomas Lucas and his wife Elizabeth, Margaret received home instruction in reading and writing, as well as in music and a number of crafts. She took an early interest in writing, and was producing books even as a young woman. Margaret was a member of the court of Queen Henrietta Maria, and was forced into exile in France along with other Royalists in the 1640s. It was there that she met and married William Cavendish, Duke of Newcastle.

While living on the European continent, Margaret Cavendish studied both science and philosophy informally, her husband encouraging and assisting her educational pursuits. Though she always recognized that her education suffered because "she did not receive a humanist's training in classical languages," Cavendish nevertheless read widely and "alludes to many works in her writings."[50] She apparently did read the Renaissance Humanist rhetoricians, and particularly admired Shakespeare and the Latin writer Ovid.

After her return to England in the early 1650s, Margaret wrote continuously. Her early works were dismissed as immature, but undoubtedly some of the criticism resulted from the fact that she dared to write and publish her works as a woman. In fact, she is reputed to be the first English woman to have written with the sole purpose of seeking publication of her works. A determined self-promoter, Cavendish ignored her critics and planned lavish and well-publicized public events featuring herself in outlandish costumes.

Cavendish was quite aware of the obstacles facing women who sought to write for public consumption, especially if their writing was overtly rhetorical. "When any of our Sex doth Write, they Write some Devotions, or Romances, or Receits of Medicines, for Cookery or confectioners, or Complemental Letters, or a Copy or two of Verses...."[51] But Cavendish was not satisfied to write devotional literature and recipe books. Rather, much of her writing, including perhaps her best known work, *The World's Olio,* "discusses her own opinions of important philosophical issues of her day." Jane Donaworth writes that Cavendish "argues both sides of the question and qualifies her answers so often as to appear a relativist, like the sophists."[52] Cavendish also penned one of the earliest works of science fiction, *The Blazing World,* in which she imagines a planet run entirely by women. Margaret Cavendish died at the age of 50 in 1673.

In spite of these examples of women who practiced rhetoric in the Renaissance, there is, according to historian George Kennedy, no woman "known to have written an account of rhetoric" in this period.[53] This is significant, for it is the theory of rhetoric rather than its practice that determines how rhetoric will be understood in a society, and ultimately how rhetoric will be used. For women to have been excluded from the domain of rhetorical *theory,* then, constituted a serious limitation on their participation in shaping the art. Nevertheless, women were instrumental in moving rhetorical practice in a more conversational and dialogic direction.

ITALIAN HUMANISM: A CATALYST FOR RHETORIC'S EXPANSION

As we saw in Chapter 6, prior to the thirteenth century the Church in Europe held sway over the academy. Scholarly attention was focused largely on theological issues, and biblical texts were taken as literally true and authoritative sources. But important intellectual changes were occurring in fourteenth- and fifteenth-century Europe that had a profound impact on both the interpretation of written texts and the role of authority in intellectual life.

Writers now known as the Italian Humanists were responsible for a resurgence of interest in the languages and texts of classical antiquity during the Renaissance period, an orientation referred to as classicism. We will take a closer look at the classicism of Renaissance Humanists in a moment. This interest in ancient texts was energized by the rediscovery of the *studia humanitatis* (humanistic studies), or studies deemed important to the development of a free and active human mind—rhetoric, poetics, ethics, and politics. These humanistic studies formed the basis of what are often referred to now as the liberal arts. Rhetoric was for the Humanists "a central preoccupation," according to renaissance scholar Don Abbott. He writes, "indeed, it is difficult to separate the study of rhetoric from the study of humanism."[54] Through their tireless research the Italian Humanists retrieved important concepts from classical rhetoric, developed methods of textual criticism for dating and interpreting ancient documents, stimulated thought about language's role in shaping human societies, and advanced theories to explain the role of emotions in the process of persuasion.

The work of the Italian Humanists during the Renaissance gained impetus from the discovery in the early fifteenth century of both Quintilian's *Institutes of Oratory* and of the complete text of Cicero's *De Oratore,* two critically important rhetorical works of ancient Rome.[55] With the recovery of these works, Italian scholars had a richer and more profound rhetorical theory available to them than the Middle Ages had bequeathed them. Moreover, the rhetoric these scholars were retrieving was largely a *Roman* rhetoric. The ruling elite of Italy's rising cities "consistently looked back to the ancient Roman republic as its model."[56] This newly discovered and largely Roman rhetorical theory provided the basis for the practice of persuasion as well as addressing important intellectual issues facing a new class of Italian politicians and scholars.

RHETORIC AS PERSONAL
AND POLITICAL INFLUENCE

Rhetoric achieved high status as a subject of study during the Renaissance for at least two reasons. First, it was viewed as an aid to moral contemplation and personal refinement. That is, through the study of rhetoric one was helped to think deeply, but also to act decorously. Though it sounds surprising, rhetoric in the Renaissance provided the basis for prescriptive manuals on how to conduct oneself in social settings. The most famous example of this phenomenon is the Italian writer Castiglione's book, *The Courtier.*[57] This book covers topics such as the appropriate way to address members of a royal court, the proper posture with which to carry oneself, and even how one's horse should behave. The standards of such personal decorum were drawn from the model of the finished orator, always a refined, well-spoken, and dignified individual. The theme of rhetoric as a source of personal power or advancement, then, marked Renaissance, as it did classical, treatments of the subject.

Second, rhetoric was considered a means of winning political power through argument and persuasion. Victoria Kahn writes that the result of these two divergent interests was that a "tension exists within the humanist tradition between rhetoric conceived as an activity of ethical deliberation, which is a good in itself, and rhetoric conceived as a neutral technique of argument."[58] This tension between rhetoric in the service of a moral goal, such as the creation of a just society, and rhetoric as a morally neutral tool of persuasion, persists in the history of rhetoric. Moreover, Renaissance rhetorical theorists found in rhetoric a source of personal and political power. As such, rhetoric was an important subject of study, but also an art with inherent dangers.

Much of Italian Humanism was Ciceronian in impulse and highly practical in conception.[59] Cities like Florence were "governed by a process of discussion, debate, and accommodation."[60] Thus, civic officials wanted a means of persuading citizens and other officials, and rhetoric provided that means. The prevailing attitude, as expressed by Vickers, was that "rhetoric is essential to governors and counsellors because it can persuade men to do what you want them to do."[61] Here we have one half of Kahn's tension-producing pair—rhetoric as a tool of persuasion. Vickers identifies this "stress on persuasion" as the principal way in which "Renaissance rhetoricians differ from their medieval counterparts."[62]

Rhetoric and the Emotions

Motivated by their strong interest in persuasion, Humanists studied human will and emotions following Book II of Aristotle's *Rhetoric,* Book II of Cicero's *De Oratore,* and portions of Quintilian's *Institutes.*[63] Humanist speculation on the topic of emotions, according to Vickers, "resulted in a new sub-discipline of rhetorical psychology, *pathologia.*"[64] The source of emotions or passions in the human mind was identified as the *affectus.* The trained orator, an individual with a properly attuned *affectus,* experienced a particular emotion with regard to a subject and sought to arouse the same emotion in his audience. This was precisely Cicero's doctrine of the emotions as well. This concern for the emotive power of language also revealed itself in the intense interest of Renaissance rhetoricians in *elocutio,* or rhetorical style. The period between 1540 and 1640 witnessed what Vickers calls an "enormous zest" for the rhetorical devices known tropes, schemes, and figures that enhanced *elocutio.*[65] So, to Lanham's earlier observation that such devices are an aid to memory and thought, we should add that rhetorical ornaments also enhance language's emotional power.

We have seen this connection between rhetoric and psychology before in Plato's discussion of a true art of rhetoric that would study the human soul, Aristotle's analysis of *pathos,* and in Cicero's treatment of emotion in *De Oratore.* We will see the interest emerge again in the British rhetoricians of the eighteenth century. The relationship between language and human emotion is, thus, a persistent theme in the history of rhetoric.

HUMANISM, RHETORIC, AND THE STUDY
OF CLASSICAL TEXTS

Also suggested by their decided interest in Cicero, another characteristic of the Italian Humanists was a preoccupation with the original texts of classical antiquity. One leading Renaissance historian, Nicholas Mann, finds such classicism to be the central defining characteristic of the Humanist movement in Europe. He writes, "Humanism is that concern with the legacy of antiquity—and in particular, but not exclusively, the literary legacy.... It involves above all the rediscovery and study of Greek and Roman texts, the restoration and interpretation of them, and the assimilation of the ideas and values that they contain."[66]

Humanists, from the fifteenth-century Italian term *umanista,* which referred to "a teacher or student of classical literature and the arts associated with it, including rhetoric," wished to read ancient works for their true meanings, rejecting the limited or false meanings attributed to them during centuries of Christian dominance in Europe.[67] Some Humanists sought a common source of both classical philosophy and Christianity, while others challenged long-accepted notions about the dating and authorship of ancient texts, including biblical texts. Both objectives threatened Christian hegemony in Europe. Recovering and interpreting ancient texts was central to Humanist thought, and so deserves closer attention.

Lauro Martines summarizes the guiding intellectual values of the Humanist movement in Italy as regards their study of ancient texts. First, the Humanists maintained "a supreme emphasis on the importance of getting the texts right." Martines adds that "this meant collating the earliest existing manuscripts and applying the finest philological techniques, with an eye to producing an authentic text." He credits the Humanists with inventing "classical scholarship."[68]

Second, the Humanists sought to place "the text in its historical context, in order to establish the correct value of words and phrases."[69] In this way they contributed to studies such as hermeneutics, the discipline of textual interpretation. As noted in the last chapter, the scholastic practice of splintering classical sources into individual statements or *sententiae* led to a loss of original meaning and even of authorial identity. Charles Nauert writes, "from Petrarch onward, humanists insisted on reading each opinion in its context, abandoning the anthologies [of passages from classical texts, called *florilegia*] and subsequent interpretations and going back to the full original text in search of the author's real meaning."[70] Consequently, classical authors "re-emerged as real human beings, living at a particular moment in history and addressing their remarks to specific issues."[71]

Third, the Humanists placed "emphasis on ascertainable facts: on words, documents, dates, events, and historical persons." As a result, in both their critical and historical writing, these scholars moved toward "exposing or challenging historical myths." Along similar lines, Nauert notes that "Humanists successfully claimed that the ancient texts...were subject to critical evaluation by the philological method invented by humanists like Lorenzo Valla and Erasmus." He adds that at this very point "the ugliest academic conflicts occurred," because Humanist scholars "insisted that any study of ancient legal or medical or even biblical sources not based on mastery of ancient languages was invalid."[72]

Fourth, the Italian Humanists revived interest in "secular history, with highlights on politics, war, biography." Thus, they "introduced the study of history into schools" while they also "freed historical writing" from its dependence on "the argument from divine intervention." Martines notes finally that "humanism gave rise to a number of new disciplines: archaeology, epigraphy, numismatics, and topography, which were aids to historical study and by-products of a new and unprecedented feeling, antiquarianism."[73]

PETRARCH AND THE ORIGINS
OF ITALIAN HUMANISM

To locate the origins of Humanism, we turn to the commercial cities of Northern Italy at the beginning of the fourteenth century. As Charles Nauert notes, in the fourteenth century "Italy became a jumble of urban republics" run by councils, committees, and members of influential families.[74] Italian Humanism developed as part of the effort to educate the leading families of Florence and other important cities in the intricacies of civic government. As in the Rome of antiquity, a few wealthy families held power in Florence, and eloquence was an aid to maintaining and exercising that power. This connection between rhetoric and power, as we have noted before, marks the entire history of rhetoric.

Crucial to the day-to-day management of Florentine civic life were the attorneys and notaries, rhetorically trained secretaries responsible for negotiating, recording, and communicating the many agreements that enabled Italian commercial cities to function. In Italy's powerful cities, "the needs of the civic administration and commerce" for educated workers "were to prove stronger than those of the Church." As the demand for these educated professionals increased, they "emerged as a new literate class" with substantial influence.[75]

The education of many of these civic officials was, perhaps not surprisingly, largely a rhetorical one. Rhetoric became "a skill for contemporary life."[76] Those who attended universities "heard lectures in Latin on rhetoric, dialectics, and the elements of law."[77] Notaries often took courses in "rhetoric emphasiz[ing] correct writing…and the art of speech making." Some of the students in these courses went on to "read more Cicero, some Virgil, and even some Seneca, but more especially certain of the late Latin writers."[78] Roman law, a complementary component of Roman rhetoric, was taken as a model for the rising cities like Florence. Again, rhetorically trained notaries and lawyers were a crucial conduit of Roman culture. "The need for lawyers and notaries to study, ponder, and apply ancient Roman law," writes Nauert, "predisposed them to develop an interest not only in the law but also in the language, literature, institutions and customs of Antiquity."[79]

One of the earliest of the Renaissance Italian Humanist writers, and the one most often associated with the origins of the movement, is Francesco Petrarca, better known as Petrarch (1303–1374). He has been called "the outstanding scholar and creative writer of his generation."[80] Born in Arezzo, Petrarch spent most of his early life in Avignon, where he was educated by a notary from Prato. During Petrarch's youth, Avignon was "the diplomatic and cultural center of the western world" due to the fact that one claimant to the title of Pope made the city his capital.[81] Thus, the city was home to a papal library containing classical texts, and Avignon became an important center of scholarship which "attracted scholars and men of letters from all over Europe."[82]

Petrarch studied, as did other privileged Italian boys of his day, "Latin grammar, elementary logic, rhetoric, and arithmetic."[83] Petrarch's own father, as well as his tutor, had rhetorical training in their backgrounds. The young Petrarch was particularly interested in the works of Cicero, writing late in his life: "I gave myself wholly to Cicero, whether through natural sympathy or at the suggestion of my father who always held the author in highest veneration."[84] Sent to study law, Petrarch continued reading Cicero and added to his literary education by studying the poetry of Virgil.

Interestingly, though he was fond of writing poetry, it was through his letters that Petrarch wielded much of his intellectual influence. One biographer writes that "his letters to friends and sympathizers and occasionally to enemies and rivals were widely circulated and they enhanced his reputation."[85] Nicholas Mann maintains that Petrarch paved the way for "the letter…to become one of the most favored and versatile literary genres of the Renaissance."[86]

Through his writings Petrarch did much to revive interest in classical, especially Ciceronian, rhetoric. "He definitely accepted Cicero as his model, and set himself the task of recovering the complete works of the master."[87] Petrarch was also an expert in Roman history and culture, and was the leading authority of his day on the Roman historical writer Livy. Petrarch personally reconstructed much of Livy's *History of Rome,* and traveled widely in search of portions of this and other Latin manuscripts. He gradually assembled the largest private collection of Roman manuscripts in his day. Petrarch's extraordinary interest in classical studies was infectious, turning even the great writer Giovanni Boccaccio (1313–1375), author of the *Decameron,* "to a career dominated by classical studies."[88]

Petrarch, like Cicero, was more interested in rhetoric's "persuasive power" than in its possibilities for "harmony and beauty of language."[89] However, Petrarch and other early Italian Humanists, such as Coluccio Salutati, feared that highly persuasive rhetoric "could be perverted if not anchored in true (Christian) wisdom."[90] Petrarch wrote that "speech can have no dignity unless the soul has dignity," a statement reminiscent of Cicero's concern for the union of wisdom and eloquence, Quintilian's dictum that rhetoric was the art of the good person speaking well, and Augustine's desire to use rhetoric in the service of God.[91] Euginio Garin sums up Petrarch's position: "[T]here is an insoluble connection between interior and exterior, between mind and speech."[92] Thus, Petrarch's claim can also be read as a statement about rhetorical aesthetics—beautiful speech issues from a beautiful soul. This connection can be traced back at least as far as Plato.

The Greatness That Was Rome

Petrarch embraced more than just the Roman rhetorical model. Realizing the civic greatness of Rome in Italy's great commercial cities became for him a guiding goal. Much of the impetus for Petrarch's work and for the Humanistic movement generally came from a growing sense that Italy could return to the greatness of its past if only it could recapture the culture of the ancient Romans. And, rhetoric was central to the great cultural achievement of Rome. As Charles Nauert comments, Petrarch "believed that the melancholy of Italy in his own time could be remedied only if Italians recaptured the moral qualities, especially the devotion to the welfare of the community, that had been the secret of Roman greatness."[93] Mann notes as well that Roman law was the basis of most Italian legal practices, and this fact combined with "the presence of many physical remains of antiquity, helped to give a sense that the civilization of the past was still alive, and this in turn led to curiosity about that civilization."[94]

Reestablishing Rome's greatness meant reviving the Ciceronian ideal of uniting wisdom and eloquence. That is, Cicero's theory of rhetoric was for Petrarch the key to Renaissance Italy's own rise to greatness. "The union of moral virtue and eloquent persuasive power was the distinctive excellence of the Rome that [Petrarch] loved." Petrarch translated this nostalgia for Rome into an educational agenda. "Roman greatness could be restored if young Italians were properly educated in wisdom and eloquence." This rhetorical turn in education would necessitate removing logic and science from their dominant positions in the universities "and to replace them with the ethical and rhetorical emphasis that had dominated ancient Roman education."[95]

PICO DELLA MIRANDOLA AND
THE MAGIC OF LANGUAGE

Another important humanist figure of the centuries following Petrarch was Pico della Mirandola (1463–1494). Pico was a fifteenth-century writer whose early philosophical training in Paris and Padua was scholastic in nature. He also studied law at Bologna when he was quite young.[96] But Pico's principal interest later in life seems to have been Greek philosophy, particularly that of Plato. Paul Askar Kristeller identifies Pico as a Platonist, placing him in the stream of Platonic, or more accurately Neoplatonic, philosophers who contributed to the Humanist movement.[97] In fact, Pico is sometimes credited with having revived interest in Neoplatonism during the Renaissance, a body of philosophic and religious ideas loosely based on Plato's idealism, but also incorporating ideas from astrology, magic, and alchemy. Pico learned much of his philosophy from Marsilio Ficino, another influential Italian Humanist and Neoplatonist.

Interest in Neoplatonism was closely aligned for Pico, as it was for many Renaissance writers, with an interest in the secret spiritual knowledge conveyed in occult works including the *Cabala,* a work of Jewish mysticism, and the *Corpus Hermeticum,* magical works of Greek and Egyptian origin. The connection between rhetoric and magic, evident in ancient rhetoricians such as Gorgias, is again expressed in Pico's lavish praise of the *Cabala* in his famous *Oration on the Dignity of Man.*[98]

Pico, Ficino, and many other Renaissance writers were as interested in magic as they were in rhetoric. In fact, to their way of thinking the two disciplines were inseparable. As the Sophist Gorgias had noted centuries earlier, rhetoric was a verbal means of altering reality, and magic often was simply another method for accomplishing the same end. William Covino writes regarding this connection that "indeed, the magician and the rhetor are similar figures, and often the same figure, throughout western intellectual history."[99]

Historian John G. Burke helps us to understand this somewhat surprising connection between rhetoric and magic, accepted as a working hypothesis by many Renaissance intellectuals. According to an ancient Egyptian legend, the god Thoth, also known as Hermes, invented language. This myth enjoyed renewed currency in the Renaissance because of the astonishing popularity of the *Corpus Hermeticum.* As the name suggests, the *Corpus Hermeticum* was attributed to the legendary Egyptian writer, Hermes Trismegistus, who supposedly manifested the language god Hermes. In fact, the Hermetic writings were composed during the first three centuries A.D. by various unidentified Greek and Egyptian writers.

Burke writes about the theory of language that developed out of such thinking: "Words, then, according to this magical view of language, are not just verbal symbols attached to things by conventional usage; they have a very real connection with things; there is a direct correspondence between a word and the divine idea it expresses."[100] Thus, when wielded by a master of rhetoric, a veritable magician of language, "words could produce extraordinary effects." People and events could literally be brought under the control of the highly skilled rhetorician. This theme is explored in many Renaissance works, including Shakespeare's play *The Tempest* and Marlowe's *Dr. Faustus.* Pico was a student of Greek philosophy, as were many humanists. But he, like several other leading Humanists, was also a student of occult religious writings, which he felt imparted secret knowledge of language's great power.

Bringing Order through Language

Important to Pico's own humanistic philosophy was the conviction that humans employ language to order the world, and to work cooperatively within it. Pico exhibited the Italian Humanists' tendency to see people as the creators of their world through the humanizing tool of language. Humans alone possess the freedom to choose their destiny, a freedom granted them by language. Kristeller writes that "Pico stresses especially man's freedom to choose his own way of life."[101] Human beings, he stressed, had been created different from the other animals, particularly as regards this ability to choose. We are not, he argued in his *Oration on the Dignity of Man* (1487), simply part of the fixed hierarchy of the universe.

Pico and other Humanists maintained that our power to choose and thus to create civilization is a direct consequence of our linguistic capacity. In fact, the civilizing force of language is nothing short of magical, language allowing humans to probe "the miracles concealed in the recesses of the world, in the depths of nature, and in the storehouses and mysteries of God."[102] Pico, like Ficino and others, intended to harness this power in rhetoric for personal as well as civic advancement.

JUAN LUIS VIVES

Juan Luis Vives (1492–1540) was born in Valencia, Spain, just two years before Pico died. His early education occurred in Spain, and, like Pico's, in the Scholastic tradition, discussed in the previous chapter. At the age of seventeen he left Spain "out of fear of the Inquisition."[103] He studied in Paris, where he was repulsed by Scholasticism and captivated by the ideas of Humanism.[104] Vives edited an edition of Augustine's *City of God.* James K. Cameron writes that Vives eventually "became the friend and disciple of Erasmus, from whom he largely assimilated the principles of humanism that formed the background of his 'grand pedagogical system.'"[105] In 1523 Vives was called to England to educate Princess Mary and to teach at Oxford University. He never returned to his homeland of Spain.

Like Quintilian in first century Rome, Vives was interested in the possibilities of rhetorical education, but he added to his curriculum the study of many other subjects as well. His works *De Disciplinis* (1531) and *Rhetoricae* (1533) set out a course of education "beginning with the initial instruction given by the mother right up to that provided for the advanced student."[106] His reliance on Cicero and Isocrates is also clear in *De Ratione Dicendi* (1532), though he claimed to be seeking to break with the classical tradition and discover a rhetoric "appropriate to the needs of the time."[107] In the process, however, he separated argument from rhetoric, leaving rhetoric mainly the territory of style. The goal of his course of study was a highly moral and articulate individual who could speak forcefully, work diligently for peace, and who embodied Christian principles of conduct. Vives died in Bruges in 1540.

RHETORIC AND THE *VITA ACTIVA*

Humanist writers found in rhetoric both a rich source for speculative thinking and the key to practical living. Petrarch and other Renaissance rhetoricians advocated the *vita activa,* the life of political and civic involvement. Rhetoric was central to this life, particularly rhetoric understood on the Ciceronian model of "the union of wisdom and eloquence." As Brian Vickers points out, "the active individual was involved in the life of the state, and rhetoric was central to such involvement. It taught one the essential powers of analysis as well as of presentation that assisted toward the solution of the practical problems facing any city or nation."[108]

The Humanist position reflects a suspicion of the contemplative life of solitary reflection advocated by some scholars of his day and elevated as the ideal life by medieval Christian society. Because Renaissance thinkers found "all forms of speech" to be crucial to the cooperative task of building a society, "to write or think purely for oneself would have been regarded as perverse."[109] For this same reason, solitude "was viewed with suspicion." Thus, the earlier Christian model of solitary contemplation of divine truth, codified in monastic rules, was rejected as antisocial, as the private use of the public property of speech (*oratio*) and reason (*ratio*).

A new ideal was developing around a conception of rhetoric as the application of reason to the solution of the practical problems of human social life. The notion of *vita activa* reflected the belief that one owed a debt to one's city or nation, that "the individual's duties should go first to the country that has given him citizenship and a language, then to his fellow-citizens, his family, his friends, and lastly to himself."[110] Rhetoric was the key to living the active life of civic involvement.

When speech is viewed as *the* characteristic human capacity, to deny speech is to deny one's humanity. Humanists affirmed the "humanizing" potential of speech for the individual and for the society. "Human conversation has the power to elevate, for conversation…soothes and shapes our minds."[111] But more than the individual intellect stood to gain from the human practices of speech. The spoken word also shapes cultures and brings into existence human civilizations. Michael Mooney writes that "at the center of this tradition is the concept of language as the bond of society and the instrument of its change."[112]

Speech, then, is the means by which human beings create civilizations, the highest human accomplishment. Thus, to avoid speech as advocates of the *vita contemplativa* recommended was to reject the essence of humanity and at the same time to undermine civilization. Rhetoric and eloquence, not prayer and meditation, brought about constructive, cooperative action on the part of the citizenry. Eloquence civilized the human mind and tamed the wilder impulses of the human heart, thus both improving the individual's existence and making social life possible.

Madame de Scudéry

Madame de Scudéry was a novelist and essayist of the mid-seventeenth century, a late Renaissance woman with a decided interest in the interpersonal and social potential in rhetoric. "In France, in treatises from the 1640s to the 1680s," writes Jane Donaworth, "Madeleine de Scudéry set out the first fully elaborated early modern theory of rhetoric by a woman." In works such as *Les Femmes Illustres* (1642), "de Scudéry encourages women to educate themselves and to seek social status through their writing rather than their beauty."[113]

Donaworth notes that in works such as *Conversations* (1680) and *Conversations Nouvelles* (1684), and in several novels, "de Scudéry lays out a rhetoric of conversation (and also letter writing) for the salon culture of Renaissance France, a theory that includes (or even centers on) women." In what amounted to a new and distinctly social approach to rhetoric, "de Scudéry imagines a world of leisure in which intellectual exploration and construction of community are carried on primarily through conversation." Indeed, conversation becomes her "model for public as well as private discourse." Donaworth adds that "central to her theory, then, is the agreeable, remaining sensitive to one's audience's interests, entertaining and not imposing one's views on the group."[114]

De Scudéry pointed the way to later developments in which "women taught and theorized conversation as an art" and "used conversation as a model for other forms of communication," and, thus, "anticipated modern theories of composition in important ways." Donaworth asks, "What does this emphasis on conversation, collaboration, and dialogue add to our conception of rhetoric?" One answer is that it, like some earlier theories—notably that of Cicero—"celebrate[s] the civilizing power of speech." She adds, "following the Greek sophists, Cicero represents language as the force that led humanity out of the wilderness into civilization, a political force through public speech that allowed peoples to make laws for themselves."[115]

For de Scudéry, then, language is "the bond that holds society together, not through public speaking but through the conversation that educates and plants morality daily in ordinary people." Donaworth finds this tendency to mark women rhetorical theorists generally. "As a group, then, women theorists bring a model of communication based on conversation, collaboration, and dialogue to our understanding of the history of rhetoric."[116]

THE TURN TOWARD DIALECTIC: RHETORIC AND ITS CRITICS

Despite its enormous success, however, rhetoric had its critics during the Renaissance period as well. Several influential writers in the fifteenth and sixteenth centuries demoted rhetoric to a set of concerns for style and expression. Logic and dialectic rather than rhetoric were taken to be the proper study of an academician, and argument in the service of disputation belonged to dialectic. As noted in Chapter 6, however, this trend actually began in the twelfth and thirteenth centuries as the result of various social forces, and was brought about as much by rhetoricians as it was by opponents of rhetoric. Two writers are particularly significant in solidifying dialectic's claim on argument during the fifteenth and sixteenth centuries.

Agricola

The first was a Dutch scholar named Roelof Huusman (1444–1485), who is better known to historians by his latinized name, Rudolph Agricola.[117] Like many other rhetorical theorists, Agricola studied law, a study he began in Italy in 1468 and that kept him in that country for ten years.[118] During his decade in Italy he also steeped himself in the study of Latin and Greek. Agricola was greatly influenced by the Italian Humanist tradition, and his ideas in turn influenced Humanist writers who "eventually succeeded in reforming scholastic education in its most important subject, dialectic."[119] He came to admire Petrarch, and even wrote a biography of Humanism's founding theorist. Under Humanist influence, Agricola's interests turned toward the classics, and especially toward rhetoric and dialectic. Like many Humanists, including Petrarch, he argued that "speaking and oration" was a gift from God for the advancement of human civilization.[120] "Thus," writes Charles Nauert, "he had a clear conception of the humanist idea of a rebirth of civilization."[121]

In 1479 Agricola completed his famous book, *On Dialectical Invention (De Inventione Dialectica)*, though it was not published until 1515, thirty years after his death in Rome at age forty-one in 1485. Nauert writes that this book was "the most important manual on logic from its publication down to the middle of the sixteenth century."[122] In this work Agricola is drawn more to the argumentative uses of speech than to the ornaments of the rhetoricians. Clear reasoning and effective teaching should be the goals of dialectic, which he made superior to rhetoric as both a study and practice. Though Agricola discussed many types of argument in *On Dialectical Invention,* he is not interested at all in stylistic considerations, which he assigns to rhetoric. A brief quotation from *On Dialectical Invention* captures his opinion of the subject. "Rhetoric," he writes, "provides us with linguistic embellishment and elegance of language, along with all the baits for capturing ears." Dialectic claims the more substantial territory of "speaking convincingly on whatever matter is included in a speech."[123] Thus, Agricola split the ancient and venerable Ciceronian pair of wisdom and eloquence, while reducing the latter to ornament and handing it over rather unceremoniously to rhetoric. Dialectic emerged the clear winner, walking away with all of the substance, the wisdom, of a speech.

As for the substance of a speech, Agricola distinguishes exposition from argument on the basis of whether one is explaining a point to a receptive audience or arguing a point before an audience that needs to be persuaded. His rhetorical theory stresses the activities of inventing and assessing arguments, and he is particularly interested in reviving the study of *topoi*.[124] Agricola also provides his readers with a discussion of the emotions more thorough than was typical even in the standard rhetoric books.

Agricola influenced prominent writers on rhetoric and dialectic including Erasmus, Philip Melancthon, Vives, and especially Peter Ramus.[125] In fact, Father Walter J. Ong writes that "it is difficult to exaggerate [Agricola's] importance." Father Ong adds that Agricola's logic "became for generations after him, in the absolute sense, logic unqualified."[126] Agricola's importance is underlined by his disciple Peter Ramus, who "has to remind his own generation that the 'true dialectic' which he professed had not sprung from nowhere, but was that of Rudolph Agricola."[127] It is to the work of this famous and influential disciple of Agricola that we now turn.

Peter Ramus

The second of these writers who secured the hold of dialectic on argument was the great French scholar Peter Ramus (1515–1572), a professor of rhetoric at the University of Paris. In the sixteenth century, scholastic university education in northern Europe followed the logical works of Aristotle. Ramus vehemently opposed scholasticism, proposing an alternative approach to learning that did not make reference to authorities such as Aristotle or Cicero at all. As Peter Mack writes, the iconoclastic Ramus "built his academic career on scandalous attacks on the academic gods of his time: Aristotle, Cicero and Quintilian."[128] He was skeptical about the value of Aristotle's and Cicero's treatment of rhetoric, calling the former "the man chiefly responsible for confusing the arts of rhetoric and dialectic," and the latter "verbose" and "unable to restrain and check himself" when making a speech.[129]

Though he owed much to Quintilian, the great Roman teacher also became Ramus' target in an angry attack entitled, *Arguments in Rhetoric against Quintilian* (1549). Ramus rejected Quintilian's famous conception of the perfect orator as a virtuous as well as an eloquent person, summed up in the Latin phrase *Vir bonus beni dicendi* ("The good man speaking well"). Such a view, which ignored the brute fact that an eloquent speaker could also be an evil person, was for Ramus simply "useless and stupid."[130] Ramus extended his disregard for the rhetorical tradition to his contemporaries as well. He was leery of the Italian brand of Humanism that was built around the study of rhetoric. Ong writes that "in a very real sense Italian humanism stood for a rhetorically centered culture opposed to the dialectically or logically centered culture of North Europe."[131] Ramus preferred the latter, less rhetorical, model of liberal education.

In 1514, the year before Ramus' birth, the Dutch Humanist Erasmus published his extremely popular work, *Praise of Folly*. In this book, "grammar and rhetoric form the basis of scholarship, and oust dialectic from its place."[132] A generation later, and as part of his reaction against the classical tradition that typified Italian Humanism, Ramus performed the opposite operation. He removed invention from the study of rhetoric, and assigned it to dialectic in his *Institutes of Dialectic* (1543). For Ramus, rhetoric was merely a kind of verbal ornamentation, and thus of little consequence. Because of Ramus' enormous intellectual influence, rhetoric suffered considerable loss of prestige as a study, following his criticisms of the art. But Ramus may have exerted an even more dramatic influence over Western education by driving a wedge between reason and language in his effort to demote rhetoric. Richard Lanham has written that Ramus "separated thought from language" by advancing a model of education in which "reason breaks free of speech."[133] Language became a neutral tool for expressing the discoveries of other disciplines, and was no longer viewed as the substance of an art worthy of mastery by an educated person for its own sake.

Rhetorical treatises after Ramus tended toward discussions of style and ornament. Rhetoric's capacity as a practical art of discourse concerned with discovering arguments toward the resolution of important issues was largely lost in such works. Rhetoric moved from being a master art, holding sway over other arts and, in some writers, over life itself, to being a marginal study with a limited practical application and a suspect heritage. But, as we saw in our discussion of Italian Humanism, and will see again when we look at rhetorical theory in the eighteenth century, rhetoric continued to exert its influence in spite of efforts to make it principally an art of dressing the insights discovered by other means, such as dialectic.[134]

RENAISSANCE RHETORICS IN BRITAIN

Whereas rhetoric was suffering under the criticism of Agricola and Ramus on the European Continent in the fifteenth and sixteenth centuries, England was developing into a particularly fertile field for the growth of interest in the art of rhetoric between 1500 and 1600.[135] A few examples of early English rhetorics serve to illustrate this point.

Leonard Cox's *The Art or Craft of Rhetoryke* (c. 1530) was the first actual rhetorical treatise written in English. The book is largely Ciceronian in its presentation of rhetoric, which it treats as consisting principally of Cicero's five canons. On the other hand, Richard Sherry's *A Treatise of Schemes and Tropes* (1550) focuses on the ornamental uses of language. Thomas Wilson's *The Arte of Rhetorique* (1553) was another important early rhetorical textbook in English. This work was used extensively as a text for teaching rhetoric under the Tudors in England, though it as actually written for people who wanted to study rhetoric on their own. As George Kennedy writes, "That such works were written is an indication that some English schoolmasters for the first time recognized a need to train students in the composition and appreciation of English."[136] Shakespeare, the great English master of classical rhetoric, was a student at around the time these works were being published.

The popularity of rhetoric in England in the sixteenth century is also suggested by the appearance of treatises such as Richard Reinolde's *A Booke Called the Foundacion of Rhetoric* (1563), and Roger Ascham's *The Scholemaster* (1570), which took a Ciceronian approach to rhetoric and presented the art as a means of promoting social refinement. Later in the century works such as Gabriel Harvey's *Rhetor* (1577) and Henry Peacham's *The Garden of Eloquence* (1577) appeared. The former was Ramistic in its approach to rhetoric, while the latter focused on the development of English prose style. As we will see in the following sections, English interest in rhetoric's capacity to enhance written and oral style, and in its ability to enhance the social refinement of its students, remained important to British interest in the subject.

CONCLUSION

Rhetoric achieved perhaps its greatest prominence as a subject of study during the period known as the Renaissance. The number of books devoted to its study, the number of people who took up the subject, and the degree to which education was rhetorically structured are all astonishing. Rhetoric was the language of education and the educated during the Renaissance. As we have seen, the movement known as Humanism, and particularly Italian Humanism, had a great deal to do with rhetoric's influence between 1300 and 1750. The attention paid to rhetoric by important intellectual figures such as Petrarch and Valla, as well as their arguments against philosophy as the foundation of study, enhanced rhetoric's status substantially.

The impulses of Italian Humanism were both iconoclastic and conservative. Humanism mixed Christian moral principles with an aggressive search for a new basis for education and inquiry that honored classical sources. Rhetoric became a tool for questioning the *status quo,* and for inaugurating new ways of thinking in Europe. But, for figures like Petrarch, Valla, and Vives, rhetoric was also a means of advancing and refining Christian principles. But, at the same time, Christian texts were made to pass the very tests applied to other ancient documents. Thus, rhetoric was, in the Renaissance, as it had been in classical Greece and Rome, elevated to a preeminent place of importance by the Humanists because of its potential both for new insight and for preserving important cultural values.

And, again as in earlier times, the Renaissance orator represented the ideal of the educated person. The true orator was a person grounded in the wisdom of the liberal arts and also highly skilled in the art of eloquence. Cicero's ideal achievement of wedding wisdom and eloquence in one individual was diligently pursued. Thus, Petrarch advocated both the *literae humanae,* or liberal arts, and the *vita activa* or active life of political involvement. Rhetoric was the means both of self-discovery and of effective government.

Toward the end of the Renaissance, the highly influential Ramus moved rhetoric's more substantial elements into the discipline of dialectic, an apparent blow to rhetoric's intellectual status. However, the sixteenth century also finds rhetoric becoming a prominent study in Britain. Rhetoric's influence in that country in the eighteenth century is the subject of the next chapter.

QUESTIONS FOR REVIEW

1. What was the status of rhetorical studies in Renaissance education?

2. What expectations regarding the writing of women did Margaret Cavendish challenge?

3. Identify some of the defining characteristics of the Italian Humanist movement.

4. What was the opinion of Valla regarding the relationship between rhetoric and philosophy?

5. What is the significance of the concept of the *vita activa* to Renaissance rhetoric?

6. What was Scholasticism, and what was the reaction of many humanists to this approach to education?

7. What orientation did Madame de Scudéry bring to rhetoric?

8. In what way are Agricola and Ramus significant to the history of rhetoric?

QUESTIONS FOR DISCUSSION

1. Is it any longer possible to speak of one discipline as somehow providing the basis for all of education? If so, what discipline might play that role? If not, what has changed since the Renaissance?

2. Respond to the idea advocated by the Italian Humanists that somehow speech is itself the means by which human beings create civilization. Is this account too simple? Are there factors other than speech that could be said to be the basis for human civilization?

3. Does the commercial life of modern capitalistic societies still depend on the language skills of a class of highly trained specialists? If so, what professions do these new notaries represent? If not, what has changed?

4. What argument could be made against Ramus' reduction of rhetoric to a concern for style and ornament in language? What argument could be made in favor of this reduction?

TERMS

Affectus: For the Italian Humanists, the source of emotions or passions in the human mind.
Classicism: A resurgence of interest in the languages and texts of classical antiquity.
Hermeneutics: The science of textual interpretation.
Literae humanae: The liberal arts.
Neoplatonism: A body of philosophic and religious ideas loosely based on Plato's idealism, but also incorporating ideas from astrology, magic, and alchemy.

Notaries: Rhetorically trained secretaries responsible for negotiating, recording, and communicating the many agreements that enabled Italian commercial cities to function.

Res: The substance matter of one's arguments.

Studia humanitatis: Humanistic studies, or studies proper to the development of a free and active human mind—rhetoric, poetics, ethics, politics.

Uomo universale: The universal man, the ideal type of an educated person in the Renaissance.

Verba: The words in which the subject matter of an argument was advanced.

Vita activa: The active life, or life of political involvement.

ENDNOTES

1. Brian Vickers, "On the Practicalities of Renaissance Rhetoric," in *Rhetoric Revalued,* ed. Brian Vickers (Binghamton, NY: Center for Medieval and Early Renaissance Studies, 1982), 133.

2. Jerrold E. Seigel, *Rhetoric and Philosophy in Renaissance Humanism* (Princeton, NJ: Princeton University Press, 1968), 200.

3. Erasmus, "The Right Way to Speak," in *Collected Works,* v. 4, ed. J. K. Sowards (Toronto: University of Toronto Press, 1985), 369. Quoted in Kelley, 89.

4. Paul Oskar Kristeller, *Renaissance Thought: The Classic, Scholastic, and Humanist Strains* (New York: Harper and Row, 1961), 13.

5. See: John Mon7asani, *George of Trebizond: A Biography and a Study of His Rhetoric and Logic* (Leiden, Netherlands: Brill, 1976).

6. George Kennedy, *Classical Rhetoric in its Secular and Christian Tradition,* (Chapel Hill, NC, 1999), 232.

7. James J. Murphy, ed. *Peter Ramus's Attack on Cicero,* trans. Carole Newlands (Davis, CA: Hermagoras Press, 1992), xv.

8. Murphy, "Introduction" to *Ramus,* xxxii.

9. Kristeller, 60–63.

10. Vickers, "Practicalities," 133.

11. Peter Mack, "Humanist Rhetoric and Dialectic," in *The Cambridge Companion to Renaissance Humanism,"* ed. Jill Kraye (Cambridge: Cambridge University Press, 1996), 88.

12. Don Paul Abbott, "Rhetoric and Writing in Renaissance Europe and England," in *A Short History of Writing Instruction,* ed. James J. Murphy (Davis, CA: Hermagoras Press, 1990), 95. See also: Wilbur Samuel Howell, *Logic and Rhetoric in England: 1500–1700* (New York: Russell and Russell, 1961).

13. Vickers, 269.

14. Thomas O. Sloane, *On the Contrary: The Protocol of Traditional Rhetoric* (Washington, DC: Catholic University of America Press, 1997), especially chap. 4, "Disputatiousness."

15. Mack, 91.

16. Kennedy, 245.

17. Richard Lanham, *A Handbook of Rhetorical Terms,* 2 ed. (Berkeley: University of California Press, 1991), 80. Lanham quotes Edward O. Wilson, *Biophilia* (Cambridge, MA: Harvard University Press, 1984), 60.

18. Donald R. Kelley, *Renaissance Humanism* (Boston: Twayne, 1991), 82.

19. Quoted in Mooney, 45.

21. Vickers, 185.

21. Kelley, 35.

22. Kelley, 35–36; Vickers, 266.

23. Mack, 86.

24. Peter Burke, "The Spread of Italian Humanism," in *The Impact of Humanism on Western Europe,* eds. Anthony Goodman and Angus MacKay (London: Longman, 1990), 1.

25. Seigel, 137.

26. Kelley, 88.

27. Quoted in Seigel, 139.

28. Vickers, 187.

29. Seigel writes that Valla "was almost certainly a loyal Christian, even though he may have been a somewhat eccentric one" (145).

30. Quoted in Seigel, 142.

31. Seigel, 142.

32. Seigel, 251.

33. Katharina Wilson, ed. *Women Writers of the Renaissance and Reformation* (Athens: University of Georgia Press, 1987), xxii–xxiii.

34. Wilson, xxiii.

35. See: *The Rhetorical Tradition: Readings from Classical Times to the Present,* eds. Patricia Bizzell and Bruce Herzberg (Boston: St. Martin's Press), 463–498. Bizzell and Herzberg include in their collection works by Christine de Pisan and Laura Cereta.

36. Wilson, xxiii. See also in this volume: Anne R. Larsen, "Les Dames des Roches," 232–259.

37. Kennedy, 231.

38. Kennedy, 231.

39. *Beyond Their Sex: Learned Women of the European Past,* ed. Patricia H. Labalme (New York: New York University Press, 1984); *Bibliotecha Lusitania,* v. III, pp. 558–559.

40. Christopher Lund, Department of Spanish and Portuguese, Brigham Young University, brought de Castro to my attention.

41. Jenny R. Redfern, "Christine de Pisan and *The Treasure of the City of Ladies:* A Medieval Rhetorician and Her Rhetoric," in *Reclaiming Rhetorica: Women in the Rhetorical Tradition,* ed. Andrea A. Lunsford (Pittsburgh, PA: University of Pittsburgh Press, 1995), 73–92.

42. Redfern, 74.

43. Redfern, 77.

44. Redfern, 74.

45. Redfern, 74.

46. Redfern, 74.

47. Redfern, 78.

48. Redfern, 75.

49. Redfern, 76.

50. Jane Donaworth, *Rhetorical Theory by Women Before 1900: An Anthology* (Lanham, MD: Rowan and Littlefield, 2002), 45.

51. Sarah Heller Mendelson, *The Mental World of Stuart Women: Three Studies* (Amherst, MA: University of Massachusetts Press, 1987), 35.

52. Donaworth, 45.

53. Kennedy, 230.

54. Don Paul Abbott, "The Renaissance," in *The Present State of Scholarship in Historical and Contemporary Rhetoric,* ed. Winifred Bryan Horner (Columbia: University of Missouri Press, 1990), 89.

55. Izora Scott, *Controversies over the Imitation of Cicero in the Renaissance* (1910; rpt. Davis, CA: Hermagoras Press, 1991), 113.

56. Charles Nauert, Jr., *Humanism and the Culture of Renaissance Europe* (Cambridge: Cambridge University Press, 1995), 25.

57. Ballasdare Castiglione, *The Courtier* (1528); G. P. Mohrmann, "The Civile Conversation: Communication in the Renaissance," *Speech Monographs* 39 (1972): 193–204.

58. Victoria Kahn, *Machiavelian Rhetoric: From the Counter-Reformation to Milton* (Princeton, NJ: Princeton University Press, 1994), 5. Also by Kahn: *Rhetoric, Prudence, and Skepticism in the Renaissance* (Ithaca, NY: Cornell University Press, 1985).

59. See: Scott, Chapter VII, "The Influence of Ciceronianism upon Educational Practice."

60. Nauert, 25.

61. Vickers, "Practicalities," 135.

62. Vickers, "Practicalities," 135.

63. On Renaissance uses of Aristotle's *Rhetoric,* see: Lawrence D. Green, "The Reception of Aristotle's *Rhetoric* in the Renaissance," in *Peripatetic Rhetoric after Aristotle,* eds. W. W. Fortenbaugh and D.C. Mirhady (New Brunswick, NJ: Transaction, 1994).

64. Vickers, "Practicalities," 136.

65. Vickers, "Practicalities," 137.

66. Nicholas Mann, "The Origins of Humanism," in *The Cambridge Companion to Renaissance Humanism,* ed. Jill Kraye (Cambridge: Cambridge University Press, 1996), 2.

67. Mann, 1.

68. Lauro Martines, *Power and Imagination: City States in Renaissance Italy* (New York: Knopf, 1979), 204.

69. Martines, Jr., 204.

70. Nauert, 18.

71. Nauert, 18.

72. Nauert, 193.

73. Martines, 204.

74. Nauert, 5.

75. Mann, 5.

76. Mann, 5.

77. Martines, 204.

78. Martines, 204.

79. Nauert, 5.

80. Mann, 9.

81. Mann, 8.

82. Mann, 8.

83. Morris Bishop, *Petrarch and His World* (Bloomington: Indiana University Press, 1963), 21.

84. Bishop, 21.

85. Gene Brucker, *Florence: The Golden Age 1138–1737* (Berkeley: University of California Press, 1969), 202.

86. Mann, 5.

87. Scott, 7.

88. Nauert, 25.

89. Seigel, 34.

90. Martines, 199.

91. Euginio Garin, *Portraits of the Quattrocentro* (New York: Harper and Row, 1963).

92. Garin, 19.

93. Nauert, 24.

94. Mann, 6.

95. Nauert, 24.

96. Walter J. Ong, S. J., *Ramus: Method and the Decay of Dialogue* (Cambridge, MA: Harvard University Press, 1983), 137.

97. Kristeller, 60–63.

98. John G. Burke, "Hermetism as a Renaissance World View," in *The Darker Vision of the Renaissance: Beyond the Fields of Reason,* ed. Robert Kinsman (Berkeley: University of California Press, 1974), 95.

99. William A. Covino, *Magic, Rhetoric and Literacy: An Eccentric History of the Composing Imagination* (Albany: State University of New York Press, 1994), 19.

100. John G. Burke, 102.

101. Kristeller, 129.

102. Pico, *Oration on the Dignity of Man.* Quoted in Anthony Grafton, "Humanism, Magic and Science," in *The Impact of Humanism on Western Europe,* eds. Anthony Goodman and Angus MacKay (London: Longman, 1990), 111.

103. Kennedy, 245.

104. James K. Cameron, "Humanism in the Low Countries," in *The Impact of Humanism on Western Europe,* 148.

105. Cameron, 30.

106. Cameron, 148.

107. Kennedy, 246.

108. Brian Vickers, *In Defense of Rhetoric* (Oxford: Oxford University Press, 1988), 182–183.

109. Vickers, 273.

110. Vickers, 271.

111. Garin, 19.

112. Michael Mooney, *Vico in the Tradition of Rhetoric* (Princeton, NJ: Princeton University Press, 1985), xii.

113. Donaworth, xxii.

114. Donaworth, xxiii.

115. Donaworth, xl.

116. Donaworth, xl.

117. For an excellent discussion of Agricola and his influence, see: Ong, chap. v.

118. George Kennedy, *Classical Rhetoric and Its Christian and Secular Tradition from Ancient to Modern Times* (Chapel Hill: University of North Carolina Press, 1980), 208–210.

119. Nauert, 104.

120. Kelley, 89.

121. Nauert, 104.

122. Nauert, 104.

123. Agricola, *De Inventione Dialectica* (Nieuwkoop, Netherlands: 1967), 192. Quoted in Mack, 86.

124. Ong, 104.

125. See: Peter Mack, *Renaissance Argument: Valla and Agricola in the Tradition of Rhetoric and Dialectic* (Leiden, Netherlands: E. J. Brill, 1993), chaps. VII and VIII.

126. Ong, 93.

127. Ong, 93.

128. Mack, 89.

129. Peter Ramus, *The Questions of Brutus* (1549) trans. Carole Newlands (Davis, CA: Hermagoras Press, 1992), 8.

130. Peter Ramus, *Rhetoricae Distinctiones in Quintilianum* (Arguments in Rhetoric against Quintilian) trans. Carole Newlands (1549; DeKalb, IL: Northern Illinois University Press, 1986), 84.

131. Ong, 49.

132. Cornelis Augustijn, *Erasmus: His Life, Works, and Influence,* trans. J. C. Grayson (Toronto: University of Toronto Press, 1991), 69.

133. Richard Lanham, *The Electronic Word: Democracy, Technology and the Arts* (Chicago: University of Chicago Press, 1993), 157–158.

134. See: Mack, chap. XVII. For another perspective on rhetoric in this period, see: Mark U. Edwards, Jr., *Printing, Propaganda, and Martin Luther* (Berkeley: University of California Press, 1994).

135. For a detailed discussion of English rhetorical works in the Renaissance, see: Arthur F. Kinney, *Humanist Poetics: Thought, Rhetoric, and Fiction in Sixteenth-Century England* (Amherst: University of Massachusetts Press, 1986).

136. Kennedy, 247.

CHAPTER EIGHT

ENLIGHTENMENT RHETORICS

All that can possibly be required of Language, is, to convey our ideas clearly to the minds of others, and, at the same time, in such a dress, as by pleasing and interesting them, shall most effectually strengthen the impressions which we seek to make.
—Hugh Blair

It is customary to locate the beginning of the "modern" age somewhere in the late seventeenth or early eighteenth century, the period known as the Enlightenment. If modernity involves questioning the received truths of Christian tradition, elevating rationality over other sources of truth, such as authority, seeking solutions to social problems by means of scientific method, and viewing the universe as governed by inviolable physical laws, then perhaps the intellectual developments in Europe in the late seventeenth and throughout the eighteenth centuries do mark a major transition in Western thought.

Several writers were particularly important in bringing about some of the changes that have traditionally been employed as markers of the modern period. Isaac Newton (1642–1727) described physical laws governing the universe in his *Principia Mathematica* (1687). John Locke (1632–1704) suggested an empirical basis of human knowing in his *Essay Concerning Human Understanding* (1690). David Hume's *Enquiry Concerning Human Understanding* (1748) explored the rational operations of the human mind. Jean-Jacques Rousseau (1712–1778) outlined a theory of government centered on the individual citizen in *The Social Contract* (1762). Francois Voltaire (1694–1778) subjected the bases of Christian belief to severe criticism in his *Dictionairre Philosophique* (1764) and several other works.

This chapter examines some developments in rhetorical theory during the eighteenth century, first on the European Continent, and then in Britain. The legacy of Renaissance Humanism is evident in writers like Giovanni Battista Vico in Italy. We will consider Vico's surprisingly modern theory of the rhetorical evolution of the human mind. Following our exploration of Vico, we will move from the European Continent to the British Isles to examine a variety of rhetorical theories that speculate about matters as disparate as psychology, argument, preaching, style, the beneficial use of leisure time, and even correcting a telltale Irish accent.

It has been noted by some scholars that the eighteenth century marks a period in which rhetorical theory turned away from its traditional concern for the invention of arguments, and toward aesthetic matters of style and good delivery. One leading expert on the period, Barbara Warnick, suggests that this shift in emphasis reflects the influence of Ramus in the sixteenth century and Descartes in the seventeenth. Both writers moved argument and proof out of the domain of rhetoric and into the domains of logic, dialectic, and mathematics. Warnick writes, "by the late seventeenth century, rhetorical logic had been displaced...." The result was the emergence of what Warnick calls a "managerial" emphasis in rhetorical studies. "During the Enlightenment, French and Scottish rhetorics turned to a managerial view of rhetoric that distinguished the discovery of knowledge through reasoning from communication of content to others." That is, in earlier periods, rhetoric had performed both functions—discovery and communication of knowledge. Eighteenth century writers often seem content to allow rhetoric only the latter responsibility. Warnick identifies a corresponding shift from rhetoric as guiding the *production* of discourse, to rhetoric as enhancing the *consumption* of discourse. "While concern for invention and the production of discourse receded, intense interest in the problem of receptive competence emerged to take its place."[1]

Though it would be an exaggeration to say that invention is completely excluded from rhetoric in eighteenth- and early nineteenth-century rhetorics, the truth of Warnick's observation often is born out in the rhetorical scholarship of this period. In the discussions that follow, note the emphasis on matters such as style, taste, delivery, and the imagination, as contrasted to earlier emphasis in rhetorical scholarship on arguments, proofs, invention, and reason. At the same time, we might also note in this period a shift from an earlier concern for rhetoric's public role as the *techne* of civil discourse and community business to a more private interest in rhetoric as a window on the human mind or a means of personal refinement.

VICO ON RHETORIC AND HUMAN THOUGHT

Among the later writers in the Italian Humanist tradition, the most important is Giambattista Vico. Vico was an Italian philosopher born in Naples in 1668.[2] Vico's father was a bookseller, and he spent a great deal of time reading as a youth. Lawyers held a prominent place in the Naples of the late seventeenth century, and Vico studied originally for a career in law. However, his interests eventually turned toward literature, history, mathematics, philosophy, and rhetoric. Something of a recluse, Vico spent long hours alone teaching himself philosophy, law, and literature. He was particularly drawn to the logical works of Peter of Spain, the speculative theology of John Duns Scotus, and the political theories and metaphysics of the Spanish writer, Francisco Suarez. Vico studied Plato, and was intrigued with the Neoplatonism of his Renaissance predecessors, Pico and Ficino.

Vico versus Descartes

Vico wrote passionately in response to the great philosopher and mathematician René Descartes, who despised rhetoric and wished to relegate it to an obscure place in the academy. In works such as *On the Study Methods of Our Time* (1708), Vico argued that the mathematical proofs of Descartes were just as reliant on symbols as were the orations of the rhetoricians. In other words, mathematics was not somehow founded on transcendent, necessary, and unchanging truths. Nevertheless, the idea that science would provide a rational basis for future societies was gaining influence, and Vico sought to answer what he viewed as a dangerous cultural development.

The study, and especially the practice, of rhetoric provided the only antidote to the broadening influence of scientific rationalism. Vico argued that rhetoric, not reason, was the basis of social life, and that the growing hegemony of scientific thinking threatened to undermine the common beliefs and values—the *sensus communis*—that provide the basis for society. Speech, especially poetic speech, provides the foundation of civilized society, not philosophical or scientific reason.

Vico's fear of the dominance of science, with its emphasis on individual reason as opposed to the common sense of the community, cannot be overstated. Descartes was his *bête noire,* and he argued strenuously that only the constructive and communal use of rhetoric provided the means of opposing the corrosive effects of the individual and sceptical use of reason advocated by Descartes.

The Rhetoric of the Imagination

Though he greatly admired the philosophy of Descartes, Vico sought answers about the nature of human thought in two unusual places—poetry and mythology. This odd approach placed him beyond the pale of Neapolitan intellectual life. Vico was seen as an eccentric and a dreamer, and his thinking was "dismissed as obscure, speculative, and unsound (*stravagante,* as the Italians put it), or even slightly mad."[3] Vico inherited much from the Italian Humanists, in whose wisdom he was schooled, but he lived too late to be considered a Renaissance figure. Though he lived during the early Enlightenment, "he was not a typical man of the Enlightenment, looking down on earlier ages as times of 'darkness' and irrationality."[4] Vico was as original in his thought as he is difficult to classify historically.

In 1697 Vico became a professor of rhetoric at Naples, a position he held for forty years. A poet himself, he held that "primitive men were necessarily poets because they possessed strong imaginations which compensated for the weakness of their reason."[5] Vico argued that language originated with rhetorical devices native to the human imagination, and maintained that language allowed people to impose order on their existence, to create meaning out of meaninglessness, and to establish society. Vico's philosophy, then, focused on human history rather than on metaphysics.[6] As Ernesto Grassi points out, for Vico "the problems that concern human beings—and these are the only kinds that can have scientific interest—are the ones that urge themselves upon us in the construction of the human world and therefore concern the realization of man as such."[7]

Pursuing this interest in human history, Vico argued in works such as his *New Science* (1725) that historical method could be just as exact as mathematics. In advancing this thesis, Vico was opposing the views of Descartes, who had affirmed that the only certain knowledge was that which could not be doubted.[8] Decisions in public life, Vico noted, were not usually based on certainties, but rather on careful weighing of options guided by prudence, or practical judgment. Vico was drawn, then, to Cicero's notion of the *perfectus orator,* or, as Michael Mooney summarizes the concept, "the 'finished orator' as a public servant whose ability with words is informed by a command of the whole cycle of learning."[9] Such a person, guided by the union of wisdom and eloquence, could provide practical and moral leadership to the society. The orator became a heroic figure, one who spoke or wrote wisely and eloquently for the benefit of the whole society. The common good was predominant in humanist thinking, and the skilled orator had greater potential for contributing to that common good than did any other citizen.

Vico held that rhetoric was essential to all of the arts and all human ways of making sense of the world. By means of language, humans have imposed order on a fundamentally disordered nature. The "humanization of nature" takes place, not through rational or inferential thought, but rather through *ingenium,* or the innate human capacity to grasp similarities or relationships. The person of practical judgment must be able to "find analogies between matters that lie far apart and are apparently unrelated...."[10] Grassi writes, "insight into relationships is not possible through a process of inference, but rather only through an original *in*-sight as invention and discovery (*inventio*)."[11]

Vico held that this innate human capacity for recognizing or grasping similarities among different objects was central to the poetic or metaphoric nature of thought. Analogic thinking allowed insights that were crucial to the ordering and humanizing of the world. Discovering "connections, and so advancing the cause of civil life, is the proper work of ingenuity [*ingenium*]."[12] Through the exercise of *ingenium,* "we surpass what lies before us in our sensory awareness."[13] And, in the act of transcending perception, we become human. The language of metaphor and poetry "is the language that constitutes humanity."[14]

Rhetoric and the Evolution of Human Thought

Thinking based on *ingenium* is more poetic than logical, more intuitive than rational, and arrives at insights rather than deductions. Such thinking is therefore actually productive of new knowledge, and not merely of reformulations of things already known. Vico, as we have noted, found direction for the development of this theory in Cicero and the rhetorical tradition rather than in the philosophers and logicians of the seventeenth and eighteenth centuries. Descartes, Vico thought, had ignored the vital rhetorical element in human thinking by focusing his attention solely on the method of demonstrable proof that moved by deduction from first principles to necessary conclusions.

Like other rhetorical theorists, Vico recognized the need for education in the arts of practical decision making about matters that did not yield to scientific analysis, issues like law, art, ethics, and politics. Human social life is lived in public space where most decisions are "contingent" or subject to various resolutions. Deductive logic is of limited use for such moral decision making, while rhetoric with its more flexible and practical characteristics, is essential.

Vico was "fascinated by the processes through which the human mind learns."[15] In an effort to understand these processes, he advanced an intriguing theory of the relationship among language, thought, and experience based on four tropes, or rhetorical devices. Mooney explains the problem with which Vico started in developing this theory: "Given the richness of nature, every language lacks words to make note of certain items of experience."[16] Thus, existing words must be imaginatively employed to allow both new modes of thinking and a broader range of expression. Tropes developed to make up for the lack of capacity in words alone. Thus, the first people "proceeded to create their world through the faculty of imagination rather than by pure abstract thought."[17] As Katherine Gilbert and Helmut Kuhn express the concept, "the poet's imagination is the natural expression of humanity's childhood."[18] It will be helpful to examine this intriguing concept in greater detail.

Vico was fascinated with early human cultures, and speculated about the evolution of language and human thought. His theory of the development of thought has been called "incomparably richer and more fully developed" than those advanced by other scholars of his generation.[19] Vico posited that during "the childhood of the world," human thinking developed first by metaphor, or a comparison of things not apparently similar. Early poets, for instance, their thought richly imaginative, compared objects to people. They thus anthropomorphized nature by attributing to inanimate objects human qualities, such as emotion. The tendency to compare dissimilar things was, according to Vico, native to the human mind and a necessary imaginative precursor to more systematic or rational thought.

Vico called the metaphorical tendency of early human poets the "poetic mode of thought."[20] He related the capacity for discovering metaphorical connections directly to "rhetorical 'wordplay', or 'wit' [*acutezza*]," also defined as acuteness or mental sharpness.[21] The notion of *acutezza* was central to sixteenth and seventeenth century humanistic writing, and was best displayed in clever metaphors. Such rhetorical devices "can only come from an alert, imaginative mind, one with a well-honed facility for seeing connections between separate and apparently unrelated things."[22] Thus, facility with words of the type taught in the rhetorical tradition was an aid to creative thought.[23]

But Vico also urged that study of the traditional *topoi* of the classical rhetoricians contributes to quick and decisive thinking. Thus, he "sought to revive the 'art of topics,'" that is, he advocated study of the topical systems of classical rhetoric.[24] He was particularly interested in the *stasis* systems of Quintilian and Cicero, built on a juridical model, that considered issues such as fact and definition. Vico's *Institutes of Oratory* (1711), the title itself drawn from that of Quintilian's *magnum opus*, treats these matters in detail. In short, Vico saw no better preparation for an active mind, one exhibiting the brilliance of *acutezza*, than the study of rhetoric.

From metaphor, "the primary operation of our mind," human thought progressed to metonym, the substitution of a part for the whole, an agent for an act, or of a sign for the thing signified. From *metonym*, thought, language, and literature moved to synecdoche, in which the whole object represents the part. Vico's final stage of linguistic development is irony, in which indirect statement carries direct meaning, or something is taken to stand for its opposite.[25]

Thus, for Vico, the "sense-making" capacity that allowed human beings to create civilization out of disordered nature was exhibited in the imaginative fantasies of poets and storytellers rather than in the premises of philosophers or the deductions of logicians. In this way he reveals the influence of earlier Humanists. Vico writes that "fantasy collects from the senses and connects and enlarges to exaggeration the sensory effects of natural appearances and makes luminous images from them."[26] That is, the imagination—guided naturally by rhetorical tropes—expands on the data of sense impressions and makes a distinctly *human* life possible. As the great French historian Paul Hazzard wrote, "If only Italy had listened to Giambattista Vico…our eighteenth century ancestors…would not have believed that reason was our first faculty, but on the contrary that imagination was."[27]

BRITISH RHETORICS IN
THE EIGHTEENTH CENTURY

We will begin our study of rhetoric in eighteenth-century Britain in the same place we have begun our discussion of rhetoric in other historical periods, with educational practice. Wilbur Samuel Howell writes that rhetoric was viewed in the eighteenth century as the means of transmitting knowledge from the learned to the general populace. Once established as the "master of the arts of popular discourse," rhetoric eventually staked a claim to being "the sole art of communication by means of language…."[28] As such, rhetoric became particularly important to influential British educational movements in the eighteenth century. But, as we shall see, rhetorical concerns also were at the heart of philosophical and psychological thinking in this period. It is perhaps appropriate to note that though the theories that follow are often labeled "British" rhetorical theories, most of the thinkers described are Scottish, and one Irish. Thus, British should not be taken to mean English when applied to eighteenth-century rhetorical theory.

Rhetoric in British Education

British education in rhetoric was pursued during the eighteenth century with various goals in view, and in response to pressing social changes. Replying to rising skepticism in Britain, writers within the Churches of England and Scotland pressed rhetoric into the service of Christian apologetic, preaching, and writing. In addition, writing and reading of English prose began to assume a new prominence during the century as British culture shifted increasingly from oral to written discourse.[29] Thus, the narrow conception of rhetoric as the study of speechmaking and argumentation was challenged, though the older view had its advocates as well.[30]

Other changes taking place in eighteenth-century England assisted rhetoric's rise to prominence in education. English was displacing Latin as the language of scholarship, which allowed access to learning to a vastly increased number of British subjects. When Adam Smith began to lecture on rhetoric in 1748, "it was largely in response to a growing need for a comprehensive, thoroughly modern treatment of English and its uses...."[31] Moreover, women were being admitted to the British universities in larger numbers during this period.[32] Finally, urbanization was bringing people from the English countryside, from Scotland, and from Ireland to urban centers such as London. Many of these new city dwellers recognized that their rustic accents limited the possibility for personal advancement in the bigger cities. The corrective they sought was education in "proper" diction, which was an element of rhetorical education. Thus, education in rhetoric was sought out by an increasingly broad cross-section of the British public during the century.

The Emerging Public, and a Changing View of Rhetoric

The idea of "the public" needs to be emphasized, for during the eighteenth century a modern sense of both the public and the public domain were taking shape in Britain and Europe. Ordinary people could speak and write their opinions in a variety of new venues, and they could engage one another's ideas in a variety of settings. Whether in the public square, the meeting hall, the coffeehouse, or the newly popular periodicals of the day, citizen addressed citizen on a range of religious and political issues.

As a result of the expanding public domain and increasingly rhetorical public, a new understanding of rhetoric and oratorical skill gradually took hold as well. One ancient model that focused on winning a debate by any means available was losing ground. A new model that saw rhetoric as an important skill of public life was developing. Kenneth Cmiel writes that the Scottish rhetorical theorists of this period—George Campbell, Adam Smith, and others—"eschewed the manipulative goals of the Ciceronians. They argued that rhetoric should teach how to forcefully communicate one's reasoned arguments."[33]

For a variety of reasons, then, rhetoric occupied a central place in British education in the eighteenth century. Winifred Horner notes that the potential for upward mobility in English society, a mobility dependent on a command of "good English," meant that there was a strong demand for language instruction, particularly instruction in writing.[34] The rise of British nationalism in this period also encouraged instruction in English. Moreover, many Scottish and English educators were members of the clergy, and "education was understandably closely connected with religion."[35] The strong emphasis on education in rhetoric spawned a variety of educational movements during the eighteenth and early nineteenth centuries.

THE ELOCUTIONARY MOVEMENT

Rhetoric has always been viewed, as we have noted at several points, as a means of personal advancement through the trained capacity to express one's views effectively, particularly in public settings. Throughout Western history, rhetoric has also functioned as a path to personal refinement and an avenue into polite social circles. The elocutionary movement of the eighteenth and nineteenth centuries draws our attention specifically to the performance side of rhetoric, and to rhetoric's use as a method for refining the public manners, poise, and expressiveness of men and women.[36]

Eighteenth-century British society was relatively open for an individual's social advancement if we compare it with other European societies of the time. Coffeehouses, lodges, freethinking clubs, and debating societies attracted individuals from a striking mix of social classes. Women often participated in these public settings as well. Though class distinctions were still rather rigid, social movement was possible, particularly if one applied oneself to personal improvement. No improvement was more important than that of one's speech. Speech marked one as belonging to a particular social class. The goal of the aspiring young urbanite, then, was to speak like a gentleman or a lady.

Moreover, an increasing number of professions—law, politics, and religion in particular—demanded skill as a public speaker. Again, demand for instruction in this highly practical art grew. We might add that famous English essayists of the day, such as Richard Steele, Joseph Addison, and Jonathan Swift, had written critically of the quality of both speaking and writing in England. Such criticism lent some urgency to the search for instruction in proper and effective management of language. English education was simply not preparing students to explore and refine the great potential in the English tongue for eloquent expression.

Thomas Sheridan

As is so often the case, rhetoric answered a strongly felt social need in the second half of the eighteenth century. Thomas Sheridan (1719–1788), an Irish actor and educator, sought to provide the ready student with a guide to proper and effective public speaking. In fact, he sought nothing less than a general reform of education in Britain so as to correct what he took to be a very serious development—the neglect of elocution or rhetorical delivery. In *British Education* (1756), Sheridan wrote that poor preaching was actually threatening the health of religion.

So deep was Sheridan's belief in the beneficial effects of powerful public speaking that he maintained the study of elocution would, in the words of G. P. Mohrmann, "improve religion, morality, and constitutional government; would undergird a refining of the language, and would pave the way for ultimate perfection in all the arts."[37] Sheridan wrote in *British Education* that oratory in the pulpit "must either effectually support religion against all opposition, or be the principal means of it's [sic] destruction."[38]

The Importance of Delivery. Good delivery was intimately connected with convincing an audience of the urgency and truthfulness of one's message. "Before you can persuade a man into any opinion, he must first be convinced that you believe it yourself. This he can never be, unless the tones of voice in which you speak come from the heart, accompanied by corresponding looks, and gestures, which naturally result from a man who speaks in earnest."[39]

Sheridan's deep concern about the poor quality of preaching in England is reflected in the following passage from his *A Discourse Introductory to a Course of Lectures* (1759):

[A] man shall rise up in a public assembly, and, without the least mark of shame, deliver a discourse to many hundred auditors, in such disagreeable tones and unharmonious cadences, as to disgust every ear; and with such improper and false use of emphasis, as to conceal or pervert the sense; and all without fear of any consequential disgrace.... [And] this is done...in the very service of the Most High![40]

Sheridan's most famous work, *A Course of Lectures on Elocution,* was published in 1762.[41] This work was a compilation of lectures Sheridan had delivered at various sites around Great Britain. In *A Course of Lectures* he set out the principles of elocution as a rhetorical study and practice. Sheridan and other elocutionists emphasized delivery over the other traditional elements in the rhetorical art, such as invention or arrangement. Certainly training of the speaking voice was important to effective public presentations, as was the proper pronunciation of words.[42] In fact, assisting young men from Ireland and Scotland to speak like educated English people so as to aid their success was one goal of the elocutionary movement. But, as one might expect from an actor, Sheridan did not view delivery simply as a matter involving the voice. Rather, the face and the body came into play in his discussion of the art of speaking in public. In fact, the instructions offered by elocutionists regarding facial expression, gesture, posture, and movement strike modern readers as something closer to instruction in acting, or even in dance, than in speaking.

Elocutionism's emphasis on delivery, and its use of teaching techniques such as the dramatic presentation of a memorized speech, led to a decline in concern for the argumentative or inventional function of rhetoric. Thus, a price was paid in the reduction of rhetoric's esteem for the benefit that came to some individuals through the honing of their presentational skills. Wilbur Samuel Howell writes that "the practices which the elocutionists encouraged inevitably led to declamation without sincere conviction and earnest feeling, as students recited discourses devised and organized by somebody else."[43] Howell's summary statement is that elocutionism was a "strange movement" that turned out to be "futureless."[44] Perhaps this reminds us that rhetoric is not simply a matter of appealing style and forceful delivery. Rhetoric divorced from the study of arguments and evidence becomes the practice of linguistic ornament.

THE SCOTTISH SCHOOL

In his excellent study, *Democratic Eloquence: The Fight over Popular Speech in Nineteenth-Century America,* Kenneth Cmiel notes the significant influence of a group of Scottish rhetorical theorists in the eighteenth century. Members of this Scottish school of rhetoric include George Campbell, Hugh Blair, Adam Smith, and others. Their new rhetorics affected British conceptions of eloquence and argument, but also shaped the teaching of rhetoric in America. Cmiel writes with regard to the early United States that "the texts of the Scottish school swept into the nation's classrooms to replace (or at least balance) the Ciceronian rhetoric used earlier. In 1783 Brown University ordered Blair's *Rhetoric* from England; in 1784 the first American edition was published." The following sections explore the new and rather different approaches to rhetoric of three Scottish theorists that were having such an impact on rhetorical education and practice.[45]

The Belletristic Movement: Kames and Blair

During the eighteenth century, British interest in literature and writing expanded. Novels achieved a high degree of popularity, satisfying an increasing public desire to read for entertainment. Books were published that promised to help the would-be writer achieve clarity, grace, and beauty. Harold Harding has observed that "in the latter half of the eighteenth century more than fifty textbooks, essays, lectures, and treatises on rhetoric and literary criticism by thirty different writers were published in England, Ireland, and Scotland. Interest in literature and the teaching of writing ran high."[46] Barbara Warnick has traced the French roots of the Belletristic Movement in Britain, suggesting that this emphasis on rhetorical style is not native to the British Isles.[47] The study of belles lettres may, then, represent an eighteenth-century effect of Pierre Ramus' much earlier efforts to remove argument and invention from rhetoric.

The study of rhetoric both shaped and was shaped by this rapidly growing interest in literature, its structure, and its effects. A literary movement devoted to the advancement of what was termed *belles lettres* (beautiful letters or language) expanded rhetoric into a study of literature, literary criticism, and writing generally. Warnick writes "Belletristic rhetoric and studies of belles lettres were particularly concerned with examining the specific qualities of discourse and their effects."[48] This approach to rhetoric "focused on reception, not production."[49] This shift from rhetoric as the study of invention or "production" of arguments, to rhetoric as the study of *effects* on readers and listeners marks an important change of emphasis for rhetorical scholarship and education. The belletristic movement represents a change in rhetoric away from the classical emphasis on developing persuasive arguments for oral public discourse, and toward the educated reception or appreciation of written and spoken discourse.

Interest in *belles lettres* grew in the 1760s and 1770s, and was marked by an increased attention to matters of style as over against invention. Douglas Ehninger notes that "the rhetoric of belles lettres was given its classic and most influential expression in Hugh Blair's *Lectures on Rhetoric and Belles Lettres*" (1783). Other important writers and works in the movement include "William Barron's *Lectures on Belles Lettres and Logic* (London, 1806), and Alexander Jameison's *A Grammar of Rhetoric and Polite Literature* (London, 1818)." Ehninger adds that "in Lord Kame's *Elements of Criticism* (Edinburgh, 1762), some 500 pages of a combined 'rhetoric and poetic' were embedded in an inquiry into the nature of beauty and the foundations of taste."[50] We will take a closer look at the work of two of these writers, Lord Kames and Hugh Blair.

Lord Kames.   As rhetoric became more closely aligned with aesthetics, questions of taste and decorum became central to rhetorical theorizing. Some rhetorical theorists such as Henry Home (1696–1782), better known by his title, Lord Kames, returned to ancient principles like sublimity in their search for an aesthetic theory suited to a new era in British literature. Kames was a Scottish philosopher and lawyer whose interests also turned to matters of literary style and aesthetics. Following the Roman writer Longinus, Kames urged in his *The Elements of Criticism*

(1762) that the quality of sublimity was conveyed by "grand" or enormous objects such as a large tree, a high cliff, or an ocean. The emotion or state of mind experienced when in the presence of such an object could be approximated in writing that attended to such aesthetic concerns. Thus, Kames notes that Shakespeare achieved this effect in his play, *Julius Caesar:*

> The pleasant emotion raised by large objects, has not escaped the poets:
>
> —*He doth bestride the narrow world*
> *Like a Colossus; and we petty men*
> *Walk under his huge legs.*
>
> *Julius Caesar, Act I, Sc. 3.*[51]

Kames also devotes a great deal of attention in the second chapter of *The Elements of Criticism* to the matter of arousing emotions, particularly through an appeal to the reader's sense of beauty. Kames pursued the notion of verbal beauty to the point of exploring the effects that the various spoken sounds have on hearers. For example, he writes with great specificity about the effects of sounds in particular words and word combinations:

> In the first place, syllables in immediate succession, pronounced each of them with the same or nearly the same aperture of the mouth, produce a succession of weak and feeble sounds; witness the French words *dit-il, pathetique:* on the other hand, a syllable of the greatest aperture succeeding one of the smallest, on the contrary, makes a succession which, because of its remarkable disagreeableness, is distinguished by a proper name, *hiatus.* The most agreeable succession is, where the cavity is increased and diminished alternately within moderate limits. Examples, *alternative, longevity, pusillanimous.*[52]

Like others in the Belletristic Movement, Kames was intrigued with the notion of "taste." Taste, or the ability to recognize and appreciate high quality in literature and other art, was in Kames's view a largely natural quality of some individuals. One would not search for taste among "those who depend for food on bodily labor," for example. If this sounds like an elitist idea, it is. Kames envisioned a refined society of individuals capable of appreciating the finer artistic achievements in literature and art. Such individuals were born, not made, though inborn capacities could be refined through proper education. As Warnick writes, "in Kames' theory is manifest an elitism that lies just below the surface of Scottish views on taste but is rarely openly articulated."[53]

Kames' interests point up again that rhetoric and a concern for written and spoken style are difficult to separate. Aristotle devoted his last book in *Rhetoric* to a consideration of stylistic matters. Moreover, at times in the history of rhetoric, matters of style become rhetoric's principal focus. Recall the Sophist Gorgias' efforts to discover a style of writing and speaking that would allow him to manipulate his audiences, to become a *psychagogos.* Kames' desire to understand the mechanisms by which speech affects thought and emotion is not far removed as a matter of inquiry, though it may be far removed in motive.

Hugh Blair.   Hugh Blair (1718–1800) was a Scottish preacher, born and educated in Edinburgh, who made important contributions to the Belletristic Movement. A famous Presbyterian preacher, in 1762 Blair was appointed to the Regius Chair of Rhetoric and Belles Lettres at the University of Edinburgh. In 1783 he published his most famous work, the *Lectures on Rhetoric and Belles Lettres*. This work was widely read in England and abroad, and went through numerous editions. Blair was a student of English literature, and an editor of Shakespeare's works. Style, taste, beauty, and decorum are central to Blair's rhetorical theory, as they were to that of Kames. And, like Kames, Blair returns to several ancient rhetoricians for ideas—writers like Aristotle, Cicero, Longinus, and Quintilian.

It is probably not an exaggeration to say that Blair wrote his *Lectures* with the goal in mind of improving the lives of his students. Much as Cicero's "perfect orator" was a person of eloquence, wisdom, grace, charm, and wit, so Blair's students developed the qualities of taste, eloquence, critical acumen, and style. Rhetoric's educational goals, then, are broader than simple preparation for professional success through making effective speeches. Rhetorical training is preparation for living the good life, the life that combines graceful and effective expression in the public sphere with contemplation and enhanced aesthetic experience in the private. However, Cicero's *perfectus orator* is a dynamic public figure employing extraordinary rhetorical skill for the greater good of society. Blair's is a more parochial, even private model—the individual citizen pursuing personal grace, leisure enjoyment, and social advancement. Much of Blair's work strikes a contemporary reader as arcane, but there is an unmistakable sincerity of conviction about the goals of education that probably should not be quickly dismissed.

As rhetorical interests grew from strictly spoken discourse to include written, a corresponding shift occurred in the perceived domain of rhetoric. Rhetoric was no longer seen as an art pertinent only to public affairs. Rhetoric was becoming part of private life as well.

Taste and Style.   This shift from public to private worlds is evident in Blair's references to the notion of taste, a developed appreciation of aesthetic experiences. Though taste is in part a matter of "natural sensibility to beauty," Blair is convinced that this capacity can be improved through experience and education.[54] Thus, Blair urges on his readers the development of their capacity for taste toward the enhancement of their private lives, their lives beyond work. "The cultivation of taste is farther recommended, by the happy effects which it naturally tends to produce in human life," writes Blair, especially in one's private life. People who live "in the most active sphere" of public life, "cannot be always occupied by business," he argues. Moreover, persons "of serious professions cannot always be on the stretch of serious thought," that is, cannot always devote their mental energies to serious topics and demanding problems. Thus, the development of taste, which enhances the enjoyment of diversions such as literature, is recommended to Blair's students as a means balancing the demands of work and the public sphere, with the retreat and enjoyments of private life.

Blair defines style as "the peculiar manner in which a man expresses his conceptions, by means of language."[55] Thus, style is for Blair a very broad category of concern. Moreover, style is related to one's "manner of thinking." Thus, "when we are examining an author's composition, it is, in many cases, extremely difficulty to separate the Style from the sentiment."[56] Blair was apparently of the opinion, then, that one's style—one's manner of linguistic expression—provided evidence of how one thought.

There are only two considerations to which the critic or student of style should attend. Blair calls these "perspicuity and ornament." "For," he writes, "all that can possibly be required of Language, is, to convey our ideas clearly to the minds of others, and, at the same time, in such a dress, as by pleasing and interesting them, shall most effectually strengthen the impressions which we seek to make."[57] Practical matters, then, are at the heart of the study of style for Blair. Rhetoric seeks to make a point persuasively. Thus, rhetorical style must attract an audience and present a case clearly. This is not bad advice to any writer or speaker, and Blair spends a good deal of time trying to explain how to make language both attractive and clear.

Of perspicuity, or clarity, Blair writes that there is no concern more central to style. After all, if clarity is lacking in a message, all is lost. Claiming that your subject is difficult is no excuse for lack of clarity according to Blair: if you can't explain a difficult subject clearly, you probably don't understand it.[58] Blair's advice on clarity includes selecting precisely the right terms to make your point, avoiding "obsolete or new-coined words," and always speaking in a manner appropriate to your audience and your subject. Much of Blair's counsel to his young readers includes such reminders as "any words, which do not add some importance to the meaning of a Sentence, always spoil it."[59] This is still good advice.

George Campbell

Some British Enlightenment rhetoricians developed new approaches to rhetoric out of a curiosity about what rhetoric revealed about the human mind. The world of the mind was beginning to be mapped using new philosophical approaches, and rhetoric was seen by some as a means of expanding our understanding of human thought itself. John Locke's psychological speculations were highly influential in scholarly circles early in the eighteenth century, while David Hume's discussion of the nature of human thought, in his *Enquiries* (1748), dominated philosophical and psychological scholarship during the second half of the century.

George Campbell (1719–1796) was one of the most important rhetorical theorists of the late eighteenth century.[60] Like several other influential English-speaking philosophers and rhetorical theorists of his day, Campbell was Scottish. Scotland's university cities—Edinburgh, Glasgow, and Aberdeen—were sites of great intellectual activity in the eighteenth century. Campbell was born in Aberdeen, where he received his early education. Later, he attended Marischal College in Aberdeen, where he studied law. His interests, however, turned toward theology, and he pursued a course of studies to prepare himself to be a minister. In 1748 he was ordained to the clergy of the Church of Scotland. In 1758 he was appointed principal of Marischal College, and later, in 1771, he was elevated to the important position of professor of Divinity at the same school. Campbell was a practicing religious polemicist who entered late into the great Deist controversy. His famous *Dissertation on Miracles* (1762) was a response to David Hume's argument against miracles. Campbell's most important work in rhetoric was his *The Philosophy of Rhetoric,* published in 1776.[61] Another important work related to rhetoric was his *Lectures on Pulpit Eloquence.*

A Scientific Rhetoric. As we have already noted, much of Campbell's work on rhetoric incorporates British philosophical thought of the seventeenth and eighteenth centuries.[62] Campbell's writing reveals the influence both of those philosophers with whom he agreed on various matters, and those with whom he took issue, especially Hobbes. Though he disagreed sharply with David Hume on a number of issues, Campbell admitted a great debt to the philosopher. In fact, the leading authority of Campbell's work, Lloyd Bitzer, writes that "Campbell's philosophy and his theory of human nature, both of which profoundly affect his treatment of rhetoric, are drawn mainly from Hume."[63] Campbell intended to offer a new rhetoric, one incorporating insights of the Enlightenment period. At the same time, he believed that he was building on the classical tradition in rhetoric by providing scientific support for classical insights. But he also hoped to move beyond those insights.

Rhetoric and philosophy were inseparably linked for Campbell, as the title of his work, *The Philosophy of Rhetoric,* suggests. Moreover, Campbell often tested his ideas on rhetoric by reading papers before the Aberdeen Philosophical Society, which he had helped to found. This Society also included thinkers such as Thomas Reid, James Beattie, and Alexander Gerard. Bitzer notes, however, that Hume "was the leading figure in the intellectual movement in which Campbell conceived and tested nearly the whole of his *The Philosophy of Rhetoric.*[64]

Campbell advanced a "scientific" rhetoric, but *science* for him meant something like what philosophy means today: an organized and rational account of a subject. "All art is founded on science," he writes in the introduction to *The Philosophy of Rhetoric,* but he counts as "the most sublime of all sciences" the studies of "*theology* and *ethics.*"[65] His rhetoric, then, reflects what were taken to be advances in fields such as ethics and psychology. "It was widely believed in the eighteenth century, even by defenders of the Ancients," writes George Kennedy, "that modern philosophy had made tremendous strides beyond the past."[66] Campbell thus sought, through new discoveries, to understand how the human mind operates and to provide instruction in eloquence based on that understanding.[67] His interest in applying new knowledge to the study of rhetoric also meant that the classical sources—Aristotle, Cicero, and Quintilian—became less important to rhetorical theory than they had been in the Middle Ages and Renaissance.[68]

Rhetoric and Psychology. Campbell connected eloquence to psychology. He defines eloquence as "that art or talent by which the discourse is adapted to its end."[69] Campbell's "theory of eloquence" was based on the belief that the mind is moved "only by those ideas it accepts as truthful and good."[70] Thus, as noted above, he sought a science of eloquence founded on the science of psychology. Campbell's rhetorical theory reflects the psychology current in Britain in the eighteenth century. Influenced by Locke, theorists divided up the mind into different capacities or "faculties."[71] In the faculty psychology view, the mind consisted of the understanding, the imagination, the passions, and the will.

For Campbell, each mental faculty spoke virtually its own language. For instance, the understanding spoke the language of logic, while the passion spoke the language of emotion. Each part also performed a distinct function. The understanding was informed and, when satisfied, responded with conviction. The imagination perceived beauty. The passions and will moved one toward action. Thus, each faculty has a part to play in the persuasive process. As he writes, "all the ends of speaking are reducible to four; every speech being intended to enlighten the understanding, to please the imagination, to move the passions, or to influence the will."[72] The relationship between eloquence and mental faculties was central to Campbell's thinking about rhetoric. "In both *The Philosophy of Rhetoric* and *Lectures on Pulpit Eloquence*," writes Barbara Warnick, "Campbell's principal aim was to describe how style and expression contributed to discourse's ability to appeal to the various faculties of its hearers."[73]

Two Types of Reasoning: Scientific and Moral.   Campbell discussed two types of reasoning that engage the faculty of the understanding: scientific and moral. Scientific reasoning, or the use of syllogistic logic, deals with demonstrable propositions of the type one encounters in mathematics and formal logic. It moves by demonstration from first principles or *axioms* to necessary conclusions or conclusions about which there can be no doubt.

But Campbell found syllogistic logic inappropriate to the kind of questions with which rhetoric typically deals. He was particularly concerned, then, with moral reasoning, by which he meant reasoning from evidence to more or less probable conclusions on practical issues.[74] We rely on moral reasoning in making practical decisions, and in most of the arenas of thought that make up daily life: politics, religion, economics. Certainty of the type sought in scientific reasoning is simply not possible given the nature of the questions and evidence with which moral reasoning typically deals, matters of faith and conduct, for instance. We reason from the available evidence to the best conclusions possible.

Campbell offers a treatment of evidence in Book I, Chapter V of *The Philosophy of Rhetoric*. His discussion takes in everything from consciousness and common sense to experience, analogy, testimony, and even statistics or "the calculation of chances."[75] In moral reasoning, there is often more than one side or case that can advance evidence in its support. A clash of views results, in a manner typical of rhetorical discourse.

A Theory of Persuasion.   One of Campbell's more famous contributions to the history of rhetoric is his theory of persuasion. As Howell explains, "[T]wo things must be done, he said, by an author who would persuade others." The first, according to Campbell, "is to excite some desire or passion in the hearers; the second is, to satisfy their judgment, that there is a connection between the action to which he would persuade them, and the gratification of the desire of passion which he excites."[76]

Campbell held persuasion to be a matter of addressing both the emotions and the reason, as people are not convinced without arguments and do not act except in response to emotions. "When persuasion is the end, passion [emotion] must be engaged," he writes.[77] Campbell explains the relationships between emotion and reason this way: "The former is effected by communicating lively and glowing ideas of the object; the latter…by presenting the best and most forcible arguments which the nature of the subject admits."[78] Thus, a speaker must know how to craft lively or "vivacious" images addressed to the passions and forceful arguments for the understanding.

Important to Campbell's thinking about persuasion was the notion of plausibility. A plausible discourse was instantly believable because of its close association with an audience's experience of their social world. As Warnick writes, "Plausibility went beyond the chronological sequencing of events in Campbell's theory.… He viewed it as arising from any description in which what was portrayed conformed to experience and expectation so as to appeal to the audience's imagination."[79] Plausibility was the feature in an orator's narration of events that corresponded to "probability" in the presentation of "sound arguments and the use of facts."[80] Thus, persuasion was a product of the probability of one's arguments, and the plausibility of one's narratives.

Education in Eloquence. Howell writes that "rhetoric and eloquence are synonymous terms with [Campbell]."[81] Thus, he was concerned that his students learn from the art of rhetoric both elocution—the ability to speak with grace, force, and clarity— and argumentation. They must know how to present a message clearly and attractively, as well how to defend a proposition with sound inference and solid evidence. Campbell's "Christian orator" had a more demanding task than did the political and judicial orators of ancient times. Why is this? Because "it is not a momentary but a permanent effect at which he aims…a thorough change of heart and disposition."[82] No demand on eloquence could be greater than "to persuade [a multitude] for the love of God, to be wise, and just and good."[83]

Of particular importance to achieving eloquence was the kind of descriptive language that would engage the imagination. Much of what we believe comes not through direct experience, but through a clear and convincing appeal to the imagination. Thus, rhetoric's appeal to imagination is crucial to persuasion. As Warnick writes, "Campbell…reminds his readers that oratory is, in a sense, painting, and that an orator must exhibit lively and glowing images of his subjects so as to bring his auditor's imaginations to the point where their representations will impress the mind as do the stimulations of sense and memory."[84] This capacity to affect the imagination is one sign of true eloquence.

Campbell's rhetoric had practical goals, and was tied most directly to the practical concerns of a public figure—the Christian minister. But any effective speaker, in Campbell's analysis, must understand both the human mind and the resources of language that can engage the mind so as to move the listener to action.

RICHARD WHATELY'S CLASSICAL RHETORIC

Despite the innovations of the Scottish school, more traditional rhetoric also survived into the nineteenth century. Richard Whately (1787–1863), an English cleric elevated to the office of Bishop of Dublin, eventually sat as a member of the House of Lords. Whately was educated at Oxford, where he taught for a time. Deeply interested in traditional logic and rhetoric, he was the author of essays, articles, and books on these topics. He argued against Campbell's rejection of syllogistic logic, contending that

Campbell misunderstood the complementary relationship of deductive and moral reasoning. Moral reasoning, Whately held, discovered the premises of arguments, while syllogistic logic provided a method for drawing conclusions from these premises, or evaluating the arguments of others.[85] "For Whately," writes Ray McKerrow, "the proper and sole role for logic was as an instrument for structuring and evaluating discourse."[86] Like Augustine, Whately was an active preacher and controversialist during much of his later life, and was a witty and even caustic polemicist. Thus, he did not only write about rhetoric, but practiced the art in a variety of public controversies.

An Ecclesiastic Rhetoric

Whately's *Elements of Rhetoric* appeared in 1828. In this important work, Whately advances what Douglas Ehninger has called "an ecclesiastical rhetoric."[87] That is, Whately's concern, one shared by other prominent rhetorical theorists of his day, was to write a treatise on the art of rhetoric that would assist both the preacher and the apologist or defender of Christianity. Rhetoric's practical and public nature is thus stressed in Whately's work, much as it had been by classical writers such as Cicero and Quintilian, and by the Renaissance humanists. But the particular role he assigns rhetoric may be more reminiscent of another ancient theorist.

Like Augustine, Whately sees rhetoric as the art as promoting and defending divine truth. Thus, rhetoric does not search for the best available truth under the circumstances, the goal of the Sophists. Nor does it reason from *doxa* or widely held opinions, as it had for Aristotle. Rather, Whately sought a systematic presentation of a practical art for expressing and defending the absolute truth handed down to humans by God in the revelation of the Bible. "With these ends in view," writes Ehninger, "Whately denies the probable or contingent nature of rhetoric."[88] Whately's theory, then, represents a break with one important emphasis of the classical tradition of Aristotle and Cicero: the tendency to see rhetoric as pursuing probable truths on debatable issues. If truth is absolute, rhetoric does not *determine* truth, though it may help to *discover* it. The view one takes of rhetoric's relationship to truth is, as we saw in the debate between Plato and the Sophists, crucial to the theory of rhetoric one accepts.

Whately on Argument

Unlike George Campbell, Whately is not particularly concerned with the larger philosophical and epistemological issues that lie at rhetoric's foundations. Whereas Campbell is concerned to understand how the mind works, Whately does not mention the issue at all. Whately's rhetoric is practical, and is particularly focused on issues of argument. In this respect, he retrieves a second emphasis of the classical tradition: the conception of rhetoric as centered on the inventional process of discovering persuasive arguments. Whately is best known for contributions such as his discussion of types of argument, like the analogy and debate principles, including presumption and burden of proof. Such issues arise out of the public practice of rhetoric as an art of argumentative disputation, and are concerns of the trained public pleader and advocate.

Analogy. One of Whately's most interesting contributions to the history of rhetoric is his discussion of analogy. Whately defines an analogy as an argument "in which the instance adduced is somewhat more remote from that to which it is applied." What does he mean by this? Whately's own example is instructive. If a physician determined that a certain substance was poisonous to human beings, this would have been learned by experience. If, however, the doctor moved to conclude that the same substance was also poisonous to animals, this conclusion would have been drawn by analogy rather than by experience.[89] Whately distinguishes this sort of direct comparison, which he terms *analogy,* from the more figurative sort of comparison that involves comparing things "that stand in similar relations to other things."[90]

Thus, following Whately's own example, an egg stands in a similar relation to a chicken as a seed stands to the plant that produced it. Both things—the seed and the egg—can produce a new member of the species that generated it. Whately finds the analogy between the body and the mind to be of the less direct, more figurative type. That is to say, the body and the mind are not literally alike, so that when we reason that, just as peoples' bodies are quite different, so must their minds be quite different, we are reasoning from an indirect or figurative analogy.

Always with the instruction of ministers in mind, Whately cautions his reader

> not to extend the Resemblance or Analogy further (*i.e.* to more particulars) than it does. The resemblance of a picture to the object it represents, is direct; but it extends no further than the one sense, of *Seeing,* is concerned. In the Parable of the unjust Steward, an Argument is drawn from Analogy, to recommend prudence and foresight to Christians in spiritual concerns; but it would be absurd to conclude that fraud was recommended to our imitation; and yet mistakes very similar to such a perversion of that Argument are by no means rare.[91]

In the parable Whately refers to, a household servant learns he is to be fired. He quickly gets his master's balance books and calls in all the people who owe the master money, and tells each one to pay a lower bill than the one recorded. In this way, the steward makes a few friends very quickly at a time when friends who feel a little indebted will soon be needed. Whately argues that the analogy employed in the story does *not* mean that Christians should be dishonest in their business dealings. Analogies may be misused and misinterpreted if we fail to see that only *some* of the similarities between the two cases, not all of them, are emphasized.

Presumption and Burden of Proof

Whately made traditional concepts of presumption and burden of proof relevant to a broad range of debates and controversies. He defines presumption as meaning a "pre-occupation of the ground, as implies that it must stand good till some sufficient reason is adduced against it."[92] That is to say, a proposition that has presumption is assumed true or reasonable until it is challenged in such a way as to raise a question about its truthfulness or reasonableness. The clearest example today is the presumption of innocence employed in our judicial system. What does it mean to say that you are "presumed innocent until proved guilty"? As Whately points out, it "does not, of course, mean that we are to *take for granted* he is innocent; for if that were the case, he would be entitled to immediate liberation." What it does mean is that the " 'burden of proof' lies with the accusers."[93] So what is the "burden of proof"?

Whately says that, in the example of the accused individual, being presumed innocent means that "he is not called on to prove his innocence, or to be dealt with as a criminal till he has done so." Thus, the burden of proof requires that the accuser cast a sufficient doubt on the accused's innocence that the accused must make an answer. Not until a reasonable person would find the evidence against the accused to be considerable has the burden of proof been satisfied. Satisfying the burden of proof does *not* mean "proving" anything. It does mean advancing evidence that, on its face (*prima facie*), raises a significant question about the accused's innocence.

Whately, as always, makes application of these principles for his readers. He cautions them not to try to prove "negative" propositions such as, "I'm not guilty." Imagine the difficulty of proving that something is *not* the case; you often end up raising more questions than you answer in such an enterprise. Let the other side answer the burden of proof as long as you enjoy presumption. Thus, with Christianity under attack, as it was in Whately's day, he thought it ill-advised to try to answer every doubt and question raised against it. Rather, Christianity enjoyed presumption, which meant that its opponents were required to raise a sufficient doubt about the religion before any defense at all was required. "Christianity *exists;* and those who deny the divine origin attributed to it, are bound to show some reasons for assigning to it a human origin; not indeed to prove that it *did* originate in this or that way, without supernatural aid; but to point out some conceivable way in which it *might* have so arisen."[94]

Whately moved the concepts of presumption and burden of proof out of the chambers of the Parliament, and made them part of public arguments about religion, justice, and politics. They have come to be important terms in both law and competitive debate. Thus, the affirmative side in a debate—the side challenging the *status quo*—must speak first in order to satisfy the burden of proof. The negative side enjoys the presumption in support of the *status quo,* and is not even required to answer until the affirmative has raised a sufficient doubt about the way things are done currently. Existing laws and institutions are also said to enjoy presumption, and if they are to be changed, the challengers have to do the work of satisfying the burden of proof before a public debate about their merits can begin.

George Kennedy calls Whately's *Elements of Rhetoric* "the last major treatment of rhetoric as a discipline in the classical tradition."[95] Rhetoric itself, Kennedy notes, "ceased to be a separate discipline in Britain and was studied, if at all, as a part of English composition" by the middle of the nineteenth century.[96] Whately's classical approach to a largely oral rhetoric was giving way to interest in writing and literary criticism.

CONCLUSION

Rhetorical scholarship in the eighteenth century reflects a wide range of concerns, from Vico's interests in the origins of human thought processes to Thomas Sheridan's search for a renewed sense of eloquence. Rhetoricians explored ancient themes, such as the importance of style to expression, the contributions of rhetorical training to personal refinement, and the standards of proof for arguments. But new territory was also being explored, as the scientific rhetoric of George Campbell illustrates.

The old order of European society makes way for a newer Anglo-American orientation in Western society during this period as well. Vico's theories hearken back to the Renaissance Humanists and eventually to Cicero and the Roman rhetoricians. On the other side of the Channel, Sheridan seeks to enhance the status of the English language and British institutions, Blair and Kames to heighten appreciation for British literature, Whately to strengthen the English Church, and Campbell to appropriate the insights of Scottish and English philosophy. Thus, a dominant concern for the British nation's development and welfare marks much of British rhetorical theory. Britain's status as a rising world empire seemed to demand the recognition of its language and institutions as equal in force to those of Europe. Even the advancement of British Protestantism required rhetorically skilled preachers.

This is not to say that the Enlightenment period represents a complete break with earlier rhetorical scholarship. George Campbell's "scientific" interest in the rhetoric of the human mind, with each faculty speaking its own language, is itself reminiscent of Plato's speculations about a complex *psyche* in which each part employs its own rhetoric. Recall that in *Phaedrus* Plato defines rhetoric as the "art of influencing the soul [*psyche:* mind] through words." Still, Campbell's treatment of rhetoric's relationship to the mind differs from Plato's in some important respects. Whately's treatment of rhetoric as centered on matters of argument is clearly rooted in a much older conception of rhetoric in which inventional concerns and skill in argument dominated, while the Belletristic Movement's interest in the power of beautiful language finds classical parallels in both Gorgias and Longinus.

Thus, the eighteenth century finds rhetoric again moved to the forefront of educational and scholarly concerns, a place it occupied many times during the course of Western history. But, as Warnick argues, in several important instances rhetoric's role shifts from producing public discourse to enhancing its consumption, from discovering knowledge to managing the discoveries of other disciplines, and from an external focus on public problems to an internal focus on the mind and imagination. Nevertheless, the wide range of ways in which rhetoric was discussed, the many concerns it was asked to address, and the energy that was expended in its discussion and dissemination, all suggest the relevance of an ancient discipline to an age in which discovery and change were hallmarks of intellectual life.

QUESTIONS FOR REVIEW

1. By what means did Vico think the mind ordered the world and made civilization possible?

2. What, according to Vico, was the human capacity of *ingenium*?

3. What were Vico's principal objections to the philosophy of Descartes?

4. What are some of the social forces that compelled British people to seek education in rhetoric during the eighteenth century?

5. What particular social developments in Britain alarmed Thomas Sheridan? What was his proposed solution?

6. What negative effects did Thomas Sheridan associate with the decline in British eloquence?

7. What were the goals of the Belletristic Movement? What effect did it have on the study of argument as a component of rhetoric?

8. Why was Hugh Blair concerned to develop the quality of taste in his students?

9. What theory of psychology influenced George Campbell's theory of rhetoric? How was this influence revealed in Campbell's theory?

10. What did Richard Whately hope to accomplish through teaching his students rhetoric?

QUESTIONS FOR DISCUSSION

1. The elocutionary movement of the eighteenth century offered training in rhetorical delivery as a means of personal refinement. Even though this particular idea may be foreign to contemporary education, are there ways in which an ability to speak clearly and effectively is still seen as a mark of personal success or social status?

2. What, for you, is the significance of style in speaking and writing? Is it important to clear communication? Is it an element in persuasion? If style is important to persuasion, should it be?

3. George Campbell built his rhetorical theory on a particular view of the human mind. We have seen something like this in the suggestions Plato made in *Phaedrus* about the nature of the human soul. What view of the human mind and its workings might a contemporary rhetorical theory reflect?

TERMS

Acutezza: Rhetorical wordplay or wit.

Axioms: Unquestioned first principles. The starting points of scientific reasoning.

Belletristic Movement: Rhetorical movement in the late eighteenth and early nineteenth centuries that emphasized considerations of style in rhetoric, expanding rhetoric into a study of literature, literary criticism, and writing generally.

Burden of proof: The responsibility to bring a case against the status quo sufficient to challenge its enjoyment of presumption.

Faculty psychology: The view that the mind consisted of "faculties" or capacities including the understanding, the imagination, the passions, and the will.

Ingenium: The innate human capacity to grasp similarities or relationships.

Irony: When indirect statement carries direct meaning, or something is taken to stand for its opposite.

Metaphor: A comparison of things not apparently similar.

Metonym: The substitution of a part for the whole.

Moral reasoning: Reasoning from evidence to more or less probable conclusions on practical issues; the kind of reasoning employed in rhetoric, and appropriate to issues such as those presented by politics, ethics, religion, and economics.

Plausibility: In Campbell's theory, discourse that is instantly believable because of its close association with an audience's experience of their social world.

Presumption: A "*pre-occupation* of the ground," in Whately's terms. An idea occupies its place as reasonable or acceptable until adequately challenged.

Prudence: Practical judgment.

Scientific reasoning: Reasoning that moves from axioms to indubitable conclusions. Syllogistic logic.

Sensus Communis: Common beliefs and values that provide the basis for society.

Synecdoche: The whole object represents the part.

Taste: In Kames and Blair, a developed appreciation of aesthetic experiences.

Tropes: Rhetorical devices.

ENDNOTES

1. Barbara Warnick, *The Sixth Canon: Belletristic Rhetorical Theory and Its French Antecedents* (Columbia: University of South Carolina Press, 1993), 129.

2. On Vico's life and relationship to rhetoric, see: Michael Mooney, *Vico in the Tradition of Rhetoric* (Princeton: Princeton University Press, 1985).

3. Peter Burke, *Vico* (Oxford: Oxford University Press, 1985), 2.

4. Burke, 55.

5. Burke, 3.

6. Ernesto Grassi, *Rhetoric as Philosophy* (University Park, PA: Pennsylvania State Press, 1980), 5.

7. Grassi, 6.

8. Mooney, 126.

9. Mooney, 8–9.

10. Mooney, 127.

11. Grassi, 7.

12. Mooney, 135.

13. Grassi, 8.

14. Mooney, 29.

15. Alessandro Giulani, "Vico's Rhetorical Philosophy and the New Rhetoric," in *Giambattista Vico's Science of Humanity,* eds. G. Tagliacozzo and D. P. Verene (Baltimore, MD: Johns Hopkins Press, 1976), 33.

16. Mooney, 79.

17. Richard Manson, *The Theory of Knowledge of Giambattista Vico* (n.p.: Archon Books, 1969), 35.

18. Katherine E. Gilbert and Helmut Kuhn, *A History of Esthetics* (Bloomington, IN: University of Indiana Press, 1953), 268. Quoted in Willson Havelock Coates, *The Emergence of Liberal Humanism* (New York: McGraw-Hill, 1966), 219.

19. Burke, 53.

20. Burke, 53.

21. Joseph Mali, *The Rehabilitation of Myth: Vico's "New Science"* (Cambridge: Cambridge University Press, 1992), 183; Mooney, 66.

22. Mooney, 66.

23. Mali, 183.

24. Mali, 184.

25. Mali, 167.

26. Vico, "Orazione in Morte di Donna Angela Cimmino Marchesa di Petrella," *Opere di G. B. Vico,* ed. Fausto Nicolini, 8 vols. in 11 (Rome: Bari Laterza, 1911–1914), 7:170. Quoted in Grassi, 7.

27. Paul Hazzard, *La Pensée Européenne au XVIIIe siécle de Montesquieu á Lessing* (Paris: Arthone Fayard, 1963), 43. Quoted in editor's introduction to Giambattista Vico, *On Humanistic Education: Six Inaugural Orations, 1699–1707,* ed. Donald Phillip Verene, trans. G. A. Pinton and A. W. Shippe (Ithaca, NY: Cornell University Press, 1993), 2–3.

28. Wilbur Samuel Howell, *Eighteenth-Century British Logic and Rhetoric* (Princeton, NJ: Princeton University Press, 1971), 6.

29. Winifred Bryan Horner, "Writing Instruction in Great Britain: Eighteenth and Nineteenth Centuries," in *A Short History of Writing Instruction,* ed. James J. Murphy (Davis, CA: Hermagoras Press, 1990), 124–125.

30. Stephen H. Browne, "Shandyean Satire and the Rhetorical Arts in Eighteenth-Century England," *Southern Communication Journal* 55 (Winter 1990): 191–205.

31. Warnick, 66. Warnick cites Richard Sher on this point.

32. Horner, 136–137.

33. Kenneth Cmiel, *Democratic Eloquence: The Fight over Popular Speech in Nineteenth-Century America* (New York: William Morrow, 1990), 36.

34. Horner, 121–150.

35. Horner, 123.

36. See: Howell, 145–256.

37. G. P. Mohrmann, introduction to Thomas Sheridan, *A Discourse Being Introductory to His Course of Lectures on Elocution and the English Language* (1759; rpt. Los Angeles: Augustan Reprint Society, 1969), ii.

38. Quoted in Howell, 155.

39. Quoted in Howell, 156.

40. Sheridan, *A Discourse,* 25–26.

41. Thomas Sheridan, *A Course of Lectures on Elocution* (London: 1762). On Sheridan's work, see: Wallace A. Bacon, "The Elocutionary Career of Thomas Sheridan," *Speech Monographs* 31 (March 1964): 1–53.

42. Thomas Sheridan, *A General Dictionary of the English Language* (London: J. Dodsley: 1780). This work was published to provide a guide to proper pronunciation of English words.

43. Howell, 145.

44. Howell, 146.

45. Cmiel, 40.

46. Hugh Blair, *Lectures on Rhetoric and Belles Lettres,* ed. Harold Harding, 2 v. (Carbondale, IL: Southern Illinois University Press, 1965), v. 1, x–xi.

47. Barbara Warnick, *The Sixth Canon: Belletristic Rhetorical Theory and Its French Antecedents* (Columbia: University of South Carolina Press, 1993), especially chap. 1.

48. Warnick, 4.

49. Warnick, 34.

50. Richard Whately, *Elements of Rhetoric,* ed. Douglas Ehninger (1828, rpt. Carbondale, IL: Southern Illinois University Press, 1963), xxiv.

51. Henry Home, Lord Kames, *The Elements of Criticism* (1761; rpt. New York: Barnes and Burr, 1865), 133.

52. Kames, 270.

53. Warnick, 112.

54. Blair, 21.

55. Blair, 183.

56. Blair, 183–184.

57. Blair, 184.

58. Blair, 185–186.

59. Blair, 226.

60. See: James L. Golden and Edward P. J. Corbett, *The Rhetoric of Blair, Campbell, and Whately* (New York: Holt, Rinehart and Winston, 1968). Other sources include: Douglas Ehninger, "George Campbell and the Revolution in Inventional Theory," *Southern Speech Journal* 15 (1950): 270–276; "Campbell, Blair, and Whately Revisited," *Southern Speech Journal* 28 (1963), 169–182; "Campbell,

Blair, and Whately: Old Friends in a New Light," *Western Speech* 19 (1955): 263–269; Douglas Mc-Dermott, "George Campbell and the Classical Tradition," *Quarterly Journal of Speech* 49 (1963): 403–409; Dominic LaRusso, "Root or Branch? A Reexamination of Campbell's 'Rhetoric,'" *Western Speech* 32 (1968): 85–91; Herman Cohen, "William Leechman's Anticipation of Campbell," *Western Speech* 32 (1968), 92–99.

61. George Campbell, *The Philosophy of Rhetoric,* ed. Lloyd F. Bitzer (Carbondale, IL: University of Southern Illinois Press, 1963). On Campbell, see: Bitzer's Introduction to *The Philosophy of Rhetoric;* Howell, 577–612.

62. Gerard Hauser, "Empiricism, Description, and the New Rhetoric," *Philosophy and Rhetoric* 5 (1972): 24–44; Lloyd Bitzer, "Hume's Philosophy in George Campbell's *The Philosophy of Rhetoric,*" *Philosophy and Rhetoric* 2 (1969): 136–166; Vincent Bevilaqua, "Philosophical Origins of George Campbell's *Philosophy of Rhetoric,*" *Speech Monographs* 32 (1965): 7–8.

63. Bitzer, introduction to *The Philosophy of Rhetoric,* xiii.
64. Bitzer, introduction to *The Philosophy of Rhetoric,* xiii.
65. Campbell, xlv.
66. George Kennedy, *Classical Rhetoric and Its Christian and Secular Tradition from Ancient Times,* 1st ed. (Chapel Hill: University of North Carolina Press, 1980), 234; See also: Thomas Conley, *Rhetoric in the European Tradition* (New York: Longman, 1990), 217–220.
67. Douglas Ehninger, introduction to Richard Whately, *Elements of Rhetoric* (1828; Carbondale, IL: Southern Illinois University Press, 1963), xxv–xxvi.
68. Kennedy, 240.
69. Campbell, 1.
70. Howell, 580.
71. Wilbur Samuel Howell, "John Locke and the New Rhetoric," *Quarterly Journal of Speech* 53 (1967): 319–321.
72. Campbell, 1.
73. Warnick, 68.
74. Ray E. McKerrow, "Campbell and Whately on the Utility of Syllogistic Logic," *Western Speech Communication Journal* (Winter 1976): 3–13.
75. Campbell, 35–61.
76. Quoted in Howell, *Eighteenth-Century,* 587.
77. Campbell, 77.
78. Quoted in Howell, *Eighteenth-Century,* 587.
79. Warnick, 67.
80. Warnick, 67.
81. Howell, *Eighteenth-Century,* 579.
82. Campbell, 108.
83. Campbell, 108.
84. Warnick, 119.
85. McKerrow, 7 ff.
86. McKerrow, 9.
87. Whately, ix.
88. Whately, xi.
89. Whately, 90.
90. Whately, 91.
91. Whately, 92.
92. Whately, 112.
93. Whately, 112–113.
94. Whately, 116.
95. Kennedy, 240.
96. Kennedy, 241.

CHAPTER NINE

CONTEMPORARY RHETORIC I: ARGUMENTS, AUDIENCES AND ADVOCACY

When Einstein discovered rationality in nature, unaided by any observation that had not been available for at least fifty years before, our positivistic textbooks promptly covered up the scandal by an appropriately embellished account of his discovery.
—Michael Polanyi, *Personal Knowledge*[1]

As was noted toward the end of the last chapter, the classical tradition in rhetoric, with its focus on oral presentations, was already beginning to decline by Whately's time. This decline in rhetoric's status as a legitimate subject of academic study continued through the end of the nineteenth century. The twentieth century opened in the Western world with interest in rhetorical theory at perhaps its lowest point since the systematic discussion of rhetoric began in ancient Greece. Scientific thinking was now ascendant, and the methods of reasoning and speaking about contingent matters that had traditionally been studied and taught under the name of rhetoric were derided as decidedly inferior to scientific method. Logical positivism, or the intellectual effort to bring scientific standards to bear on the resolution of all issues, had apparently rendered rhetoric obsolete.

However, as the twentieth century progressed, confidence in scientific thinking as appropriate to the solution of human social and moral problems began to diminish. Events such as World War II, and "scientific" approaches to social structuring such as those undertaken by fascists in Europe, left the intellectual world reeling. In addition, as news of Stalin's often brutal tactics started to reach the West, many intellectuals began to question whether "scientific socialism" could indeed be a viable response to fascism and the inequalities of industrial capitalism. Whereas science had made major advances in such areas as medicine, it had failed to provide solutions to persistent human problems like aggression, racism, economic exploitation, and class polarization.

Perhaps science could not provide solutions to these problems, for its methods of reasoning were suited to investigating natural rather than social phenomena, and it dealt best with clear cases of physical causation. Science did not provide a means of investigating human motivation, the place of values in human choice-making, the intricacies of how power is achieved and maintained, or how political leaders come to wield the kind of massive influence that had been a major factor in bringing the world to war.

A new means of discussing human values was required, one suited specifically to resolving perennial problems that engaged human values and moral commitments. Recognizing the importance of everyday reasoning processes to our deliberations about such problems, some thinkers turned their attention to the structures that undergird "everyday" or "marketplace" arguments. Others looked to the classical tradition in rhetoric for help in discovering a new language, a new rhetoric, of human values. In this search for a new logic and a new rhetoric, attention was focused on two foundational components of rhetoric: argumentation and the audience.

Not only had science not provided solutions to social problems, but also scientists were increasingly willing to admit as the twentieth century progressed that much of the discourse of science was not formulary, clinical, and syllogistic, but decidedly strategic, argumentative, and rhetorical. The theory that "won out" over competing theories in scientific debates was often the theory presented in the most persuasive manner, not the one supported by the greatest weight of evidence. Moreover, human motives were seen to play an enormous role in interpreting data, creating the institutional arrangements in which science was practiced, allocating funding to research, and even in the process of formulating theories. Science, it turned out after more than a century of intellectual dominance, was in several important respects rhetorical. Scholars in fields as varied as economics, astronomy, psychology, literature, and even biology and mathematics were acknowledging that rhetoric played a major role in their professional lives.

ARGUMENTATION AND RATIONAL DISCOURSE

One of the important accomplishments of twentieth-century rhetorical studies has been to examine and provide a means of discussing the structure of everyday argumentation. The work of scholars such as Stephen Toulmin and Chaim Perelman has been directed toward revealing the logical structure of everyday arguments, demonstrating the place of values in such arguments, and providing a theory about the conditions under which such arguments are most equitably advanced. The goal of this important intellectual work has been to improve the practice of discourse in contemporary society, and to thus improve the quality of human social life.

PERELMAN AND OLBRECHTS-TYTECA:
A NEW RHETORIC

Chaim Perelman (1912–1985) was a Belgian philosopher and legal theorist who became interested in the question of how moral claims can be proven rational in a culture in which there are few agreements about values. He and colleague Madame L. Olbrechts-Tyteca searched for a nonscientific but also nontheistic foundation for discourse involving values.[2] This search led them to the ancient discipline of rhetoric and, more specifically, to argumentation and the audience. "What we preserve of the traditional rhetoric," they write in their major work, *The New Rhetoric,* "is the idea of the audience, an idea immediately evoked by the mere thought of a speech."[3] Sounding like rhetoricians from classical Greek or Rome, they write that "knowledge of those one wishes to win over is a condition preliminary to all effectual argumentation."[4]

Perelman and Olbrechts-Tyteca begin with the assumption that no claim or conclusion is self-evidently true, and that resort to absolutes such as God or a specific revealed truth will not uphold arguments about important issues of value in our contemporary, pluralistic social setting. Only through a sustained process of public argumentation could propositions of value and policy be tested and established as sufficiently reasonable, or rejected as lacking rational merit. Thus, their particular concern is the argumentative processes involved in testing ideas by engaging and convincing audiences.[5] Much of their groundbreaking book, *The New Rhetoric,* is a catalog of various types of arguments common to everyday discourse, along with discussions of how different arguments achieve their effects and examples of each type.

Perelman and Olbrechts-Tyteca, as we shall see, place great emphasis on the audience. "All argumentation," as they see it, "aims at gaining the adherence of minds, and, by this very fact, assumes the existence of intellectual contact."[6] That is, rhetoric inseparably intertwines the concepts of audience and argumentation. Moreover, these writers contend that the quality and significance attributed to an argument depend on the astuteness and skill of the audience it succeeds in persuading. As Perelman and Olbrechts-Tyteca put the point, the audience "will determine to a great extent both the direction the arguments will take, and the character, the significance that will be attributed to them."[7] The audience, then, plays a role equal to that of the orator in the testing of ideas publicly. A closer look at Perelman and Olbrechts-Tyteca's theory of audience is in order, as theirs is perhaps the best developed analysis of this topic in contemporary rhetorical theory.[8] A closer look at their theory of audience will be helpful to understanding their rhetorical theory.

The Centrality of Audience

Three audiences are particularly important in Perelman and Olbrechts-Tyteca's theory of rhetoric. This is because these three audiences can reliably test the rational quality of arguments. "The first such audience," they write, "consists of the whole of mankind, or at least, of all normal, adult persons; we shall refer to it as the universal audience."[9] The universal audience is advanced as a possible test of the reasonableness of arguments that transcends local and personal biases.[10] The second audience they consider is "the single interlocutor whom a speaker addresses in a dialogue," while the third audience that can test the reasonableness of arguments is "the subject himself when he deliberates or gives himself reasons for his actions."[11] We will examine in some detail their discussion of these and other audiences, and consider how audiences may enhance the quality of public rhetoric.

Particular Audiences, Starting Points, and Values.   Though the universal audience, the audience of the single interlocutor, and the audience of self provide important checks on the reasonableness of arguments, Perelman and Olbrechts-Tyteca locate social and personal values in particular audiences. A particular audience is the actual audience of persons one addresses when advancing an argument publicly. In fact, this regard for particular audiences and their "opinions and values" is what Perelman and Olbrechts-Tyteca see as distinguishing a rhetorical approach to argument from other possible approaches. "What...characterizes the rhetorical point of view in philosophy is a fundamental concern with the opinions and values of the audience that the speaker addresses, and more particularly with the intensity of his audience's adherence to each of these invoked by the speaker."[12]

When we recall the importance of public values as starting points of argument in Greek and Roman theories of rhetoric, we recognize Perelman and Olbrechts-Tyteca's debt to these theories. Whether in ancient or modern settings, rhetors must attend to what real audiences believe and value, and adapt their arguments to the beliefs of particular audiences. "Every social circle or milieu is distinguishable in terms of its dominant opinions and unquestioned beliefs, of the premises that it takes for granted without hesitation." Does one, then, question such beliefs as simply the shifting opinions of the public, as Plato did, or take them as the basis of rhetorical appeals, as Aristotle did? Perelman and Olbrechts-Tyteca apparently side with Aristotle. "These views form an integral part of its culture, and an orator wishing to persuade a particular audience must of necessity adapt himself to it."[13]

Perelman and Olbrechts-Tyteca devote considerable time in *The New Rhetoric* to the notion of the starting points of argument. Starting points are points of agreement between a rhetor and an audience that allow for argumentation to develop. Because of their interest in forging a rhetoric that allows for a rational discussion of human values, the concept of starting points as places for finding agreement between disagreeing parties is important to Perelman and Olbrechts-Tyteca's rhetorical theory. "The unfolding as well as the starting point of argumentation," they write, "presupposes indeed the agreement of the audience."[14]

Perelman and Olbrechts-Tyteca divide starting points into two general classes. The first class of starting points they call simply "the real," which includes "facts, truths, and presumptions." The other category they call "the preferable," which takes in "values, hierarchies, and lines of argument relating to the preferable."[15] Thus, one source of the agreements needed to begin constructive argumentation is found in what both speaker and audience accept as well-established facts, widely accepted truths, or uncontested commitments, called presumptions. Recall that presumptions were discussed in the last chapter when we considered the argument theory of Hugh Blair. The clearest example of a presumption accepted by most Americans is the presumption of innocence in judicial settings. A second source of starting points is discovered in commonly held values, values arranged into hierarchies, and preferences such as the preference for group over individual decision making in an organization. From such points of agreement, further agreements may be reached through the processes of argumentation. Again, the central concern of these authors is to establish a rational method for discussing questions of value in a modern, pluralistic social setting. Their call for renewed attention to classical theories of argumentation is a major part of this effort.

Perelman and Olbrechts-Tyteca recognized the very serious problems associated with arguments about matters of value before real audiences. Rhetoric based strictly on the beliefs of a particular group may be biased, narrow, and parochial. Arguments capable of winning the adherence of *only* a particular audience often are not acceptable to most reasonable people. To solve this problem associated with arguments addressed to particular audiences, Perelman and Olbrechts-Tyteca introduced what was to become their most famous concept.

The Universal Audience

Who decides which ideas are truly rational, if the judgments of different particular audiences clash? In some instances we turn to elite audiences. These are audiences of trained specialists in particular disciplines who can assist in "the attempt to formulate norms and values such as could be proposed to every reasonable being."[16] But even the judgments of experts must be brought back to the test of the particular audience. Otherwise we run the "risk of the philosopher-king who would use the political authority and power of the State" to impose one set of values on everyone.[17]

The universal audience is also important in the effort to develop sound arguments for particular audiences without bowing to the local prejudices these audiences often endorse. Looking beyond persuading only their immediate audience, conscientious rhetors will consider how an imagined audience of highly rational individuals would respond to a particular argument. In his book, *Justice,* Perelman writes, "I do not see [reason] as a faculty in contrast to other faculties.... I conceive of it as a privileged audience, the universal audience."[18] Perelman and Olbrechts-Tyteca seek an imagined audience of reasonable people available at all times, and not subject to the limitations and biases of any particular audience.

In the universal audience, Perelman and Olbrechts-Tyteca reveal their conviction that a reasonable and moral advocate must possess a vision of rationality that transcends particular social groups or geographical locations. A rational advocate "seeks to conform to principles of action which are acceptable to everyone [and] considers as unreasonable a rule of action which cannot be universalized."[19] The reasonable advocate looks beyond the immediate and recognizes that "a principle of action which others would consider acceptable and even reasonable cannot arbitrarily favor certain people or certain situations: what is reasonable must be able to be a precedent which can inspire everyone in analogous circumstances."[20]

The "highest point" of assurance that an argument is reasonable "is reached when there is agreement of the universal audience," which audience is "a universality and unanimity imagined by the speaker, to the agreement of an audience which should be universal."[21] Argumentation which wins the assent of the universal audience must reach a very high standard indeed. It must "convince the reader that the reasons adduced are of a compelling character, that they are self-evident, and possess an absolute and timeless validity independent of local or historical contingencies."[22]

The Audience of One

How can we know, in a practical sense, if our arguments are ready for appeal to the universal audience? Though Perelman and Olbrechts-Tyteca are not explicit in their answer to this question, there are some clear suggestions in *The New Rhetoric* about practical tests of one's arguments. One of these is the careful scrutiny that takes place when one person argues directly with another. "Argumentation before a single hearer" can also make a special claim to reasonableness, and provides another kind of test of arguments. In *The New Rhetoric,* Plato's *Gorgias* is an example of the role of the audience of a single hearer: "Each of Socrates' interlocutors is the spokesman...of a particular viewpoint and their objections must first be disposed of in order to facilitate public adherence to the proposed theses."[23]

The single hearer sometimes acts like an audience of one's opponents by advancing the counterarguments to one's own arguments. The single listener or reader carefully checks each step in the argumentation, raising objections to it, asking for clarifications, providing arguments in response.[24] The individual listener can in some cases fulfill this role so well that he or she represents the universal audience. "The hearer is assumed to have the same reasoning power at his disposal as the other members of the universal audience."[25] Thus, if our arguments succeed before an audience of a single, careful critic, they may be ready for the test of the universal audience.

The Self as Audience

We are all familiar with argumentation before a large audience, and each of us has likely advanced arguments before an audience of a single hearer. But do we typically think of ourselves as an audience for our own arguments? Perelman and Olbrechts-Tyteca wish to draw our attention to this audience as well, the audience of the self. "The self-deliberating subject," they write, "is often regarded as an incarnation of the universal audience."[26] The individual "endowed with reason" who directs her own arguments privately to herself "is bound to be contemptuous of procedures aimed at winning over other people." Moreover, such an individual "cannot avoid being sincere" in this process, and "is in a better position than anyone else to test the value" of her arguments.[27]

Self-deliberation is crucial to the process of inventing or coming up with arguments. It is also important to justifying arguments as reasonable. We might say that the self is the first audience whose adherence is sought in argumentation, and, for reasons Perelman and Olbrechts-Tyteca articulate, among the most important. Of course, even in self-deliberation, reasons may be invented simply to justify a particular decision rather than reasonably to explore options.

The universal audience consists of the speaker's conception of all rational people. Reasons addressed to this audience are to be compelling, self-evident, and timeless, thus independent of local concerns. The speaker's character is reflected in the conception she forms of the universal audience. The audience of the single hearer provides a check on each step in the reasoning process. The goal of discourse addressed to this audience is not to "win" a debate, but to engage in dialogue leading to a reasonable decision. The interlocutor may be seen as a manifestation of all reasonable people, as an instance of the universal audience. Self-deliberation is viewed as a kind of argumentation, and not as a distinct cognitive activity. We employ the same arguments to persuade others that we use to persuade ourselves. The secrecy of a personal, internal debate is seen as a guarantee of its sincerity, as we are not interested in deceiving ourselves.

Regardless of the type of discourse one advances—scientific, political, judicial, religious—an audience is being addressed. Argumentation, for Perelman and Olbrechts-Tyteca, cannot be adequately understood apart from a theory of audience. Discourse is not simply addressed to, but adapted to and affected by its audience. Here is both a fact about rhetoric and a criticism of it that has been advanced ever since Plato raised the concern in *Gorgias*. But, does this fact mean that argumentation must then be unreasonable? Perelman and Olbrechts-Tyteca think not, and they respond with both a theory of audiences and of arguments intended to secure the rationality of discourse about moral issues that engages values and beliefs. And finding a rational approach to moral discourse is perhaps the most pressing problem of rhetorical theory in the twentieth century.

Presence

We have considered Perelman and Olbrechts-Tyteca's theory of audience and its centrality to their "new rhetoric." Another of their concepts has also been influential and deserves attention. Perelman and Olbrechts-Tyteca call this concept "presence." The immediate goal of argumentation, according to Perelman and Olbrechts-Tyteca, is to make certain facts present to an audience. Establishing presence involves the choice to emphasize certain ideas and facts over others, thus encouraging an audience to attend to them. Perelman and Olbrechts-Tyteca write that presence "is an essential factor in argumentation and one that is far too much neglected in rationalistic conceptions of reasoning."[28] The presence of a fact or an idea is almost a sensory experience rather than a purely rational one; "presence," they write, "acts directly on our sensibility."[29]

Thus, in argumentation a rhetor seeks to bring his or her audience to the point of seeing the relevant facts, or experiencing the truthfulness of an idea. Thus, Perelman and Olbrechts-Tyteca can write, "one of the preoccupations of a speaker is to make present, by verbal magic alone, what is actually absent" but what is considered "important to [the] argument."[30] This statement, particularly with its reference to rhetoric as a kind of magic, sounds like something the Sophist Gorgias or a Renaissance humanist like Ficino might say. Indeed, Perelman and Olbrechts-Tyteca share Gorgias' and the humanists' intrigue with rhetoric's power to direct thought, particularly rhetoric in the control of a skilled rhetorician. But their confidence in argumentation as a *rational* foundation of discourse is decidedly stronger than was Gorgias'.

STEPHEN TOULMIN AND THE USES OF ARGUMENT

In 1958, British philosopher and scientist Stephen Toulmin published his ground-breaking study of argumentation, *The Uses of Argument.*[31] Thus, his work appeared in England just one year before *The New Rhetoric* of Perelman and Olbrechts-Tyteca. His analysis of everyday or marketplace arguments on a model derived from logical studies is reminiscent of Aristotle's reference to the enthymeme as a "rhetorical syllogism." Toulmin also drew on the study of legal argumentation in establishing his system for assessing arguments.[32] However, he affirmed that the standards for assessing arguments varied depending on the subject matter under consideration. The authors of *Handbook of Argumentation Theory* write, "Toulmin's central thesis is that every sort of argumentation can in principle claim rationality and that the criteria to be applied when determining the soundness of the argumentation depend on the nature of the problem to which the argumentation relates."[33] To demonstrate this possibility, Toulmin developed a scheme for analyzing arguments that has become extremely popular, and which we will review momentarily.

Argument Fields

Toulmin questioned the ancient idea of logical validity as applicable to the analysis of ordinary arguments. In order to make his case, Toulmin introduced the concept of argument fields into his discussion of arguments. "The first problem we have set ourselves," writes Toulmin in *The Uses of Argument,* "can be re-stated in the question, 'What things about the form and merits of our arguments are field-invariant and what things about them are field-dependent?'" Toulmin explains the distinction in the following way:

> What things about the modes in which we assess arguments, the standards with reference to which we assess them and the manner in which we qualify our conclusions about them, are the same regardless of field (field-invariant), and which of them vary as we move from arguments in one field to arguments in another field (field-dependent)?[34]

Specifically, "two arguments will be said to belong to the same field when the data [evidence] and conclusions in each of the two arguments are, respectively, of the same logical type (emphasis added)."[35] Geometrical proofs, navigational calculations, arguments from statistical data, arguments based on criteria for inclusion in a category, and arguments applying laws to particular cases—all of these, according to Toulmin, belong to different fields. Thus, some of the criteria relevant to evaluating each type of argument will *differ* from some of the criteria appropriate to evaluating any of the others. That is, not all arguments are subject to evaluation by the same criteria or standards. Thus, Toulmin rejects the logician's idea that validity—a concern for an argument's structure without consideration of its content—is the single universal standard of argument analysis. But, even within a particular domain of argument, law, for example, arguments may belong to different fields. Thus, arguments about whether to apply a particular law to a particular action, and judicial arguments based on generalizations about human character, would belong to different fields. Arguments are from the same field when it makes sense to compare them to one another and to judge them by similar special criteria.

Field-Dependent and Field-Invariant Standards

Toulmin introduces the concept of field, then, for a particular reason: He wishes to explore the rational standards by which arguments can be assessed. Some standards for assessing arguments belong specifically to a particular field, and these standards Toulmin called field-dependent. Other standards for assessing arguments apply regardless of the field in which the argument is advanced. Toulmin called these standards field-invariant. Thus, in an argument about whether a particular law should be applied to a particular action, standards appropriate to the interpretation of law would be among the field-dependent factors that might come into play. Standards regarding the underlying logic of the arguments advanced—for example, whether a logical fallacy had been committed—would be among the field-invariant standards that could be applied to the arguments on both sides.

Modal Qualifiers

As one application of his idea that some of the standards by which arguments are assessed vary with argument fields, Toulmin expresses interest in certain terms "which have always been of interest to philosophers and have come to be known as modal terms."[36] Modal qualifiers, words that indicate the degree of confidence or force assigned to a conclusion, include terms such as *must, possibly, probably, certainly,* and *cannot.* The "force" of these terms does not vary from one field of argument to another, "but the criteria applied in order to determine whether a given modal term has been used rightly or wrongly in a given context are field-dependent."[37] In modals, Toulmin sees a reflection of the rational processes involved in decision making and an important clue to the nature of everyday reasoning.[38] The standards used to assess whether a modal has been properly employed will vary with a variation in the argument's field. For example, the term *must* is justified by the rules of mathematics in the following example from Toulmin: "In view of the preceding steps in the argument, the square of the hypotenuse of a right-angled triangle must be equal to the sum of the squares of the other two sides."[39] However, the term *must* is justified by rules of professional behavior in the statement, "You must not make demeaning comments to your colleagues at work." Toulmin takes this variation from one field to another to be one typical use of modals.

But notice the different sense of *must* in the following example from *The Uses of Argument:* "Under the circumstances, there is only one decision open to us; the child must be returned to the custody of its parents."[40] Imagining a judicial setting for the discussion of a child's custody, advocates may employ modals such as this one to indicate their confidence that certain evidence and certain laws must, that is, *ought to be,* interpreted in a particular way. But *must* in this example does not mean "by logical necessity" as it does in the first example drawn from mathematics. Thus, modal qualifiers play various roles in arguments. Again, the field or domain of argument must be considered in interpreting a modal qualifier's meaning.

Toulmin's Famous Model

Toulmin's concern for the structure of arguments and for modal terms come together in his famous model of argument. The Toulmin Model identifies a variety of elements in an argument, and arranges these elements on a diagram. Briefly, Toulmin noted that arguments consist of a claim, or conclusion, some data, or evidence to support the claim, and a warrant, or generalization that tends to link some data to a claim. Toulmin also noted the presence of backing, or support for the warrant, rebuttals, or potential conditions on the acceptance of the claim, and modal qualifiers in his model. Toulmin presents the following example to introduce his model:

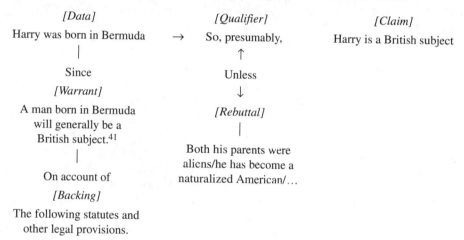

[Data]		*[Qualifier]*	*[Claim]*
Harry was born in Bermuda	→	So, presumably,	Harry is a British subject

Since   Unless

[Warrant]

A man born in Bermuda
will generally be a
British subject.[41]

[Rebuttal]

On account of

Both his parents were
aliens/he has become a
naturalized American/…

[Backing]

The following statutes and
other legal provisions.

This model became popular for two reasons. First, it allowed scholars to label and discuss the components of everyday arguments. Second, the model, coupled with Toulmin's analysis of modals and fields, provided a means of evaluating the rationality of everyday arguments. This possibility was important to those interested in informal or marketplace arguments, because logicians under the influence of logical positivism had charged that such arguments can stake no claim to being rational. Thus, Toulmin's analysis of arguments was highly influential on both U.S. and European thinkers.

ARGUMENTATION AND SCIENTIFIC INQUIRY

Recently, rhetorical theorist Herbert Simons has written that "it is generally acknowledged that…scholars have no choice but to rely on rhetorical appeals and arguments in the forging of a discipline."[42] This is a remarkable statement coming at the end of a century in which the natural and social sciences have presented themselves as intentionally nonrhetorical. As Simons suggests, scholars increasingly are recognizing that the methods, procedures, and languages of the academic disciplines are rhetorical in nature.[43] This observation has been particularly difficult for some members of the natural and social science communities to accept, for these academic endeavors have promoted themselves on the claim of investigative objectivity and aloofness from the messy, irrational realm of persuasion. But, this claim of objectivity may itself be rhetorical in nature, intended to persuade the general public that science is the one arena of human activity in which rhetorical analysis is inappropriate. Science thus assumes the status of a protected domain in which critical examination of human motives and human persuasive abilities must not intrude. Such a protected, unexamined scientific community would in this way recognize a corresponding increase in its social power. As rhetorical critic John Lyne has written, "I investigate scientific arguments because the discourses of science have substantial impact on thought, action and culture in our time—and that influence will be all the stronger if we accept the opinion that they have little to do with persuasion in the public space."[44]

Historically, scientific discourse has been portrayed as "concerned with things rather than words," and thus "innocent of rhetorical seductions."[45] The social sciences sought rational respectability by imitating this antirhetorical quality of the natural sciences. Nevertheless, some members of natural and social science disciplines recently have shown a decided interest in rhetoric as a means of understanding how their own disciplines operate.[46] Increasingly, scientists are willing to acknowledge, as Charles Willard has written, that "personal preferences and quirks, conventional wisdom, professional politics, and the need for popularization to secure funding, all play a part in the puzzles scientists find interesting."[47] That is, the conduct of science, if we take a broad view of the enterprise, is as disorderly, irrational, and contaminated by human biases at times as is politics. This means that a rhetorical understanding of science can open new perspectives on this most powerful intellectual enterprise of our age.

An understanding of the rhetorical nature of scientific discourse is particularly important when we consider the enormous power of scientific institutions in contemporary culture, a power founded directly on the image of the natural sciences as immune to the ambiguities and contingencies that mark other arenas of human social life. Scholars in the rhetoric of science have opened a vast territory for exploration, hoping to reveal the place of persuasion and linguistic strategy in the writing of science, and even in the decisions that determine which projects scientists will undertake. Moreover, some scholars recently have pointed out that certain dangers are present when we fail to identify the assumptions at work beneath the surface of scientific texts. Susan Wells, for example, argues that the appearance of neutrality and objectivity in scientific discourse may be a reason for concern. "The scientific text," she writes, "reductively segments nature into connected objects of knowledge, open to manipulation in time and capable of being transformed without affecting the knowing subject." That is, scientific discourse "objectifies" everything it touches, and in this way insulates the scientist from the very object of scientific study. As Wells points out, historians Max Horkheimer and T. W. Adorno argue that the "practices of language most closely associated with the physical sciences were those which, when transferred to the social, rationalized domination and the Holocaust: Enlightenment in its moment of triumph emerged as chaos and terror."[48] Others have argued a similar hypothesis, that scientific rationality and objectivity, cut free from the shaping influence of human motives, values, and beliefs, may produce a dangerously "objective" outlook on nature and even on human beings themselves.[49]

Perhaps our failure to subject scientific discourse to careful rhetorical analysis does have serious social consequences. This failure may result from a long tradition of attributing to scientific texts a special status as "purely rational discourse," a status *not* conferred on political, judicial, and religious discourse. But the pristine rationality of scientific texts is now widely challenged by rhetoricians and others. Scientific discourse's special status has also to do with the fact that "no other discursive formation is so relentlessly inaccessible to the public, so exclusively addressed to practitioners of scientific disciplines."[50] To write about the rhetoric of science, then, means first learning a great deal about a particular scientific endeavor, and then translating that endeavor into language accessible to readers not trained in that discipline. Despite the problems facing the rhetorician who ventures to study scientific discourse, this difficult work of analysis and translation is being pursued, and admirably so in many cases. In the following pages we will examine a few of the scholarly initiatives in the new and rapidly growing area of research known as the rhetoric of science.

Advocacy in the Sciences

What are the specific qualities that make academic disciplines rhetorical? Perhaps the most significant quality is *advocacy* itself, an activity hardly captured in the more usual description of scientific activity as *investigation*. Herbert Simons writes that "one common thread in the rhetoric of inquiry movement is its rejection of the conventional split between inquiry and advocacy."[51] The point here is that natural and social scientists function as advocates for points of view, theories, and differing interpretations of data. Moreover, a scientist's political perspective and even her personal commitments can influence how data are collected and interpreted.

We can take this notion of advocacy a little further, and explore some specific ways that a scientist's advocacy can be worked out rhetorically. First, scientists make decisions about which questions they will investigate. Sometimes these decisions are connected to current political controversies that generate funds to support some research projects and deny funding to support others. The scientist's choice of a project, and certainly the presentation of a rationale for a line of research, immediately take on a rhetorical aspect. In addition, the scientist's presentation of data and its interpretations must be persuasive, must gain a hearing among colleagues and, perhaps, eventually the general public.

In addition to the presence of outright advocacy in the sciences, John Lyne notes that science is rhetorical because it "is a collective enterprise that is sustained only within a highly specialized network of communication."[52] That is, scientists must remain in constant communication with other scientists, and this communication is seldom devoid of the motives and strategies we associate with rhetoric. Lyne writes, "Participation in that network is the very sine qua non of scientific practice.... Add to this the presence of interpersonal competition, inflated egos, and the constant need to justify expenditures, and one has an area rife not only with communication but with rhetorical practice."[53]

Lyne draws our attention to a third way in which we might view science as rhetorical. Science, he writes, "is also a part of the very fabric of our public discourse as well." Because we live in an age in which a staggering amount of technical information is available to all of us, "scientific information can be called upon by almost anyone." Thus, scientific talk has become part of the fabric of political talk, religious talk, educational talk, and economic talk. In virtually any forum we enter where people are seeking to persuade one another, "one usually finds modern science deployed as a resource of persuasion."[54] To take seriously the study of the rhetoric of science is to become more aware of "the sort of powers that are unleashed in the very language of science."[55] Ultimately, the language of science—its rhetoric—affects actions and decisions in arenas we do not typically identify as scientific at all. "We who take an interest in public discourse," writes Lyne, "must be concerned with how the discourses of scientific knowledge may mesh with the discourses of value and action, because, one way or another, they will."[56]

We have considered some ways in which science is rhetorical. It will be helpful at this point to explore some specific instances of the rhetoric of science. I have gathered these examples from both the social and the natural sciences.

DEIRDRE MCCLOSKEY AND THE RHETORIC OF ECONOMICS

Some social scientists have found a rhetorical approach to their disciplines liberating in that it allows them both to admit and to appreciate some of the rhetorical dimensions of their work. Economist Deirdre McCloskey of the University of Iowa has written that a rhetorical approach to economics "is not an invitation to irrationality in argument," as some economists might presume. "Quite the contrary," she adds, "it is an invitation to leave the irrationality of an artificially narrowed range of argument and to move to the rationality of arguing like human beings." She adds that a rhetorical approach to her discipline "brings out into the open the arguing that economists do anyway."[57]

What is Professor McCloskey saying about the rhetoric of economics? At least this: that economists argue among themselves about economic theories, and that they seek to persuade one another using arguments and strategies that are not linked directly to the methods of economics. The arguments of economists frequently are, that is, persuasively intended, strategically framed, stylistically shaped, and reflective of individual biases, preferences, and values. Is this surprising? Probably not, but it also is not typically admitted as part of "doing economics" when an economist goes public with a theory. At the point of going public, the economist must adopt the voice of the objective investigator whose "discoveries" are based strictly on an investigation of the best available evidence. Some scientists are threatened by the thought of revealing the rhetorical nature of their enterprises, and McCloskey thinks they ought not to be. Acknowledging the rhetorical nature of academic inquiry can actually serve to enhance one's understanding of what it means to be a scientist, and can actually advance the scientific project.

CLIFFORD GEERTZ AND RHETORIC
IN ANTHROPOLOGY

"The narrative and rhetorical conventions assumed by a writer...shape ethnography," writes John Van Maanen of the rhetorical nature of ethnographic research. That is, the manner or style in which an ethnographer's report of fieldwork has much to do with that report's acceptance by the scholarly community. Thus, the rhetoric of reporting one's experience is as much a part of anthropology as is careful observation of a culture. Van Maanen explains:

> Ways of personal expression, choice of metaphor, figurative allusions, semantics, decorative phrasing or plain speaking, textual organization, and so on all work to structure a cultural portrait in particular ways. Style is just as much a matter of choice when the experimentalist writes in a self-conscious, hyper-realistic, attention grabbing, dots-and-dashes fashion...as when the traditionalist falls back on a neutral, pale-beige, just-the-facts fashion of reporting. Some styles are, at any given time, more acceptable in ethnographic circles than others.[58]

In similar fashion, anthropologist Clifford Geertz has written about the role of persuasion in anthropology. "The ability of anthropologists to get us to take what they say seriously," he urges, "has less to do with either a factual look or an air of conceptual elegance than it has with their capacity to convince us that what they say is a result of their having actually penetrated...another form of life, of having, one way or another, truly 'been there.'" Thus, the popular image of the anthropologist-as-scientist reporting "only the facts" to an audience, of a dispassionate observer unmoved by linguistic strategies of persuasion, is, for both Van Maanen and Geertz, not an accurate one. To understand the work of the anthropologist, one must understand rhetoric.

Rhetoric seeking persuasion, according to Geertz, enters the picture explicitly as anthropologists sit down to write about their experiences in the field. "Persuading us that this offstage miracle has occurred, is where the writing comes in."[59] Thus, the successful anthropologist must also be a rhetorician, a writer writing to "convince" and to "persuade" an audience of colleagues that her or his work is worthy. Geertz acknowledges the presence of the even larger audience of the educated reader. He writes, "the most direct way to bring field work as personal encounter and ethnography as reliable account together is to make the diary form...something for the world to read."[60] Thus, even the anthropologist's choice of the diary form, the most objective and intimate of prose genres, can be a strategic and persuasive one. To let the reader peer over my shoulder as I record my most private observations with no apparent audience in mind is, according to Geertz, a rhetorical act.

MICHAEL BILLIG AND THE RHETORIC
OF SOCIAL PSYCHOLOGY

Some members of the social scientific community, then, have recognized the rhetorical aspects of their work, and have benefited by that recognition. Others have employed rhetoric to gain insights into the phenomena that they study. Michael Billig, for instance, has used rhetoric's appreciation for argument to explore human social behavior, and to point up some problems in the language of social psychology.[61]

Billig, an English social psychologist teaching at Loughborough University, maintains in his book, *Arguing and Thinking,* that ancient rhetorical theory is a source of rich insights for the social psychologist.[62] After all, the problems of ancient rhetoric and modern social psychology are essentially the same: understanding why people act as they do, what they believe, and how they are persuaded to their actions and beliefs. Billig quotes Rom Harre to the effect that people are "rhetorician[s]—all of life is rhetorical, and we are mainly advocates. This is not a sideline, it is the very business of life."[63]

Billig was initially drawn to the observation of the Sophist Protagoras that arguments are available for and against any particular claim. Billig dubs this the principle of rhetorical opposition.[64] He suggests that this represents a striking and important insight about human thought, that every form of thought is contrasted with an opposing one. For instance, categorization is opposed by particularization. Pushing the observation further, Billig argues that even what we call "common sense" contains oppositions.[65] Thus, an advocate may argue that "a desperate man may violate his cherished principles," a maxim of common sense. But common sense also provides us with the opposite notion: "Even a desperate man may adhere to his principles."

Thinking, like rhetoric, is characterized by logos and the antilogos, that is, by argument and counterargument. As Protagoras pointed out, the human capacity for "contradiction" suggests that our minds by nature contrive oppositions. Billig concludes from this observation that we learn to think as we learn to argue, not vice versa.[66] But there is more to these observations than simply an analysis of human thought. If Billig is correct, then the power of speech is the power to challenge silent obedience by advancing counterarguments. Billig's view of the human mind, then, develops around this innately human rhetorical capacity to "argue back."

Audiences have always been central to the study of rhetoric, and the concept of audience, like that of argument, provides Billig a second link between ancient rhetoric and modern social psychology. Though Plato held out hope of a perfect science of persuasion (a frightening prospect), the Roman rhetorician Quintilian recognized that this was not likely given the infinite variety of human responses to any persuasive case. Billig calls this Quintilian's uncertainty principle. We may formulate the principle this way: Given the great and unpredictable variety of possible human responses to any situation, the rules of rhetoric must always be provisional, never absolute.[67] The greatest guard against rhetorical manipulation, then, is the fact that any particular audience is capable of subverting through counterargument the principle of persuasion being employed to gain their assent.

Plays and Games without Arguments?

Billig also argues in *Arguing and Thinking* that the two dominant metaphors for contemporary social psychologists are the theater and games. These metaphors have provided social scientists a vocabulary for explaining human social behavior. But

Billig finds both metaphors to miss the rhetoric of our mental and social lives.[68] From theater are borrowed such concepts as scripts, roles, scenes, and episodes; from games concepts such as rules, laws, and violations. But, though some human social behaviors yield to these metaphors, they lack a crucial component for explaining most of what we do on a daily basis. Billig points out that theatre and game metaphors are not adequate even to describe the worlds of theater and of games, let alone the drama and sport of real life. What is that missing element? For Billig, it is the essentially rhetorical feature of argument.

Billig argues that the theater and sport metaphors draw attention to life's regularities.[69] But life, as we experience it on a daily basis, is not all that regular. Disagreements are a regular feature of our social lives, and even of the private life of thought. The theater metaphor, Billig notes, fails to explain even the life of the theater. Rather, it explains only the regularities of a performance during which actors recite their parts and deliver their lines. But what about the disagreements regarding lighting, sound, casting, and staging that arise as a play is prepared for presentation?[70] The theater metaphor describes human social life as if it were a scripted performance during which a "deliberate suppression of argument" is required. But such a situation is decidedly unlike our ordinary social lives.

The game or sport metaphor runs into similar problems. It focuses on the sporting contest itself, ignoring all the human interactions surrounding the contest. Even the effort to win is downplayed in this metaphor, as are disagreements about strategies and rules.[71] Conversation is one social interaction often explained using game metaphor. But argument frequently is a component of conversation, and one for which the game metaphor does not account. Even initial agreements in conversation can reemerge as disagreements.[72] And the notion that conversation *requires* agreement may itself be an exaggeration suggested by the game metaphor. Thus, Billig finds that social psychology's dominant metaphors reveal a serious flaw: the fundamental inability to account for the rhetoric of human social life.

JOHN CAMPBELL ON THE RHETORIC OF CHARLES DARWIN

Rhetorical analysis has also been applied to argumentation in the natural sciences. The degree to which sciences such as biology, chemistry, physics, and astronomy proceed rhetorically often has not been well understood, or readily admitted. However, the work of scholars such as John Angus Campbell has helped to illuminate the rhetorical nature of these disciplines. Campbell's studies of the work of Charles Darwin in advancing his theory of natural selection stand as a good example of the rhetorical analysis of discourse in the natural sciences.[73]

Campbell notes that Darwin faced a practical problem when he believed he had discovered the mechanisms of interspecial change, or evolution. Neither the scientific world of the middle of the nineteenth century, nor the general public were ready to accept that changes from one species to another take place by virtue of natural processes. How, then, could Darwin make this idea persuasive to these two very different audiences?

Darwin's answer to this problem was the notion of natural selection, which was, Campbell argues, a rhetorical invention designed to accomplish a specific persuasive end. Moreover, Darwin knew that the metaphor of natural selection—which compared domestic animal breeding to evolutionary processes—was a somewhat misleading rhetorical strategy. By this metaphorical comparison of two fundamentally dissimilar notions, Darwin transformed the gloomy doctrine of "survival of the fittest" into a hopeful and thus persuasive prospect.

Why was evolution a "gloomy doctrine"? "Natural selection," explains Campbell, "is the application to evolution of Malthus's doctrine of population dynamics."[74] Malthus has observed that "food supply increases arithmetically while population increases geometrically." The result is that "not as many organisms live as are born."[75] That is, evolution is predicated on the certain premature death from starvation of many members of any given species. One of Darwin's argumentative moves was to add to "this thoroughly negative doctrine" the notions of "variation and inheritance." Campbell notes that "when one combines variation, inheritance, and the struggle for existence, one is left with differential reproduction. Allow differential reproduction to continue over virtually unlimited time in an unlimited variety of changing environments and the result is organic change or evolution."[76]

What many readers import to Darwin's argument—a conclusion not present in the argument itself—is progress, that is, that interspecial change implies successive improvement in species. But evolution under the Darwin doctrine is random and undirected. Biological life is not headed anywhere in particular, is not "progressing"; it just happens. This notion was unacceptable to most people in Darwin's day, and thus posed a serious rhetorical problem for Darwin. He was convinced that his theory was accurate, but unless he could persuade both the scientific community and general public, evolution would remain only an intellectual curiosity. Darwin's rhetorical problem demanded a rhetorical solution.

Natural Selection and the Religious Audience

One strategy Darwin chose was to argue on religious grounds to the highly religious audience of the public. In one such argument, Darwin sought to make evolution through "natural selection" appear benevolent by arguing that certain decidedly unpleasant natural states were not finished works of God, as his opponents argued, but rather steps along the way to more "advanced" life. As Campbell writes, "Darwin takes several of nature's ingenious adaptations and underscores the embarrassment they cause to the customary belief in divine goodness."

For instance, the cuckoo bird lays its eggs in the nests of other birds. When the chicks hatch, they destroy their host's eggs, and allow their adopted mother to nurture them instead. Darwin argues, "to my imagination it is far more satisfactory to look at such instincts as the young cuckoo ejecting its foster-brothers—ants making slaves—the larvae of the ichneumonidae feeding within the live bodies of caterpillars—not as especially endowed or created instincts, but as small consequences of one general law, leading to the advancement of all organic beings."[77] In other words,

God did not specifically design cuckoos, some species of ant, and certain wasps to be cruel to other species. Rather, God allows such cruelties as are necessary in the vast evolutionary process because they will eventually yield more advanced forms of life.

A second strategy employed to persuade a reluctant audience involved helping readers to "see" evolution take place by writing as a simple eyewitness to objective facts that required no interpretation. Campbell writes that "Darwin's skill in setting forth in colloquial language a case for a mechanism plausibly capable of bringing about evolutionary change successfully persuaded many of his readers...." The key to this strategy "was to present evolution by natural selection as though it could be seen—indeed, to convince the reader that his theory was not an inference from facts but a fact the reader had witnessed."[78] Thus, in his writing Darwin "stresses facts and observations," "minimizes theory," and removes the narrator/interpreter from the story of evolution.

But the master strategy behind Darwin's success was the metaphor of natural selection itself, an implied comparison of undirected natural processes to the highly intentional work of the animal breeder. In employing this metaphor, Darwin walked a fine line between rhetorical stratagem and outright deception. This point requires some explanation.

Campbell writes, "[I]n Darwin's theory, nature is like the breeder in that both in nature and in domestication there is an unstaunchable supply of variation; nature is further like the breeder in that both eliminate certain individuals from their breeding stocks." But, Campbell adds, "nature is not like the breeder in that nature does not consciously choose certain animals or plants to achieve a foreseen end." But, as Darwin tells the story of evolution, "Nature"—an entity created strictly for the purposes of his argument—and the breeder are essentially similar.

Has Darwin stepped over an ethical boundary line? Campbell concludes that "for Darwin to equate Malthus' laws of population," which teach that some members of a species must starve, with the appealing notion of selection "is to use words in a sense that is unusual and technically false." Campbell also calls Darwin's metaphor "misleading" and "inaccurate." And, we should add, enormously successful. After all, Darwin convinced many readers who, frankly, did not understand his argument, that his "observations" led directly and without interpretation to his theory.

Campbell's work on Darwin illustrates some of the critical possibilities inherent in a rhetorical approach to scientific discourse. Campbell shows us a famous and highly influential scientist operating as a skilled and highly successful rhetorician. Moreover, Campbell asks his readers to participate in both the rhetorical dilemma and accompanying ethical conundrum Darwin faced. After reading Campbell's accounts, it is difficult ever again to see Darwin simply as a scientist. Or, perhaps it is more accurate to say that Campbell helps us to see that science itself is inherently rhetorical.

Under the classical conception, rhetoric dealt only with contingent and public issues, a view that persisted in rhetorical studies well into the second half of the twentieth century. Scientific discourse, it was thought, operated in a distinct rational realm governed by rigid rules of inference and under the watchful eye of highly trained experts. Recently that conception of scientific rhetoric has come under intense scrutiny. Scientists have come to acknowledge the degree to which rhetorical influences shape science itself. Rhetoricians have extended the analysis to other disciplines that were also considered to operate outside the realm of the rhetorical, including, as we have seen, to economics, anthropology, psychology, and biology.

CRITICISMS OF THE RHETORIC OF SCIENCE

Some rhetorical scholars have seen in the application of rhetorical insights to the study of scientific texts a risky expansion of the term *rhetoric* from its classical definition as a practical art of civic discourse. Prominent among these critics is the historian of rhetoric, Dilip Gaonkar. In his 1993 essay, "The Idea of Rhetoric in the Rhetoric of Science," Gaonkar notes that "it is a habit of our time to invoke rhetoric, time and again, to make sense of a wide variety of discursive practices that beset and perplex us, and of discursive artifacts that annoy and entertain us.... Rhetoric is a way of reading the endless discursive debris that surrounds us."[79]

Gaonkar notes that in writing about scientific discourse as rhetorical, "we have extended the range of rhetoric to include discourse types...that the ancients would have regarded as falling outside its purview."[80] For example, recall that Aristotle said that rhetoric was the system we use to make decisions when we *do not* have other arts or sciences to guide us. Moreover, Gaonkar finds the extent of rhetoric's current reach to be unprecedented. "Never before in this history of rhetoric, not even during its glory days of the Italian Renaissance, did its proponents claim for rhetoric so universal a scope" as do some contemporary scholars.[81] Gaonkar also notes that what he terms "the promiscuous invocation of rhetoric" to account for anything and everything in all symbolic realms, while exciting to those who study rhetoric, might "only succeed in trivializing rhetoric."[82] Thus, he expresses concern that "the seemingly careless and ubiquitous uses of rhetoric" and the "sheer multiplicity of its uses" may lead the "overwhelmed reader [to] abandon the hope of ever finding what motivates and steers rhetoric."[83]

So, Gaonkar raises important concerns about what he terms the "globalization of rhetoric," its expansion from its earlier status as a "discourse practice" into a "hermeneutic metadiscourse"—an interpretive scheme that unlocks all symbolic activity. "Globalization," he writes, "severely undermines rhetoric's self-representation as a situated practical art."[84]

Should rhetoric's role be limited to the practical considerations of conducting government and business, or should it be accepted as an approach to understanding all of the many and varied symbolic worlds in which we live, including science, music, medicine, and penology? Does using the label, "The Rhetoric of X," where X can mean anything, trivialize rhetoric? Dilip Gaonkar's criticisms have prompted a reevaluation of writing in the rhetoric of science, but certainly has not served to dampen interest in this growing field of research.

CONCLUSION

One of the dominant interests in twentieth century rhetorical theory has been argument. This interest is linked by Perelman and Olbrechts-Tyteca, as we have seen, to a theory of audiences. The interaction of arguments and audiences is their solution to one of the central intellectual problems of the twentieth century: finding a means of testing and verifying value claims without reference to an absolute such as divinity or scientific method.

Stephen Toulmin, like Perelman and Olbrechts-Tyteca, sought a means of assessing and discussing the rational merits of arguments in nontechnical domains, and even in ordinary conversation. His book, *The Uses of Argument,* and the model of argument he there advanced, greatly influenced thinking about the underlying structure of everyday arguments and how the reasonableness of such arguments might be assessed.

Rhetoric's persistent concern for argument has been applied in the twentieth century to the study of various social and natural sciences. Scholars in the academic movement known as the "rhetoric of inquiry" have examined the fundamentally rhetorical ways that scientists pursue their work. For those who have read and been persuaded by the work of Geertz, McCloskey, Billig, Campbell, and many others writing on the rhetoric of science, the discourse of the sciences can never sound the same. Clearly, there is more to the pursuit of scientific truth than conducting experiments and publishing results. Science, it appears, is as rhetorical as are other human pursuits.

Nothing is more central to the classical conception of rhetoric than is argument. It is intriguing that this essential aspect of the original study of persuasive discourse should now play a prominent role in some of the most original and insightful of recent rhetorical scholarship. Some scientists have found the claim that science is rhetorical to be overstated, perhaps because the claim, if true, threatens our very conception of science. The authors discussed in the second half of this chapter do, however, make a compelling case for a rhetorical dimension in the sciences.

QUESTIONS FOR REVIEW

1. What do Perelman and Olbrechts-Tyteca mean by their concept of the "universal audience," and why is it important to their theory of argument?

2. What, according to Perelman and Olbrechts-Tyteca, are the advantages of argumentation before a single listener?

3. Into what two categories do Perelman and Olbrechts-Tyteca divide the starting points of argumentation? What specific sources of agreement are placed under each heading?

4. What are the constituent elements of an argument, according to Toulmin? How is each defined?

5. In Toulmin's system, what is the difference between field-dependent and field-invariant standards for assessing arguments?

6. What concern does Michael Billig have about the game metaphor that he had about the theater metaphor? What key factor in human interaction do these metaphors miss?

7. In what different ways are the natural and social sciences presented as rhetorical by writers discussed in this chapter?

8. What concern does Dilip Gaonkar raise regarding the rhetoric of science movement?

QUESTIONS FOR DISCUSSION

1. Perelman and Olbrechts-Tyteca consider self-deliberation a kind of argumentation. Do you agree that you can "reason with yourself"? Is this, as they claim, a particularly reliable way of testing our reasoning?

2. Michael Billig introduces the concepts of *logoi* and *antilogoi* to express what he takes to be the inevitable two-sidedness of human thought. Do you agree that our thinking is "dialogic" or inherently two-sided? Are we always discovering counterarguments for the arguments we hear, or even for the ones we ourselves use?

3. Are you persuaded by the arguments of scientists like Geertz, McCloskey, and Campbell that the natural and social sciences have a distinctly rhetorical dimension to them? Does such an idea violate your notion of science as objective? Should it?

TERMS

Argument field: In Toulmin's theory, arguments that can be said to be "of the same logical type."

Backing: Toulmin's term for support for an argument's warrant.

Claim: Toulmin's term for an argument's conclusion.

Data: Toulmin's term for the evidence to support the claim.

Elite audience: In Perelman and Olbrechts-Tyteca, an audience of trained specialists in a discipline.

Field-dependent: Toulmin's term for standards of argument assessment that belong specifically to a particular field.

Field-invariant: Toulmin's term for standards of argument assessment that apply regardless of the field in which the argument is advanced.

Ideology: Irrational or unexamined system of thinking.

Intersubjective agreements: Agreements forged among independent participants in dialogue on the basis of open and fairly conducted argument.

Logical positivism: The intellectual effort to bring scientific standards to bear on the resolution of all issues.

Modal qualifiers: Words that indicate the degree of confidence one takes in a conclusion; terms such as "must," "possibly," and "probably."

Particular audience: The actual audience of persons one addresses when advancing an argument publicly.

Presence: In Perelman and Olbrechts-Tyteca, the choice to emphasize certain ideas and facts over others, thus encouraging an audience to attend to them.

Quintilian's uncertainty principle: In Billig, the notion that the variety of possible human responses to any situation means that the rules of rhetoric must always be provisional, never absolute.

Rebuttal: Toulmin's term for potential conditions on the acceptance of the claim.

Rhetorical opposition: In Billig, the observation of the Sophist Protagoras that there are two sides to every question, because every form of human thought has its opposite

Starting points: In Perelman and Òlbrechts-Tyteca, points of agreement between a rhetor and an audience that allow argumentation to develop.

Toulmin Model: Identifies the claim, data, warrant, backing, qualifier, and rebuttal in an argument, and arranges these elements on a diagram.

Universal audience: In Perelman and Olbrechts-Tyteca, an imagined audience of highly rational individuals; and audience of all normal, adult persons.

Validity: A concern for an argument's structure without consideration of its content.

Warrant: Toulmin's term for a generalization that tends to link some data to a claim.

ENDNOTES

1. Michael Polanyi, *Personal Knowledge* (Chicago: University of Chicago Press, 1962), 11.
2. For a good collection of essays on Perelman's rhetorical theory, see: *The New Rhetoric of Chaim Perelman,* ed. Ray D. Dearin (Lanham, MD: University Press of America, 1989).
3. Chaim Perelman and L. Olbrechts-Tyteca, *The New Rhetoric: A Treatise on Argumentation,* trans. John Wilkinson and Purcell Weaver (Notre Dame, IN: University of Notre Dame Press), 6.
4. Perelman and Olbrechts-Tyteca, 20.
5. Perelman and Olbrechts-Tyteca, 4.
6. Perelman and Olbrechts-Tyteca, 14 (emphasis in original).
7. Perelman and Olbrechts-Tyteca, 30.
8. On Perelman's rhetorical theory, see: The *New Rhetoric of Chaim Perelman: Statement and Response,* ed. Ray D. Dearin (Lanham, MD: University Press of America, 1989). On Perelman and Olbrechts-Tyteca's theory of argument, see: Alan Gross, "A Theory of the Rhetorical Audience: Reflections on Chaim Perelman," *Quarterly Journal of Speech* 85 (May 1999): 202–211.
9. Perelman and Olbrechts-Tyteca, 30.
10. If you would like to read more about the concept of the universal audience, see: John R. Anderson, "The Audience as a Concept in the Philosophic Rhetoric of Perelman, Johnstone, and Natanson," *Southern Speech Communication Journal* 38 (Fall 1972): 39–50; Lisa S. Ede, "Rhetoric vs. Philosophy: The Role of the Universal Audience in Chaim Perelman's *The New Rhetoric,*" *Central States Speech Journal* 32 (Summer 1981): 118–125; John W. Ray, "Perelman's Universal Audience," *Quarterly Journal of Speech* 64 (December 1978): 361–375; Allen Scult, "Perelman's Universal Audience: One Perspective," *Central States Speech Journal* 27 (Fall 1976): 176–180.
11. Perelman and Olbrechts-Tyteca, 30.
12. Chaim Perelman, *The New Rhetoric and the Humanities,* trans. William Kluback (Dordrecht, Holland: D. Reidel, 1979), 46.
13. Perelman and Olbrechts-Tyteca, 20–21.
14. Perelman and Olbrechts-Tyteca, 65.
15. Perelman and Olbrechts-Tyteca, 66.
16. Chaim Perelman, *Justice* (New York: Random House, 1967), 78.
17. Perelman, *Justice,* 78.
18. Perelman, *Justice,* 82.
19. Perelman, *Rhetoric and Humanities,* 118.
20. Perelman, *Rhetoric and Humanities,* 119.
21. Perelman and Olbrechts-Tyteca, 31.
22. Perelman and Olbrechts-Tyteca, 32.
23. Perelman and Olbrechts-Tyteca, 36.
24. Perelman and Olbrechts-Tyteca, 36.
25. Perelman and Olbrechts-Tyteca, 37.
26. Perelman and Olbrechts-Tyteca, 40.
27. Perelman and Olbrechts-Tyteca, 40.

28. Perelman and Olbrechts-Tyteca, 117.

29. Perelman and Olbrechts-Tyteca, 116.

30. Perelman and Olbrechts-Tyteca, 117.

31. Stephen Toulmin, *The Uses of Argument* (Cambridge: Cambridge University Press, 1958).

32. Toulmin, 7.

33. Frans H. van Eemeren, Rob Grootendorst, Tjark Kruiger, *Handbook of Argumentation Theory* (Dordrecht, Holland: Foris Publications, 1987), 163.

34. Toulmin, 15.

35. Toulmin, 14 (emphasis added).

36. Toulmin, 17–18.

37. van Eemeren, Grootendorst, Kruiger, 173.

38. Toulmin, 22–30.

39. Toulmin, 20.

40. Toulmin, 20.

41. Toulmin, 99.

42. *The Rhetorical Turn: Invention and Persuasion in the Conduct of Inquiry,* ed. Herbert Simons, (Chicago: University of Chicago Press, 1990), 8.

43. See, for instance: Thomas Kuhn, *The Structure of Scientific Revolutions,* 2d ed. (Chicago: University of Chicago Press, 1970); Evelyn Fox Keller, "Secrets of Life, Secrets of Death," in *The Rhetoric of the Human Sciences,* eds. J. Nelson, A. Megill, and D. McCloskey (Madison: University of Wisconsin Press, 1987); Charles Bazerman, *Shaping Written Knowledge: The Genre and Activity of the Experimental Article in Science* (Madison: University of Wisconsin Press, 1988); Lawrence Prelli, *A Rhetoric of Science: Inventing Scientific Discourse* (Columbia: University of South Carolina Press, 1989); Alan Gross, *The Rhetoric of Science* (Cambridge, MA: Harvard University Press, 1990).

44. John Lyne, "Rhetoric and Scientific Communities," in *Rhetoric and Community: Studies in Unity and Fragmentation,* ed. Michael J. Hogan (Columbia: University of South Carolina Press, 1998), 266.

45. Wells, 93.

46. See: Kenneth Gergen and Mary Gergen, "Narrative Form and the Construction of Psychological Sciences," in *Narrative Psychology,* ed. T. R. Sarbin (New York: Praeger Press, 1986), 22–44; Lisa J. Disch, "More Truth than Fact: Storytelling as Critical Understanding in the Writings of Hannah Arendt," *Political Theory* (1994): 665–694.

47. Charles Arthur Willard, "Argumentation and Postmodern Critique," in *Perspectives on Argumentation: Essays in Honor of Wayne Brockriede* (Prospect Heights, IL: Waveland, 1990), 221–231, p. 225.

48. Wells, 56.

49. See, for example: Stephen B. Katz, "The Ethic of Expediency: Classical Rhetoric, Technology, and the Holocaust," *College English* 54 (March 1992): 255–275. Katz argues that the objectification of human beings in Nazi rhetoric, often in the name of expediency and technology, contributed to bringing about the Holocaust.

50. Wells, 56.

51. Simons, 4.

52. Lyne, 268.

53. Lyne, 268–269.

54. Lyne, 272–273.

55. Lyne, 273.

56. Lyne, 275.

57. D. N. McCloskey, *The Rhetoric of Economics* (Madison: University of Wisconsin Press, 1985), 36. Quoted in Herbert W. Simons, "The Rhetoric of Inquiry as an Intellectual Movement," *The Rhetorical Turn,* ed. Herbert W. Simons (Chicago: University of Chicago Press, 1990), 1–31, p. 9.

58. John Van Maanen, *Tales of the Field* (Chicago: University of Chicago Press, 1988), 5.

59. Clifford Geertz, *Works and Lives* (Stanford, CA: Stanford University Press, 1988), 4–5.

60. Geertz, 84. For other views of rhetoric's role in anthropology, see: Renato Rosaldo, "Where Objectivity Lies," in *The Rhetoric of the Human Sciences,* 87–110; *Narrative in Culture,* eds. Christo-

pher Nash and Martin Warner (London: Routledge, 1988); Alessandro Duranti, *From Grammar to Politics: Linguistic Anthropology in a Western Samoan Village* (Berkeley: University of California Press, 1994).

61. Michael Billig, "Psychology, Rhetoric, and Cognition" *History of the Human Sciences* 2: 289–307.

62. Michael Billig, *Arguing and Thinking* (Cambridge: Cambridge University Press, 1987), 2.

63. Billig, *Arguing and Thinking*, 4.

64. Billig, *Arguing and Thinking*, 5.

65. Billig, *Arguing and Thinking*, 6.

66. For another discussion of the relationship between rhetoric and psychology, see: Kenneth Gergen and Mary M. Gergen, "Narrative Form and the Construction of Psychological Sciences," in *Narrative Psychology* (New York: Praeger Press, 1986), 22–44. On related topics, see: J. A. Barnes, *A Pack of Lies: Towards a Sociology of Lying* (Cambridge: Cambridge University Press, 1994); Frank Stringfellow, *The Meaning of Irony: A Psychoanalytic Investigation* (State University of New York Press, 1994).

67. Billig, *Arguing and Thinking*, 62.

68. Billig, *Arguing and Thinking*, 10.

69. Billig, *Arguing and Thinking*, 13.

70. Billig, *Arguing and Thinking*, 15.

71. Billig, *Arguing and Thinking*, 20.

72. Billig, *Arguing and Thinking*, 25.

73. See: John Angus Campbell, "Darwin, Thales, and the Milkmaid: Scientific Revolution and Argument from Common Beliefs and Common Sense," in *Perspectives on Argument,* eds. Robert Trapp and Janice Schuetz (Prospect Heights, IL: Waveland, 1990), 207–220; "Scientific Discovery and Rhetorical Invention: The Path of Darwin's Origin," *The Rhetorical Turn,* 58–90.

74. Campbell, "Darwin, Thales," 209.

75. Campbell, "Darwin, Thales," 209.

76. Campbell, "Darwin, Thales," 210.

77. Quoted in Campbell, "Darwin, Thales," 213.

78. Campbell, "Darwin, Thales," 214.

79. Dilip Parameshwar Gaonkar, "The Idea of Rhetoric in the Rhetoric of Science," *Southern Communication Journal,* 58, 4 (Summer, 1993): 255–327, p. 259. Also published in *Rhetorical Hermeneutics: Invention and Interpretation in the Age of Science,* eds. Alan G. Gross and William M. Keith (Albany: State University of New York Press, 1997).

80. Gaonkar, 258.

81. Gaonkar, 259.

82. Gaonkar, 266.

83. Gaonkar, 267.

84. Gaonkar, 292.

CHAPTER TEN

CONTEMPORARY RHETORIC II: RHETORIC AS EQUIPMENT FOR LIVING

*[Language] may be treated as an instrument developed through its
use in the social processes of cooperation and competition....
Such considerations are involved in what I mean by the "dramatistic,"
stressing language as an aspect of "action," that is, as "symbolic action."*
—Kenneth Burke, *Language as Symbolic Action*

A word is a bridge thrown between myself and another.
—Mikhail Bakhtin

In the last chapter we considered rhetorical scholarship focusing on argumentation as rhetoric's defining feature. Writers like Perelman, Toulmin, and Billig emphasize a particular resource of rhetoric—the argument—as it is employed to solve practical problems associated with human social life. Other rhetorical scholars, however, have focused on rhetoric as a means of understanding and living successfully in a world of symbols. Rather than focusing on a single defining element such as the argument or the audience, these rhetorical theories emphasize larger issues such as the cultural contexts and general structures of rhetoric. This chapter considers several twentieth-century rhetorical theories that provide us with what these thinkers consider our essential rhetorical equipment for living.

RHETORIC IN ITS SOCIAL CONTEXT: THE DRAMATIC AND SITUATIONAL VIEWS

Several contemporary rhetorical theorists emphasize the context or situation in which rhetoric occurs. James L. Kinneavy writes that "certainly one of the most overpowering concepts in contemporary rhetoric, obvious in many different disciplines, is the notion that a piece of discourse must be judged against the cultural and situational contexts in which it was produced and in which it is being interpreted."[1]

Two of the most prominent representatives of this approach to rhetoric are Kenneth Burke and Lloyd Bitzer.

KENNETH BURKE AND RHETORIC
AS SYMBOLIC ACTION

Kenneth Burke (1897–1993) was perhaps the most influential of U.S. rhetorical theorists.[2] A writer of wide-ranging interests, Burke drew freely on disciplines as diverse as philosophy, drama, religion, political science, literature, and rhetoric. His thinking also reveals the influence of a variety of political, philosophical, literary, and religious perspectives.[3] Burke's work and thought is so vast in scope as to defy summary, his influence so pervasive and fundamental as to be impossible to estimate, his writing and vocabulary so idiosyncratic as to render understanding his thought difficult at best. Sidney Hook has written, "the greatest difficulty that confronts the reader of Burke, is to find out what he means."[4] The ordinarily circumspect writer George Kennedy calls Burke a "sometimes quirky writer."[5] Yet despite the difficulties associated with Burke's writing, the effort to understand him is repaid with genuine insights into the nature of rhetorical discourse. We will begin with his most foundational ideas: that rhetoric makes human unity possible, that language use is symbolic action and that rhetoric is symbolic inducement.

Identification

Among the most famous lines in the great corpus of Kenneth Burke's work is this statement: "You persuade a man only insofar as you can talk his language by speech, gesture, tonality, order, image, attitude, idea, identifying your ways with his."[6] So critical was this notion to Burke's thought that Lloyd Bitzer calls Identification, "the key term in Burke's theory of rhetoric."[7] This is the case because Burke found the most serious human problem to be alienation or separation, and rhetoric to be that problem's only solution. Burke wrote in his highly influential work, *A Rhetoric of Motives,* "If men were not apart from one another, there would be no need for the rhetorician to proclaim their unity. If men were wholly and truly of one substance, absolute communication would be of man's very essence."

   Burke's long interest in rhetoric was in large measure an interest in finding symbolic means of bringing people back together. Identification, he writes, "is affirmed with earnestness precisely because there is division. Identification is compensatory to division," that is, it is the antidote or necessary remedy for our alienation from one another.[8] Bitzer adds, however, that we experience "a constant condition of both division and community; our efforts to bridge gaps, even when successful, sometimes create others; and some of our most exhausting labor towards cooperation only anticipates division, as when we take great pains to rally ourselves to war." Rhetoric is needed "to find common meaning, unifying symbols, and ways of acting together, and thus promoting cooperation."[9] But that cooperation will never be complete.

"Identification," writes Burke, "ranges from the politician who, addressing an audience of farmers, says, 'I was a farm boy myself,' through the mysteries of social status, to the mystic's devout identification with the source of all being."[10] Symbolic interaction is possible, according to Burke, precisely because it recognizes and appropriates the hidden sources of identification among human beings as symbol users. Moreover, for Burke identification is possible because we share a quality he labeled using the essentially religious term *consubstantiality,* or commonality of substance. That is, we have in common certain substances including physical embodiment, common aspirations, and language itself. By recognizing and building on our consubstantiality, identification among people—and thus healing from the wound of our separation—becomes a rhetorical possibility.

Rhetoric's goal, then, is to bring together individuals separated from one another by alienation and competition. Burke sometimes called this condition of human alienation "warfare," and directed his work "toward the elimination of warfare."[11] And yet, Burke recognized that struggle and separation were inherent to the human condition, and that there could be no perfect rhetorical solution to that problem. After all, rhetoric itself embodied struggle. Thomas Farrell writes, "the very meaning of *symbolic action*" in Burke's thinking "must include notions of identification and *division,* struggle, and tension...." Still, rhetoric is both our most characteristically human activity, and our best hope of avoiding self-destruction. As Farrell writes, for Burke "there is no contradiction ultimately between discourse practice that is always suspect and practice that is the best human embodiment of human civility."[12] We as humans are always seeking something better, always "rotten with perfection," according to Burke. And through symbolic interaction we continuously press on toward unattainable perfection—and always imperfectly.

Rhetoric as "Symbolic Inducement"

There is at the center of Kenneth Burke's massive project, as we have seen, an unyielding interest in the symbol, and a corresponding interest in its use by human agents to change themselves and their communities. Burke's lasting hope was that the power of strategic language or rhetoric could be harnessed to move human beings in the direction of cooperation and ultimately of peace. Thus, Burke chose the Latin phrase *ad bellum purificandum*—toward the elimination of war—to introduce his rhetorical investigations in his work of 1945, *A Grammar of Motives.*

For Burke, "rhetoric" was the use of symbols to shape and change human beings and their contexts. Burke early turned his attention to three fundamental elements of human social and private existence that knowledge of rhetoric helped us to understand: (1) The symbolic means by which we define ourselves and our communities, (2) the nature of meaning as a matter of interpreting symbols, and (3) human motivation and action. He sometimes employed the phrase symbolic inducement to sum up this central activity of rhetoric, garnering cooperation by the strategic use of symbols. Perhaps his most famous definition of rhetoric occurs in *A Rhetoric of Motives* (1950), a definition that gives us an inkling both of Burke's thinking, and of the difficulty he sometimes poses to his interpreters. Burke writes: *"Rhetoric...is rooted in an essential function of language itself, a function that is wholly realistic, and is continually born anew; the use of language as a symbolic means of inducing cooperation in beings that by nature respond to symbols* [emphasis in original]."[13]

"Wholly realistic"? "Continually born anew"? These and many other "Burkisms" have always challenged Kenneth Burke's readers. Perhaps for now we can say that Burke believed that language was a concrete aspect of our existence and not merely conceptual or abstract, and at the same time that meaning is always being developed anew out of human social interaction. Understanding such facts of our symbolic existence was, for Burke, understanding rhetoric. Let's look a little further into his theory of rhetoric.

Terministic Screens and Being Human

Burke defined human beings in terms of their natural tendency to use symbols. But symbol use was, for Burke, an indication of both the best and the worst qualities of human beings. To be human was to be "the symbol-using (symbol-making, symbol misusing) animal," and to be the "inventor of the negative." Human beings also are "separated from [our] natural existence by instruments of [our] own making." That is, we create a world of objects that separates us from the natural world. Finally, human beings are "goaded by a spirit of hierarchy" and "rotten with perfection."

Language is the mechanism we employ in our continuous effort to order the world, and even this act of ordering reveals our drive to impose perfection on our surroundings. Burke wrote, "the mere desire to name something by its 'proper' name…is intrinsically 'perfectionist.' "[14] Language is at the very center of our being as humans, and it reveals much about us—our desire for order, our wish to control the natural world by naming its contents, our capacity to use and to misuse symbols. Language that names another as enemy in order to make their destruction possible would be an example of misusing symbols. It will be helpful to an understanding of Burke's rhetorical theory to explore his theory of language.

For Burke, language is not a neutral tool used to describe an objective existence. Rather, symbols are the essence of existence, the mechanisms by which we understand ourselves and our world, and the means by which we affect change. And language always has a strategic dimension for Burke. The linguistic choices we make as we speak shape our perceptions and reveal our intentions. In *Language as Symbolic Action* (1966) Burke wrote that "even if any given terminology is a *reflection* of reality, by its very nature as a terminology it must be a *selection* of reality; and to this extent it must function also as a *deflection* of reality."[15] What does Burke mean by this sentence that appears at first glance to be merely a play on words?

Here is one possible explanation of Burke's claim. Any set of terms used to describe an object, event, or person simultaneously directs attention *toward* some factors and *away from* others. Thus, all language is inherently rhetorical or strategic. For instance, if I describe an individual as a "consumer" rather than as a "citizen" I reveal my preference (at that moment) for economic over political descriptions of people. At the same time, I strategically direct attention *toward* the fact of a person's economic activity and *away from* their political activity. Thus, the choice of *consumer* over *citizen,* a choice evident in many media discussions of Americans, is *neither neutral nor objective.* Rather, it is a significant rhetorical positioning of both a speaker and the subject of the speaker's attention. Every set of terms or symbols, thus, becomes a particular kind of screen through which we perceive the world. Burke writes of the origin of his own label for this phenomenon, terministic screens, that it was suggested by a photographic exhibit:

> When I speak of "terministic screens," I have particularly in mind some photographs I once saw. They were *different* photographs of the *same* objects, the difference being that they were made with different color filters. Here something so "factual" as a photograph revealed notable distinctions in texture, and even in form, depending upon which filter was used for the documentary description of the event being recorded.[16]

Similarly, the terms we employ in thought, and thus in perception, function as filters of our experience. Again, language does not just "reflect" reality, it "selects" reality.

Language, then, does not just describe truths, experiences, or ideas. Rather, it directs us to *look at* some things and *overlook* others. This idea is not new with Burke, though he presented it clearly and persuasively. Burke relates a satirical use of the basic notion of terministic screens from the seventeenth-century French writer, Blaise Pascal. The Catholic Church in France had outlawed dueling, but this had done little to stop the practice. Pascal suggested that persons "intending to take part in a duel," might rather "merely go for a walk to the place where the duel was to be held." Moreover, "they would carry weapons as a precautionary means of self-protection in case they happened to meet an armed enemy." In this way "they could have their duel" without breaking the law. Writers of Pascal's day called this strategy "directing the intention," but, according to Burke, language has a similar effect at all times.[17] Burke summarizes the concept of terministic screens in *Language as Symbolic Action* this way: "We *must* use terministic screens, since we can't say anything without the use of terms; whatever terms we use, they necessarily constitute a corresponding kind of screen; and any such screen necessarily directs attention to one field [way of seeing] rather than another."[18]

Burke's Pentad

Burke's most famous contribution to rhetorical theory is known as his dramatistic pentad, presented in his work, *A Grammar of Motives* (1945).[19] As the name *dramatistic pentad* implies, the concept is drawn from the world of drama and divides rhetorical situations into five constituent elements for analysis. Burke sought in the pentad a "*grammar of motives,*" that is, a means of understanding human motivation. Burke begins his discussion of the pentad with a question: "What is involved, when we say what people are doing and why they are doing it?" He believed that the language of the drama provided a means of assessing rhetorical settings in order to come to some understanding of why people choose the actions they do.

The five elements of the pentad are *the act, the scene, the agent, agency, and purpose.* Briefly, the act is what was done or is being done. The scene is the location of the act, its setting. The agent is the person performing the action, while the agency is the means by which the agent performs the act. Finally, the purpose is the reason for the action, the intended goal. Burke drew an important distinction between simple "motion" and purposeful "action," the principal difference being the presence of a motive in the latter. A motive lies behind an action such as voting for president or leaving a job. Motives make human life and interaction strategic and intentional, that is, rhetorical. Thus, to understand human acts, one must understand human motives, and Burke's grammar of motives, his pentad, is advanced as an aid to such understanding.

Burke suggested that the pentad is most helpful when the elements are combined as ratios to demonstrate the dynamics of a particular rhetorical act. He writes: "We want to inquire into the purely internal relationships which the five terms bear to one another, considering their...range of permutations and combinations—and then to see how these various resources figure in actual statements about human motives."[20] This idea is best understood when applied to examples of human motivation.

For instance, one might emphasize the scene/act ratio when explaining a speaker's decision to redefine the physical setting of a speech. Thus, in his speech at Gettysburg, Abraham Lincoln sought to transform a battleground into a sacred setting in which fallen heroes could be honored. Through the act of making his speech, the scene—the battleground—is transformed into hallowed ground, thus making it a symbol of national redemption by Lincoln's act of speaking. The motive behind the rhetorical "act" of Lincoln's speech is thus best understood in the direct relationship to the "scene" in which the act is both being *per*formed and by which that same scene is being *trans*formed.

Or, alternatively, a rhetorical critic might wish to emphasize the scene/agent ratio in order to reveal how the scene of a rhetorical act reveals the character of the agent. Martin Luther King speaking before the Lincoln Memorial one hundred years after Lincoln spoke at Gettysburg is an instance of an agent interacting with a scene for rhetorical purposes. King stood in front of Lincoln's statue in the Lincoln Memorial in 1963 as he delivered his famous address to more than a quarter of a million people. He began by emphasizing his own rhetorical act as transpiring in a particular scene: "Five score years ago, a great American in whose symbolic shadow we stand today, signed the Emancipation Proclamation." King's opening line reverberates with the cadence and sound of Lincoln's own opening, "Four score and seven years ago." The agent, King, speaks in a particular scene, the Lincoln Memorial grounds, and the ratio of these two elements allows us to glimpse King's motives in speaking: to advance the work of justice that Lincoln himself had initiated a hundred years earlier.

As we have seen, the elements of the pentad can be employed to understand human motivation. But, they can also be used strategically to persuade audiences. A ratio of elements from the pentad may be highlighted as part of a rhetorical strategy. How might a politician accused of dishonesty set a scene for his oratorical defense that suggested that he, as agent, is honest? Perhaps a bust of Lincoln on a bookshelf behind him would make the point, something Richard Nixon attempted in one of his Watergate defense speeches. The scene is strategically redefined through the agency of the statue. Or, how might a politician accused of feathering her own nest with public moneys set a scene so as to show that she is a woman of modest means who has not benefited from anyone else's money? Perhaps her advisers might set as the scene for the speech a small auditorium filled with union workers. Setting the agent in this scene makes her appear less likely to have taken advantage of ordinary people.

The two ratios, "scene/act" and "scene/agent," says Burke, "are at the very center of motivational assumptions." Perhaps Burke meant that rhetoric is always situated discourse, and that acts and agents are always interacting with the rhetorical setting. Burke, like many rhetorical theorists throughout history, was concerned about the problem of justice and its relationship to rhetoric. He apparently held to a materialist explanation of justice. That is, justice can never transcend the material situation or circumstances of people's actual lives. By the reasoning of the scene/act ratio, to put people in the right scene is to encourage them to act justly, while to put them in the wrong scene is to encourage them to act unjustly. It follows that if you wish to change a person, you must change her or his context.

An example of a rhetorical situation in which Burke's dramatistic analysis provides various perspectives on human motivation is found in the confirmation hearings of Supreme Court Justice Clarence Thomas, and the controversy these hearings raised in 1991 over his relationship with Anita Hill. Hill accused Thomas of sexual harassment over a long period of time when she worked as his assistant at the law school at which he was teaching. Various accounts of Thomas's and Hill's actions developed out of the hearings resulting from Hill's charges. Some accounts found Hill to be the victim of a predatory male employer. Other accounts cast Hill as an aggressive young attorney currying favor with a boss on his way to significant power. How were the motives of these two people explained by various observers? Here are four possibilities suggested by Burke's pentadic analysis:

1. Thomas was a male employer taking advantage of a female employee in the workplace. The agent—Thomas—is placed in a particular scene—the workplace—to suggest a motive that might have been behind his actions, and to make Thomas culpable.
2. Thomas and Hill were in a work environment in which such acts are common, understandable, and even encouraged. Now the scene becomes preeminent. It is placed in ratio with the act, rendering the act excusable.
3. Hill was a scheming woman trying to seduce and entrap a successful man she admired. Here the act—defined as seduction—is attributed to a particular kind of agent—a "scheming woman." Hill is culpable in this strategy.
4. Hill is a black liberal trying to discredit an influential black conservative, Thomas. Thomas at one time referred to the efforts to prevent his confirmation as "a high-tech lynching," suggesting that his political enemies were out to sabotage his career for reasons related to race. Here is another strategic possibility for the act/agent ratio. This time, however, the act is redefined as a "lynching" and attributed to an agent defined as a ruthless political opponent.

Burke's pentad suggests how rhetorical strategists may answer crucial questions for an audience about an agent's motives. How was Thomas portrayed by his supporters? How was he portrayed by opponents? Similarly, in what ways was Hill portrayed by supporters and opponents, and toward what rhetorical ends? What defining terms were used to describe the agents and their acts? Were the hearings portrayed as a particular kind of scene? What elements in the scene—objects, events, and people—were manipulated to create an impression of guilt or innocence on the part of either agent? Burke wrote, "both act and agent require scenes that contain them."[21] Clearly there were actual actions performed and motives at work in the events that led to the hearings. But Burke's analysis helps us to see the rhetorical strategies at work as different terms are employed to influence how we perceive and understand those actions and motives.

Form

Burke's notion of form is another influential concept he introduced into the twentieth-century discussion of rhetoric and literary criticism.[22] In one of his earliest works, *Counter Statement* (1931), Burke identifies several "aspects" of form, which he defines as *"an arousing and fulfillment of desires."*[23] *Form* helps one to understand the underlying structure of appeals in rhetoric, and thus the rhetor's persuasive approach to her audience.

The first of these formal aspects Burke termed "syllogistic form," which he describes as "the form of a perfectly conducted argument, advancing step by step."[24] A drama or a rhetorician's case may unfold according to the structure of a logical proof, with reasons set out before an audience in an orderly fashion. The second form "is subtler" than a syllogism. Burke calls it "qualitative progression," by which he means that "one incident in a plot prepares us for some other incident of plot."[25] Thus, when an innocent victim has been harmed, we expect a scene in which the perpetrator is brought to justice. Similarly, when a politician identifies a particular group—say, drug traffickers—as perpetrating a harm on society, we expect a call to arms against that group.

"Repetitive form" is "the consistent maintaining of a principle under new guises."[26] Different images or arguments may be employed to make the same point repeatedly. When he ran for president, Ronald Reagan employed repetitive form in repeatedly making the point that the federal government was too big. Reagan employed arguments, anecdotes, statistics, and even jokes to suggest to his audience that U.S. government was a "bloated bureaucracy."

Some types of form are used so often that they achieve the status of a "conventional form." Thus, we expect introductions at the beginnings of speeches, emotional stories toward the end of a lengthy appeal, and illustrations following the introduction of a general claim.[27] Finally, "minor or incidental form" occurs any time we encounter such devices as "metaphor, paradox, disclosure, reversal" or any number of other recognizable approaches to securing or illustrating a point. The very fact that we recognize metaphor *as* metaphor reveals its status as form—we know what's coming. If I were to say with the poet Robert Burns, "My love is like a red, red rose, freshly sprung in June," and a friend replied, "Have you watered her lately?" the metaphor was not, for him, an instance of form.

Kenneth Burke's contributions to the field of rhetorical studies are as varied as they are rich, and we have just introduced a few of them here. Richard Lanham maintains that the powerful hypothesis that "rhetorical analysis can be used on nonliterary texts and on the conventions of social life is the pivotal insight of Burkean dramatism."[28] In other words, Burke opened new vistas for rhetorical and literary studies by demonstrating that *all* human symbolic behavior, not just linguistic behavior, was rhetorical. But despite such extravagant praise, Burke has not escaped criticism for his unusual language and method of presenting his ideas. As noted earlier, George Kennedy calls Burke a "sometimes quirky writer," employing a terministic screen that directs us to see Burke's excesses as excusable and even charming. Others treat Burke less indulgently. Brian Vickers, for example, calls Burke's rhetorical theory "free-wheeling, allusive, unhistorical philosophizing that rearranges the components of classical rhetoric so idiosyncratically as to be virtually unusable."[29] Certainly Vickers' "terministic screen" directs our attention in a slightly different direction than does Kennedy's, but neither assessment is flattering of Burke.

At the heart of Burke's massive project, developed in more than twenty-five books written over a span of more than sixty years, is a fascination with both human symbolic behavior and the sheer power of language. For Burke, the strategic use of language was the very essence of human personal and social existence. Like the Sophist Gorgias in the fifth century B.C. and the Renaissance humanists of the fifteenth century, Burke found rhetoric to be a kind of verbal magic that created meaning and reality out of the immateriality of the word. Explaining Burke's view of language, William Covino writes, "Language *creates,* and so every utterance is always a magical decree [emphasis added]."[30] Burke himself affirmed in his book, *The Philosophy of Literary Form,* "The magical decree is implicit in all language."[31] Thus, Burke retrieves to view in the twentieth century an ancient and venerable orientation to rhetoric that sees it as actually creating the substance of our lives through "symbolic action." The influence of his thought regarding such symbolic action, regarding rhetoric, has been great.

LLOYD BITZER AND RHETORIC AS SITUATIONAL

Lloyd Bitzer's 1968 article, "The Rhetorical Situation," marked a turning point in the U.S. study of rhetorical theory.[32] Bitzer's relatively brief essay sought to define rhetoric as discourse responsive to a particular kind of situation. "Rhetorical discourse, I shall argue, obtain[s] its character-as-rhetorical from the situation which generates it."[33] Calling rhetoric "a mode of altering reality...by the creation of discourse which changes reality through the mediation of thought and action," Bitzer argued that a rhetorical situation is defined by three elements: an audience, an exigence, and constraints.

The Exigence

Bitzer defined an exigence as "an imperfection marked by urgency; it is a defect, an obstacle, something waiting to be done, a thing which is other than it should be."[34] Not all exigencies, however, contribute to rhetorical situations. The particular exigence in question must be one capable of modification by discourse. For instance, the onset of winter cannot be altered by a speech, though the exigence of inadequate snow removal by an inept city government may be an exigence that can be modified by discourse. "An exigence is rhetorical when it is capable of positive modification and when positive modification requires discourse or can be assisted by discourse."[35] The national crisis arising immediately after the assassination of President John Kennedy in 1963 stands for Bitzer as an example of a *rhetorical* exigence. Speeches by Lyndon Johnson and others helped to ameliorate or improve the situation rhetorically.

The Audience

The second element in the rhetorical situation is the audience. However, it is again important to point out that not all audiences are rhetorical audiences from Bitzer's point of view. "Properly speaking," he writes, "a rhetorical audience consists only of those persons who are capable of being influenced by discourse and of being mediators of change."[36] In other words, you are *not* a member of a rhetorical audience merely because you heard a rhetorical appeal. A citizen of Canada listening to a campaign speech by a U.S. presidential candidate is not part of the rhetorical audience because she cannot vote in the United States, and thus can do nothing to alter the exigence facing the candidate or the United States. One must be capable of acting in a manner directly relevant to improving the exigence in order to qualify as a member of the rhetorical audience.

Constraints

Finally, Bitzer maintains that rhetorical situations exhibit constraints. This is the third and probably the most difficult to understand of the three elements of a rhetorical situation. The word "constraint" conjures up a problem or a restriction on one's actions. But Bitzer also has in mind enabling factors when he writes of constraints. He writes, "besides exigence and audience, every rhetorical situation contains a set of *constraints* made up of persons, events, objects, and relations which are parts of the situation because they have the power to constrain decision and action needed to modify the exigence."[37]

Bitzer compares constraints to the artistic and inartistic proofs of Aristotle's *Rhetoric*. He apparently has in mind, then, that constraints are any factors that a rhetorician must contend with in the inventional process. They are factors both limiting and liberating the rhetor as arguments and appeals are discovered, arranged, and delivered to the rhetorical audience. Thus, one's own rhetorical abilities (or lack thereof) is a constraint, as is available evidence, possible arguments, audience beliefs, and a range of other factors that the rhetor must take into account while composing a rhetorical message. Constraints may be thought of as the boundaries within which rhetoric is both created and advanced.

The Fitting Response

Bitzer argued that the rhetorical situation actually "dictates" or "prescribes" the response appropriate to it. It is on this point that his theory may be open to the most telling criticism. "If it makes sense to say that situation invites a 'fitting' response, the situation must somehow prescribe the response which fits [emphasis added]."[38]

This notion of rhetoric that fits a particular rhetorical situation is reminiscent of Hugh Blair's notion that rhetoric's style ought to be fitting to its purposes and occasion. Bitzer imagines a process by which the rhetor assesses the elements of the rhetorical situation—the audience, the exigence, and the constraints. Having assessed these elements, the astute rhetor discovers the limits of what can properly or effectively be said to improve that particular situation. The rhetor then composes the right rhetorical response by uttering rhetoric that is dictated to her or him by the elements of audience, exigence, and constraints.

Lloyd Bitzer's theory of the rhetorical situation provided an accessible yet powerful tool for assessing a wide variety of rhetorical events. To speak of the rhetorical situation has become an inherent aspect of much U.S. rhetorical theory and criticism. Bitzer's basic insight—that rhetoric is discourse situated in and responsive to particular settings—has been an extraordinarily suggestive one.

RHETORIC AND NARRATION

One important movement in twentieth-century rhetorical theory developed at the confluence of rhetoric and narrative.[39] The connection between rhetoric and story is an ancient one. It shows up, for instance, in Plato's *Phaedrus,* where Socrates relates stories to argue for a particular view of the human soul (the myth of the charioteer) or to suggest the dangers inherent in moving from oral to written discourse (the myth of the Egyptian god Thoth). Some recent theorists have expanded the concept of narration to the point that it subsumes all of rhetoric, while others have discovered a rhetorical dimension in the writing of all fiction.

How does one determine what written and spoken texts *mean*? How can interpretive practices accommodate the increasing difficulty of defining a "source" and an "audience" in rhetorical settings? How does rhetorical theory, rooted in classical thinking, come to recognize and appreciate the multiple meanings evident in rhetorical texts advanced by diverse social groups? As the power of public discourse to shape values and thus action becomes increasingly clear, how are the social functions of discourse best explained?

As the practice of rhetoric has changed in the modern period, some rhetoricians have found in narrative theories the flexible structure necessary to account for new rhetorical functions. Susan Wells, for instance, finds narrative to be "central to the discourses of modernity because of its heterogeneity, its complex articulations of time, and its construction of the narrator's fluid subject position."[40] Narrative, according to Wells, is "marked by deep diversity of styles, forms of argument, and rhetorical relations," and offers ways to "organize separate trajectories of knowledge and reflection."[41] Some narrative theories of rhetoric have developed in response to diverse cultural settings demanding a highly adaptable method of analysis. We will explore four such narrative theories in the following pages.

MIKHAIL BAKHTIN AND THE POLYPHONIC NOVEL

Although his work has only recently begun to influence the study of rhetoric, Russian linguist Mikhail Bakhtin (1896–1975) was one of the earliest of the contemporary European thinkers to turn his attention to problems of discourse in cultural contexts.[42] Bakhtin, according to Michael Holquist, "seek[s] to grasp human behavior through the use humans make of language."[43]

Bakhtin's work, while preserving significant tenets of Marxist theory, represents a departure from the Marxist orthodoxy of his time. He was suspicious of the possibility of "objectivity" in writing, that is, suspicious of the claim that art can convey an unambiguous, monolithic knowledge of the truth. For instance, perhaps a story simply obscures economic relations while ostensibly presenting them as matters of fact. Bakhtin questioned whether any writer or philosopher represented the "correct view" of the human condition. Does Marxist analysis, for example, present a true picture of social circumstances simply because it has shaken off the ideological trappings of capitalist thinking? Bakhtin thought not.

Discourse as Ideological and Social

For Bakhtin, all discourse is inherently ideological in two senses. First, in a way reminiscent of Kenneth Burke, Bakhtin held that language does not merely reflect an objective world. Rather, words participate in *constructing* that world as well. To use language is to engage in a construction process, and what is constructed is our view of the world we inhabit. Thus, speaking and writing are *never* neutral or value-free activities.[44] Second, to speak is to articulate a position. Thus, for Bakhtin, when we speak or write we give voice to our own system of beliefs. To create discourse is to engage in a process of self-disclosure.

Bakhtin argues that language use is inherently ideological, but it is also inherently social or dialogic. This is true for two reasons. First, we fashion speech out of preexisting, historically bound, linguistic material. That is, the very substance of speech is a product of previous social processes. We never invent speech out of a vacuum: All of our words are marked by the meanings and intentions of many people who spoke before we did.

Second, every utterance or "word" "*is a two-sided act.*" That is, the word's meaning "is determined equally by *whose* word it is and *for whom* it is meant." This means that by its very nature as a word "it is precisely *the product of the reciprocal relationship between speaker and listener, addresser and addressee....*" Consequently, "a word is a bridge thrown between myself and another. If one end of the bridge depends on me, then the other depends on my addressee. A word is a territory shared by both addresser and addressee, by the speaker and his interlocutor."[45] Meanings, therefore, are negotiated territories always involving the participation of more than one person. Thus, discourse always performs a social or relational function; it responds to, or anticipates a response from, another person.

Polyphonic Discourse: Hearing Many Voices in the Novel

From Bakhtin's perspective, multiple "voices" or positions constitute the social world. But, while multiple voices are always present, not all voices are valued equally. In the continual process of dialogue, which may be friendly or not, the relative value of voices is continually asserted and contested. Bakhtin sought to free discourse from the "constraints" that rendered some voices more valued than others. Consequently, Bakhtin focused on examining dialogues—chains of assertion and response—and on freeing the different voices present in a dialogue, perhaps especially those which may pass unnoticed.

Language as a dialogic phenomenon is virtually a site of political struggle as each of us "seeks to infuse language with [our] own intentions."[46] Moreover, meaning is corporately constructed as communication takes place, the listener becoming as important to the process as the speaker, the reader as crucial as the author. For these reasons, when describing the basic unit of discourse Bakhtin preferred the term *utterance* with its implied sense of a personal statement full of potential meanings, to the fixed meaning implied by the word *sentence.*

Bakhtin recognized that the dialogic aspect of language can be subverted by official efforts to suppress its inherent possibilities for diversity of expression. He thus elevated a concept he termed *heteroglossia,* that is, the vast variety of language use always evident in any culture. A moment's reflection reveals that each one of us, in fact, employs various "languages" everyday depending on our audience, the social setting, and the issues being addressed. To heteroglossia, Bakhtin contrasted *monologia,* or the univocal, fixed meaning of the state or official language. Thus, the "official" language of a nation might be opposed to the innumerable group and individual variations on that language as heard in dialects, slang, or the special vocabulary of an occupational group.

Because of this great interest in language's capacity for diversity of expression, Bakhtin took a decided interest in the novel. The novel became for Bakhtin a way of demonstrating, studying, and even celebrating the dialogic nature of language, and to oppose monologic models. Josephine Donovan writes that Bakhtin viewed the novel as "an anarchic, insubordinate genre that reflects a kind of popular resistance to centralizing official establishments and unifying disciplines...."[47] Of particular interest to Bakhtin were the novels of Dostoevsky.

Novels do not reflect an objective view of reality, for, as literary critic Wayne Booth points out, "the author's voice is always present, regardless of how thoroughly it is disguised."[48] Even the forms that discourse takes are infused with meaning, are "ideological" in their tendency to communicate a point of view. "The quality pursued by Bakhtin," writes Booth, "is a kind of 'sublimity of freed perspectives' that will always, on all fictional occasions, be superior to every other."[49] Thus, Bakhtin sought the possibility of a full voice for various perspectives in order that, as part of the Great Dialogue that is human existence, we might discover "the best possible avenues to truth."[50]

It is for these reasons that Bakhtin admired the polyphonic nature of Dostoevsky's novels, the quality of each character being fully developed and speaking fully his or her perspective on the world.[51] Bakhtin writes that "a plurality of independent and unmerged voices and consciousness, a genuine polyphony of fully valid voices is in fact the chief characteristic of Dostoevsky's novels."[52] Bakhtin, then, saw the works of Dostoevsky as a model for allowing equal voice to varied perspectives in the continuous dialogue among people about their conditions and the truths by which they live.

Bakhtin has interested students of rhetoric because of his focus on dialogue and discourse as means of answering some of the most pressing private and public questions of the twentieth century. What is the nature of truth? For Bakhtin, "truth" is a process, a dialogic negotiation, a contest rather than an outcome, a conversation rather than a proposition. Insofar as Bakhtin equated a community's capacity to accommodate multiple voices with that community's health, he challenges rhetorical theorists and critics to ask: How can varied perspectives on truth be allowed equal access to the great dialogue? In what ways can a society accommodate and even nurture differentness?

Bakhtin's ideas also challenge rhetorical theorists to listen to marginalized voices and to consider how social and political life is transformed as these voices confront those spoken from society's "center." Moreover, Bakhtin's conception of the self as constituted in the dialogic process presents a challenge to traditional understandings of "sources" and "audiences."

WAYNE BOOTH AND THE RHETORIC OF FICTION

A U.S. writer with interests in both rhetoric and narrative, and one who admired the work of Bakhtin, is Wayne Booth. Booth, a literary critic, is perhaps best known for his rhetorical approach to the study of fictional writing. In *The Rhetoric of Fiction,* he examines the relationship between author and narrator, and between authorial intent and textual content. Booth notes that some works of fiction pretend to an "authorial objectivity or impersonality."[53] That is, authors pretend not to be present in the voices of their characters. However, Booth affirms that, the rhetoric of fiction is that "the author's judgment is always present, always evident to anyone who knows how to look for it.... We must never forget that though the author can to some extent choose his disguises, he can never choose to disappear."[54]

Booth sought to answer writers like Sartre who had argued that the author must "give the illusion" of not even existing. If there is an author present "controlling the lives of the characters, they will not seem to be free," argued Sartre.[55] But, responds Booth, not only are authors present in their work, they *should* be in order to provide the reader relief from the "dramatic vividness" of "pure showing." Authors cannot be excised from their writings. "The author's voice is never really silenced. It is, in fact, one of the things that we read fiction for, and we are never troubled by it unless the author makes a great to-do about his own superior naturalness."[56]

Booth, like Bakhtin, also questioned whether a writer could adopt a value-neutral stance in writing. Sartre had contended that "a writer...must know that dung-heaps play a very respectable part in a landscape, and that evil passions are as inherent in life as good ones."[57] However, Booth counters that even such a claim elevates one set of values over another, and thus advocates the former. Such advocacy is a fundamentally rhetorical activity. Could an author, then, achieve neutrality about values by casting main characters as "everyperson," an ordinary member of the human race? Booth responds to this possibility, "Even among characters of equal moral, intellectual, or aesthetic worth, all authors inevitably take sides."[58]

Wayne Booth has played a major role, then, in sensitizing the literary world to the presence of the author's rhetorical voice in works of fiction. In his interest in discovering motives in the symbolic arena of literature, Booth can be seen as contributing to the larger project of Kenneth Burke and others who would have us attend to the presence of the rhetorical in all symbolic realms.

Booth's interest in narrative again underlines the interest of the U.S. rhetorical community in the relationship between narration and rhetoric. Wayne Booth's attention to narrative underlines the interest of rhetorical scholars in the relationship between rhetoric and the story. Seeing rhetoric through the lens of narration, and vise versa, provides yet another practical approach to navigating the world of symbols which we all inhabit.

JURGEN HABERMAS AND THE CONDITIONS
OF RATIONAL DISCOURSE

Jurgen Habermas (b. 1929) like virtually every European intellectual who lived through the disaster, was greatly affected by the experience of World War II. Extending the work of the Frankfurt School, he employed an analysis influenced by Marx and Freud to argue that political corruption, criminality, and class warfare were the major problems to be addressed by the humanities. Habermas, like Michael Foucault (discussed in the next chapter), believed that "critical rationality consists in the unflinching examination of our most cherished and comforting assumptions."[59] But beyond this point of agreement, these writers' approaches to reason and society "diverge dramatically." Finding Marx's idea of economic determinism too limited, Habermas sought to develop a theory of communication rooted in a concept of an "ideal speech community," a theory that has as its ultimate goal emancipation of the self.[60] Habermas begins with a critique of the sources of human knowledge.[61] His critical work is guided by a vision of a functional and just human society rooted in the rational tradition of Western philosophy and in a Marxism analysis of social justice. He credits Stephen Toulmin as one of the people who did important work in understanding the logical foundations of natural language.[62] Though he was not especially enamored of the rhetorical tradition, Habermas was deeply concerned with some of the same issues that have concerned many rhetorical theorists.

Communicative Action and the Rational Society

Habermas was born in Düsseldorf, and studied philosophy at Göttingen and Bonn. He became acquainted with the philosopher Theodor Adorno at the Institute for Social Research. During the 1960s and 1970s, Habermas taught at the Universities of Heidelberg and Frankfurt, and was for a time the director of the Max Planck Institute.

Habermas's rational society is built on the foundation of rationally liberated individuals speaking to one another as equals toward the goal of agreement and, thus, action. To Habermas's way of thinking, establishing a rational society requires both the correct interpretation and the subsequent transformation of the present society. In a rational society, individuals are allowed a greater degree of choice across a wider range of options, resulting in personal emancipation. In such a society, "assent secured by custom or tradition is replaced by...rational evaluations of claims," a view that places Habermas squarely in the Enlightenment tradition of confidence in reason as emancipating.[63] All views are *not* equally rational; each claim or proposition must pass muster before it assumes the title "rational." Thomas McCarthy, a leading expert on Habermas's thought, writes that Habermas insists on the validity of "the distinctions between truth and falsity, right and wrong."[64] But, then, how does one know which claims are "truer" than others?

For Habermas, claims are subject to proof or refutation through the process of communication itself. We must also subject our received cultural traditions to a process of scrutiny through argumentative discourse, perhaps especially those ideas that lead to economic injustice. "The ideas of reason, truth, justice...serve as ideals with reference to which we can criticize traditions we inherit."[65] Habermas writes that "dramatic examples" of this critical process occur when "the validity claims of mythical and religious world-views could be systematically questioned and tested; we understand this as the beginnings of philosophy in the Athens of the classical period."[66] Thus, the critique of ideologies is central to the evolution of Habermas's rational society.

Habermas found the interactive process of critical argumentation a key to overcoming the problems of ideological domination—the situation that obtains when a society is no longer rational. He called such critical discourse by the name communicative action.[67] Susan Wells writes that communicative action is "the interaction of at least two people who establish a relationship," and who "try to come to a common understanding of the situation in which they are acting through interpretation." The goal of such associations is "to act together, which means they must agree on how to act."[68] Communicative action comes about as "a shared recognition that speech is subject to criteria of truth, appropriateness, and sincerity" that emerges from communication.[69] The activity of communication is central, then, to Habermas's theory of rationality. His interest in communication reflects his recognition of the inherently rhetorical nature of all free and open human interactions.

The Universality of the Rhetorical

Though he does not specifically write about rhetoric, Habermas holds that no aspect of human endeavor is rationally pure or nontendentious. Thus, philosophy is just as rhetorical as art, which is no more rhetorical than is science.[70] Consequently, each arena must test its own propositions in debate or dialogue according to standards appropriate to that arena. This orientation places Habermas close to the English pragmatic or problem-solving philosophy of language, in opposition to the largely aesthetic approaches to language of Continental linguists and critical theorists.

Habermas found in argumentative dialogue a path to rationality. Dialogue affords the opportunity to test propositions and their underlying values. The goal of such argumentative exchanges is intersubjective agreements, that is, agreements forged among independent participants in dialogue on the basis of open and fairly conducted argument. McCarthy writes that Habermas views reason as "a healing power of unification and reconciliation." But, such unification is not for him discovered in a mystical "Absolute," but rather in "the unforced intersubjectivity of rational agreement." A claim to having made a true statement, what Habermas calls a validity claim, can "in the end be redeemed only through intersubjective recognition brought about by the unforced force of reason."[71] Thus, unity and healing in society require voluntary, mutual, or "intersubjective" agreements achieved through rational argument.

Rational communication, which Habermas defines much as Aristotle or Cicero would have defined *rhetoric,* develops around the "'unforced force of the better argument,' with the aim of coming to an agreement about the validity or invalidity of problematic claims."[72] Claims about what is true can be, must be, tested in "argumentative discourse."[73] Habermas holds out for the utility of both reason and discourse to solve practical and pressing human problems. Though he agrees that some contemporary criticisms of the limits of reason are just, he is not ready to give up on the possibility that reason, tested in discourse, can provide us with desperately needed answers to the problems that face us.

Universal Pragmatics and Communicative Competence

Habermas is best known among rhetoric scholars for his theory of universal pragmatics. This technique, important to his critical theory, sets out the rules for using and understanding language rationally. The goal of universal pragmatics is open, equitable, ethical, and thus rational discourse aimed at freeing human beings from dominance. Such discourse takes place in what Habermas called the public sphere, a place of discussion among individuals unrestrained by the dominating influence of political systems and the interests of the state. "In the public sphere," writes Susan Wells, "the problems of politics, society, and culture are represented in general terms and opened to rational discussion."[74]

Habermas also discussed, in connection with universal pragmatics, the notion of communicative competence, the conditions under which rational communication is possible. Communicative competence involves three elements, according to Habermas. First, a truth claim is shared by speaker and hearer. A speaker makes a claim that both speaker and listener understand in a similar fashion. A failure to accurately interpret truth claims would, then, constitute a failure in communication competence. Second, the hearer is led to understand and accept the speaker's intention. Beneath the truth claim, the competent listener understands the operation of a motive. Here, again, we find Habermas to reflect a traditionally rhetorical orientation, attention to the underlying motives that drive human communication. As a third element in communication competence, Habermas finds that the speaker adapts to the hearer's world view. Again, this is a concern for audience adaptation that has been part of rhetorical thinking for centuries.[75]

By Habermas's account, disagreement about the truth or appropriateness of statements leads to discourse or argumentation. In order for communicative transactions to be rational, they must meet three conditions. These include, first, that the discussion be unrestrained, which means that all participants are allowed to speak freely and to present their positions without fear of being restricted. Second, all advocates must have a right to self-representation, that is, the freedom to speak for themselves. Third, a full complement of norms and expectations must be in place under the conditions of rational discourse. Everyone should communicate on an equal footing, and no one can command the other parties to listen to them without an equal communicative opportunity being extended to those others.

Critical Theory and the Critique of Ideology

Critical theory, the systematic means of analyzing discourse for its hidden assumptions and implications, clears the way for liberation by providing criticism of ideologies, defined as irrational, unexamined, or coercive systems of thinking. For instance, technological thinking becomes an ideology as it closes off certain possibilities in a society's discourse. When educational reform is considered under technological ideology, as an example, some possibilities are excluded and others are given privilege. Education moves toward the service of technology with emphasis and funding going to studies such as mathematics and science, while disciplines such as philosophy and literature are relegated to the position of inconsequential ornaments to education. Nor is the influence of ideology felt only at the level of policy. The problem of ideological dominance goes as deep as the human psyche. For Habermas, false ideologies lead to false thinking, which in turn leads to false consciousness, a flawed and thus distorting view of reality, of the world, and of people. Critical theory seeks, through the analysis of ways we talk and think, a new and liberating consciousness. McCarthy writes: "Habermas's argument is, simply, that the goal of critical theory—a form of life free from unnecessary domination in all its forms—is inherent in the notion of truth; it is anticipated in every act of communication."[76]

His critics have alleged that his theory is naive in its failure to account for the real differences among people as regards access to channels of communication, ability to communicate, and social power.[77] His vision of rational citizens talking as equals, the critics respond, neglects the massive social inequities that prevent just this sort of conversation from taking place. In addition, his theory of communicative action is sometimes seen as favoring "the specific structures of rationality associated with technological cultures of Europe and North America," which opens Habermas to the charge of "paternalistic guidance" when standards employed in "other regions of the world" are taken to represent an underdeveloped rationality.[78] In spite of these criticisms, Habermas argues that as we enter dialogue under the conditions of communicative competence, we afford ourselves a greater opportunity to interact, and to act interdependently, free of the constraints of ideology. Habermas's concern for a more rational society led him to advance a theory of rational communication that shares some elements in common with rhetorical theories, such as an account of how assertions are supported and of the ethical conduct of persuasion.

CONCLUSION

Theories focusing on rhetoric as basic equipment for living have opened a broad avenue of insight for rhetorical theorists. Recall that Aristotle's account of the art of rhetoric describes it as an art that allows one to understand and respond well to various real life settings—the court, the legislature, the public ceremony.

Perhaps, then, the theories we have considered in this chapter rediscover the relationships between rhetoric and life as we encounter it in the symbolic world. Kenneth Burke has drawn attention to the symbolic nature of our lives and how symbols and human motives interact. Lloyd Bitzer's situational approach also sees rhetoric as revealing a structure in which human agents respond rhetorically to events out of the desire to improve on an imperfect situation. Rhetoric is seen as a response to a particular kind of setting, and as structured by that setting in predictable ways.

Early in this century, Mikhail Bakhtin opened a discussion about the rhetorical nature of narrative. His interest in the polyphonic possibilities in the novel prompted discussion about the relationship between rhetoric and narrative generally. Wayne Booth has pursued Bakhtin's vision of narrative as rhetoric. Finally, Jurgen Habermas has suggested the means by which we might equip an entire society to conduct more rational discourse.

QUESTIONS FOR REVIEW

1. What are the key terms in Burke's dramatistic pentad? What do the terms describe?
2. What is Wayne Booth's position on the possibility of an author of fiction being "invisible"?
3. What are the three essential components of Bitzer's "rhetorical situation"?
4. What quality did Mikhail Bakhtin find intriguing in the novels of Dostoevsky?
5. Why did Bakhtin consider that discourse is always ideological and social?
6. Why was Bakhtin drawn to the novels of Dostoevsky?
7. What is the ultimate goal of Habermas's theorizing?

QUESTIONS FOR DISCUSSION

1. After reading this chapter, what argument could be made for broadening the conception of rhetoric beyond public speeches or widely circulated written documents?
2. In your opinion, what kinds of rhetoric would Kenneth Burke's theory be most likely to help one to understand?

3. Which theorist in this chapter did you find the most helpful or interesting? Why?

4. What is your reaction to Jurgen Habermas's search for universal guidelines of argumentative practice that might help assure rational and just discourse? Is such a system possible, or is this a utopian dream that does not have any application to the real world of rhetorical interactions?

TERMS

Communicative action: In Habermas, the interactive process of critical argumentation; a key to overcoming the problems of ideological domination.

Communicative competence: The conditions under which rational communication is possible.

Constraints: In Bitzer, "persons, events, objects, and relations which are parts of the situation because they have the power to constrain decision and action needed to modify the exigence."

Consubstantiality: Commonality of substance.

Critical theory: The systematic means of analyzing discourse for its hidden assumptions and implications.

Dialogues: In Bakhtin, chains of assertion and response that reveal the presence of different voices.

Dramatistic pentad: Burke's "grammar of motives," consisting of act, scene, agent, agency, and purpose.

Exigence: In Bitzer, "an imperfection marked by urgency;...a defect, an obstacle, something waiting to be done, a thing which is other than it should be."

False consciousness: In Habermas, a flawed and thus distorting view of reality, of the world, and of people.

Fitting response: In Bitzer, rhetoric that is dictated to the rhetor by the rhetorical situation.

Form: In Burke, "an arousing and fulfilling of a desire in an audience."

Heteroglossia: The many languages that proliferate in any culture (Bakhtin).

Polyphonic: "Many voiced;" Bakhtin's term for quality of narrative in which each character is fully developed and speaks fully his or her perspective on the world.

Rhetorical audience: In Bitzer, "those persons who are capable of being influenced by discourse and of being mediators of change."

Rhetoric of fiction: Booth's insight that, in narrative, "the author's judgment is always present."

Symbolic inducement: Burke's definition of rhetoric. Garnering cooperation by the strategic use of symbols.

Terministic screens: Burke's term to describe the fact that every language or choice of words becomes a filter through which we perceive the world.

Utterance: A personal statement full of potential meaning. For Bakhtin, the basic unit of discourse.

ENDNOTES

1. James L. Kinneavy, "Contemporary Rhetoric," in *The Present State of Scholarship in Historical and Contemporary Rhetoric,* ed. Winifred Bryan Horner (Columbia: University of Missouri Press, 1990), 192.

2. Burke's numerous works include: *Counter-Statement* (Berkeley: University of California Press, 1931); *Language as Symbolic Action* (Berkeley: University of California Press, 1937); *A Grammar of Motives* (Berkeley: University of California Press, 1945); *A Rhetoric of Motives* (Berkeley: University of California Press, 1950); *The Rhetoric of Religion* (Berkeley: University of California Press, 1961).

3. See, for example: Don Abbott, "Marxist Influences on the Rhetorical Theory of Kenneth Burke," *Philosophy and Rhetoric* 4 (1974): 217–233.

4. Sidney Hook, "The Technique of Mystification" *Critical Responses to Kenneth Burke,* ed. William H. Ruckert (Minneapolis: University of Minnesota Press, 1969), 89. Quoted in Abbott, 217.

5. George Kennedy, *Classical Rhetoric and Its Christian and Secular Tradition* (Chapel Hill: University of North Carolina Press, 1999), 94.

6. Kenneth Burke, *A Rhetoric of Motives* (Berkeley: University of California Press, 1969), 55.

7. Lloyd Bitzer, "Political Rhetoric," in *Landmark Essays on Contemporary Rhetoric,* ed. Thomas Farrell (Mahwah, NJ: Lawrence Earlbaum, 1998), 1–22, p. 9.

8. Burke, *Rhetoric of Motives,* 22.

9. Bitzer, 9–10.

10. Burke, *Rhetoric of Motives,* xiv.

11. Burke, used the Latin phrase, *ad purificandum bellum.*

12. Thomas Farrell, *Norms of Rhetorical Culture* (New Haven: Yale University Press, 1993), 204.

13. Kenneth Burke, *A Rhetoric of Motives* (Berkeley: University of California Press, 1950), 43.

14. Burke, *Language as Symbolic Action,* 16.

15. Burke, *Language as Symbolic Action,* 45.

16. Burke, *Language as Symbolic Action,* 45.

17. Burke, *Language as Symbolic Action,* 45.

18. Burke, *Language as Symbolic Action,* 50.

19. Burke, *A Grammar of Motives* (1945; Berkeley: University of California Press, 1969).

20. Burke, *Grammar of Motives,* xvi.

21. Burke, *Grammar of Motives,* 15.

22. Burke, *The Philosophy of Literary Form: Studies in Symbolic Action* (1941; Berkeley: University of California Press, 1973), 3rd ed. Also: *Counter-Statement.*

23. Kenneth Burke, *Counter-Statement* (1931; Berkeley: University of California Press, 1968), 124.

24. Burke, *Counter-Statement,* 124.

25. Burke, *Counter-Statement,* 124.

26. Burke, *Counter-Statement,* 125.

27. Burke, *Counter-Statement,* 126.

28. Richard Lanham, *The Electronic Word: Democracy, Technology and the Arts* (Chicago: The University of Chicago Press, 1993), 56.

29. Brian Vickers, *In Defense of Rhetoric* (Oxford: Oxford University Press, 1988), 441.

30. William A. Covino, *Magic, Rhetoric and Literacy: An Eccentric History of the Composing Imagination* (Albany: State University of New York Press, 1994), 93.

31. Kenneth Burke, *The Philosophy of Literary Form,* 4. Quoted in Covino, 91.

32. Lloyd Bitzer, "The Rhetorical Situation," *Philosophy and Rhetoric* 1 (December 1968), 1–14.

33. Bitzer, 3.

34. Bitzer, 6.

35. Bitzer, 7.

36. Bitzer, 8.

37. Bitzer, 8.

38. Bitzer, 10.

39. Sources on rhetoric and narration include: Anne Dipardo, "Narrative Knowers, Expository Knowledge," *Written Communication* 7 (January, 1990): 59–95; Doug Hesse, "Aristotle's Poetics and Rhetoric: Narrative as Rhetoric's Fourth Mode," in *Rebirth of Rhetoric: Essays in Language, Culture, and Education,* ed. Richard Andrews (London: Routledge, 1992); Albert R. Jonsen and Stephen Toulmin, *The Abuse of Casuistry* (Berkeley: University of California Press, 1988); Allan Megill, "Recounting the Past: Description, Explanation, and Narrative in Historiography," *American Historical Review* 94 (1989): 627–653; *Narrative and Argument,* ed. Richard Andrews (Milton Keynes, UK: Open University Press, 1989); Renato Rosaldo, "Where Objectivity Lies," in *The Rhetoric of the Human Sciences,* ed. John Nelson, Allen Megill, Donald McCloskey (Madison: University of Wisconsin Press, 1987), 87–110; Misia Landau, "Paradise Lost: The Theme of Terrestriality in Human Evolution," *Rhetoric of the Human Sciences,* 111–124.

40. Susan Wells, *Sweet Reason: Rhetoric and the Discourses of Modernity* (Chicago: University of Chicago Press, 1996), 49.

41. Wells, 49.

42. On Bakhtin's thought, see: Michael Holquist, *Dialogism: Bakhtin and His World* (London: Routledge, 1990).

43. Holquist, 15.

44. Bakhtin, *Marxism and the Philosophy of Language,* trans. L. Matejka and I. R. Titunik (New York: Seminar Press, 1973), 9.

45. Mikhail Bakhtin, *Marxism,* 86.

46. Charles Schuster, as quoted in editor's introduction to *Landmark Essays on Bakhtin, Rhetoric, and Writing,* ed. Frank Farmer (Mahwah, NJ: Hermagoras Press, 1998), 3.

47. Josephine Donovan in *Feminism, Bakhtin, and the Dialogic,* eds. Dale M. Bauer and S. Jaret McKinstry (Albany: State University of New York, 1991), 86.

48. Mikhail Bakhtin, *Problems of Dostoevsky's Poetics,* ed. and trans. Caryl Emerson (Minneapolis: University of Minnesota Press, 1984), xix.

49. Bakhtin, *Dostoevsky,* xx.

50. Bakhtin, *Dostoevsky,* xxv.

51. Bakhtin, *Dostoevsky,* 3.

52. Bakhtin, *Dostoevsky,* 6.

53. Wayne Booth, *The Rhetoric of Fiction* (Chicago: University of Chicago Press, 1961), 16. See also: *Now Don't Try to Reason with Me* (Chicago: University of Chicago Press, 1970); *Modern Dogma and the Rhetoric of Assent* (Chicago: University of Chicago Press, 1974).

54. Booth, *Fiction,* 20.

55. Booth, *Fiction,* 50.

56. Booth, *Fiction,* 60.

57. Booth, *Fiction,* 69.

58. Booth, *Fiction,* 78.

59. Hubert L. Dreyfus and Paul Rabinow, "What is Maturity? Habermas and Foucault on 'What is Enlightenment?'" in *Foucault: A Critical Reader,* ed. David Couzens Hoy (Oxford: Basil Blackwell, 1986), 110.

60. Dreyfus and Rabinow, 110. For a discussion of Foucault's ideas, see Chapter 11 of this text.

61. See: Jurgen Habermas, *Toward a Rational Society,* trans. Jeremy J. Shapiro (Boston: Beacon Press, 1970); *Knowledge and Human Interests,* trans. Jeremy J. Shapiro (Boston: Beacon Press, 1971); *Theory and Practice,* trans. John Viertel (Boston: Beacon Press, 1973).

62. Jurgen Habermas, *Communication and the Evolution of Society,* trans. Thomas McCarthy (Boston: Beacon Press, 1979), 7.

63. Susan Wells, *Sweet Reason: Rhetoric and the Discourse of Modernity* (Chicago: University of Chicago Press, 1996), 114.

64. Jurgen Habermas, *The Philosophical Discourse of Modernity: Twelve Lectures,* trans. Frederick Lawrence (Cambridge, MA: MIT Press 1987), ed. Thomas McCarthy, x.

65. Thomas McCarthy, introduction to Habermas, *Philosophical Discourse,* x.

66. Jurgen Habermas, *Theory and Practice,* trans. John Viertel (Boston: Beacon Press, 1973), 25.

67. McCarthy in editor's introduction to *Philosophical Discourse,* x.

68. Susan Wells, 115.

69. Wells, 103.

70. McCarthy in editor's introduction to *Philosophical Discourse,* xii.

71. McCarthy in editor's introduction to *Philosophical Discourse,* xvi.

72. Thomas McCarthy, *The Critical Theory of Jurgen Habermas* (Cambridge, MA: MIT Press, 1978), 292.

73. McCarthy, *Critical Theory,* 294.

74. Wells, 119.

75. Sonja K. Foss, Karen A. Foss, Robert Trapp, *Contemporary Perspective on Rhetoric,* 2d ed. (Prospect Heights, IL: Waveland, 1991), 241–272.

76. McCarthy, *Critical Theory,* 273.

77. See, for example: Dick Howard, "A Politics in Search of the Political," *Theory and Society* 1 (Fall 1974): 271–306.

78. Wells, 116.

■ ■ ■ ■ ■

CHAPTER ELEVEN

CONTEMPORARY RHETORIC III: TEXTS, POWER, AND ALTERNATIVES

Now 'everyday language' is not innocent or neutral.
—Jacques Derrida

Men have an ancient and honorable rhetorical tradition.
—Karlyn Kohrs Campbell

A powerful intellectual movement took shape in Europe and the United States in the twentieth century, centered on the relationships among language, culture, and power. Scholars such as Ferdinand de Saussure, Claude Levi-Strauss, and Jacques Lacan explored language's role in shaping human thinking, and even in the construction of our sense of self. Interest in language has led to renewed interest in persuasive discourse and the strategies by which individuals and groups achieve power.[1] This international discussion of discourse by philosophers, linguists, communication theorists, historians, and literary critics has again placed the ancient discipline of rhetoric at the center of academic debate, a position it has not occupied for two centuries. The conclusions derived from this debate are still finding their way into the mainstreams of communication teaching and research.

This chapter overviews some of the contributions of two of the more important European writers on the subject of language and meaning during the past three decades—Michel Foucault and Jacques Derrida. These theorists resist simple labels and standard classifications; their ideas have been called radical and conservative, sophisticated and naive, oppressive and liberating, brilliant and confused. Nevertheless, important issues such as the nature of power, the sources of knowledge, and the structures of social life animate the debate sparked by their work.

A third theorist interested in the relationship between rhetoric and political power is also considered. Richard Weaver defended a politically conservative view of rhetoric that has implications for education and the maintenance of culture. If our first two writers are involved in the work of cultural criticism through and exploration of the nature of language, knowledge, and power, Weaver is concerned for the corrosive effects of modernism on Western culture. He sees the study of traditional rhetoric as a means of combating modernism and of upholding the traditional values of Western culture.

This chapter also explores the most powerful and influential application of the insights provided by Foucault, Derrida, and others into rhetoric's relationship to power—the feminist movement in the West. We will focus particular attention on feminist criticism of the rhetorical tradition itself. Feminist scholars have employed the critique of power and language to analyze perhaps the most sustained source of male power ever developed: the Western rhetorical tradition. This chapter closes with a consideration of non-Western alternatives to the Western rhetorical tradition.

POSTMODERNISM

Postmodernism is a reaction to the intellectual values and philosophical goals of the European Enlightenment of the eighteenth and early nineteenth centuries, values said to have inaugurated the modern age. During this period reason was elevated as our best hope of solving ancient human problems and creating a rational society. Thinkers such as French satirist and playwright Voltaire (1694–1778), British empirical philosopher David Hume (1711–1776), and German philosopher Immanuel Kant (1724–1804) represent the great intellectual luminaries of the period.

In addition to ultimate trust in reason, the hallmarks of modernity include belief in the fixed meanings of symbols, confidence in sense perception and direct observation, and the reliability of the individual human subject pursuing truth. Under the commitments of modernity, academic disciplines were viewed as moving along a clear line of progress. Enlightenment scholars studied subjects such as history, anthropology, sociology, physics, and literature as they pursued the rational project of delivering humanity from the oppression of earlier superstitions and false beliefs, especially those beliefs associated with the Christian tradition. Though the Age of Enlightenment is conventionally held to have ended with the French Revolution (1792–1794), modernist confidence in reason and progress as the twin means of solving human problems and resolving moral dilemmas persisted well into the twentieth century.

The nineteenth-century German philosopher Friedrich Nietzsche (1844–1900) had already begun to question Enlightenment assumptions, and thus provided the seeds of a new or "postmodern" system of thought. He attacked the grand explanatory narratives of Christianity and Judaism, and strongly opposed all overarching philosophical frameworks. Morality and social principles were relative and only served the "will to power" of those who sought power. Twentieth-century thinkers built on these criticisms of Enlightenment thought. Finally, in the 1960s Europe a view that has come to be known as Postmodernism began to shake the very foundations of modernity. Postmodernism incorporated insights from philosophy, sociology, history, literature, and the social sciences.

Postmodern thought questions both reason and progress, and rejects what Jean-Francois Lyotard termed, in his seminal work *The Postmodern Condition,* "meta-narratives," those grand explanatory schemes such as Christianity or capitalism that claim to account for the entirety of human history and the human condition. Postmodernism rejected even the notion of the autonomous subject or "self" as a sociolinguistic construction. In other words, Postmodernism—a general name for a host of intellectual, artistic, and cultural trends—challenged the very foundations of Western philosophy.

Claudia Moscovici writes that for Lyotard, "inquiries into the nature of reality," the very goal of modern thinking, are merely "futile pursuits." In fact, "Lyotard advises readers against accepting the concepts of reality, truth, and morality" at all because the sources of each have traditionally been "meta-narratives." Armed with such basic assumptions, Lyotard suggested that "to enter the postmodern era...we must overcome our enlightenment legacy by abandoning the quest for truth."[2] So, again, Postmodernism had in its sights the Enlightenment project that elevated reason. Moreover, Lyotard challenged the Enlightenment figure he termed "the hero of knowledge," that careful employer of reason in the pursuit of truth who "works toward a good ethical–political end."[3] It is also the case that Lyotard found language to constitute the worlds we inhabit, not fixed and external realities. And, the possibilities in language for creating realities were numerous. He wrote that "there are many different language games," that is, "ways of creating a reality out of the units of language."[4]

This chapter considers several writers whose works are associated with the development of postmodern thought, and who have contributed in important ways to our understanding of how we employ language in both private and public settings. We will also examine the feminist critique of the European rhetorical tradition, one of the more powerful and socially significant applications of postmodern criticism.

MICHEL FOUCAULT: DISCOURSE, KNOWLEDGE, AND POWER

The French scholar Michel Foucault (1926–1984) is probably the most influential European intellectual figure of the last half of the twentieth century. So sweeping has been his influence that C. G. Prado writes that Michel Foucault "changed the basis of the work of all scholars."[5] This writer who changed how so many other writers do their work is himself difficult to categorize. He was a philosopher, social historian, semiotician, and social critic, though he might have rejected all four labels. Even his biographers sometimes confess "ignorance about what Foucault is really doing."[6] Foucault held various academic positions around Europe between 1955 and 1969, settling eventually at the highly acclaimed College de France where he held the chair of Professor of the History of the Systems of Thought. Here he taught and wrote until his death from AIDS in 1984.

Some of his works, such as *Madness and Civilization* (1961), *The Order of Things* (1966), and *The Archaeology of Knowledge* (1969) are sweeping in scope: the first traces the history of the idea of insanity, the second the development of the human sciences, the third the processes by which people come to achieve knowledge.[7] Others, such as *The Birth of the Clinic* (1963), a work that examines a century in the history of medicine, are focused on single subjects.[8] Toward the end of his life Foucault wrote the three-volume work *The History of Sexuality* (1976–1984), a pioneering effort to understand how the concept of sexuality has been defined in discourse throughout human history. What makes these works part of a common corpus other than shared authorship?

Power and Discourse

One of Foucault's consuming interests is clearly evident in much of his writing over more than thirty years: the "central problem of power," its uses, and its relationship to discourse.[9] Foucault investigated in particular the relationship between power and language, and has been called the "first major writer to pose the question of power in relation to discourse."[10] More specifically, Foucault pondered how power "installs itself and produces real material effects."[11] That is, he wondered about how power comes to be concentrated in certain institutions, and the ways that such concentration of power affects how we live our daily lives. One expert on his work writes that Foucault "does not approach the question of power in terms of some fundamental principle from which its manifestations may be deduced." Rather, Foucault addresses the phenomenon "in terms of the concrete mechanisms and practices through which power is exercised, and in terms of the play of historical forces which orient that exercise."[12]

We might say that for Foucault, power happens. It is not the result of "conscious or intentional decision," but rather of a complex and almost indecipherable set of language practices within a culture. Thus, "he does not ask: who is in power? He asks how power installs *itself* and produces real material effects."[13] Who is a criminal? What is considered appropriate punishment for a criminal? Who is insane? How are the insane to be treated?[14] These and similar questions intrigued Foucault. Who is president? How are bills passed into law? Questions of this type Foucault considered misleading, for they suggest that power is a fixed, predictable, objective fact. Power, for Foucault, is not imposed from above through social structures and hierarchies. Rather, power is fluid, and flows from discourse—with systems of talk within the limits of particular disciplines or practices.[15] Thus, modern Western medicine would constitute for Foucault a "discourse," while medicine as practiced in eighteenth-century Europe would constitute a different discourse.

It is important to understand, however, that Foucault considered discourse to be more than symbolic representation of real, objective facts in the world of experience. He held that discourse did not "merely represent 'the real'" but was, in fact, "part of its production."[16] That is, how we talk about a concept like power was actually an important part of creating and sustaining genuine power. He wrote, "although power is an omnipresent dimension in human relations, power in a society is never a fixed and closed regime, but rather an endless and open strategic game."[17] *Game* here should be taken to mean something closer to "contest" than to "amusement."

Power is a matter of which ideas prevail at the moment.[18] Systems of discourse come to control how we think and what we claim to know, Foucault argued. Most people assume that the reverse is true: that what we claim to know governs how we talk. But for Foucault, rules of discourse are always present, and because these rules govern knowledge they are the essence of power. The actual material effects of power—for example, how criminals are treated—follow from the rules of discourse in place at a particular time. McHoul and Grace write, "events, no matter how specific, cannot happen just anyhow. They must happen according to certain constraints, rules or conditions of possibility."[19]

Thus, power and knowledge are inextricably bound together for Foucault: Power is understood as the discursive constraint on what can be known, and what can be known determines the allocation of power in the material realm. Thus, "power and knowledge directly imply one another."[20] Moreover, on this view power becomes a productive force: It generates ideas and concepts that are worked out materially in a culture. Despite his suspicion of its concentration, Foucault does not understand power principally as a repressive force, but rather as a generative one.

Escape

Nevertheless, we *are* constrained by the power generated by systems of discourse. Thus, the theme of escape or emancipation is also constant in Foucault's work, and closely related for him to the problem of power. In fact, "Foucault said that he wrote to escape from himself, to become other than he was."[21] Two related goals, then, emerge from his writing. First, Foucault seeks to reveal how knowledge constrains human freedom, that is, how knowledge and power are related. Second, he wishes to provide his readers the intellectual resources necessary for escaping these constraints.[22]

Foucault's interest in captivity and escape may explain why he was drawn to institutions in which people were literally held captive, prisons (*Discipline and Punish*) and mental asylums (*Madness and Civilization*). The prison and the asylum symbolized for Foucault the results of certain ways of talking—or systems of discourse—that made it possible for some individuals to decide the status and treatment of others.

And yet, for all his penetrating analysis and his interest in offering a critique of Western institutions, Foucault seldom argued explicitly for or against particular social practices. As one commentator notes, even in *Discipline and Punish,* a book that deals with the horrific treatment of criminals and prisoners, Foucault is "hardly polemical, rarely mentions transgression and confines himself to descriptions of the past."[23]

Archaeology of Knowledge: In Search of the Episteme

In his intellectual career Foucault had come to reject conservatism, structuralism, Marxism, and anarchism. He was influenced by studies as diverse as archaeology, anthropology, medicine, psychiatry, and sociology, as well as by a wide range of writers including Marx, Freud, Nietzsche, and Levi-Strauss. The "three contemporary thinkers to whom he felt he owed the greatest debt" were Georges Dumezil, Georges Canguilhem, and Jean Hyppolite.[24]

Foucault denied that he had a methodology that could be classified as historical or philosophical. But he believed that discourse—understanding the term broadly enough to include a range of social documents and practices—represented a kind of archaeological artifact. Thus, Foucault sought to reveal an "archaeology of knowledge" through the study of various discursive texts.[25] "What I am doing is neither a formalization nor an exegesis," he writes, "but an archaeology." As he used the term, *archaeology* is not the exploration of ancient sites in search of physical objects. Rather, archaeology is "the description of an archive." What is an archive? Not so much a specific collection of documents such as one might find in a library, but rather "the set of rules which at a given period and for a given society" define, among other things, "the limits and forms of the sayable" and "the limits and forms of conversation [emphasis added]."[26] Notice that an archive is specific to a particular time and location, and does not take in an entire culture or historical era.

An archive, then, reveals what could be said in a particular society at a particular time, and thus what could be *known* at that time and in that place. Knowledge, for Foucault, is "a matter of the social, historical and political conditions under which, for example, statements come to count as true or false."[27] At a level more general than the archive, Foucault's archaeological study pursued the episteme of a culture and an age, that is, the totality of discursive practices of a culture over an extended period of time.[28] Karlis Racevskis defines an episteme as "a field of epistemological possibilities structured in a way that will determine the particular mode in which knowledge is to be achieved in a given culture and age."[29] And David R. Shumway points out that "each *episteme* is like a stratum of earth in which the artifacts uncovered are the products of a distinct historical period."[30] As Foucault moved through the various historical strata, he sought to "show the conditions that allowed the particular ways of dealing with [knowledge and discourse] to come about."[31]

Foucault, as we have noted, selected the metaphor of archaeology to describe much of his investigative work aimed at discovering the discursive rules in place at different points in history. He was attracted to archaeology for a number of reasons, perhaps principally because archaeology is less concerned with the particular events than it is with general cultural trends. Archaeology thus accommodates contradictions in its search for governing patterns and principals, and doesn't seek to avoid them like so many other disciplines. Archaeology asks how change was possible, rather than looking at change as a matter of sequence. In sum, archaeology seeks to understand the totality of a culture rather than to account for minor manifestations of it, and Foucault sought a similarly comprehensive description of possible knowledge in a culture.

Was Foucault simply studying intellectual history, trends, and connections in the world of ideas? His work could be described this way, but it is more accurate to say that Foucault sought the history of rational *possibilities;* that is, sought the underlying potentialities that made certain thoughts possible at a given time in human history. What possibilities of human rationality, for instance, result in present penal institutions in the West in which a prisoner's body is incarcerated, but in which outright physical torture, so common in earlier ages, is uncommon? Why did our present method of treating the criminal become a rational possibility? Or, why did previous ages find rational treating the insane as sources of amusement, while we presently employ clinical metaphors and thus treat the insane like hospital patients rather than clowns?

Foucault wished to expose the forces that set the rational boundaries of "the present." In the process he hoped to demonstrate that "the present"—a taken-for-granted and unassailable fact—is not inevitable. That is, Foucault sought to show that how we talk, how we think, and what we say we know might be other than they are.

An episteme is a way of organizing knowledge by regulating discourse, but it is more. It is an underlying and probably largely subconscious set of assumptions and operating hypotheses that make thought and social life possible. A culture only operates on the basis of one episteme at a time; to think in two different ways at the same moment is impossible. Moreover, each episteme is likely unrelated to the others, constituting a radically new and different viewing of the world rather than an evolving view.

Foucault, then, was interested in the discursive practices within a culture that provided the framework for knowledge, meaning, and power. Knowledge is a product of *what* can be discussed and *how* topics may be discussed. As such, knowledge is constantly being reconfigured as the rules governing discourse change over time. But this does not mean simply that people in different historical epochs have known different facts. Foucault always sees a direct link between knowledge and power, so differences in knowledge always imply differences in the ways power is distributed in a culture. Thus, these "reorganizations of knowledge also constituted new forms of power and domination."[32]

Excluded Discourse

For Foucault, knowledge is not simply available for the taking. Rather, the historical record of what has been said on a particular topic at a particular time, that is, of knowledge, is largely a result of a "set of rules (neither grammatical nor logical) to which speakers unwittingly conform."[33] Some of these rules dictate which topics can (or cannot) be discussed, and the language that may be used to discuss them. Excluded discourse is Foucault's term for discourse that is controlled by being prohibited.[34] And, for Foucault, such prohibitions always govern our knowledge of the world. Of course, only that which can be discussed can be "known," for we cannot "know" something that cannot be expressed symbolically. Knowledge and the rules governing discourse are inseparable, because the content of the former is governed by the latter.

Concerning rules of discourse, Foucault explains that "in every society the production of discourse is at once controlled, selected, organized and redistributed according to a certain number of procedures, whose role is to avert its powers and its dangers."[35] Discourse—and thus knowledge, and power—is governed by rules, though these rules often are not consciously adhered to or openly articulated. There are, for instance, discursive rules governing who may talk, what can be talked about, and in which settings. Some subjects, or certain positions on those subjects, are not recognized as within the realm of legitimate discourse. Other issues may not be considered proper topics of conversations in certain settings. Sexually transmitted diseases, for example, cannot be discussed among some groups of people within the bounds of acceptable discourse, or may not be discussible in some contexts. In the eighteenth century the Church of England tried to restrict the kind of language that could be employed to speak about God. Blasphemy charges were sometimes brought against those who violated the prevailing rules for theological discourse.

Foucault was intrigued by the connections between rules of discourse and judgments about an individual's sanity. "From the depths of the Middle Ages," he writes, "a man was mad if his speech could not be said to form part of the common discourse of men. His words were considered null and void, without truth or significance, worthless as evidence."[36] Thus, by the unspoken rules of discourse, the words of some people carry no weight, are not to be credited as reliable. Prisoners, children, women, the insane are all groups that have been silenced in some cultural settings. Unspoken rules govern many other aspects of discourse as well, such as the qualifications one must have to speak in certain contexts and the places from which discourse may originate.

Power and Institutions

Foucault was also interested in institutions and their relationship to power. However, power does not *originate with* institutions such as the government or church. Rather, institutions are *subject to* power just as individuals are. John Caputo and Mark Yount write that "power is the thin, inescapable film that covers all human interactions, whether inside institutions or out." Thus, Foucault "situated institutions within the thin but all-entangling web of power relations."[37] Power shapes institutions and shapes the relationships among individuals within institutions. Consequently, "institutions are the means that power uses, and not the other way around, not the sources or origins of power."[38]

Institutions in our own era manifest power as surely as they did in the past. In a capitalist society, "production" dominates economic thinking. Our democratic political system demands that "control" and "order" are crucial political concerns. Finally, the regime of scientific thinking requires physical explanations for everything, including human behavior. A modern prison reflects how the "discourses" of capitalism, democracy, and science are translated into power within an institution, rather than being produced by the institution.

"Production" as a guiding economic value leads to the practice of locking up a person's body to "extract" time and labor, fundamental commodities of capitalism. "Control" and "order" as rational democratic values suggest that "surveillance" rather than torture is appropriate for prisoners. Consequently, prisons are built so that prisoners can be easily watched and kept in their proper places, while torture chambers, common in earlier times, seldom show up in the blueprints for new penitentiaries. The science of human thought and behavior—psychiatry—requires an explanation for criminal behavior, as well as a correction of that behavior. Thus, psychiatrists analyze prisoners as a condition of their incarceration. In the Middle Ages, keeping a prisoner in a room and providing for regular visits by a physician to explain the prisoner's behavior would have been unthinkable. In the nineteenth and twentieth centuries, such practices have been common, and are viewed as "reasonable." The material outworking of these discourses and the power they produce are the actual events of the modern prisoner's daily life—being confined to a room by himself, watched day and night, and psychoanalyzed on occasion.[39]

Some of his critics have claimed that Foucault's detached, archaeological approach to historical analysis leaves him unable or unwilling to judge one ethic of discourse and action as morally preferable to another. Thus, a follower of Foucault's critical work might be left unable to make decisive moral judgments and to act morally. However, supporters of his project have countered that "like the pre-Platonic rhetoricians, Foucault uses language to articulate an understanding of our situation which moves us to action."[40] Indeed, Foucault's explorations of the relationships among language, rules of discourse, and the appropriation of power have informed a variety of critiques of contemporary social practices and much attendant action. The feminist critique of ways of talking about women and their roles in society, which we will consider later in this chapter, has benefited from Foucault's insights. Similarly, his view of power and language could be applied fruitfully to the analysis of political practices, religious discourse, and the uses of the mass media to shape opinion. Foucault provides a wide range of possibilities to those interested in the uses of discourse in shaping culture and distributing power.

Queer Theory

Michel Foucault's original insight into the intimate connection between language and power, between the symbolic action and social arrangements, has had a profound influence on a variety of important intellectual movements. He was, for instance, one of the major shaping forces in the development of feminist theory in the 1970s and 1980s. His insight was also foundational to a critical movement known as Queer Theory that began to take shape around 1990. Invention of the actual term *Queer Theory* and of its basic premises is attributed to Teresa de Lauretis and her landmark 1991 essay, "Queer Theory: Lesbian and Gay Sexualities."[41] Interestingly, only a few years after introducing the term, de Lauretis jettisoned it as having taken on its own fixed meaning.

Queer theory is often associated with the advent of academic departments of lesbian and gay studies, but its implications for our uses of language extend beyond issues directly related to homosexuality. This theoretical framework shares with feminist critical theories the notion that gender itself is not so much a fixed fact about individuals as it is a social construct. That is, queer theory sees gender as a product of symbolic interaction and the social negotiation of meaning. Queer theory questions even the idea that there is anything fixed or essential about our conceptions of self, arguing that the "self" is, like gender and sexuality, socially constructed. Thus, discourse in the public arena—one definition of rhetoric—becomes crucial to the construction of gender as to all other components of the self. Queer theory, then, emphasizes the social constructedness of gender, sexual identity, and the self. Each is a matter, not of natural conditions, but rather of symbolically based meanings negotiated in public as well as private settings.

Queer theory began by questioning the allegedly stable meanings associated with sexuality, sexual activity, and gender. But it soon extended this analysis of our social existence to questions regarding everything previously taken as essential and unchanging in personal identity.

JACQUES DERRIDA: TEXTS, MEANINGS, AND DECONSTRUCTION

The French philosopher Jacques Derrida was born in Algiers in 1930, and studied at Harvard in the 1950s. Derrida and his controversial method of reading texts, known as "deconstruction," have done more to influence literary and philosophical studies than perhaps any other forces in the second half of the twentieth century.[42] His many books, including *Speech and Phenomena, Of Grammatology,* and *Writing and Difference* (all of which originally appeared in 1967) advance a wide-ranging and novel analysis of the hidden operations of language and discourse, matters that have long interested students of rhetoric. Many contemporary rhetorical theorists and critics have made use of Derrida's insights, as have scholars in a number of disciplines. In fact, the volume of literature commenting on Derrida and his work is astonishing. Two scholars recently recorded "1,322 books or contributions to books, and 1,152 articles on Derrida" published as of 1991.[43]

What were the ideas that prompted such an outpouring of academic as well as of popular interest and, occasionally, scorn? Derrida held that language—especially *written* language—cannot escape the built-in biases of the cultural history that produced it. "Now 'everyday language' is not innocent or neutral," he commented in an interview in the early 1970s. Derrida explains why he makes this charge about "everyday language": "It is the language of Western metaphysics, and it carries with it not only a considerable number of presuppositions of all types, but also presuppositions inseparable from metaphysics, which, although little attended to, are knotted into a system."[44] Derrida, then, sought to reveal the underlying assumptions and even the irrationalities of Western philosophical and political writing, writing that influences the thinking of all of us.

While it is risky to generalize about the goals of a writer of Derrida's scope, complexity, and difficulty, I will venture to say that among his goals in developing deconstruction are: (1) to reveal the hidden mechanisms subtly at work influencing meaning in written language; (2) to demonstrate the concealed power of symbols to shape thinking; and (3) to underline the fact that no one escapes these elusive qualities of language. By pursuing these goals, Derrida hopes to make fresh reading a possibility, reading that is not merely "handing on ready made results, passing along finished formulas for mechanical repetition and recitation."[45]

To read a text for what a traditional reading would overlook, dismiss, or omit Derrida referred to as transgression, that is, violating the received interpretation of a text in search of its submerged meanings. Derrida's defenders are quick to assert that he does not promote "saying whatever comes into your head about the text, however absurd and ridiculous," nor discovering by dint of extraordinary cleverness a transcendent and utterly true meaning in a text.[46] We will take a closer look at the approach that prompts such defenses, but first it will be helpful to address a preliminary question.

Authors Out of Control

How does Derrida's approach intersect with the rhetorical tradition? If rhetoric teaches us the power of intentional structuring of texts, Derrida and deconstruction teach us that no author is in complete, intentional, conscious control of the meanings of any written text. John Caputo puts this point well when he writes: "A deconstructive reading, Derrida says, always settles into the distance between what the author consciously intends or means to say (*vouloir-dire*), that is, what she 'commands' in her text, and what she does not command, what is going on in the text, as it were, behind her back…."[47] Derrida adds a dimension to our thinking about rhetoric, calling attention to the fact that each of us is "embedded in various *networks*" of meaning, some of which we are not conscious of as we write.[48]

Thus, even the most skilled rhetorician—one who manages even those hidden persuasive devices operating below the audience's level of conscious awareness— creates a text carrying meanings that resist even *her* conscious control. Derrida finds his approach to texts to move the self out of the way, and thus to make room for "the other," the voice in the text that is not the author's own narcissistic voice. The rhetorical tradition, on the other hand, elevates the self as controlling agent of the text and all of its meanings, and thus as controlling agent of the audience.

Deconstructing Texts

We might see Derrida as providing an important counterpoint to the thinking of Jurgen Habermas discussed in Chapter 10, and, on a larger scale, a counterpoint to the entire Western rational tradition in philosophy.[49] Habermas has been said to be completing the modernist project of establishing the supremacy of rationality, while Derrida is sometimes called *post*modern in his tendency to undermine the foundations of Western rationalism.

While Habermas looks to stabilize discourse by outlining conditions under which it can proceed rationally and with relative freedom from ideological coercion, Derrida wishes to destabilize or "deconstruct" discourse by challenging traditional assumptions concerning language and meaning. His work of destabilizing discourse by dissecting its underlying structures of meaning and implication has been called deconstruction. But Derrida insisted "that deconstruction was a process, an activity of reading irreducible to a concept or method."[50] Neither does Derrida accept that deconstruction is a method of criticism or interpretation of texts. It is only, he claims, a process of reading. Thus, any fixed definition of deconstruction must be held somewhat tentatively.

Unstable Meanings.   The object of Derrida's attention is language itself, especially written language.[51] His principal goal "is to remain acutely sensitive to the deeply historical, social and linguistic 'constructedness' of our beliefs and practices."[52] One type of discourse was of particular concern to Derrida—Western philosophical discourse. Derrida was determined to show that philosophy, not less than any other enterprise that relies on writing, is not a "privileged, truth-seeking discourse immune from all the vagaries of writing."[53] The "vagaries" of meaning occupied Derrida's attention, and it is to his particular concerns about meaning that we now turn.

Derrida did not see language simply as a system of signifying words, but rather as "a system of relations and oppositions" that must be continually defined.[54] Derrida refuses to accept the "reality" of established social structures, unexamined, standardized meanings, and well-worn oppositions such as "mind and body," "form and content," "nature and culture," or "faith and reason." For instance, he seeks to "steer clear of the simple opposition of reason and faith" suggested by Enlightenment writers, exposing instead "the extent to which reason is deeply saturated by faith."[55] Derrida argues that traditional notions like "structure," "opposition," and even "meaning" force stability on concepts that are fundamentally unstable, and obscure the operations through which the *appearance* of stability is created. Meaning is always "the product of a restless play within language that cannot be fixed or pinned down for the purposes of conceptual definition."[56] This may be why Derrida was so reluctant to define the concept, "deconstruction," preferring rather to call it a "process." One of the goals of the deconstruction of discourse is to reveal "those blind-spots of argument" that result from rigid, unexamined meanings attributed to terms.[57]

Deconstruction seeks, then, to examine the "oppositions" embedded in a discourse that provide it with its potential for meaning, to point out how concepts are invested with meaning by contrast with their opposites. When such oppositions have been brought to light, a text may appear self-contradictory. Thus, "to deconstruct a discourse," writes Jonathan Culler, "is to show how it undermines the…oppositions on which it relies, by identifying in the text the rhetorical operations that produce the supposed ground of the argument, the key concept or premise."[58] In deconstructing the discourse of nuclear deterrence, a particular interest of Derrida's, he shows the "logical incoherence" of the central concept itself. An apparently stable term like *war* is understood or defined only in contrast to the assumed opposite, *peace.* In a curious way, then, an argument for the possibility of war becomes dependent on the opposite concept, peace. Moreover, Derrida sought to demonstrate through deconstructive practices how the entire argument for nuclear deterrence rested on an "elaborate fiction" of nuclear attack and defense.[59] The "rational" and deadly serious rhetoric of nuclear deterrence, then, is built on unstable meanings and irrational assumptions.

James Aune suggests that the political ideology of Ronald Reagan might also stand as an example of what deconstruction reveals about the oppositions that define rhetorical texts. "Something as relatively straightforward as the political ideology of Ronald Reagan does not exist in and of itself," writes Aune. "It consists of a set of rhetorical idioms (fierce nationalism, free-market capitalism, a Protestant view of family and work) which are defined only in relation to one another, and by that to which they are opposed."[60] If this is so, then, "there is a strange way in which someone like Reagan *needs* Communists, Democrats, and feminists to define himself. If they were to disappear, which is presumably the ultimate goal of his political practice, he would disappear, too."[61]

Derrida, then, questions the very components of traditional argument that were so important to the writers in Chapter 9, Perelman, Olbrechts-Tyteca, and Toulmin.

For Derrida, the foundations of argument—stable meanings, the appeal to reason, the unambiguous nature of principles such as "equality," and the reality of rigid oppositions like "labor" versus "capital"—are the *effects* of rhetorical interactions rather than the objective foundations of arguments. Deconstruction, both as philosophy and as critical method thus involves exposing the fundamental variability, what Derrida calls the "undecidability," of meanings. Derrida asks us to consider the following questions: "What if the meaning of *meaning* 'is infinite implication'" and the "force" of meaning "is a certain pure and infinite equivocalness, which gives signified meaning no respite…?"[62]

Derrida's critics, especially in the discipline of philosophy, have sometimes seen him as exacting "literature's revenge upon philosophy," and as something of a "mischievous latter-day sophist bent upon reducing every discipline of thought to a species of rhetorical play."[63] Moreover, Derrida's ideas have often been misinterpreted as warranting a free-ranging, unrestrained, and undirected dismantling of written texts, a "farewell to rigorous protocols of reading."[64] His defenders adamantly deny these charges, but deconstruction remains an unwelcome guest in the academy to some.

Criticism and misunderstanding notwithstanding, Derrida may be correct that meanings are not fixed, and that constructing meanings involves an ongoing process of social negotiation. His insight suggests that language and discourse contain embedded structures that reveal the ways in which our thinking is directed by the very terms we use to communicate. Derrida's work of deconstruction has had a considerable impact on thinking about discourse, how it works, and the nature of meaning. It has also, like the work of Foucault, provided critical tools for writers wishing to challenge the ideological status quo of Western society.

Derrida and deconstruction have been widely criticized, even in the popular media. They "have been blamed for almost everything. For ruining American departments of philosophy, English, French, comparative literature, for ruining the university itself [and] for dimming the lights of the Enlightenment…."[65] Deconstruction has been viewed by many as "some sort of intellectual 'computer virus'" that destroys everything with which it comes in contact.[66] And why is this? Because nothing is more crucial to traditional philosophic, political, and literary discourse than the assumption of fixed meanings, unless it is the complementary assumption that authors control those meanings. By violating both sacred ideas at once, Derrida has made himself the *bête noir* of many who cherish these two ancient verities.

But Derrida considers himself a friend of philosophy, if "philosophy is the right to ask any question about all that we hold sacred, even and especially about reason and philosophy itself." Derrida does what he does in the name of "a love for what philosophy loves—knowledge and truth."[67] His iconoclastic approach to reading certainly has upset many traditionalists (and others), but it also has been heralded as providing an important corrective to rigid readings that concentrate power in authors and their conscious control of texts. In this respect, deconstruction is a counterpoint to the rhetorical tradition itself, or, perhaps, the cutting edge of a new way in rhetoric.

RICHARD WEAVER: RHETORIC
AND THE PRESERVATION OF CULTURE

The tradition of rhetoric has stimulated the thinking of both liberal and conservative theorists. The former—Foucault and Derrida are examples—see in critical studies the possibility for challenging the *status quo,* the latter find a method for preserving and propagating cultural values. Among the latter is the U.S. rhetorical theorist and literary critic, Richard Weaver, most of whose works on rhetoric appeared between 1948 and 1965.[68]

Critique of Modernism

Weaver is perhaps most famous for his attacks against "modernism." Modernism, for Weaver, involved a faith in reason and scientific advancement to bring about a better society, and a corresponding break with the traditions of Western culture. As a conservative social critic he "sought to clarify the role of rhetoric in improving a declining modern culture."[69] "The apostles of modernism," Weaver writes, "usually begin their retort [against conservatism] with catalogues of modern achievement."

However, Weaver is unimpressed with the evidence of Western cultural advancement. Modernists, who believe in the advancement of culture by embracing science and rejecting tradition, do not realize that they are parochial thinkers "immers[ed] in particulars." That is, liberals stand to lose everything because they see only the events and accomplishments of contemporary culture. They have no sense of history and culture, in part through their disregard for rhetoric.[70]

Weaver argued for "the restoration of values," and was "met with the objection that one cannot return" to the past. He responded to this criticism by arguing that "the philosophic position of modernism" assumes that "we are prisoners of the moment." However, "the believer in truth…is bound to maintain that the things of highest value are not affected by the passage of time; otherwise the very concept of truth becomes impossible."[71]

True to his conservative orientation, Weaver's interest in rhetoric was largely an interest in the means by which a society refines and perpetuates its traditional values. In preserving the past, a culture achieves stability and insight. Modernism, on the other hand, "is in essence a provincialism, since it declines to look beyond the horizon of the moment." Thus, modernism also reveals a lack of interest in, and naivete about, rhetoric.[72]

Critique of Scientism

Weaver argues his famous essay, "Language is Sermonic," that "our age has witnessed the decline of a number of subjects that once enjoyed prestige and general esteem, but no subject, I believe, has suffered more amazingly in this respect than rhetoric."[73] He traces this dramatic decline in disciplinary esteem for rhetoric directly to the modernist tendency to see human beings in a new and "scientistic" way. Scientism he defines as *"the application of scientific assumptions to subjects which are not wholly comprised of naturalistic phenomena* [emphasis added]."[74] Once scientism reached a position of dominance in Western intellectual circles, toward the end of the nineteenth century, rhetoric, with its emphasis on human values and motives, was relegated to the status of an antique academic curiosity. But, in Weaver's estimation, a great deal was lost to both the academy and Western society in this relegation.

Weaver on Education

Weaver's interest in the relationships among values, culture, and rhetoric led him to be fiercely interested in both rhetoric and education. For Weaver, education ought to be employed to transmit cultural values. "It has been said countless times in this country that democracy cannot exist without education. The truth concealed in this observation is that only education can be depended on to bring men to see the hierarchy of values."[75] The argument is frequently made, he continues, that "education should serve the needs of the people," but what are their needs, and what type of education best serves those needs? Is scientific education "the answer," as many recent reports on the dire state of U.S. education might suggest? In Weaver's opinion "this reliance upon science and scientism" in "modern education" is just a matter of "cultural fashion."[76]

What, then, is the purpose of education? Weaver's answer to this question is emphatic but also somewhat ambiguous. "The purpose of an education is to make a human being more human."[77] Of course, such a view requires a consensus on what it means to be fully human. In Weaver's estimation, Western culture has provided an answer to the question of our humanness, though scientism fails to recognize that answer. Scientism's naive reliance on science to bring about a utopian society leads us to ignore our cultural history as a source of insights into our humanness. Instead, it asks us to rely on "an intuition about the immanent nature of reality."[78] Thus, "even in everyday speech the word *fact* has taken the place of *truth*."[79] Weaver is interested in truth, not mere facts of science. Substituting one for the other is indeed dangerous, even fanatical. Thus, we must "recognize the peril in which science and technology have placed our souls."[80]

A True Rhetoric

So, where does rhetoric fit in with Weaver's critique of modernism and scientism? Sounding much like the Italian Humanist writers of the Renaissance, he writes that "language has been called 'the supreme organon of the mind's self-ordering growth.' It is the means by which we not only communicate our thoughts to others but interpret our thoughts to ourselves."[81] Thus, the study of language and its use—that is, of rhetoric—is the most vital component of education, for this learning determines the nature of all other learning. Rhetoric is both cultural and personal power. Speech is "the vehicle of order, and those in command of it," he writes, have "superior insight...into the necessary relationship of things."[82]

Thus, a morally informed rhetorical education about the subtleties of language and its potentialities, which is by definition the study of rhetoric, is at the very heart of education itself. But this rhetorical education must have as its goal the production of rhetoricians committed to practicing a true rhetoric. In an essay entitled, "The *Phaedrus* and the Nature of True Rhetoric," Weaver disavows sophistic uses of rhetoric that deal in illusions and falsehoods. When sophistic rhetoric is practiced "rhetoricians are persons of very low responsibility and their art a disreputable one." But, "the discourse of the noble rhetorician…will be about real potentiality or possible actuality…."[83] True rhetoric, then, is a morally grounded endeavor that literally makes a connection to "the Good." Weaver writes as a Platonist, and, like Plato, longs for a rhetoric that brings moral healing to souls.[84]

We see, then, that rhetoric is for Weaver the master study that governed the study of all other arts. Weaver's goal in advocating a return to the study of rhetoric is the enhancement of human life through the perpetuation of culture. The writers to be considered in the next section would strongly disagree with Weaver in this regard. Their argument is that his celebrated "traditional Western culture" is, in fact, a male culture built on a male rhetoric.

FEMINISM AND RHETORIC: CRITIQUE AND REFORM IN RHETORIC

A survey of virtually any history of rhetoric—including this one—will reveal that the vast majority of writers who have been acknowledged as shaping this field of study were men. Recently, the problems for women that emerge from a male rhetorical history have been pointed out by a number of astute critics and theorists of rhetoric, and their acuity of insight into the masculine history of rhetoric has made feminist criticism perhaps the most powerful recent movement in rhetoric.[85] Some of the same writers who have raised serious questions about the traditionally male rhetorical theory and practice of the Western world have also suggested that women have their own ways of speaking and of knowing, that is, their own rhetoric.[86]

Many theorists analyzing the male tradition of Western rhetoric and its effects on social structures and discursive practices have employed the insights of Foucault and Derrida in carrying out their critical work. But Jana Sawicki notes that "the work of Foucault has been of special interest to feminist social and political theorists."[87] She adds that his historical work has served to "free [his readers] for new possibilities of self-understanding, new modes of experience, new forms of subjectivity, authority, and political identity."[88]

The Need for a Woman's Voice

The feminist critique of Western rhetoric has been both sweeping and powerful. But, then, feminist critics have identified rhetoric as a particularly destructive influence on the fortunes of women in the West. For example, Leslie Di Mare writes, "although other disciplines (history, philosophy, art, film, and so on) have been used by the patriarchy to create the perception that women function best biologically, none has been used so effectively as the discipline of rhetoric."[89] It will be helpful, before proceeding, to become oriented to the project of feminist criticism of rhetoric.

Sonja Foss writes that "two assumptions that connect gender with rhetoric undergird feminist criticism: (1) women's experiences are different from men's; and (2) women's voices are not heard in language."[90] Foss points out that "much inquiry into rhetorical processes...is inquiry into men's experiences," which are in turn assumed to be "universal."[91] But women's experience of the world, she writes, differs from that of men for a number of reasons, some less obvious than others. Biological differences may be obvious, but less obvious are the socialization processes that both men and women undergo, and that teach women to be quieter than men and to assume positions of service.

More to the point for the consideration of rhetoric, women's "perceptions, experiences, meanings, practices, and values—are not incorporated into language." Thus, women, as Foucault would argue, are denied a voice in culture, because their discourse has been excluded from the public realm.[92] Moreover, they have been denied access to power because they have been denied access to rhetoric. "Language, then," Foss asserts, "features men's perspectives and silences women's." Moreover, Adrienne Rich asserts that "in a world where language and naming are power, silence is oppression, is violence."[93]

The exclusion of women from the rhetorical mainstream has resulted in the loss of women's meanings, and thus, it is argued, in the loss of women themselves as members of the social world. One critic writes, "[because] women have been unable to give weight to their symbolic meanings they have been unable to pass on a tradition of women's meanings to the world...they have been cut off from the mainstream of meaning and therefore have frequently been lost."[94] Another writes of the "strong voices" of social leadership, that "when these strong voices are feminine, the words are less often recorded and analyzed."[95] Victoria DeFrancisco and Marvin Jensen point out that speeches by women are infrequently recorded and studied when compared to those by men.[96] Such facts regarding systematic exclusion of women from the history of rhetoric and public address are significant for a variety of reasons, but of perhaps the most immediate concern is the role of women as contributors to a democratic society. "Women will not be equal participants or successful negotiators," writes Sally McConnell-Ginet, "if the language code does not serve them equally."[97]

A society's rhetorical practices would have to be considered part of a larger language code. Some scholars contend that language itself, by its words and its structures, reflects a male view of the world.[98] Moreover, students of language and culture, including perhaps especially rhetorical critics, have not viewed women's rhetorical practices as significant. As a result, women have been left out of the history of rhetorical practice. Foss suggests that feminist critics have sought to correct this error. "Rather than assuming, for example, that significant rhetorical artifacts are speeches made in public contexts by famous rhetors...the feminist critic seeks out symbolic expressions considered significant in women's lives in the context in which they are likely to occur."[99]

Reconceptualizing Rhetoric: Voice, Gender, Invitation

Foss urges that the feminist perspective on rhetoric seeks nothing less than "the reconceptualization of rhetorical theory." "Feminist criticism," she writes, "does not simply involve the grafting on of women's perspectives to the existing framework of rhetorical theory. Rather, it challenges the theoretical tenets of the rhetorical tradition because they were developed without a consideration of gender."[100] This does not mean that feminist rhetoricians discard the history of rhetoric, though that history "was created largely by men to deal with their interests and concerns." The feminist perspective, however, "encourages us to examine the rhetorical tradition with a new consciousness of its less attractive features and implications, and to create a new body of rhetorical theory that is more satisfying to and reflects the perspectives of all people."[101]

The feminist rhetorical theorist, then, might be particularly interested in the rhetorical practices of any group of people who have systematically been denied access to rhetorical power. For instance, Karlyn Kohrs Campbell has written of the persuasive efforts of early feminist advocates: "Given the traditional concept of womanhood, which emphasized passivity, submissiveness, and patience, persuading women that they could act was a precondition for other kinds of persuasive efforts."[102] Other groups facing rhetorical exclusion would include racial minorities, the illiterate, the poor, and children. The rhetorical techniques directed to such groups might differ from those used to motivate empowered groups. Campbell comments, "Because oppressed groups tend to develop passive personality traits, consciousness-raising is an attractive communication style to people working for social change."[103] Thus, the feminist perspective is driven by a social and intellectual agenda rhetoric that extends to the interests of persons who may not be women.

Constructing Gender Rhetorically

One social and thus rhetorical phenomenon of particular interest to feminist rhetoricians is the construction of gender. "Feminist critics," writes Foss, "examine how masculinity and femininity have been created and ask that these fundamental constructions of gender be changed" when they tend to silence or otherwise degrade women. "Thus," Foss asserts, "feminist rhetorical criticism is activist—it is done not just *about* women but *for* women—it is designed to improve women's lives."[104]

Julia T. Wood has also pointed out the highly rhetorical nature of gender construction, noting that "social views of gender are passed on to individuals through communication by parents, peers, and teachers."[105] Wood is asserting nothing less than that the notions of masculinity and femininity are rhetorically derived, that they are constructed through persuasive communication. "For instance, in the early 1800s, masculinity was equated with physical potency, but today masculinity is tied to economic power and success." What accounts for this change? "Changes such as these do not just happen. Instead, they grow out of rhetorical movements that alter cultural understandings of gender and, with that, the rights, privileges, and perceptions of women and men."[106] Thus, Wood concludes, "any effort to understand relationships among gender, communication, and culture must include an awareness of how rhetorical movements sculpt social meanings of men and women."[107]

From Conquest to Invitation

The history of gender is, then, a rhetorical history that must be studied rhetorically. But perhaps new methods of rhetorical criticism and history are needed to do justice to this study of gender. Feminist critics writing during the past twenty years have called in question the standard, male-dominated "history" of rhetoric written along the lines followed in, for example, this text. In 1979, for instance, Sally Miller Gearhart argued that the history of rhetorical theory is, in fact, a history of *male* rhetorical theory and practice, and as such says little if anything about women's understanding of or practice of critical thought and persuasion.

Gearhart begins her argument with the provocative assertion that "My indictment of our field of rhetoric springs from my belief that any intent to persuade is an act of violence."[108] Gearhart points out that the men who have written the history of rhetoric have "taken as given that it is a proper and even necessary function to attempt to change others."[109] As a direct result of this attitude, rhetoric "has spent whole eras examining and analyzing its eloquence, learning how to incite the passions, move the will." She adds, "of all the human disciplines, it has gone about its task of educating others to violence with the most audacity."[110]

Gearhart affirms that her concern is not so much with the study of rhetoric itself, but rather with the underlying "*intent* to change people and things, of our attempt to educate others in that skill."[111] Rhetoric, or at least the rhetoric propounded by male theorists such as Aristotle and Perelman, does not mind its own business, but rather minds the business of other people. In this office as meddler into the affairs of others, rhetoric is aggressive, violent.

Gearhart may find support for her position in a comment about the source of the Western rhetorical tradition by the eminent historian of rhetoric, George Kennedy. In his early study of Greek oratory, *The Art of Persuasion in Greece,* Kennedy wrote that "some of the Greek love of speech and argumentation is probably derived from a feeling that oratory is a contest in which man exhibits something of his manliness. Phoenix taught Achilles to be a doer of deeds and a speaker of words. Circumstances of a less heroic age robbed many Greeks of the opportunity to be the former and these made up for it by exercise of the latter."[112] Thus, oratory was a kind of battle using words rather than swords, one in which one man sought to defeat another by a skill that drew applause rather than blood.

Indeed, rhetoric-as-male-art is built on what Gearhart terms "the *conquest* model of human interaction" which finds its most egregious manifestation in "the *conversion* model of human interaction." The conversion model holds that the goal of rhetoric is to convert others to one's own views. Gearhart takes this activity to be fundamentally an act of violence not unlike rape. When I convert another to my views, this critique affirms, I conquer the other under the justification that the conquest is actually good for the conquered, and is, in fact, what the conquered wanted.[113] The rhetoric of the courtroom, the rhetoric of the legislature, the rhetoric of the pulpit all "demonstrate precisely a violence not just of conquest but also of conversion." The conquest model of rhetoric is itself rooted in the human tendency to want to conquer the natural world. Gearhart finds all such efforts at forceful change to be fundamentally violent.

Having set out her basic argument against the violence of persuasion, Gearhart suggests that there is an alternative to such communication, "a non-persuasive notion of communication."[114] The alternative is a theory of communication as information for or assistance to others. "Communication can be a deliberate creation or co-creation of an atmosphere in which people or things, if and only if they have the internal basis for change, may change themselves...." Encouragement, the recognition of differentness among participants, enhancing the other's feeling of power, and a willingness to yield to others all are important commitments of participants in such communication.[115] Communication must come to be viewed as a "matrix" in which individuals are nurtured to become whole people. Such communication Gearhart describes as an "essentially...womanlike process," and the changes Gearhart calls for would bring about "the womanization of that discipline" of rhetoric.[116] She concludes, "in order to be authentic, in order to be nonviolent communicators, we must all become more like women."[117]

Can there be a nonpersuasive practice of rhetoric, or does this question suggest a contradiction? Recently, Sonja Foss and Cindy Griffin have outlined what they term an invitational rhetoric, one that does not require or assume intent to persuade on the part of a source.[118] "One manifestation of the patriarchal bias that characterizes much of rhetorical theorizing," they write, "is the definition of rhetoric as persuasion."[119] Following Gearhart's analysis, these authors conclude that such a view of rhetoric and communication "disallow[s]...the possibility that audience members are content with the belief systems they have developed, function happily with them, and do not perceive a need to change."[120]

An invitational view of rhetoric, Foss and Griffin's proposed solution to the received, male-controlled model centered on persuasion, "is an invitation to understanding as a means to create a relationship rooted in equality, immanent value, and self-determination."[121] Rhetoric, understood in this way, seeks not to persuade, but rather to invite audience members "to enter the rhetor's world, and see it as the rhetor does."[122] Does such rhetoric seek change in the audience? Foss and Griffin suggest that "change may be the result of invitational rhetoric, but change is not its purpose."[123]

Feminist writers have focused their energies on a critique of the Western tradition of rhetoric in the effort to reveal the ways in which this tradition was both male-generated and male-serving in its tendencies. Their work has had tremendous impact on rhetorical studies over the past twenty-five years, having influenced not just the writing of rhetorical history, but the practices of doing rhetorical theory and criticism. It remains to be seen whether an entirely different model of communicative interaction, perhaps the invitational model of Foss and Griffin, will influence the public practice of rhetoric as well.

It is undeniable that women were not allowed to play a substantial role in either Western rhetorical theory or practice prior to the end of the nineteenth century. This fact had enormous consequences for social practice, as language and power are inextricably linked. Feminist rhetoricians have worked diligently to make clear to the academic world and to the public generally that women must be afforded a rhetorical voice, and that a women's rhetoric will not resemble the male-constructed rhetoric we have received from our intellectual fathers. Their work has also opened up a vast field of rhetorical analysis of discourse by and for socially oppressed groups. The influence of the feminist critique has been, and will continue to be, profound.

"Works," "Texts," and the Work of Reading

Diane Helene Miller writes that feminist scholars working in one important tradition have "uncovered the operation of patriarchal systems" that have functioned throughout Western history to exclude women from language-based disciplines such as rhetoric and literature. These same scholars have also "chronicled the precise ways in which women's voices were suppressed or omitted from the historical record...."[124] The critical task of discovering exactly what challenges women faced was seen to precede the work of developing a distinctly feminist theory of rhetoric. Miller adds that in this way "the justification for feminist intervention" in telling rhetoric's story was "abundantly provided by observing that women had been silenced and that, even when they found or created opportunities to speak, their words were largely erased from or hidden by history." She adds that, as a result of taking this approach, the task that "has largely guided feminist rhetorical criticism thus far" has been "excavating and revaluing women's texts."[125]

However, a problem arises: this approach, according to Miller and others, can become yet another way of marginalizing women by the very tendency to demonstrate how the structures of Western intellectual inquiry have left women out of the picture. Assembling the scattered evidences of women's contributions *does not affect the patriarchal structures themselves,* does not reveal that "[women's] silencing is effected by configurations of gender that are built into the very definition of rhetoric as it has been conceived in Western society from the beginning."[126]

Miller refers to the highly influential work of Roland Barthes in suggesting another trajectory for future rhetorical investigations by feminist scholars. Barthes famously distinguished a "work" from a "text"—referring by both terms to the same artifact. That is, the relatively fixed meaning or reading of a literary "work" and its free or alternate interpretation as a "text" when read by a skilled critic in search of other meanings. Miller writes that for Barthes "language is viewed as 'polysemic' and unstable, comprised of dominant meanings that can remain privileged only so long as they continually suppress alternate meanings."[127] The work of the feminist rhetorician is to draw out these alternate meanings in such a way as to reveal the structures of male privilege hidden in texts.

This work of textual deconstruction, then, results in more than one reading of a single artifact. Miller writes, "deconstruction thereby introduces the possibility of reading a text *both* in a manner that exposes the workings of the dominant culture *and* for the purpose of generating resistant readings that oppose or modify that dominant meaning."[128] The skilled work of the reader or critic becomes paramount in approaching a "text." In this respect, power may be viewed as shifting from the author to the critic, as the author is not the sole or even the most important determiner of meaning. Following such an approach, even classic "works" such as Plato's dialogues may be read as "texts" that reveal hidden meanings and assumptions about rhetoric, the Western intellectual tradition, and the treatment women have received from both. Quoting Jane Sutton, Miller writes, "'Plato's writing resists his intentions' with respect to the taming of desire, rhetoric, and of woman."[129] Critics like Sutton, Susan Jarratt, and John Fiske find "language as the source of potentially empowering contradictions."[130] "Ultimately," writes Miller, "it is not only the opportunity for critique but the potential for reinvention that provides the impetus for a feminist engagement with the texts of the rhetorical tradition."[131]

In proposing this approach, then, Miller advocates an alternative to prior feminist scholarship in this history of rhetoric that had aimed principally at compiling catalogues of women's contributions. Such efforts may inadvertently create a false impression about social structures that worked systematically to exclude women's voices from the rhetorical domain, even as they occasionally allowed women themselves to speak in that domain.

GEORGE KENNEDY AND
COMPARATIVE RHETORIC

Feminist critics have highlighted the specifically male nature of Western rhetoric. George Kennedy, in a groundbreaking new study, has emphasized the specifically Western, especially Greek, nature of the rhetorical tradition.[132] Kennedy accomplishes this goal by comparing the Western world's rhetoric with that of other cultures, and even with the communication behaviors of some animals. The result is a view of rhetoric as universal to human cultures, and perhaps as universal to any sign using biological life. Kennedy's work in this regard, and the work of many scholars he cites, will require the attention of all students of rhetoric as we enter a new millennium of rhetorical study.

Kennedy finds an evolutionary basis for rhetoric, writing that "the probable source of such basic emotions, and thus of rhetoric, is the instinct for self-preservation, which in turn derives from nature's impulse to preserve the genetic line." If this is the case, then "rhetoric is a natural phenomenon: the potential for it exists in all life forms that can give signals, it is practiced in limited forms by nonhuman animals, and it contributed to the evolution of human speech and language from animal communication."[133] In fact, Kennedy explores the origins of rhetorical expression in the communication patterns of various species.

Kennedy's project takes him on an excursion into a number of cultures whose rhetorical history is little understood by Western scholars. He examines Native American, Aboriginal Australian, Chinese, Indian, Egyptian, Mesopotamian, Aztec, and other rhetorical traditions. His findings about other rhetorical traditions are fascinating and instructive, especially when contrasted to the Western and largely Greek tradition we have been examining in this book. A few examples will help to illustrate Kennedy's work.

In his study of ancient Aztec rhetoric, Kennedy finds a highly developed practice of what the Greeks would have termed *epideictic* oratory. So well-developed is this tradition of speaking that Kennedy writes, "the speeches reveal the great importance of formal speech in Aztec culture, both in public and private life."[134] Though their predominant form of speaking resembles epideictic oratory, their approach to issues such as proof varies dramatically from that of the Greeks. "The predominant means of persuasion in Aztec oratory is ethical and pathetical," writes Kennedy. "Speakers usually proclaim a thought authoritatively and provide no supporting reasons."[135] This is because *ethos* was the basis of rhetorical persuasion. "The primary means of persuasion is the authority of the speaker, who is regularly an older individual of high status, wise in the ways of the culture."[136]

One of Kennedy's contributions in *Comparative Rhetoric* is to collect the findings of many scholars working in a variety of disciplines. For example, Michael J. Fox is a scholar in Near Eastern languages who has studied ancient Egyptian rhetorical practices. Fox finds that elaborate displays of oratorical skill were not valued in Egypt, but that self-restraint typically won the day. Argument, the centerpiece of Greek rhetoric, was not carefully studied in Egyptian rhetoric. Fox writes, "it does not teach how to formulate arguments because it is not argumentation but rather the ethical stance of the speakers that will maintain harmony in the social order, and that is the ultimate goal of Egyptian rhetoric.[137]

Rhetoric in Ancient China

Moving from Egypt to China, Kennedy discovers that the very conditions that encouraged a sophistic movement in fifth- and fourth-century B.C. Greece were also present in fourth-century B.C. China, and to similar effect. "All these conditions existed in China in the fourth century" leading to a Chinese sophistical movement similar to that in Greece. India also experienced a sophistic movement, though a little later than China and Greece.

Among Chinese writers interested in rhetoric was the sage known as Han Fei-tzu. His book, *Records of the Grand Historian,* was written around 280 B.C. Among the observations that Han Fei-tzu offers is the following. "On the whole, the difficult thing about persuading others is not that one lacks knowledge needed to state his case nor the audacity to exercise his abilities to the full. On the whole, the difficult thing is to know the mind of the person one is trying to persuade and to be able to fit one's words to it."[138] Kennedy notes that "the history of rhetoric in China in the more than two millennia since Han Fei has not yet been written," something that could be said of many other rhetorical traditions.[139]

"Private Speaking"

As Kennedy points out, the practice of rhetoric was certainly known in ancient China, but took rather different forms than in Greece and Rome. For instance, there was considerably more interest in writing than in speaking in China. Public oratory of the traditional Greco-Roman variety was virtually unknown, though persuasion was widely practiced and studied. The actual activity of persuasion often took place in private settings as a professional adviser sought to persuade a highly placed official to take a particular course of action. James Crump, another scholar with an interest in Chinese rhetoric, writes that "there is a vast amount of material…which demonstrates quite clearly that the Chinese counterpart for Greek public speaking was Chinese 'private-speaking' in the form of advice to a patron, remonstrating with a ruler, or persuasion of a prince."[140] Apparently, however, ancient Chinese scholars were less interested in theorizing about rhetoric than were their Greek and Roman counterparts, for treatises on the theory of rhetoric are lacking despite the survival of a vast literature covering many other topics.

Chinese Sophists and the *Intrigues of the Warring States*

Based on evidence concerning the practice of rhetoric in China, Crump contends that something closely resembling sophistry was not limited to Greece.[141] Conditions that favored the appearance of sophistry were present in China in the fourth and third centuries B.C.E., including (1) an increasingly diverse social setting, (2) an unstable political situation, (3) the presence of a significant number of foreigners, and (4) radical changes in the moral and religious environment. In fact, some sinologists acknowledge the word *sophist* as "an acceptably accurate and handy term to designate a stage in the growth of Chinese intellectual life."[142] It appears that what has traditionally viewed as a distinctly Western phenomenon—sophistry understood as interest in the study and practice of techniques of argumentation and persuasion— may in fact have been considerably more widespread in the ancient world.

One important ancient Chinese work in particular has the appearance of being a manual for rhetorical training. The *Intrigues of the Warring States* reports on events that occurred in China during an early period in which a number of principalities were contending for control of the nation. Crump finds in this work a fully developed art of rhetoric, something long held not to have existed in ancient China. He writes that "every conceivable stylistic device is employed in its stories," and that that the *Intrigues* exhibits a pronounced "attention to polished language" that renders it "completely analogous" to Greek and Roman rhetorical treatises. Among the rhetorical devices Crump finds displayed in the *Intrigues* are rhythm, antithesis, symmetry, consonance and, in fact, "all the other devices peculiar to the orator's self-conscious and somewhat fulsome use of language."[143] He concludes that the *Intrigues* must have been intentionally written as a manual or handbook for teaching effective rhetoric, comparing it to the *suasoria* used in Rome, books of example speeches and debates to be memorized and practiced by young students of rhetoric.

Jian, Shui, Pien, and the Traveling Persuaders

Jian is a Chinese word that means persuasion and advice-giving, and its ancient practitioners were known as *jian shi* or *ke qing,* terms sometimes translated as "traveling persuaders." These same rhetoricians were also skilled in *shui,* or persuasion, and *pien,* or disputation. The *jian shi* were essentially itinerant political advisers who "traveled from state to state attempting to persuade the rulers to adopt their ideas and strategic plans."[144] Crump writes that political advising was "what the entire field of rhetoric was designed for in China."[145]

Rhetorical scholar Xing Lu writes that "*jian*-related activities included alerting the king to wrong or inappropriate actions, and reminding the king of considerations for the future."[146] As Chinese leaders looked to the actions of ancient "sage kings" for direction, the arguments of these professional advisers often relied on analogies to the decisions of such wise rulers of antiquity, especially the legendary Kings of Zhou. Lu writes that "the goal of *jian* was to give advice in order to correct the past wrongdoings of the king, while the purpose of *shui* was to provide a concrete plan or clever scheme regarding military or foreign affairs for the future benefit of the state." She adds that "both jobs were highly skillful and professional occupations receiving much respect in ancient Chinese society...."[147]

Re-Visioning the Greek Tradition

After his survey of rhetoric in many world cultures, Kennedy offers some general conclusions about comparative rhetorical studies. One striking conclusion is that "generally speaking, throughout the non-Western world, rhetoric has been used for purposes of agreement and conciliation, and emotionalism, except in the case of lamentation for the dead, is regarded as in poor taste."[148] This sets many other rhetorical traditions in sharp contrast to the highly competitive Greek approach with which the West is most familiar. Kennedy notes that "contentiousness found an important outlet in athletics, esteemed and organized by the Greeks on a scale not known elsewhere, and in oratorical contests."[149]

In fact, the Greek tradition, which Kennedy has done so much to illuminate throughout his career, does not come in for much praise from the eminent historian of rhetoric when he contrasts it to other rhetorical traditions. "Personal invective and mud-slinging is also a regular feature of Greek deliberative oratory from the beginning," he notes, "and becomes a regular feature of judicial oratory...."[150] Moreover, "the Greeks delighted in contentious argument; they often put a relatively low priority on telling the truth if a lie would be more effective; slanderous invective was not out of order in a court of law."[151] The contentious nature of Greek rhetoric likely derived from a much broader cultural love of competition that other scholars have noted. "Greek society was characterized by a contentiousness that is expressed in mythology, poetry, athletics, democratic government, and public address. Personal invective was acceptable to a degree not commonly found elsewhere."[152]

Because ancient Greek rhetoric had such a dominant influence on subsequent Western rhetorical theory and practice, we have grown accustomed to some of its peculiarities. For instance, "Western rhetorical practices differ from other traditions in being more tolerant of contention, personal invective, and flattery."[153] Perhaps in other ways Western culture has institutionalized the ancient Greeks' ways. Kennedy writes that "Greek orators were characteristically quarrelsome and emotional, inclined to bitter personal attacks on each other, highly resentful of such attacks on themselves but tolerant of verbal fights by others. Alone among ancient civilizations the Greeks also developed competitive athletics."[154]

But, the picture of a Western rhetoric derived from an unusually contentious Greek rhetoric is not a completely bleak one for Kennedy. Competitiveness brings a certain vigor and energy to Western rhetoric, and Greek competitiveness may actually have led to the development of democratic institutions as a means of avoiding outright violent conflict. "As an answer to sharp political differences the Greeks invented decision-making by majority," Kennedy notes.[155]

One distinct impression created by Kennedy's work on comparative rhetoric is that through the study of the rhetorics of other cultures the West may learn rhetorical practices relying less exclusively on a model of competition and seeking the goal of victory over rivals. In this way, the goals of the new rhetoric suggested by feminist critics and the comparative rhetorical approach of Kennedy may converge.

CONCLUSION

The writers considered in this chapter have analyzed how we use discourse in the effort to address a range of problems, including the distribution of power, the pathologies of public debate about issues such as nuclear deterrence, and how gender is rhetorically constructed. Writers like Foucault, Derrida, Weaver, the feminist critics, and George Kennedy have examined the uses of language to discover, challenge, or preserve sources of power and knowledge.

The scholars discussed in this chapter have sought answers for crucial questions such as: How is power achieved, preserved, and challenged in contemporary society? How do particular discourses or "ways of talking" advance the interests and political fortunes of certain social groups? Where does knowledge come from in a culture? How can culture be preserved? Their work has been widely influential in changing how we think about our uses of persuasive discourse generally.

Feminist rhetoricians have sought, through a rigorous historical and cultural criticism of the rhetorical tradition, to open a way for women to enter public debate on an equal footing with men. They have urged women to engage the public rhetorical sphere, and to do so with confidence of being heard and making a difference. It may be the case that the public sphere itself, to the degree that it has been a sphere of "debate," will be reconfigured as a result of feminist criticism. Kennedy's initial study of comparative rhetoric suggests a similar direction for the future of rhetorical theory and practice. As more non-western rhetorics are retrieved to view, western rhetoric itself may be radically reevaluated. Are we entering the age of a truly new rhetoric?

QUESTIONS FOR REVIEW

1. Why, generally, was Foucault interested in language and discourse? What is discourse's relationship to knowledge? To power?

2. What is an "episteme" in Foucault's theory? Why is he interested in discovering the episteme of an age?

3. What did Foucault mean by an "archaeology of knowledge"?

4. What is Derrida's goal in "deconstruction"? How do his goals differ from those of Habermas?

5. What is Richard Weaver's goal in advocating the study of rhetoric?

6. In your own words, what is the basic feminist criticism of the Western rhetorical tradition?

7. Why does Sally Gearhart find traditional rhetoric to be a form of violence?

8. What do Foss and Griffin mean by the phrase "invitational rhetoric"?

9. What is unusual in the Greek tradition of rhetoric when compared to other rhetorical traditions?

10. Who were the *jian shi* in ancient China?

QUESTIONS FOR DISCUSSION

1. Is Foucault convincing in his argument that language and power are intimately connected?

2. What is your response to Foucault's claim that power is not the product of institutions such as a government, but that it is a product of the ways in which we talk?

3. What is your response to Derrida's suggestion that the meanings of words are fundamentally unstable?

4. Richard Weaver argues that Western education should give privileged position to the inherited culture of the West, and perhaps particularly to Western rhetorical traditions. Do you agree that this is the avenue to perpetuating Western values? What might a feminist critic say in response to Weaver's case?

5. Some feminist theorists have called for an "invitational" rather than a combative rhetoric. Is such a rhetoric possible? Does the nature of rhetoric itself, or of human beings, render this suggestion impracticable?

6. What is your response to George Kennedy's claim that the Western rhetorical tradition is unusually aggressive and competitive when contrasted to other traditions?

TERMS

Archive: For Foucault, "the set of rules which at a given period and for a given society" define, among other things, "the limits and forms of the sayable" and "the limits and forms of conversation."

Conversion model: In Gearhart's critique of traditional rhetoric, the model that holds that the goal of rhetoric is to convert others to one's own views.

Deconstruction: In Derrida, the work of destabilizing discourse by dissecting its underlying structures of meaning and assumption.

Discourse: For Foucault, systems of talk within the limits of particular disciplines or practices.

Episteme: The totality of discursive practices of a society over an extended period of time.

Excluded discourse: In Foucault, discourse that is controlled by being prohibited.

Invitational rhetoric: In Foss and Griffin, a rhetoric that does not require or assume intent to persuade on the part of a source.

Jian shi: In ancient China, itinerant political advisors.

Modernism: For Weaver, the philosophy that involved a faith in reason and scientific advancement to bring about a better society, and a corresponding break with the traditions of Western culture.

Pian: In ancient China, the art of disputation.

Scientism: In Weaver, the application of scientific assumptions to subjects which are not wholly comprised of naturalistic phenomena.

Shui: In ancient China, the art of persuasion.

Transgression: To read a text for what a traditional reading would overlook, dismiss or omit; violating the received interpretation of a text in search of its submerged meanings.

ENDNOTES

1. For a good survey of these developments, see: Ann Gill, *Rhetoric and Human Understanding* (Prospect Heights, IL: Waveland, 1994). See also: Charles C. Lemert and Garth Gillan, *Michel Foucault: Social Theory as Transgression* (New York: Columbia University Press, 1982), chap. 1, "Foucault's Field."

2. Claudia Moscovici, *Double Dialectics: Between Universalism and Relativism in Enlightenment and Postmodern Thought* (Lanham, MD: Rowman and Littlefield, 2002), 2.

3. Jean-Francois Lyotard, *The Postmodern Condition: A Report on Knowledge.* Trans. Geoff Bennington and Brian Massumi (Minneapolis: University of Minnesota Press, 1988), xxiii.

4. Lyotard, xxiv. Quoted in Moscovici, 3.

5. C. G. Prado, *Starting with Foucault: An Introduction to Genealogy* (Boulder, CO: Westview, 1995), 1.

6. James W. Bernauer, *Michel Foucault's Force of Flight: Toward an Ethics of Thought* (Atlantic Highlands, NJ: Humanities Press, 1990), 2.

7. Michel Foucault, *The Order of Things: An Archaeology of the Human Sciences* (*Les Mots et les Chose* 1966; New York: Random House, 1970); *The Archaeology of Knowledge,* trans. A. M. Sheridan Smith (*L'Archaeology du Savoir,* 1969; New York: Random House, 1972).

8. Michel Foucault, *The Birth of the Clinic: An Archaeology of Medical Perception,* trans. A. M. Sheridan Smith (New York: Random House, 1973).

9. *Michel Foucault: Power, Truth, Strategy,* eds. Meaghan Morris and Paul Patton (Sydney, Australia: Feral Publications, 1979), 32.

10. Alec McHoul and Wendy Grace, *A Foucault Primer: Discourse, Power and the Subject* (New York: New York University Press, 1997), 22.

11. McHoul and Grace, 22.

12. *Power, Truth, Strategy,* 8.

13. McHoul and Grace, 21.

14. On Foucault's study of madness, see: Gutting, chap. 2, "Madness and Mental Illness."

15. For a very sophisticated discussion of the meaning of *discourse* in Foucault's works, see: Manfred Frank, "On Foucault's Concept of Discourse," in *Michel Foucault: Philosopher,* trans. Timothy J. Armstrong (New York: Routledge, 1992), 99–116.

16. McHoul and Grace, 35.

17. Bernauer, 5.

18. Lemert and Gillan, 6.

19. McHoul and Grace, 39.

20. Foucault, *Discipline and Punish: The Birth of the Prison* (London: Allen Lane, 1975), 29. Quoted in McHoul and Grace, 59.

21. *Routledge Encyclopedia of Philosophy,* ed. Edward Craig (London: Routledge Press, 1998), 708.

22. Gary Gutting, *Michel Foucault's Archaeology of Scientific Reason* (New York: Cambridge University Press, 1989), 2.

23. McHoul and Grace, 18.

24. For the influences of Foucault's thought, see: Bernauer, 96–100.

25. See: Gutting, Chap. 6: "The Archaeology of Knowledge."

26. *The Foucault Effect,* eds. Graham Burchell, Colin Gordon and Peter Miller (Chicago: University of Chicago Press, 1991), 59–60.

27. McHoul and Grace, 29.

28. Karlis Racevskis, *Michel Foucault and the Subversion of Intellect* (Ithaca, NY: Cornell University Press, 1983), 58. See also: Lemert and Gillan, chap. 2, "Historical Archaeology."

29. Racevskis, 59.

30. David R. Shumway, *Michel Foucault* (Charlottesville: University Press of Virginia, 1989), 56.

31. Shumway, 56.

32. Joseph Rouse, "Power/Knowledge," in *The Cambridge Companion to Foucault,* ed. Gary Gutting (Cambridge: Cambridge University Press, 1994), 92.

33. Gutting, 231.

34. Michel Foucault, "Discourse on Language," published with *Archaeology of Knowledge* (NY: Random House, 1972), 215–237, p. 216.

35. Foucault, "Discourse on Language," 216.

36. Foucault, *Archaeology of Knowledge,* 217.

37. *Foucault and the Critique of Institutions,* eds. John Caputo and Mark Yount (University Park, PA: Pennsylvania State University Press, 1993), 4.

38. Caputo and Yount, 4.

39. For a detailed discussion of these and similar practices see: Foucault, *Discipline and Punish.* Select passages from the work appear in *The Foucault Reader,* ed. Paul Rabinow (New York: Pantheon, 1984), 169–256.

40. Hubert L. Dreyfus and Paul Rabinow, "What is Maturity? Habermas and Foucault on 'What is Enlightenment?'" in *Foucault: A Critical Reader,* ed. David Couzens Hoy (Oxford: Basil Blackwell, 1986), 114.

41. Teresa de Lauretis, "Queer Theory: Lesbian and Gay Sexualities," *differences: A Journal of Feminist Cultural Studies* (1991: 3, 2), iii–xviii. See also Teresa de Lauretis, "Habit Changes," *differences: A Journal of Feminist Cultural Studies* (1994: 6, 2–3), pp. 296–313; David Halperin, *Saint Foucault: Towards a Gay Hagiography* (New York: Oxford University Press, 1995); Judith Butler, *Bodies That Matter: On the Discursive Limits of "Sex"* (New York: Routledge, 1994).

42. See: Gayatri Spivak, translator's preface to: Jacques Derrida, *Of Grammatology* (*De la Grammatologie,* 1967; Baltimore, MD: Johns Hopkins University Press, 1976).

43. *Deconstruction in a Nutshell: A Conversation with Jacques Derrida,* ed. John D. Caputo (New York: Fordham University Press, 1997), 79.

44. Jacques Derrida, *Positions,* trans. and ed. Alan Bass (1972; Chicago: University of Chicago Press, 1981), 19.

45. *Deconstruction,* 205.

46. John Caputo in *Deconstruction,* 79.

47. *Deconstruction,* 78.

48. *Deconstruction,* 78.

49. On Derrida's relationship to Habermas, see: Bill Martin, *Matrix and Line* (Albany: State University of New York Press, 1992), chap. 3, "What is the Heart of Language? Habermas, Davidson, Derrida."

50. Christopher Norris, *Derrida* (Cambridge, MA: Harvard University Press, 1987), 27.

51. Jacques Derrida, *Speech and Phenomena,* trans. David Allison (*La Voix et le Phénomène,* 1967; Evanston, IL: Northwestern University Press, 1973).

52. *Deconstruction,* 52.

53. Norris, 22.

54. James A. Aune, "Rhetoric after Deconstruction," in *Rhetoric and Philosophy,* ed. Richard A. Cherwitz (Hillsdale, NJ: Lawrence Erlbaum, 1990), 253–273, p. 256.

55. *Deconstruction,* 55.

56. Norris, 14.

57. Norris, 163.

58. Jonathan Culler, *On Deconstruction* (Ithaca, NY: Cornell University Press, 1982), 86.

59. Norris, 165–166.

60. Aune, 257.

61. Aune, 257.

62. Jacques Derrida, *Writing and Difference,* trans. Alan Bass (*L'écriture et la Différence;* Chicago: University of Chicago Press, 1978), 42.

63. Norris, 23, 21.

64. Norris, 43.

65. *Deconstruction,* 41.

66. *Deconstruction,* 49.

67. *Deconstruction,* 55.

68. Richard M. Weaver, *Ideas Have Consequences* (Chicago: University of Chicago Press, 1948); *The Ethics of Rhetoric* (Chicago: Regnery, 1953); *Composition: A Course in Writing and Rhetoric* (New York: Holt, Rinehart and Winston, 1957); *Language is Sermonic: Richard M. Weaver on the Nature of Rhetoric,* ed. Richard L. Johannesen, Rennard Strickland, Ralph T. Eubanks (Baton Rouge: Louisiana State University Press, 1970).

69. Johannesen, et al., *Language is Sermonic,* 8.

70. Weaver, *Ideas,* 12.

71. Weaver, *Ideas,* 52.

72. Weaver, *Ideas,* 67

73. Richard Weaver, "Language is Sermonic" in *Language is Sermonic,* 201.

74. Weaver, "Language is Sermonic," 203.

75. Weaver, *Ideas,* 49

76. Richard Weaver *Visions of Order* (Baton Rouge: Louisiana State University Press, 1964).

77. Richard Weaver, *Life Without Prejudice and Other Essays* (Chicago: University of Chicago Press, 1965), 44.

78. Weaver, *Ideas,* 18.

79. Weaver, *Ideas,* 58.

80. Weaver, *Ideas,* 60.

81. Weaver, *Life Without Prejudice,* 51.

82. Weaver, *Ideas,* 148.

83. Richard Weaver, *The Ethics of Rhetoric* (1953; Chicago: Regnery, 1968), 19–20.

84. Weaver, *Ethics,* 23.

85. In addition to the other sources discussed in this section, see: Elizabeth A. Fay, *Eminent Rhetoric: Language, Gender, and Cultural Tropes* (Westport, CT: Bergen and Garvey, 1994); Deborah Tannen, *Gender and Discourse* (Oxford: Oxford University Press, 1994).

86. General studies of the issue of the differences between men's and women's ways of speaking and knowing can be found in: Carol Gilligan, *In a Different Voice* (Cambridge, MA: Harvard University Press, 1982); Janice Moulton, "A Paradigm of Philosophy: The Adversary Method"; Genevieve Lloyd, "The Man of Reason," and Alison M. Jaggar, "Love and Knowledge" in *Women, Knowledge and Reality: Explorations in Feminist Philosophy,* eds. Ann Gary and Marilyn Pearsall (New York: Routledge, 1989); Maryann Ayim, "Violence and Domination as Metaphors in Academic Discourse," in *Selected Issues in Logic and Communication,* ed. Trudy Govier (Belmont, CA: Wadsworth, 1988), chap. 16.

87. Jana Sawicki, "Foucault, Feminism and Questions of Identity," in *The Cambridge Companion to Foucault,* 290.

88. Sawicki, 288.

89. Leslie Di Mare, "Rhetoric and Women: The Private and Public Spheres," in *Constructing and Reconstructing Gender: The Links Among Communication, Language, and Gender,* eds. Linda A. M. Perry, Lynn H. Turner, and Helen M. Sterk (Albany: State University of New York Press, 1992), 47.

90. Sonja Foss, *Rhetorical Criticism* (Prospect Heights, IL: Waveland, 1989), 151–152.

91. Foss, 152.

92. Foss, 152.

93. Dale Spender, *Man Made Language* (Boston: Routledge and Kegan Paul, 1980), 59.

94. Spender, 52.

95. *Women's Voices in Our Time: Statements by American Leaders,* eds. Victoria L. DeFrancisco and Marvin D. Jensen (Prospect Heights, IL: Waveland, 1994), ix.

96. DeFrancisco and Jensen, ix. They cite studies by Karlyn K. Campbell, "Hearing Women's Voices," *Communication Education* 40 (January 1991): 33–48; and K. S. Vonnegut, "Listening for Women's Voices," *Communication Education* 41 (January 1992): 26–39.

97. Sally McConnel-Ginet, et al., *Women and Language in Literature and Society* (New York: Prager, 1980), 66.

98. Barrie Thorne and Nancy Henley, *Language and Sex: Difference and Dominance* (Rowley, MA: Newberry House, 1975).

99. Foss, 153.

100. Foss, 154.

101. Foss, 154.

102. Karlyn Kohrs Campbell, *Man Can Not Speak for Her: A Critical Study of Early Feminist Rhetoric* (New York: Greenwood Press, 1989), 14.

103. Campbell, 14.

104. Foss, 155.

105. Julia T. Wood, *Gendered Lives* (Belmont, CA: 1994), 91.

106. Wood, 91.

107. Wood, 91–92.

108. Sally Gearhart, "The Womanization of Rhetoric," *Women's Studies International Quarterly* 2 (1979): 195–201, p. 195.

109. Gearhart, 195.

110. Gearhart, 195.

111. Gearhart, 196.

112. George Kennedy, *The Art of Persuasion in Ancient Greece* (Princeton, NJ: Princeton University Press, 1963), 189.

113. Gearhart, 196.

114. Gearhart, 198.

115. Gearhart, 199.

116. Gearhart, 200.

117. Gearhart, 201.

118. S. J. Foss and C. L. Griffin, "Beyond Persuasion: A Proposal for an Invitational Rhetoric," *Communication Monographs* 62 (March 1995): 2–18.

119. Foss and Griffin, 2.

120. Foss and Griffin, 3.

121. Foss and Griffin, 5.

122. Foss and Griffin, 5.

123. Foss and Griffin, 6.

124. Diane Helene Miller, "The Future of Feminist Rhetorical Criticism," in *Listening to Their Voices: The Rhetorical Activities of Historical Women* (Columbia: University of South Carolina Press, 1997), 359–380, pp. 361–362.

125. Miller, 362.

126. Miller, 363.

127. Roland Barthes, "From Work to Text," in *Textual Strategies,* ed. Josue V. Harari, 73–81. Quoted in Miller, 366.

128. Miller, 367.

129. Jane Sutton, "The Taming of *Polos/Polis:* Rhetoric as an Achievement without Woman," in *Southern Communication Journal* (57:2), 97–119, p. 112. Quoted in Miller, 370.

130. Miller, 370.

131. Miller, 371.

132. George Kennedy, *Comparative Rhetoric: An Historical and Cross-Cultural Introduction* (New York: Oxford University Press, 1998).

133. Kennedy, *Comparative,* 4.

134. Kennedy, *Comparative,* 101.

135. Kennedy, *Comparative,* 103.

136. Kennedy, *Comparative,* 105.

137. Michael J. Fox, "Ancient Egyptian Rhetoric," *Rhetorica* 1 (1983): 21–22. Quoted in Kennedy, *Comparative Rhetoric,* 131.

138. Burton Watson, *Basic Writings of Mo Tzu, Hsun Tzu, and Han Fei-Tzu* (New York: Columbia University Press, 1967) 73. Quoted in Kennedy, *Comparative Rhetoric,* 163–164.

139. Kennedy, *Comparative Rhetoric,* 164.

140. James Crump, *Intrigues: Studies of the Chan-Kuo Tse* (Ann Arbor: University of Michigan Press, 1964), 100.

141. Crump, 93.

142. Crump, 97.

143. Crump, 100.

144. Crump, 117.

145. Crump, 100.

146. Xing Lu, *Rhetoric in Ancient China, Fifth to Third Century, B.C.E.: A Comparison with Classical Greek Rhetoric.* (Columbia: University of South Carolina Press, 1998), 79.

147. Lu, 81. On Chinese rhetorical practices, see also Mary Garrett, "Classical Chinese Conceptions of Argumentation and Persuasion," *Argumentation and Advocacy* 29 (1993): 105–115.

148. Kennedy, *Comparative Rhetoric,* 198.

149. Kennedy, *Comparative Rhetoric,* 199.

150. Kennedy, *Comparative Rhetoric,* 199.

151. Kennedy, *Comparative Rhetoric,* 203.

152. Kennedy, *Comparative Rhetoric,* 211.

153. Kennedy, *Comparative Rhetoric,* 217.

154. Kennedy, *Comparative Rhetoric,* 221.

155. Kennedy, *Comparative Rhetoric,* 221.

GLOSSARY

Acutezza [Italian]: In Vico, rhetorical wordplay or wit.

Aesthetics: Study of the persuasive potential in the form, beauty, or force of symbolic expression.

Affectus [Latin]: For the Italian Humanists, the source of emotions or passions in the human mind.

Ambigua [Latin]: In Cicero's theory of humor, the source of humor inherent in words.

Animorum motus [Latin]: The emotions.

Ante rem [Latin]: In one Roman topical system, events *preceding an act* in one *loci* system.

Antilogike [Greek]: The creation of arguments for and against a claim.

Apologia [Greek]: Defense. One type of pleading common to forensic oratory, the other being accusation.

Aporia: Placing a claim in doubt by developing arguments on both sides of the issue.

Appeals: Symbolic methods that aim either to elicit an emotion or to engage the audience's loyalties or commitments.

Archive: For Foucault, rules of discourse that define and limit what can be said during a given period in a particular society.

Arete [Greek]: An ability to manage one's personal affairs in an intelligent manner and to succeed in public life. Excellence. Natural leadership ability. Virtue. A component of *ethos.*

Argument: Discourse characterized by reasons advanced to support conclusions.

Argument field: In Stephen Toulmin's theory, arguments that can be said to be "of the same logical type."

Arrangement [Latin *dispositio*]: The distribution of arguments in the most effective order. The planned ordering of components in a message to achieve the greatest persuasive effect, whether of persuasion, clarity or beauty. The second of Cicero's five canons of rhetoric as set out in *De Inventione.*

Artistic proofs [Greek *entechnoi pisteis*]: Proofs or means of persuasion taught specifically by the art of rhetoric. In Aristotle's rhetorical theory these include *logos, pathos,* and *ethos.*

Audience adaptation: Changes made in a message to tailor it to a particular audience.

Axioms: Unquestioned first principles, the starting points of scientific reasoning.

Backing: Toulmin's term for support for an argument's warrant.

Bases: In Quintilian's system for teaching argument, the specific issues needing to be addressed in arguing a judicial case.

Belletristic Movement: Rhetorical movement in the late eighteenth and early nineteenth centuries that emphasized considerations of style in rhetoric, expanding rhetoric into a study of literature literacy criticism, and writing generally.

276

Burden of proof: In the argument theory of Richard Whately, the responsibility to bring a case against the status quo sufficient to challenge its enjoyment of presumption.

Captatio benevoluntatiae [Latin]: Section of a letter securing goodwill of recipient.

Chiasmus: Rhetorical device that takes its name from the reversing of elements in parallel clauses, forming an X (*chi*) in the sentence.

Circa rem [Latin]: In one Roman topical system, the circumstances *surrounding the act.*

Claim: Stephen Toulmin's term for an argument's conclusion.

Classicism: A resurgence of interest in the languages and texts of classical antiquity that characterized Renaissance Humanism.

Common Topics [Greek *koinoi topoi*]: In Aristotle's *Rhetoric,* arguments and strategies useful in a variety of rhetorical settings.

Communicative action: In Jurgen Habermas, the interactive process of critical argumentation crucial to overcoming ideological domination.

Communicative competence: In Habermas, the particular conditions under which rational communication is possible.

Consubstantiality: Commonality of substance.

Conclusio [Latin]: The conclusion of a letter.

Confirmatio [Latin]: In Roman rhetorical theory, the section of a judicial speech offering evidence in support of claims advanced during the statement of the facts, or *narratio.*

Confutatio [Latin]: In Roman rhetorical theory, the section in a judicial speech that advances counterarguments in response to the opposition's case.

Conjectural issues: In Cicero's stasis system, questions of fact, such as "What occurred?" and "When did it occur?"

Constraints: In Lloyd Bitzer's situation theory of rhetoric, "persons, events, objects, and relations which are parts of the situation because they have the power to constrain decision and action needed to modify the exigence."

Contingent matters: Matters in which decisions must be based on probabilities, because absolute certainty is not possible.

Conversio [Latin]: A teaching method in which the structure of a sentence was varied so as to discover its most pleasing form.

Conversion model: In Sally Gearhart's critique of traditional rhetoric, the model that holds that the goal of rhetoric is to convert others to one's own views.

Critical theory: The systematic means of analyzing discourse for its hidden assumptions and implications.

Data: Stephen Toulmin's term for the evidence to support the claim.

Deconstruction: In Derrida, the work of destabilizing discourse by dissecting its underlying structures of meaning and assumption.

Deduction: Reasoning moving from a general premise, through a specific application of that premise, to a specific conclusion.

Definite questions: In Quintilian's system, issues concerning specific individuals, facts, places, and times.

Definition: In Quintilian's system, a concern for categorizing an event.

Delectare [Latin]:   To delight. One of Cicero's three functions or goals of rhetoric.

Deliberative Oratory: Oratory that occurs in legislative assemblies and that addresses questions concerning the appropriate use of resources.

Delivery [Latin ***pronuntiatio***]:   The control of voice and body in a manner suitable to the dignity of the subject matter and the style. The fifth of Cicero's five canons of rhetoric.

Demos [Greek]:   The people.

Dialectic [Greek ***dialektike***]:   Rigorous, critical questioning. A method of reasoning from common opinions, directed by established principles of reasoning to probable conclusions about general questions. Also, the method of investigating philosophical issues by the give and take of argument. Also, a teaching method involving arguing either side of a case. For Aristotle, a method of debating issues of general interest starting from widely accepted propositions.

Dialogues: In Mikhail Bakhtin, chains of assertion and response that reveal the presence of different voices.

Dianoia [Greek]:   True meaning, as opposed to false (*eristic*) arguments.

Dictaminis (Ars) [Latin]:   Medieval art of letter writing.

Dictatores [Latin]:   In the Middle Ages, teachers of letter writing.

Differentia [Latin]:   Topics of Boethius divided according to major premises.

Dikanikon [Greek]:   Courtroom or forensic oratory.

Discourse: Symbols intentionally organized into a message. Also, the systems of talk within the limits of certain disciplines and practices.

Dispositio [Latin]:   Arrangement. Cicero's term for the effective ordering of arguments and appeals making up the substance of a persuasive case. The second of his five canons of rhetoric.

Dissoi logoi [Greek}:   Contradictory arguments.

Docere [Latin]:   To teach. One of Cicero's three functions or goals of rhetoric, the other two being to persuade (*movere*) and to delight (*delectare*).

Doxa [Greek]:   A belief or opinion. Also, mere opinion.

Dramatistic pentad: Kenneth Burke's "grammar of motives," consisting of act, scene, agent, agency, and purpose.

Dunamis [Greek]:   Faculty, power, ability, or capacity. Aristotle defined rhetoric as the *dunamis,* or faculty of discovering the available means of persuasion in any given situation.

Eidei topoi [Greek]:   The special topics of Aristotle, appropriate to special rhetorical settings such as the courtroom. Contrasted to the *koinoi topoi* or common topics.

Elite audience: In Perelman and Olbrechts-Tyteca's rhetorical theory, an audience of trained specialists in a discipline.

Elocutio [Latin]:   Style. Cicero's term to designate the concern for finding the appropriate language or style for a message. One of his five canons of rhetoric.

Endoxa [Greek]:   The probable premises from which dialectic began—widely held opinions, or the opinions of the wisest people.

Enthymeme [Greek ***enthymema***]:   A rhetorical syllogism. An argument built from values, beliefs, or knowledge held in common by a speaker and an audience.

Epainos [Greek]:   Praise. One of two functions of epideictic oratory, the other being blame (*psogos*).

Epideictic Oratory [Greek *epideiktikon*]:   The kind of speaking characteristic of public ceremonies such as funerals or events commemorating war heroes.

Epideixis [Greek]:   a speech prepared for a formal occasion.

Episteme [Greek]:   Plato's term for true knowledge.

Eristic [Greek]:   Discourse's power to express, to captivate, to argue, or to injure.

Ethos [Greek]:   The study of human character. The persuasive potential of the speaker's character and personal credibility. One of Aristotle's three artistic proofs.

Eudaimonia [Greek].   Human well-being or happiness. The goal of legislation and thus the central concern of deliberative oratory.

Eunoia [Greek]:   Goodwill. Along with practical wisdom (*phronesis*) and virtue (*arete*), a component of *ethos,* or good character.

Excluded Discourse: In Foucault, discourse that is controlled by being prohibited.

Exigence: In Lloyd Bitzer's situation theory of rhetoric, "an imperfection marked by urgency…a defect, an obstacle, something waiting to be done, a thing which is other than it should be."

Existence: In Quintilian, a question of fact.

Exordia [Latin]:   Introductions designed to dispose the audience to listen to a speech or to secure a reader's goodwill.

Expression: [Latin: *elocutio*] Fitting proper language to arguments; The Third of Cicero's five canons of oratory.

Facetiae [Latin]:   Wit or humor.

Faculty psychology: The eighteenth-century view that the mind consisted of "faculties" or capacities including the understanding, the imagination, the passions, and the will.

False consciousness: In Jurgen Habermas's work, a flawed and thus distorting view of reality, of the world, and of people.

Field-dependent: Stephen Toulmin's term for standards of argument assessment that belong specifically to a particular field.

Field-invariant: Stephen Toulmin's term for standards of argument assessment that apply regardless of the field in which the argument is advanced.

Fitting response: In Lloyd Bitzer's situational theory, a rhetorical response that is dictated by components of the rhetorical situation, including exigence, audience, and constraints.

Forensic Oratory (*dikanikon*):   Courtroom speaking.

Form: In Kenneth Burke, "an arousing and fulfilling of a desire in an audience."

Gens [Latin]:   A clan, a group of influential families in Rome.

Hermeneutics: The science of textual interpretation.

Heteroglossia: The many languages that proliferate in any culture (Bakhtin).

Heuristic [Greek]:   Discourse's capacity for discovery, whether of facts, insights, or even of self-awareness.

Hypothesis: In Hermagoras' system, a conclusion drawn from a thesis or general premise combined with a particular premise that applies the thesis to a given case.

Hypsos [Latin]: Sublimity or great writing, the theme of Longinus' *On the Sublime.*

Ideology: A system of belief, or a framework for interpreting the world. Also, an irrational or unexamined system of thinking.

Imitatio [Latin]: Imitation or mimicry.

Inartistic proofs [Greek *atechnoi pisteis*]: In Aristotle's *Rhetoric,* proofs not belonging to the art of rhetoric.

Indefinite questions: In Quintilian's system of rhetoric, questions discussed without specific reference to persons, time, place, or other particular limitation.

Ingenium [Latin]: In Vico, the innate human capacity to grasp similarities or relationships.

In re [Latin]: In one Roman topical system, arguments concerning what occurred in *the act itself.*

Intersubjective agreements: Agreements forged among independent participants in dialogue on the basis of open and fairly conducted argument.

Invention [Latin *Inventio*]: Cicero's term describing the process of coming up with the arguments and appeals in a persuasive case. The first of his five canons of rhetoric.

Invitational rhetoric: In Foss and Griffin, a rhetoric that does not require or assume intent to persuade.

Ioci [Latin]: Jokes. Discussed in Cicero's theory of humor presented in *De Oratore.*

Irony: When indirect statement carries direct meaning, or something is taken to stand for its opposite. In Vico, the final stage in the development of human language and thought.

Issues: Hermagoras of Temnos' *topoi,* which included three classifications of judicial arguments. The three types include (1) conjectural issues or a concern for matters of fact, (2) legal issues or a concern for the interpretation of a text or document, and (3) juridical issues or a concern for the rightness or wrongness of an act.

Issues of definition: Questions rejonding by what name an act should be called.

Issues of fact: Questions concerning such questions as "What occured?" and "When did it occur?"

Issues of quality: Questions concerning the severity of an act.

Jian shi: In ancient China, itinerant political advisors.

Kairos [Greek]: Rhetoric's search for relative truth rather than absolue certainty. A consideration of opposite points of view, as well as attention to such factors as time and circumstances. An opportune moment or situation.

Kategoria [Greek]: Accusation. One of the two functions of forensic oratory, the other being defense or *apologia.*

Koinoi topoi [Greek]: Aristotle's universal lines of argument. Arguments useful in any setting.

Kolakeia: Flattery. Promising people what they want without regard for what is best for them. Plato argued that rhetoric succeeded by employing flattery.

Literae humanae [Latin]: The liberal arts.

Loci communes [Latin]:   Commonplaces. Types of arguments.

Logical positivism: The intellectual effort to bring scientific standards to bear on the resolution of all issues.

Logos, pl. *logoi* [Greek]:   The study of arguments. One of Aristotle's three artistic proofs, the other two being *pathos* (the study of emotion) and *ethos* (the study of character). Also, an account, or a clear and logical explanation. Also, a word or an argument. Also, a transcendent source of truth for Plato.

Memory [Latin *memoria*]:   The firm mental grasp of the content of a speech. The fourth of Cicero's five canons of rhetoric.

Meta-narratives: Grand explanatory schemes that claim to account for the entirety of human history and the human condition.

Metaphor: A comparison of things not apparently similar.

Metonym: The substitution of a part for the whole.

Metron [Greek]:   Measure. From Protagoras' famous statements that "man is the measure [*metron*] of all things; of things that are not, that they are; of things that are, that they are."

Modal qualifiers: In Stephen Toulmin's theory of argument, words that indicate the degree of confidence one takes in a conclusion. Examples include *must, possibly, probably,* and *certainly.*

Modernism: For Richard Weaver, the philosophy that involved a faith in reason and scientific advancement to bring about a better society, and a corresponding break with the traditions of Western culture.

Modus inveniendi [Latin]:   In St. Augustine, material for understanding scripture.

Modus proferendi [Latin]:   In St. Augustine, the means of expressing the ideas found in scripture.

Moral reasoning: Reasoning from evidence to more or less probable conclusions on practical issues. The kind of reasoning employed in rhetoric, and appropriate to issues such as those presented by politics, ethics, religion, and economics.

Motives: Commitments, goals, desires, or purposes when they lead to action.

Movere [Latin]:   To persuade or move an audience's emotions. One of Cicero's three functions or goals of rhetoric.

Narratio [Latin]:   In judicial speech, a statement of essential facts. In a letter, the body setting and details of the problem to be addressed.

Neoplatonism: A body of philosophic and religious ideas loosely based on Plato's idealism, but also incorporating ideas from astrology, magic, and alchemy.

Nomos [Greek]:   Social custom or convention. Rule by agreement among the citizenry.

Notaries: Rhetorically trained secretaries responsible for negotiating, recording, and communicating the many agreements that enabled Italian commercial cities to function.

Paradeigma [Greek]:   Argument from an example or examples to a probable generalization. The inductive argument that complements the deductive enthymeme.

Particular audience: In Perelman and Olbrechts-Tyteca, the actual audience of persons one addresses when advancing an argument publicly.

Pathos [Greek]:   The study of psychology of emotion; one of the three artistic proofs of Aristotle.

Perfectus orator [Latin]:   The complete or finished orator. In Roman thought, an eloquent leader embodying and articulating the society's values.

Peroratio [Latin]:   The conclusion or final section of a judicial speech in which the orator re-iterated the full strength of a case.

Petitio [Latin]:   Request, demand, or announcement in a letter.

Phronesis [Greek]:   Practical wisdom. Good sense. In Aristotle, a component of *ethos*.

Physis [Greek]:   The law or rule of nature under which the strong dominate the weak.

Pian: In ancient China, the art of disputation.

Pistis [Greek]:   Mere belief.

Plausibility: In Campbell's rhetorical theory, discourse that is instantly believable because of its close association with an audience's experience of their social world.

Poetriae, Ars [Latin]:   Art of poetry. One of three medieval rhetorical arts. Highly prescriptive approaches to writing poetry.

Polis [Greek]:   The city–state, particularly the people making up the state.

Polyphonic: Having many voices. Mikhail Bakhtin's term for quality of narrative in which each character is fully developed and speaks fully his or her perspective on the world.

Postmodernism: A twentieth-century intellectual movement that rejected the Enlightenment ideals of progress and reason, and questioned all "metanarratives."

Post rem [Latin]:   In one Roman topical system, the *following an act.*

Praedicandi, Ars [Latin]:   Preaching. One of three medieval rhetorical arts.

Presence: In Perelman and Olbrechts-Tyteca, the choice to emphasize certain ideas and facts over others, thus encouraging an audience to attend to them.

Presumption: A *"pre-occupation* of the ground," in Richard Whately's terms. The principle that an idea occupies its place as reasonable or acceptable until adequately challenged.

Pronuntiatio [Latin]:   Delivery. The control of voice and body in a manner suitable to the dignity of the subject matter and the style.

Protreptic [Greek]:   The potential in language for persuasion.

Prudence: Practical judgment.

Psogos [Greek]:   Blame. One of two functions of epideictic oratory, the other being praise (*epainos*).

Psychagogos [Greek]:   A poet. A "leader of souls" through incantation.

Psyche [Greek]:   Mind or soul.

Public sphere: A place of discussion among individuals unrestrained by the dominating influence of political systems and the interests of the state.

Quadrivium [Latin]:   The four major studies in medieval schools, consisting of arithmetic, geometry, music, and astronomy.

Quaestiones [Latin]:   Debatable points suggested by passages from ancient authorities.

Quality: In Quintilian's system of bases, a concern for the severity of the act, once defined or categorized.

Quintilian's uncertainty principle: In Michael Billig, the notion that the variety of possible human responses to any situation means that the rules of rhetoric must always be provisional, never absolute.

Rebuttal: Stephen Toulmin's term for potential conditions on the acceptance of the claim.

Res [Latin]: The substance of one's arguments.

Rhetor: Anyone engaged in preparing or presenting rhetorical discourse.

Rhetores [Greek]: Rhetors or orators. Those making their living and wielding power by means of persuasive words. Also, politicians.

Rhetoric: As an art, the study and practice of effective symbolic expression. As a type of discourse, goal-oriented speaking or writing that seeks, by means of the resources of symbols, to adapt ideas to an audience.

Rhetorical audience: In Lloyd Bitzer's situational theory, "those persons who are capable of being influenced by discourse and of being mediators of change."

Rhetorical discourse: Discourse crafted according to the principles of the art of rhetoric.

Rhetorical opposition: In Michael Billig, the observation of the Sophist Protagoras that there are two sides to every question, because every form of human thought has its opposite.

Rhetorical Theory: The systematic presentation of the art of rhetoric, descriptions of rhetoric's various functions, and explanations of how rhetoric achieves its goals.

Rhetoric of fiction: Wayne Booth's insight that in narrative, "the author's judgment is always present."

Salutatio [Latin]: The greeting in a letter.

Sannio [Latin]: A clown or buffoon. For Cicero, a classification the orator must avoid in using humor.

Scholasticism: A closed and authoritarian approach to education centered on disputation over a fixed body of premises derived largely from the teachings of Aristotle.

Scientific reasoning: Reasoning that moves from axioms to indubitable conclusions.

Scientism: In Weaver, the application of scientific assumptions to subjects which are not wholly comprised of naturalistic phenomena.

Senatus [Latin]: Senate. Roman governing body. Literally, a council of elders.

Sensus Communis: Common beliefs and values that provide the basis for society.

Sententiae [Latin]: Isolated statements from ancient authorities.

Shui: In ancient China, the art of persuasion. Also, the formulation of concrete plans of action.

Sophistes, pl. *sophistae* [Greek]: An authority, an expert, a teacher of rhetoric.

Starting points: In Perelman and Olbrechts-Tyteca, points of agreement between a rhetor and an audience that allow for argumentation to develop.

Stasis **system:** Method for discovering arguments by identifying points at which clash or disagreement was likely to occur in a case or debate.

Studia humanitatis [Latin]: Humanistic studies, or studies proper to the development of a free and active human mind—rhetoric, poetics, ethics, politics.

Syllogism: A deductive argument moving from a general premise, through a specific application of that premise, to a specific and necessary conclusion.

Symbol: Any mark, sign, sound, or gesture that represents something based on social agreement.

Symbolic inducement: Kenneth Burke's definition of rhetoric. Garnering cooperation by the strategic use of symbols.

Sympheron [Greek]: Advantageous course of action and actions.

Synecdoche: The rhetorical device in which the whole object represents one part.

Taste: In Lord Kames and Hugh Blair, a developed appreciation of aesthetic experiences.

Techne [Greek]: A true art or discipline. A scientific or systematic pursuit of a full account and arriving regularly at a good product or outcome.

Terministic screens: Kenneth Burke's term to describe the fact that every language or choice of words becomes a filter through which we perceive the world.

Theme: A biblical text providing the basis for developing a sermon.

Thesmos: Law derived from the authority of Kings.

Thesis: A general premise in an argument under Hermagoras' system.

Topical maxim: In Boethius, rational principle or major premises in arguments.

Topical systems [Latin *topica*]: Systematic methods for discovering arguments.

Topos: A line of argument.

Toulmin Model: Stephen Toulmin's diagram of an argument that identifies components including the claim, data, warrant, backing, qualifier, and rebuttal.

Transgression: To read a text for what a traditional reading would overlook or omit; violating the received meaning of a text in search of its submerged meanings.

Translative issue: Issues of procedure, objections regarding how a case is being pursued.

Trivium [Latin]: Three minor studies of grammar, rhetoric, and logic in medieval schools.

Tropes: Rhetorical devices.

Universal audience: In Perelman and Olbrechts-Tyteca, an imagined audience of highly rational individuals; an audience of all normal, adult persons.

Universal pragmatics: In Jurgen Habermas's works, rules for using and understanding language rationally.

Uomo universale [Italian]: The universal man, the ideal type of an educated person in the Renaissance.

Utterance: A personal statement full of potential meaning. For Bakhtin, the basic unit of discourse.

Validity: A concern for an argument's structure without consideration of its content.

Validity claim: In Jurgen Habermas's works, a claim to having made a true statement.

Verba [Latin]: The words in which the subject matter of the argument was advanced.

Vita activa [Latin]: The active life, or life of political and civic involvement.

Warrant: Stephen Toulmin's term for a generalization that links some data to a claim.

BIBLIOGRAPHY

■ ■ ■ ■ ■

Abbott, Don Paul. "Marxist Influences on the Rhetorical Theory of Kenneth Burke," *Philosophy and Rhetoric* 4 (1974): 217–233.
———. "Rhetoric and Writing in Renaissance Europe and England." *A Short History of Writing Instruction.* Ed. James J. Murphy. Davis, CA: Hermagoras Press, 1990.
Agricola, Rudolph. *De Inventione Dialectica.* Nieuwkoop, Holland: B. de Graaf, 1967.
Anderson, Graham. *Sage, Saint, and Sophist: Holy Men and Their Associates in the Early Roman Empire.* London: Routledge, 1994.
Anderson, John R. "The Audience as a Concept in the Philosophic Rhetoric of Perelman, Johnstone, and Natanson." *Southern Speech Communication Journal* 38 (1972): 39–50.
Andrews, Richard, ed. *Narrative and Argument.* Milton Keynes, UK: Open University Press, 1989.
———. ed. *Rebirth of Rhetoric: Essays in Language, Culture, and Education.* London: Routledge, 1992.
Aristotle. *Rhetoric.* Trans. W. Rhys Roberts. New York: Modern Library, 1954.
———. *Rhetoric.* Trans. Lane Cooper. New York: Appleton-Century-Crofts, 1932.
Arnhart, Larry. *Aristotle on Political Reasoning: A Commentary on the Rhetoric.* DeKalb, IL: Northern Illinois University Press, 1981.
Augustijn, Cornelis. *Erasmus: His Life, Works, and Influence.* Trans. J. C. Grayson. Toronto: University of Toronto Press, 1991.
Augustine. *On Christian Doctrine.* Trans. D. W. Robertson. Indianapolis, IN: Library of Liberal Arts, 1958.
Aune, James A. "Rhetoric after Deconstruction." *Rhetoric and Philosophy.* Ed. Richard A. Cherwitz. Hillsdale, NJ: Lawrence Erlbaum, 1990: 253–273.
Bacon, Wallace A. "The Elocutionary Career of Thomas Sheridan." *Speech Monographs* 31 (1964): 1–53.
Bakhtin, Mikhail. *Marxism and the Philosophy of Language.* Trans. L. Matejka and I. R. Titunik. New York: Seminar Press, 1973.
———. *Problems of Dostoevsky's Poetics.* Ed. and trans. Caryl Emerson. Minneapolis, MN: University of Minnesota Press, 1984.
Barilli, Renato. *Rhetoric.* Trans. Giuliana Menozzi. Minneapolis, MN: University of Minnesota Press, 1989.
Barnes, John A. *A Pack of Lies: Towards a Sociology of Lying.* Cambridge: Cambridge University Press, 1994.
Barnes, Jonathan, ed. *The Cambridge Companion to Aristotle.* Cambridge: Cambridge University Press, 1995.
Barrett, Harold. *The Sophists.* Novato, CA: Chandler and Sharp, 1987.
Barthes, Roland. "From Work to Text." *Textual Strategies.* Ed. Josue Harari. Ithaca NY: Cornell University Press, 1979.
Bauer, Dale M. and S. Jaret McKinstry, eds. *Feminism, Bakhtin, and the Dialogic.* Albany, NY: State University of New York Press, 1991.
Bazerman, Charles. *Shaping Written Knowledge: The Genre and Activity of the Experimental Article in Science.* Madison, WI: University of Wisconsin Press, 1988.

285

Benardete, Seth. *The Rhetoric of Morality and Philosophy: Plato's Gorgias and Phaedrus.* Chicago: University of Chicago Press, 1991.

Benson, T. and M. Prosser, eds. *Readings in Classical Rhetoric.* Boston: Allyn and Bacon, 1969.

Berlin, James A. "Revisionary Histories of Rhetoric: Politics, Power, and Plurality." *Writing Histories of Rhetoric.* Ed. Victor Vitanza. Carbondale, IL: Southern Illinois University Press, 1994: 112–127.

Bernauer, James W. *Michel Foucault's Force of Flight: Toward an Ethics of Thought.* Atlantic Highlands, NJ: Humanities Press, 1990.

Bevilaqua, Vincent. "Philosophical Origins of George Campbell's *Philosophy of Rhetoric.*" *Speech Monographs* 32 (1965): 7–8.

Billig, Michael. *Arguing and Thinking.* Cambridge: Cambridge University Press, 1989.

———. *Ideology and Opinion.* London: Sage, 1991.

———. "Psychology, Rhetoric, and Cognition." *History of the Human Sciences* 2 (1989): 289–307.

Bishop, Morris. *Petrarch and His World.* Bloomington, IN: Indiana University Press, 1963.

Bitzer, Lloyd. "Aristotle's Enthymeme Revisited," *Quarterly Journal of Speech* 45 (1959): 399–408.

———. "Hume's Philosophy in George Campbell's *The Philosophy of Rhetoric,*" *Philosophy and Rhetoric* 2 (1969): 136–166.

———. "The Rhetorical Situation." *Philosophy and Rhetoric* 1 (1968): 1–14.

———. "Rhetoric and Public Knowledge." *Rhetoric, Philosophy, and Literature: An Exploration.* Ed. Don Burks. West Lafayette, IN: Purdue University Press, 1978: 67–93.

———. "Political Rhetoric." *Landmark Essays on Contemporary Rhetoric.* Ed. Thomas Farrell. Mahwah, NJ: Hermagoras Press, 1998: 1–22.

Bizzell, Patricia and Bruce Herzberg. *The Rhetorical Tradition: Readings from Classical Times to the Present.* Boston: St. Martin's Press, 1990.

Black, Edwin. "Plato's View of Rhetoric." *Quarterly Journal of Speech* 44 (December 1958): 361–374.

Blair, Hugh. *Lectures on Rhetoric and Belles Lettres.* Ed. Harold Harding. Carbondale, IL: Southern University Press, 1965.

Boethius. *De Topicis Differentiis.* Trans. Eleanor Stump. Ithaca, NY: Cornell University Press, 1978.

Booth, Wayne. *Modern Dogma and the Rhetoric of Assent.* Chicago: University of Chicago Press, 1974.

———. *Now Don't Try to Reason with Me.* Chicago: University of Chicago Press, 1970.

———. *The Rhetoric of Fiction.* Chicago: University of Chicago Press, 1961.

———. *The Vocation of a Teacher.* Chicago: University of Chicago Press, 1988.

Bowersock, G. W. *Greek Sophists in the Roman Empire.* Oxford: Clarendon Press, 1969.

Breitman, George, ed. *Malcolm X Speaks.* New York: Grove Press, 1966.

Browne, Stephen H. "Shandyean Satire and the Rhetorical Arts in Eighteenth-Century England." *Southern Communication Journal* 55 (1990): 191–205.

Brucker, Gene. *Florence: The Golden Age 1138–1737.* Berkeley: University of California Press, 1969.

Brummett, Barry. *Rhetoric in Popular Culture.* New York: St. Martin's Press, 1994.

Burchell, Graham, Colin Gordon and Peter Miller, eds. *The Foucault Effect.* Chicago: University of Chicago Press, 1991.

Burke, Kenneth. *Counter-Statement.* 1931. Berkeley: University of California Press, 1968.

————. *A Grammar of Motives.* 1945. Berkeley: University of California Press, 1969.

————. *Language as Symbolic Action.* 1937. Berkeley: University of California Press, 1966.

————. *The Philosophy of Literary Form: Studies in Symbolic Action.* 1941. Berkeley: University of California Press, 1973.

————. *A Rhetoric of Motives.* Berkeley: University of California Press, 1950.

————. *The Rhetoric of Religion.* Berkeley: University of California Press, 1961.

Burke, Peter. "The Spread of Humanism." *The Impact of Humanism in Western Europe.* Eds. Anthony Goodman and Angus MacKay. London: Longman, 1990.

————. *Vico.* Oxford: Oxford University Press, 1985.

Butler, Judith. *Bodies that Matter: On the Discursive Limits of Sex.* New York, NY: Routledge, 1994.

Campbell, George. *The Philosophy of Rhetoric.* 1776. Ed. Lloyd F. Bitzer. Carbondale, IL: University of Southern Illinois Press, 1963.

Campbell, John Angus. "Darwin, Thales, and the Milkmaid: Scientific Revolution and Argument from Common Beliefs and Common Sense." *Perspectives on Argument: Essays in Honor of Wayne Brockriede.* Eds. Robert Trapp and Janice Schuetz. Prospect Heights, IL: Waveland, 1990: 207–220.

————. "Scientific Discovery and Rhetorical Invention: The Path of Darwin's Origin," *The Rhetorical Turn.* Ed. Herbert Simon. Chicago: University of Chicago Press, 1990: 58–90.

Campbell, Karlyn K. "Hearing Women's Voices." *Communication Education* 40 (1991): 33–48.

————. *Man Can Not Speak for Her: A Critical Study of Early Feminist Rhetoric.* New York: Greenwood Press, 1989.

Caputo, John D., ed. *Deconstruction in a Nutshell: A Conversation with Jacques Derrida.* New York: Fordham University Press, 1997.

————and Mark Yount. *Foucault and the Critique of Institutions.* University Park: Pennsylvania State University Press, 1993.

Carleton, Walter. "What is Rhetorical Knowledge?" *Quarterly Journal of Speech* 64 (1978): 313–328.

Casson, Lionel. *Selected Satires of Lucian.* New York: Norton, 1968.

Castiglione, Ballasdare. *The Courtier.* n.p.: 1528.

Charles, David. *Aristotle's Philosophy of Action.* Ithaca, NY: Cornell University Press, 1984.

Cialdini, Robert. *Influence: The Psychology of Persuasion.* New York: William Morrow, 1993.

Cicero. *De Inventione.* Trans. H. M. Hubbell. Cambridge, MA: Loeb Classical Library, 1976.

————. *De Oratore.* Trans. E. W. Sutton and H. Rackham. Cambridge, MA: Loeb Classical Library, 1976.

Cicero. Ed. T. A. Dorey. New York: Basic Books, 1965.

Clark, Martin L. *Rhetoric at Rome.* New York: Barnes and Noble, 1953.

Cmiel, Kenneth. *Democratic Eloquence: The Fight over Popular Speech in Nineteenth-Century America.* New York: William Morrow, 1990.

Coates, Willson Havelock. *The Emergence of Liberal Humanism: An Intellectual History of Western Europe.* New York: McGraw Hill, 1966.

Cohen, Herman. "William Leechman's Anticipation of Campbell." *Western Speech* 32 (1968): 92–99.

Cole, Percival. *Later Roman Education in Ausonius, Capella, and the Theodosian Code.* New York: Columbia University Press, 1909.

Conley, Thomas M. "'Logical Hylomorphism' and Aristotle's *Koinoi Topoi.*" *Central States Speech Journal* 29 (1978): 92–97.

————. *Rhetoric in the European Tradition.* New York: Longman, 1990.

Corbett, Edward P. J. "The *Topoi* Revisited." *Rhetoric and Praxis: The Contribution of Classical Rhetoric to Practical Thinking.* Ed. Jean Deitz Moss. Washington, DC: Catholic University Press of America, 1986.

Covino, William A. *Magic, Rhetoric and Literacy: An Eccentric History of the Composing Imagination.* Albany: State University of New York Press, 1994.

Craig, Christopher P. *Form as Argument in Cicero's Speeches: A Study of Dilemma,* American Classical Studies, #31. Atlanta: Scholars Press, 1993.

Craig, Edward, ed. *Routledge Encyclopedia of Philosophy.* London: Routledge Press, 1998.

Crombie, I. M. *An Examination of Plato's Doctrines.* London: Routledge and Kegan Paul, 1961.

Crump, James. *Intrigues: Studies of the Chan-Kuo Tse.* Ann Arbor, MI: University of Michigan Press, 1964.

Culler, Jonathan. *On Deconstruction.* Ithaca, NY: Cornell University Press, 1982.

Curran, Jane V. "The Rhetorical Technique of Plato's *Phaedrus*," *Philosophy and Rhetoric* 19 (1986): 66–72.

Dearin, Ray D., ed. *The New Rhetoric of Chaim Perelman: Statement and Response.* Lanham, MD: University Press of America, 1989.

DeFrancisco, Victoria and Marvin Jensen, eds. *Women's Voices in Our Time.* Prospect Heights, IL: Waveland, 1994.

de Lauretas, Teresa. "Habit Changes." *differences: A Journal of Feminist Cultural Studies* 6 (1994), 296–313.

————. "Queer Theory: Lesbian and Gay Sexualities." *difference: A Journal of Feminist Cultural Studies* 3 (1991), iii–xviii.

de Romilly, Jacqueline. *The Great Sophists in Periclean Athens.* Trans. Janet Lloyd. Oxford: Clarendon Press, 1992.

————. *Magic and Rhetoric in Ancient Greece.* Cambridge, MA: Harvard University Press, 1975.

Derrida, Jacques. *Of Grammatology* (*De la Grammatologie*). Trans. Gayatri Spivak 1967. Baltimore, MD: Johns Hopkins University Press, 1976.

————. *Positions.* Trans. and Ed. Alan Bass. 1972. Chicago: University of Chicago Press, 1981.

————. *Speech and Phenomena* (*La Voix et le Phénomène*). Trans. David Allison 1967. Evanston, IL: Northwestern University Press, 1973.

————. *Writing and Difference* (*L' écriture et la Différence*). Trans. Alan Bass. Chicago: University of Chicago Press, 1978.

Despland, Michael. *The Education of Desire: Plato and the Philosophy of Religion.* Toronto: University of Toronto Press, 1985.

Dickinson, Emily. *The Poems of Emily Dickinson.* Ed. Thomas H. Johnson. Cambridge, MA: Belknap Press of Harvard University, 1983.

Dipardo, Anne. "Narrative Knowers, Expository Knowledge." *Written Communication* 7 (1990): 59–95.

Disch, Lisa J. "More Truth than Fact: Storytelling as Critical Understanding in the Writings of Hannah Arendt." *Political Theory.* 1994: 665–694

Donaworth, Jane, ed. *Rhetorical Theory by Women before 1900.* Lanham, MD: Rowman and Littlefield, 2002.

Donovan, Josephine. "Feminism, Bakhtin, and the Dialogic." Eds. Dale M. Bauer and S. Jaret McKinstry. Albany, NY: State University of New York Press, 1991.

Duranti, Alessandro. *From Grammar to Politics: Linguistic Anthropology in a Western Samoan Village.* Berkeley: University of California Press, 1994.

Ede, Lisa S. "Rhetoric vs. Philosophy: The Role of the Universal Audience in Chaim Perelman's *The New Rhetoric.*" *Central States Speech Journal* 32 (1981): 118–125.

Edwards, Mark U., Jr. *Printing, Propaganda, and Martin Luther.* Berkeley: University of California Press, 1994.

Ehninger, Douglas. "Campbell, Blair, and Whately: Old Friends in a New Light," *Western Speech* 19 (1955): 263–269.

———. "Campbell, Blair and Whately Revisited." *Southern Speech Journal* 28 (1963): 169–182.

———."George Campbell and the Revolution in Inventional Thinking." *Southern Speech Journal* 15 (1950): 270–276.

Enos, Richard Leo. *Greek Rhetoric before Aristotle.* Prospect Heights, IL: Waveland, 1993.

Erasmus. "The Right Way to Speak." *Collected Works,* v. 4. Ed. J. K. Sowards. Toronto: University of Toronto Press, 1985.

Erickson, Keith V., ed. *Aristotle: The Classical Heritage of Rhetoric.* Metuchen, NJ: The Scarecrow Press, 1974.

Faral, Edmond. *"Les Artes Poetique du XIIe et XIIIe Siecle."* (1924) Paris, n.p.: 1971.

Farmer, Frank, ed. *Landmark Essays on Bakhtin, Rhetoric and Writing.* Mahwah, NJ: Hermagoras Press, 1998.

Farrell, Thomas. "Social Knowledge II." *Quarterly Journal of Speech* 64 (1978): 329–334.

Faulhaber, Charles. "The Origins of Humanism." *Medieval Eloquence: Studies in the Theory and Practice of Medieval Rhetoric.* Ed. James J. Murphy. Berkeley: University of California Press, 1978: 85–111.

Fay, Elizabeth A. *Eminent Rhetoric: Language, Gender, and Cultural Tropes.* Westport, CT: Bergen and Garvey, 1994.

Ford, Andrew. "The Price of Art in Isocrates: Formalism and the Escape from Politics." *Rethinking the History of Rhetoric.* Ed. Takis Poulakos. Boulder, CO: Westview, 1992.

Fortenbaugh, W. W. *Aristotle on Emotion.* New York: Barnes and Noble, 1975.

———and D.C. Mirhady, eds. *Peripatetic Rhetoric after Aristotle.* New Brunswick, NJ: Transaction, 1994.

Foss, Sonja. *Rhetorical Criticism.* Prospect Heights, IL: Waveland, 1989.

———and C. L. Griffin. "Beyond Persuasion: A Proposal for an Invitational Rhetoric," *Communication Monographs* 62 (1995): 2–18.

———, Karen A. Foss, and Robert Trapp. *Contemporary Perspective on Rhetoric.* 2d ed. Prospect Heights, IL: Waveland, 1991.

Foucault, Michel. *The Archaeology of Knowledge (L'Archáeologie du Savoir).* Trans. A. M. Sheridan Smith. 1969. New York: Random House, 1972.

———. *The Birth of the Clinic: An Archaeology of Medical Perception.* Trans. A. M. Sheridan Smith. New York: Random House, 1973.

———. *Discipline and Punish: The Birth of the Prison.* London: Allen Lane, 1975.

———. *The Order of Things: An Archaeology of the Human Sciences (Les Mots et les Chose).* 1966. New York: Random House, 1970.

Fox, Michael J. "Ancient Egyptian Rhetoric." *Rhetorica* 1 (1983): 21–22.

Frank, Manfred. "On Foucault's Concept of Discourse." *Michel Foucault: Philosopher.* Trans. Timothy J. Armstrong. New York: Routledge, 1992: 99–116.

Fredborg, Karin Margareta. "Twelfth-Century Ciceronian Rhetoric: Its Doctrinal Development and Influences." *Rhetoric Revalued.* Ed. Brian Vickers. Binghamton, NY: Center for Medieval and Early Renaissance Studies, 1982, 87–97.

Fuhrmann, Manfred. *Cicero and the Roman Republic.* Trans. W. E. Yuill. Oxford: Blackwell, 1992.

Gadamer, Hans-George. *The Idea of the Good in Platonic-Aristotelian Philosophy.* New Haven, CT: Yale University Press, 1986.

Gagarin, Michael. *Antiphon and the Athenians: Oratory, Law and Justice in the Age of the Sophists.* Austin, TX: University of Texas Press, 2002.

Gallo, Ernest. "The *Poetria Nova* of Geoffrey of Vinsauf." *Medieval Eloquence: Studies in the Theory and Practice of Medieval Rhetoric.* Ed. James J. Murphy. Berkeley: University of California Press, 1978: 68–84.

Gaonkar, Dilip Parameshwar. "The Idea of Rhetoric in the Rhetoric of Science." *Southern Communication Journal* 58 (1993): 255–327.

Garin, Euginio. *Portraits of the Quattrocentro.* New York: Harper and Row, 1963.

Garry, Ann and Marilyn Pearsall, eds. *Women, Knowledge and Reality: Explorations in Feminist Philosophy.* New York: Routledge, 1989.

Gearhart, Sally Miller. "The Womanization of Rhetoric." *Women's Studies International Quarterly* 2 (1979): 195–201.

Geertz, Clifford. *Works and Lives.* Stanford, CT: Stanford University Press: 1988.

Geoffrey of Vinsauf. *Documentum do Modo et Arte Dictandi et Versificandi.* Trans. Roger P. Parr. Milwaukee, WI: Marquette University Press, 1968.

Gergen, Kenneth and Mary M. Gergen. "Narrative Form and the Construction of Psychological Sciences." *Narrative Psychology,* ed. T. R. Sarbin. New York: Praeger Press, 1986: 22–44.

Gilbert, Katherine E. and Helmut Kuhn. *A History of Esthetics.* Bloomington, IN: University of Indiana Press, 1953.

Gill, Ann. *Rhetoric and Human Understanding.* Prospect Heights, IL: Waveland, 1994.

Gilligan, Carol. *In a Different Voice.* Cambridge: Harvard University Press, 1982.

Glenn, Cheryl. "Locating Aspasia on the Rhetorical Map." *Listening to their Voices.* Ed. Molly Meijer Wertheimer. Columbia, SC: University of South Carolina Press, 1997: 19–41.

Golden, James L. and Edward P. J. Corbett. *The Rhetoric of Blair, Campbell, and Whately.* New York: Holt, Rinehart and Winston, 1968.

Goodman, Anthony and Angus MacKay, eds. *The Impact of Humanism on Western Europe.* London: Longman, 1990.

Gorgias. *Encomium on Helen.* Trans. LaRue VanHook. *The Classical Weekly* 6 (1913): 122–123.

Gotoff, Harold C. *Cicero's Caesarian Speeches: A Stylistic Commentary.* Chapel Hill: University of North Carolina Press, 1993.

Govier, Trudy. *Selected Issues in Logic and Communication.* Belmont, CA: Wadsworth, 1988.

Grassi, Ernesto. *Rhetoric as Philosophy.* University Park, PA: Pennsylvania State University Press, 1980.

Gregg, Richard B. *Symbolic Inducement and Knowing: A Study in the Foundations of Rhetoric.* Columbia, SC: University of South Carolina Press, 1984.

Grimaldi, Michael. *Aristotle, Rhetoric I: A Commentary.* New York: Fordham University Press, 1980.

———. "The Aristotelian Topics." *Traditio* 14 (1958): 1–16.

Gronbeck, Bruce E. "Gorgias on Rhetoric and Poetic: A Rehabilitation." *Southern Speech Communication Journal* 38 (1972): 27–38.

Gross, Alan. *The Rhetoric of Science.* Cambridge: Harvard University Press, 1990.

———. "A Theory of the Rhetorical Audience: Reflections on Chaim Perelman." *Quarterly Journal of Speech* 85 (1999): 202–211.

Grube, G. M. A. *The Greek and Roman Critics.* Toronto: University of Toronto Press, 1965.

———. Introduction to Longinus, *On the Sublime.* Indianapolis IN: Library of Liberal Arts, 1957.

———. *Plato's Thought.* 1935. Boston: Beacon Press, 1958.

Guthrie, W. K. C. *The Sophists.* Cambridge: Cambridge University Press, 1971.

Gutting, Gary, ed. *The Cambridge Companion to Foucault.* Cambridge: Cambridge University Press, 1994.

———. *Michel Foucault's Archaeology of Scientific Reason.* New York: Cambridge University Press, 1989.

Habermas, Jurgen. *Communication and the Evolution of Society.* Trans. Thomas McCarthy. Boston: Beacon Press, 1979.

———. *Toward a Rational Society.* Trans. Jeremy J. Shapiro. Boston: Beacon Press, 1970.

———. *Knowledge and Human Interests.* Trans. Jeremy J. Shapiro. Boston: Beacon Press, 1971.

———. *Theory and Practice.* Trans. John Viertel. Boston: Beacon Press, 1973.

———. *The Philosophical Discourse of Modernity: Twelve Lectures.* Ed. Thomas McCarthy. Trans. Frederick Lawrence. Cambridge, MA: MIT Press, 1987.

Habicht, Christian. *Cicero the Politician.* Baltimore, MD: Johns Hopkins University Press, 1990.

Halperin, David. *Saint Foucault: Toward a Gay Hagiography.* New York, NY: Oxford University Press, 1995.

Hare, R. M. *Plato.* Oxford: Oxford University Press, 1982.

Hauser, Gerard. "Empiricism, Description and the New Rhetoric." *Philosophy and Rhetoric* 5 (1972): 24–44.

———. "The Example in Aristotle's *Rhetoric:* Bifurcation or Contradiction?" *Philosophy and Rhetoric* 1 (1968): 78–90.

Hazzard, Paul. *La Pensée Européenne au XVIIIe siècle de Montesquieu à Lessing.* Paris: Arthone Fayard, 1963.

Hill, Forbes I. "The Rhetoric of Aristotle." *A Synoptic History of Classical Rhetoric.* Davis, CA: Hermagoras Press, 1983.

Hogan, Michael J., ed. *Rhetoric and Community: Studies in Unity and Fragmentation.* Columbia, SC: University of South Carolina Press, 1998.

Holquist, Michael. *Dialogism: Bakhtin and His World.* London: Routledge, 1990.

Home, Henry: Lord Kames. *The Elements of Criticism.* 1761. New York: Barnes and Burr, 1865.

Horner, Winifred Bryan, ed. *The Present State of Scholarship in Historical and Contemporary Rhetoric.* Columbia, MO: University of Missouri Press, 1990.

Howard, Dick. "A Politics in Search of the Political." *Theory and Society* 1 (1974): 271–306.

Howell, Wilbur Samuel. *Eighteenth-Century British Logic and Rhetoric.* Princeton, NJ: Princeton University Press, 1971.

———. "John Locke and the New Rhetoric." *Quarterly Journal of Speech* 53 (1967): 319–321.

———. *Logic and Rhetoric in England: 1500–1700.* New York: Russell and Russell, 1961.

Hoy, David Couzens. *Foucault: A Critical Reader.* Oxford: Basil Blackwell, 1986.

Hubbard, B. A. F. and E. S. Karnofsky. *Plato's Protagoras: A Socratic Commentary.* Chicago: University of Chicago Press, 1982.

Jarratt, Susan. *Rereading the Sophists: Classical Rhetoric Refigured.* Carbondale, IL: Southern Illinois University Press, 1991.

———and Rory Ong. "Aspasia: Rhetoric, Gender, and Colonial Ideology." *Reclaiming Rhetorica: Women in the Rhetorical Tradition.* Ed. Andrea Lunsford. Pittsburgh, PA: University of Pittsburgh Press, 1995: 9–24.

Jennings, Margaret, C. S. J. "The *Ars Compendi Sermones* of Ranulph Higden." *Medieval Eloquence: Studies in the Theory and Practice of Medieval Rhetoric.* Ed. James J. Murphy. Berkeley: University of California Press, 1978: 112–126.

Johannesen, Richard L., Rennard Strickland and Ralph T. Eubanks, eds. *Language is Sermonic: Richard M. Weaver on the Nature of Rhetoric.* Baton Rouge: Louisiana State University Press, 1970.

Johnson, W. R. "Isocrates Flowering: The Rhetoric of Augustine." *Philosophy and Rhetoric* 9 (1976): 217–231.

Jonsen, Albert R. and Stephen Toulmin. *The Abuse of Casuistry.* Berkeley: University of California Press, 1988.

Kahn, Victoria. *Rhetoric, Prudence, and Skepticism in the Renaissance.* Ithaca, NY: Cornell University Press, 1985.

———. *Machiavelian Rhetoric: From the Counter-Reformation to Milton.* Princeton, NJ: Princeton University Press, 1994.

Katula, Richard and James J. Murphy, eds. *A Synoptic History of Classical Rhetoric.* Davis, CA: Hermagoras Press, 1995.

Katz, Stephen B. "The Ethic of Expediency: Classical Rhetoric, Technology, and the Holocaust." *College English* 54 (1992): 255–275.

Kraye, Jill, ed. *The Cambridge Companion to Renaissance Humanism.* Cambridge: Cambridge University Press, 1996.

Kelley, Donald R. *Renaissance Humanism.* Boston: Twayne Publishers, 1991.

Kennedy, George, trans. *Aristotle on Rhetoric: A Theory of Civic Discourse.* New York: Oxford University Press, 1991.

———. *The Art of Persuasion in Ancient Greece.* Princeton, NJ: Princeton University Press, 1963.

———. *Classical Rhetoric and Its Secular and Christian Tradition.* Chapel Hill, NC: University of North Carolina Press, 1980.

———. *Classical Rhetoric and Its Secular and Christian Tradition,* 2d ed. Chapel Hill, NC: University of North Carolina Press, 1999.

———. *Comparative Rhetoric: An Historical and Cross-Cultural Introduction.* New York: Oxford University Press, 1998.

Kenny, Anthony. *Aristotle on the Perfect Life.* Oxford: Clarendon Press, 1992.

Kerferd, G. B. *The Sophistic Movement.* Cambridge: Cambridge University Press, 1981.

Kinney, Arthur F. *Humanist Poetics: Thought, Rhetoric, and Fiction in Sixteenth-Century England.* Amherst, MA: University of Massachusetts Press, 1986.

Kinsman, Robert, ed. *The Darker Vision of the Renaissance: Beyond the Fields of Reason.* Berkeley: University of California Press, 1974.

Kitto, H. D. F. *The Greeks.* Baltimore, MD: Penguin Books, 1968.

Kristeller, Paul Oskar. *Renaissance Thought: The Classic, Scholastic, and Humanist Strains.* New York: Harper and Row, 1961.

Kuhn, Thomas. *The Structure of Scientific Revolutions,* 2d ed. Chicago: University of Chicago Press, 1970.

Labalme, Patricia H. *Beyond Their Sex: Learned Women of the European Past.* New York: New York University Press, 1984.

Landau, Misia. "Paradise Lost: The Theme of Terrestriality in Human Evolution." *The Rhetoric of the Human Sciences.* Eds. John Nelson, Allen Megill, and D. N. McCloskey. Madison, WI: University of Wisconsin Press, 1987: 111–124.

Lanham, Richard. *The Electronic Word: Democracy, Technology and the Arts.* Chicago: University of Chicago Press, 1993.

———. *A Handbook of Rhetorical Terms.* Second ed. Berkeley CA: University of California Press, 1991.

LaRusso, Dominic. "Root or Branch? A Reexamination of Campbell's 'Rhetoric.'" *Western Speech* 32 (1968): 85–91.

Leff, Michael. "The Logician's Rhetoric: Boethius' *De Differentiis Topicis,* Book IV." *Medieval Eloquence: Studies in the Theory and Practice of Medieval Rhetoric.* Berkeley: University of California Press, 1978: 3–24.

———. "The Topics of Argumentative Invention in Latin Rhetorical Theory from Cicero to Boethius." *Rhetorica* 1 (1983): 23–44.

Lemert, Charles C. and Garth Gillan. *Michel Foucault: Social Theory as Transgression.* New York: Columbia University Press, 1982.

Lincoln, Abraham. "Second Inaugural Address." *The World's Great Speeches.* Ed. Lewis Copeland. New York: Dover, 1958: 316–317.

Lloyd, G. E. R. *Aristotle: The Growth and Structure of His Thought.* Cambridge: Cambridge University Press, 1968.

Locke, John. *Essay on Human Understanding.* London: 1690.

Lodge, Rupert C. *Plato's Theory of Art.* 1953. New York: Russell and Russell, 1975.

Longinus, *On the Sublime.* Ed. and Trans. G. M. A. Grube. Indianapolis, IN: Library of Liberal Arts, 1957.

Lu, Xing. *Rhetoric in Ancient China, Fifth to Third Century,* B.C.E. Columbia, SC: University of South Carolina Press, 1998.

Lunsford, Andrea A. *Reclaiming Rhetorica: Women in the Rhetorical Tradition.* Pittsburgh, PA: University of Pittsburgh Press, 1995.

Lyotard, Jean-Francois. *The Postmodern Condition: A Report on Knowledge.* Trans. Geoff Bennington and Brian Massumi. Minneapolis, MN, 1988.

Mack, Peter. *Renaissance Argument: Valla and Agricola in the Tradition of Rhetoric and Dialectic.* Leiden, Holland: E. J. Brill, 1993.

Mali, Joseph. *The Rehabilitation of Myth: Vico's "New Science."* Cambridge: Cambridge University Press, 1992.

Manson, Richard. *The Theory of Knowledge of Giambattista Vico.* Hamden, CT: Archon Books, 1969.

Martin, Bill. *Matrix and Line.* Albany, NY: State University of New York Press, 1992.

Martines, Lauro. *Power and Imagination: City States in Renaissance Italy.* New York: Knopf, 1979.

May, James M. *Trials of Character: The Eloquence of Ciceronian Ethos.* Chapel Hill, NC: University of North Carolina Press, 1988.

McCarthy, Thomas. *The Critical Theory of Jurgen Habermas.* Cambridge, MA: MIT Press, 1978.

―――, ed. *The Philosophical Discourse of Modernity: Twelve Lectures.* Trans. Frederick Lawrence. Cambridge, MA: MIT Press, 1987.

McCloskey, D. N. "The Neglected Economics of Talk." *Planning for Higher Education* 22 (1994): 11–16.

―――. *The Rhetoric of Economics.* Madison, WI: University of Wisconsin Press, 1985.

McConnell-Ginet, Sally, Ruth Borker and Nelly Furman. *Women and Language in Literature and Society.* New York: Prager, 1980.

McDermott, Douglas. "George Campbell and the Classical Tradition." *Quarterly Journal of Speech* 49 (1963): 403–409.

McHoul, Alec and Wendy Grace. *A Foucault Primer: Discourse, Power and the Subject.* New York: New York University Press, 1997.

McKeon, Richard. *Rhetoric: Essays in Invention and Discovery.* Ed. Mark Backman. Woodbridge, CT: Ox Bow Press, 1987.

McKerrow, Ray E. "Campbell and Whately on the Utility of Syllogistic Logic," *Western Speech Communication Journal* 40 (1976): 3–13.

Meador, Prentice A. "Quintilian and the *Institutio Oratoria.*" *A Synoptic History of Classical Rhetoric.* Davis, CA: Hermagoras Press, 1983: 151–176.

Megill, Allan. "Recounting the Past: Description, Explanation, and Narrative in Historiography." *American Historical Review* 94 (1989): 627–653.

Mendelson, Sarah Heller. *The Mental World of Stuart Women: Three Studies.* Amherst, MA: The University of Massachusetts Press, 1987.

Miller, Diane Helene. "The Future of Feminist Rhetorical Criticism." *Listening to their Voices: The Rhetorical Activities of Historical Women.* Ed. Molly Meijer Wertheimer. Columbia, SC: University of South Carolina Press, 1997.

Miller, J., M. Prosser and T. Benson, eds. *Readings in Medieval Rhetoric.* Bloomington, IN: Indiana University Press, 1974.

Mohrmann, G. P. "*The Civile Conversation:* Communication in the Renaissance." *Speech Monographs* 39 (1972): 193–204.

Moline, Jon. *Plato's Theory of Understanding.* Madison, WI: University of Wisconsin Press, 1981.

Monfasani, John. *George of Trebizond: A Biography and a Study of his Rhetoric and Logic.* Leiden, Holland: Brill Publishers, 1976.

Mooney, Michael. *Renaissance Thought and Its Sources.* New York: Columbia University Press, 1979.

―――. *Vico in the Tradition of Rhetoric.* Princeton, NJ: Princeton University Press, 1985.

Morris, Meaghan and Paul Patton, eds. *Michel Foucault: Power, Truth, Strategy.* Sydney: Feral Publications, 1979.

Moscorici, Claudia. *Double Dialectics: Between Universalism and Relativism in Enlightened and Postmodern Thought.* Lanham, MD: Rowman and Littlefield, 2002.

Moss, Jean Deitz, ed. *Rhetoric and Praxis: The Contribution of Classical Rhetoric to Practical Reasoning.* Washington, DC: Catholic University of America Press, 1986.

Murphy, James J., ed. *Medieval Eloquence: Studies in the Theory and Practice of Medieval Rhetoric.* Berkeley: University of California Press, 1978.

―――. ed. *Peter Ramus's Attack on Cicero.* Trans. Carole Newlands. Davis, CA: Hermagoras Press, 1992.

―――. *A Synoptic History of Classical Rhetoric.* Davis, CA: Hermagoras Press, 1983.

―――. ed. *A Short History of Writing Instruction.* Ed. James J. Murphy. Davis, CA: Hermagoras Press, 1990.

————. "Saint Augustine and the Debate about a Christian Rhetoric." *Quarterly Journal of Speech* 46 (1960): 400–410.

————. *Three Medieval Rhetorical Arts.* Berkeley: University of California Press, 1971.

Nash, Christopher and Martin Warner, eds. *Narrative in Culture.* London: Routledge, 1988.

Nauert, Charles G., Jr. *Humanism and the Culture of Renaissance Europe.* Cambridge: Cambridge University Press, 1995.

Nelson, John, Allen McGill and D. N. McCloskey, eds. *The Rhetoric of the Human Sciences.* Madison, WI: University of Wisconsin Press, 1987.

Norris, Christopher. *Derrida.* Cambridge, MA: Harvard University Press, 1987.

Nothstine, William, Carole Blair and Gary Copeland. *Critical Questions.* New York: St. Martin's Press. 1994.

Ober, Josiah. *Mass and Elite in Democratic Athens: Rhetoric, Ideology, and the Power of the People.* Princeton, NJ: Princeton University Press, 1989.

Ochs, Donovan J. "Aristotle's Concept of Formal Topics." *Speech Monographs* (36) 1969: 419–425.

————. "Cicero's *Topica:* A Process View of Invention." *Explorations in Rhetoric: Essays in Honor of Douglas Ehninger.* Glenview, IL: Scott, Foresman, 1982.

Ong, Walter J., S. J. *Ramus: Method and the Decay of Dialogue.* Cambridge, MA: Harvard University Press, 1983.

Perelman, Chaim. *The Idea of Justice and the Problem of Argument.* New York: Random House, 1963.

————. *Justice.* New York: Random House, 1967.

————. *The New Rhetoric and the Humanities.* Trans. William Kluback. Dordrecht, Holland: D. Reidel, 1979.

————, and Lucy Olbrechts-Tyteca. *The New Rhetoric: A Treatise on Argumentation.* 1958. Trans. John Wilkinson and Purcell Weaver. Notre Dame, IN: University of Notre Dame Press, 1969.

Perry, Linda A. M., Lynn H. Turner, and Helen M. Sterk, eds. *Constructing and Reconstructing Gender: The Links among Communication, Language, and Gender.* Albany, NY: State University of New York Press, 1992.

Philostratus. *Lives of the Sophists.* Trans. W. C. Wright. London: Loeb Classical Library, 1965.

Plato. *Gorgias.* Trans. W. C. Helmbold. Indianapolis, IN: Bobbs-Merrill, 1952.

————. *Gorgias.* Trans. T. Irwin. Oxford: Clarendon Press, 1979.

————. *Phaedrus.* Trans. W. C. Helmbold and W. G. Rabinowitz. Indianapolis, IN: Liberal Arts Press, 1956.

————. *Protagoras.* Trans. C. C. W. Taylor. Oxford: Clarendon Press, 1991.

————. *Sophist.* Trans. William S. Cobb. Savage, MD: Rowman and Littlefield, 1990.

Plochmann, George Kimball and Franklin E. Robinson. *A Friendly Companion to Plato's Gorgias.* Carbondale, IL: Southern Illinois University Press, 1988.

Polanyi, Michael. *Personal Knowledge.* Chicago: University of Chicago Press, 1962.

Poulakos, John. *Sophistical Rhetoric in Classical Greece.* Columbia, SC: University of South Carolina Press, 1995.

————. "Terms for Sophistical Rhetoric." *Rethinking the History of Rhetoric: Multidisciplinary Essays on the History of Rhetoric.* Ed. Takis Poulakos. Boulder, CO: Westview, 1993: 53–74.

————. "Toward a Sophistic Definition of Rhetoric." *Philosophy and Rhetoric* 16 (1983): 35–48.

Prado, C. G. *Starting with Foucault: An Introduction to Genealogy.* Boulder, CO: Westview, 1995.

Prelli, Lawrence. *A Rhetoric of Science: Inventing Scientific Discourse.* Columbia, SC: University of South Carolina Press, 1989.

Putnam, L. L. and M. E. Pacanowsky, eds. *Communication and Organizations: An Interpretive Approach.* Newbury Park, CA: Sage, 1983: 99–122.

Quandahl, Ellen. "Aristotle's *Rhetoric:* Reinterpreting Invention." *Rhetoric Review* 4 (1986): 128–137.

Quintilian. *Institutio Oratoria.* 4 vol. Trans. H. E. Butler. Cambridge, MA: Loeb Classical Library, 1959–1963.

———. *On the Early Education of the Citizen Orator.* Ed. James J. Murphy. Trans. John S. Watson. Indianapolis, IN: Library of Liberal Arts, 1965.

Rabinow, Paul, ed. *The Foucault Reader.* New York: Pantheon Books 1984.

Racevskis, Karlis. *Michel Foucault and the Subversion of Intellect.* Ithaca, NY: Cornell University Press, 1983.

Ramus, Peter. *The Questions of Brutus.* 1549. Trans. Carole Newlands. Davis, CA: Hermagoras Press, 1992.

———. *Rhetoricae Distinctiones in Quintilianum* (Arguments in Rhetoric against Quintilian). Trans. Carole Newlands. 1549. DeKalb, IL: Northern University Press, 1986.

Randall, John H. *Aristotle.* New York: Columbia University Press, 1960.

Rankin, H. D. *Sophists, Socratics and Cynics.* London: Croom Helm, 1983.

Ray, John W. "Perelman's Universal Audience." *Quarterly Journal of Speech* 64 (1978): 361–375.

Redfern, Jenny R. "Christine de Pisan and *The Treasure of the City of Ladies*: A Medieval Rhetorician and her Rhetoric." *Reclaiming Rhetorica: Women in the Rhetorical Tradition.* Ed. Andrea A. Lunsford. Pittsburgh, PA: University of Pittsburgh Press, 1995: 73–92.

Richardson, Malcom. "Women, Commerce, and Rhetoric in Medieval England." *Listening to their Voices: The Rhetorical Activities of Historical Women.* Ed. Molly Meijer Wertheimer. Columbia, SC: University of South Carolina Press, 1997: 133–149.

Sallis, J. *Being and Logos.* Atlantic Highlands, NJ: Humanities Press, 1986.

Schiappa, Edward. "Did Plato Coin *Rhetorike*?" *American Journal of Philology* 111 (1990): 457–470.

———. *Protagoras and Logos.* Columbia, SC: University of South Carolina Press, 1991.

Scott, Izora. *Controversies over the Imitation of Cicero in the Renaissance.* 1910. Davis, CA: Hermagoras Press, 1991.

Scott, Robert L. "On Viewing Rhetoric as Epistemic," *Central States Speech Journal* 18 (1967): 9–16.

———, and Wayne Brockriede. *The Rhetoric of Black Power.* New York: Harper and Row, 1969: 132

Scult, Allen. "Perelman's Universal Audience: One Perspective." *Central States Speech Journal* 27 (1976): 176–80.

Segal, Charles P. "Gorgias and the Psychology of the *Logos*," *Harvard Studies in Classical Philology* 66 (1962): 99–155.

Seigel, Jerrold E. *Rhetoric and Philosophy in Renaissance Humanism.* Princeton, NJ: Princeton University Press, 1968.

Shackleton-Bailey, D. R. *Cicero.* New York: Charles Scribner's Sons, 1971.

Sher, Richard B. *Church and University in the Scottish Enlightenment.* Edinburgh: Edinburgh University Press, 1985.

Sheridan, Thomas. *A Course of Lectures on Elocution.* London: 1762.

———. *A Discourse Being Introductory to his Course of Lectures on Elocution and the English Language.* 1759. Los Angeles: Augustan Reprint Society, 1969.

———. *A General Dictionary of the English Language.* London: 1780.

Shumway, David R. *Michel Foucault.* Charlottesville, VA: University Press of Virginia, 1989.

Simons, Herbert W., ed. *The Rhetorical Turn.* Chicago: University of Chicago Press, 1990.

Sloane, Thomas O. *On the Contrary: The Protocol of Traditional Rhetoric.* Washington, DC: Catholic University of America Press, 1997.

Spender, Dale. *Man Made Language.* Boston: Routledge and Kegan Paul, 1980.

Spitzer, Adele. "The Self-Reference of the *Gorgias.*" *Philosophy and Rhetoric* 8 (1975): 1–22.

Stringfellow, Frank. *The Meaning of Irony: A Psychoanalytic Investigation.* Albany, NY: State University of New York Press, 1994.

Sullivan, Dale. "*Kairos* and the Rhetoric of Belief," *Quarterly Journal of Speech* 78 (1992): 317–332.

Sutton, Jane. "The Marginalization of Sophistical Rhetoric and the Loss of History." *Rethinking the History of Rhetoric.* Ed. Takis Poulakos. Boulder, CO: Westview Press, 1993: 75–90.

———. "The Taming of *Polos/Polis*: Rhetoric as an Achievement without Woman." *Southern Communication Journal* (57:2), 97–119.

Swearingen, Jan. "A Lover's Discourse: Diotima, Logos, and Desire." *Reclaiming Rhetorica,* ed. Andrea Lunsford. Pittsburgh, PA: University of Pittsburgh Press, 1995: 25–51.

———. *Rhetoric and Irony: Western Literacy and Western Lies.* Oxford: Oxford University Press, 1991.

Tagliacozzo, G. and D. P. Verene, eds. *Giambattista Vico's Science of Humanity.* Baltimore: Johns Hopkins Press, 1976.

Tannen, Deborah. *Gender and Discourse.* Oxford: Oxford University Press, 1994.

Thorne, Barrie and Nancy Henley. *Language and Sex: Difference and Dominance.* Rowley, MA: Newberry House, 1975.

Tompkins, Jane P., ed. *Reader Response Criticism.* Baltimore, MD: Johns Hopkins University Press, 1980.

Toulmin, Stephen. *The Uses of Argument.* Cambridge: Cambridge University Press, 1958.

Trapp, Robert and Janice Schuetz, eds. *Perspectives on Argument: Essays in Honor of Wayne Brockriede.* Prospect Heights, IL: Waveland Press, 1990.

Troup, Calvin. *Temporality, Eternity, and Wisdom: The Rhetoric of Augustine's Confessions.* Columbia, SC: University of South Carolina Press, 1999.

Untersteiner, Mario. *The Sophists.* Oxford: Oxford University Press, 1954.

van Eemeren, Frans H., Rob Grootendorst and Tjark Kruiger. *Handbook of Argumentation Theory.* Dordrecht, Holland: Foris Publications, 1987.

Van Maanen, John. *Tales of the Field.* Chicago: University of Chicago Press, 1988.

Vasaly, Ann. *Representations: Images of the World in Ciceronian Oratory.* Berkeley: University of California Press, 1993.

Verene, Donald Philip, ed. Giambattista Vico, *On Humanistic Education: Six Inaugural Orations, 1699–1707.* Trans. G. A. Pinton and A. W. Shippe. Ithaca: Cornell University Press, 1993.

Vickers, Brian, ed. *Rhetoric Revalued: Papers from the International Society for the History of Rhetoric.* Binghamton, NY: Center for Medieval and Early Renaissance Studies, 1982.

————. *In Defense of Rhetoric.* Oxford: Oxford University Press, 1988.

Vico, Giambattista. *On Humanistic Education: Six Inaugural Orations, 1699–1707.* Ed. Donald Phillip Verene. Trans. G. A. Pinton and A. W. Shippe. Ithaca, NY: Cornell University Press, 1993.

————. "Oratzione in Morte did Donna Angela Cimmino Marchesa did Petrella." *Opere di G. B. Vico.* Ed. Fausto Nicolini. Rome: Bari Laterza, 1911–1914.

Vitanza, Victor, ed. *Writing Histories of Rhetoric.* Carbondale, IL: Southern Illinois University Press, 1994

Vonnegut, K. S. "Listening for Women's Voices." *Communication Education* 41 (1992): 26–39.

Ward, John O. "From Antiquity to the Renaissance: Glosses and Commentaries on Cicero's Rhetorica." *Medieval Eloquence.* Ed. J. J. Murphy. Berkeley: University of California Press, 1978. 25–67.

————. "Magic and Rhetoric from Antiquity to the Renaissance: Some Ruminations," *Rhetorica* 6 (1988): 57–118.

Warnick, Barbara. *The Sixth Canon: Belletristic Rhetorical Theory and Its French Antecedents.* Columbia, SC: University of South Carolina Press, 1993.

Watson, Burton. *Basic Writings of Mo Tzu, Hsun Tzu, and Han Fei Tzu.* New York: Columbia University Press, 1967.

Weaver, Richard M. *Composition: A Course in Writing and Rhetoric.* New York: Holt, Rinehart and Winston, 1957.

————. *The Ethics of Rhetoric.* 1953. Chicago: Regnery, 1968.

————. *Ideas Have Consequences.* Chicago: University of Chicago Press, 1948.

————. *Life Without Prejudice and Other Essays.* Chicago: University of Chicago Press, 1965.

————. *Visions of Order.* Baton Rouge, LA: Louisiana State University Press, 1964.

Welch, Kathleen E. *The Contemporary Reception of Classical Rhetoric: Appropriations of Ancient Discourse.* Hillsdale, NJ: Lawrence Erlbaum, 1990.

Wells, Susan. *Sweet Reason: Rhetoric and the Discourses of Modernity.* Chicago: University of Chicago Press, 1996.

Wenzel, Joseph. "Three Perspectives on Argument." *Perspectives on Argumentation: Essays in Honor of Wayne Brockriede.* Eds. Robert Trapp and Janice Schuetz. Prospect Heights, IL: Waveland, 1990: 9–26.

Whately, Richard. *Elements of Rhetoric,* Ed. Douglas Ehninger. 1828. Carbondale, IL: Southern Illinois University Press, 1963.

Willard, Charles Arthur. "Argumentation and Postmodern Critique." *Perspectives on Argumentation: Essays in Honor of Wayne Brockriede.* Prospect Heights, IL: Waveland, 1990: 221–231.

Wilson, Katharina, ed. *Women Writers of the Renaissance and Reformation.* Athens: University of Georgia Press, 1987.

Wood, Ellen Meiksins. *Peasant–Citizen and Slave: The Foundations of Athenian Democracy.* London: Verso, 1988.

Wood, Julia T. *Gendered Lives.* Belmont, CA: Wadsworth, 1994.

Woods, Marjorie Currie. "The Teaching of Writing in Medieval Europe." *A Short History of Writing Instruction.* Ed. James J. Murphy. Davis, CA: Hermagoras Press, 1990, 77–94.

INDEX

299